A. Activism; iii. Legal/Politics

The Courage of Their Convictions

Peter Irons

THE FREE PRESS
A Division of Macmillan, Inc.
NEW YORK

Collier Macmillan Publishers
LONDON

The Free Press
A Division of Macmillan, Inc.
866 Third Avenue, New York, N. Y. 10022

Collier Macmillan Canada, Inc.

Printed in the United States of America

Printing number
1   2   3   4   5   6   7   8   9   10

Library of Congress Cataloging-in-Publication Data

Irons, Peter H.
   The courage of their convictions.

   1. Civil rights—United States—Cases. 2. United
States. Supreme Court. I. Title.
KF4748.I76   1988   342.73'085   88–21406
ISBN 0-02-915670-X   347.30285

The line from "i sing of Olaf glad and big," which appears on p. xiv, is reprinted from *Viva, poems by E.E. Cumings,* edited by George James Firmage, by permission of Liveright Publishing Corporation. Copyright 1931, 1959 by E. E. Cummings. Copyright © 1979, 1973 by the Trustees for the E. E. Cummings Trust. Copyright © 1979, 1973 by George James Firmage.

FOR HOWARD ZINN

"Are we historians not humans first,
and scholars because of that?"

—Zinn, *The Politics of History*

Contents

Preface

On the morning of March 29, 1965, I stepped into the witness box of the federal district court in Cincinnati, Ohio. I took the stand as a criminal defendant, charged with two counts of violating the draft law: failing to report for a physical exam, and then for induction in 1963 at Fort Knox, Kentucky. Although I had dutifully registered with my draft board in a Cincinnati suburb in 1958, two years later I returned my card to the board, with a letter which explained why I would not carry it. Unwilling to apply for exemption as a conscientious objector, I chose to risk prosecution and prison for my stand against the draft.

My noncooperation began a month after I registered, with my exposure at Antioch College to pacifists, socialists, civil-rights activists, and other critics of the Cold War America in which I was raised. But I did not share the conservative values of most of my suburban, middle-class neighbors—the values of the country club, corporate offices, and comfortable churches. Although I lived like my neighbors and looked like them, white and well-dressed, I was "different" in ways that made me a good candidate for conversion at Antioch—once an Underground Railroad stop in Yellow Springs, Ohio—to rebellion and resistance. My family was Unitarian, from a church which stressed both tolerance and searching inquiry into ultimate questions. During a Sunday-school study of "The Church Across the Street," I visited Jewish temples, black pentecostal churches, Eastern Orthodox services, and Buddhist ceremonies.

My parents also raised me (and six brothers and sisters) to abhor racism. I attended segregated schools in Delaware before the 1954 Supreme Court decision in the *Brown* case, and I could not understand why the kids who lived down the road in the black hamlet of Buttonwood could not attend my schools. During the Little Rock school crisis in 1957, I wrote to a local right-wing newspaper columnist—he screamed "Wake Up, Americans!" every morning—who denounced the Supreme Court as Communist. I defended the Court against his "Paleolithic" views and suggested that "the duty of the Supreme Court is to redefine the purport of the law in light of changing social trends." Much to my surprise, my letter appeared in his column, with a sinister question at the end: "Obviously, this boy has been taught these things. By whom?" One of my teachers wrote back this answer: "He was taught by Jefferson, by Tom Paine, and by Emerson and Thoreau." The teacher did not know I wrote the letter—the columnist did not reveal my name—but he was right.

Three years later, in October 1960, I drove with several black and white friends from Washington, D.C. to Atlanta for the first national meeting of the Student Nonviolent Coordinating Committee. I had already been briefly jailed for joining sit-ins in suburban Maryland, where I worked at an Antioch co-op job and lived with black students from Howard University. The SNCC convention in Atlanta—my first trip to the Deep South—moved and inspired me. Speeches by apostles of Gandhi such as Martin Luther King, James Lawson, and Richard Gregg prompted me, once I returned to Washington, to return my draft card as a tangible symbol of a system which relied on force to defend a country still practicing legal apartheid.

Back at Antioch in 1961, I wrote a leaflet called "An Alternative to the Draft—A Statement to Young Men." It urged a mass return of draft cards by students who "agree with the nonviolent, direct action methods of the sit-in movement, those students who feel that a law which violates the moral precepts they hold so deeply must be broken, and the consequences accepted." Although friends and I circulated 5,000 copies to Midwest college campuses, I don't know whether anyone who read it joined my stand. But it did attract two FBI agents, who showed up at Antioch, identical in snap-brim hats and trenchcoats. They grilled me for two hours and promised to return with a warrant for my arrest on sedition charges. They never returned.

Four years later, still wondering where the FBI agents were, I went on trial before Judge John W. Peck. My lawyer advised me to waive a jury; federal jurors in Cincinnati were mostly retired American Legion members. This decision made no difference to the outcome. Judge Peck bristled with hostility. Since I did not deny my draft-law violations, I took the stand to explain why. My defense was based on my objection to the "Supreme Being" clause of the draft law, restricting exemption as conscientious objectors to those who swore a belief in God. I considered this unconstitutional—I had done research on Supreme Court precedent—and I argued to Judge Peck that the Court's 1961 opinion in *Torcaso* v. *Watkins* had outlawed any religious tests for public office or service. Roy Torcaso had refused to affirm belief in God to obtain a Maryland notary-public commission, and the Supreme Court had upheld his objection.

Judge Peck endured my lecture on constitutional law with obvious impatience. When I finished, he looked down from the bench and asked me a scornful question: "Young man, where did you attend law school?" His tone, and his summary dismissal of my position, left me feeling indignant and angry. He found me guilty and sentenced me to three years in federal prison. My lawyer asked the federal appellate court to reverse Judge Peck, arguing that the Supreme Court decision in the *Seeger* case, issued just weeks before my trial, struck down the "Supreme Being" clause. The appellate judges split 2-to-1, ruling that, unlike Dan Seeger, I had refused to apply for exemption, and that therefore my reasons for objecting to the religious test were irrelevant. The lone dissenter, Judge George Edwards, suggested that my refusal had been prompted by futility, and that I should now be allowed to apply for exemption under the *Seeger* test.

After this defeat, I decided to serve my sentence. My lawyer held out little hope for victory in the Supreme Court; I had no funds for another appeal; the American Civil Liberties Union had refused to help me. (I have since forgiven the ACLU, and now serve on the board of its San Diego affiliate.) Between 1966 and 1969, I spent more than two years in federal prison. After my release I attended graduate school in political science at Boston University, receiving a Ph.D. in 1973. Five years later I graduated from Harvard Law School.

During my law training I sought reversal of my draft convictions: After my prison term the Supreme Court ruled that punitive inductions were unlawful, and I proved from draft-board and

FBI records that mine was intended to punish me for anti-draft agitation. A federal judge in Cincinnati erased my conviction for refusing Army induction. I was still angry at Judge Peck. I wrote to him that I had graduated from Harvard Law School and that my conviction had been vacated. I asked if he had any second thoughts about my case and about Vietnam, now that the war was lost. His reply was terse—no and no. One last word about Judge Peck and my trials: Indignation and anger can be valuable emotions if they are channeled into constructive outlets. I think this book is such an outlet.

I relate this personal story to help explain why I began this book; why I wanted to meet and talk with people who, unlike me, took their cases to the Supreme Court. During my law-school years I read hundreds of Supreme Court opinions, and noticed the lack of any description of the parties in most opinions. They were simply names on paper. After I began teaching law, I decided to write a book about three of the Court's worst decisions, those that upheld in 1943 and 1944 the wartime internment of Japanese Americans. I tracked down the original defendants—Gordon Hirabayashi, Min Yasui, and Fred Korematsu—and learned from talking with them about their courage in facing prison for resisting the concentration camps into which their families and friends had been herded at gunpoint.

My research for that book, *Justice at War,* uncovered clear evidence that government lawyers had lied to the Supreme Court in all three cases. Aided by teams of young lawyers whose parents had been incarcerated, I helped Gordon, Min, and Fred to get their criminal convictions vacated with the same legal tools I had used in my own draft case. While their cases plodded through the courts—they began in 1983 and ended in 1988—it struck me that many other Americans had displayed equal courage in asking the Supreme Court to uphold their rights under the Constitution. I decided to find and talk with a number of these people and to put their stories into a book.

I chose sixteen cases which I considered important and interesting. They spanned five decades, and involved four major issues: religion, race, protest, and privacy. I felt that these sixteen cases would adequately represent those years and issues. Some I chose because of personal connections: I represented Gordon Hirabayashi; I joined sit-ins as had Robert Mack Bell; my draft case relied on Dan Seeger's; I used Barbara Elfbrandt's case to undo a loyalty oath in New Hampshire. These are not, I know, the same cases that others would choose; there are dozens of equally significant cases from the past fifty years, and many fascinating people who began them. But one point of this book is that in fact *thousands* of Americans have taken courtroom stands on principle and conscience. Not all have reached the Supreme Court, but all have shared a belief in a living Constitution.

Senator John F. Kennedy published his book *Profiles in Courage* in 1955. He painted sympathetic portraits of eight Americans— all white, all men, all Senators. The sixteen people in this book more accurately reflect America's diversity. They include women and men. They are black, white, Hispanic, and Asian. They are gay and straight. They are carpenters, bartenders, doctors, and lawyers. They live in all sections of our country. They profess many religions and none. They are united only by their diversity.

I have many debts to acknowledge in bringing this book to life. Going back to the beginning, Alda and Rusty Irons raised me the right way. Howard Zinn answered my letters written from prison, arranged my admission to graduate school, and served as mentor, friend, and model of the engaged scholar. Indeed, he dedicated a book to me before we even met! Now, twenty years later, I can repay that debt of gratitude. Working as one of Howard's graduate assistants in his "Justice in America" course at Boston University helped me to understand, as he wrote, that "the small circles of our daily life might be the beginning of justice."

Laurence H. Tribe taught me a great deal about constitutional law at Harvard. Larry also taught me that the "living Constitution" needs constant nurture from its friends, and protection from its enemies. My work on the internment cases gave me the friendship of Dale Minami, Don Tamaki, Lori Bannai, Dennis Hayashi, Peggy Nagae, Rod Kawakami, Mike Leong, and many other people I did not grow up with in White America. Krista Kiger has infused my life with the spirit of "hesed" that makes her a wonderful person and pastor. Lloyd Gardner invited me to Rutgers in 1988 as the Raoul Wallenberg Distinguished Visiting Professor of Human Rights, an honor which I hope this book repays. Dick McCormick and the Rutgers history department have given me a warm reception. Harry Hirsch, my colleague at the University of California, San Diego, and Paul Clemens, David Oshinsky, and Lloyd Gardner at Rutgers have made valuable comments on the manuscript of this book. My Rutgers graduate assistant, Richard Moser, helped locate photographs for the book. My editor, Joyce Seltzer, has supported me with judicious (forgive the pun, Joyce) criticism and bubbling enthusiasm. George Rowland gave the manuscript the scrutiny of a careful copyediting. Priscilla Long has cared for me for almost half of my life. She has shared my doubts, disappointments, and discouragements. Now that this book is done, she can share my happiness.

I must finally thank the sixteen people who speak in this book. They welcomed me to their cities and towns, shared their stories with me, bared emotions which had been hidden from family and friends, and revealed the courage and conviction that animated both their cases and their lives. They led me across this vast and beautiful country, to such cities as New York, Chicago, St. Louis, and Miami, to Little Rock, Mobile, Tucson, Salt Lake City, St. Paul, and more. In crossing America—by plane, train, subway, and Greyhound bus—to visit these remarkable people, I found the roots of my own convictions.

Let me end this preface with two statements which have animated my own life. One is profane and one is profound; both are important to me. First: Writing of "Olaf, the Conscientious Objector," the poet e. e. cummings declared that "there is some shit I will not eat." Each person in this book refused to accept some indignity, some act of intolerance. Finally: Speaking to the graduates of Antioch College in 1859, Horace Mann gave them this admonition: "Be ashamed to die until you have won some victory for humanity." All the people who tell their stories in this book have won a victory for humanity.

Prologue

"Emotions Bubble and Tempers Flare"

Brown v. *Board of Education*. *Miranda* v. *Arizona*. *Roe* v. *Wade*. Most Americans recognize these decisions of the United States Supreme Court. Few would dispute that they are among the most significant that the Court has issued over the past five decades. Racism, crime, and abortion are issues which continue to raise passions in our society. Each of these decisions provoked both praise and protest at the time the Court ruled; politicians, preachers, and pundits joined the chorus of comment. And each decision led to calls for constitutional amendments to reverse the rulings. Although none has succeeded, campaigns to curb the Court have been launched in every session of Congress in this century. Hardly any significant decision of the Supreme Court fails to stir controversy, from pornography to presidential power.

Linda Carol Brown. Ernesto Arturo Miranda. Norma McCorvey. Few Americans can recollect the names of these people who began important Supreme Court cases. Hardly anyone, aside from family and friends, knows anything of their lives. The Supreme Court tells us very little about the people whose cases the justices decide. All the Court wrote about Linda Brown and the other black children who challenged school segregation in Kansas was that "the plaintiffs are Negro children of elementary school age residing in Topeka." The Court described Ernesto Miranda, who after a relentless police grilling confessed to rape, simply as an "indigent Mexican defendant" who was "a seriously disturbed individual with pronounced sexual fantasies." Norma McCorvey, seeking an abortion and using the pseudonym "Jane Roe" to protect her privacy, was described in the Court's opinion as "a single woman

3

who was residing in Dallas County, Texas" and who "alleged that she was unmarried and pregnant."

Almost without exception, the notoriety of Supreme Court cases is matched by the obscurity of the people who began them. Even when the networks and newsweeklies fulfill Andy Warhol's prediction that everyone will be famous for fifteen minutes, it is generally lawyers who speak for their clients. Thirty seconds on television, or three inches in a newspaper or magazine, can hardly tell the public more than a person's name, the barest facts of their case, and perhaps a brief quote about their reaction to the Court's decision. We usually learn nothing of their background, their family, why they brought the case, how it affected their life, and the future impact of the case. What little we do learn is distorted by the media's lust for the sensational and the trivial. Hardly anyone who has initiated an important Supreme Court case—or even an "average" case—has spoken directly and at length to other Americans.

This book presents the stories, in their own words, of sixteen Americans whose acts of resistance or affirmation led to the Supreme Court in Washington, D.C. These accounts are intended to remove what John Noonan, once a law professor and now a federal judge, called the "masks of the law" from the faces of real people. They attempt also to break down some of the myths that surround the Court. Anthropologists who have studied tribal ceremonies tell us that masks are often used to conceal the emotion of anger, and to act out tribal mythology. We are raised to believe that anger is an inappropriate response to the law's promise of impartiality. The rationale for the masking ceremony of the Supreme Court is expressed in the truism that we have "a government of laws, not of men." Or of women and children, for that matter. Justice is blindfolded. The Supreme Court is not concerned with a person's race or religion or gender or income or education.

"Our Constitution is color-blind," Justice John Marshall Harlan wrote in 1896, "and neither knows nor tolerates classes among citizens." Like most constitutional myths, the Court's claim of impartiality is suspect. Justice—as does each of the justices—peeks past the blindfold to see who stands before the bench. In many cases, it *does* make a difference in the outcome whether the party who seeks relief is white or black, believer or atheist, male or female, rich or poor, educated or ignorant.

Another constitutional myth is that the Court decides only issues of law, not questions of character. Justice Felix Frankfurter once disparaged the defendants in a murder case as "worthless creatures." Nonetheless, he wrote proudly, "the fact that worthless creatures may invoke the protection of the Constitution is not the least of the glories of our country." But the justices often comb through case records looking for evidence of moral depravity. People who engage in acts such as sodomy cannot celebrate our country's glories with those of more conventional morality!

A third constitutional myth is that the Court decides cases without reference to politics. Justice Frankfurter, perhaps the Court's leading mythmaker, once likened his colleagues to monks who took vows of silence and lived in solitude. Frankfurter wrote that "this Court has no excuse for being unless it's a monastery." This is the easiest myth to demolish. Frankfurter himself relished politics and peppered his old friend, President Franklin Roosevelt, with advice on policy. Justice Abe Fortas, who later sat in Frankfurter's seat, provided his old friend, President Lyndon Johnson, with advice on Vietnam and other issues. Not only is the Supreme Court a political institution, but its members often play political roles. And cases are often decided along political lines. Presidents tend to place members of their party on the Court, and justices often—although not invariably—vote along partisan lines.

Confronted with ceremonial masking and constitutional myth, what can we learn from the sixteen cases in this book? We learn first that the Supreme Court's profession of "color-blindness," the ideal of impartiality, has moved in the past fifty years from solicitude for wealth toward partiality to the victims of prejudice. The Court's historic malevolence against minorities, exposed in the "separate but equal" doctrine of the infamous *Plessy* decision in 1896, turned to benevolence in 1938. Justice Harlan Fiske Stone, writing for the Court in an "easy" regulatory case, *United States* v. *Carolene Products*, suggested that his colleagues strip "the presumption of constitutionality" from legislation that "appears on its face" to violate any provision of the Bill of Rights. Stone urged, in Footnote Four of this historic opinion, that the burden of proof in such cases be shifted from the challenger to the government.

Stone urged that "more exacting judicial scrutiny" be applied to laws that restricted political rights such as voting, free speech and press, organizing, and peaceful assembly. The formula later devised to implement Stone's test required government officials to demonstrate a "compelling state interest" in restricting such rights. Stone also sheltered religious, ethnic, and racial minorities under the Constitution's protective umbrella, along with other "discrete and insular minorities" who had experienced prejudice. All such minority groups, named and unnamed, could ask the Supreme Court for "more searching judicial inquiry" of laws which singled them out for discrimination. Again, Stone's formula required government officials to present "compelling" reasons for disparate treatment of minorities.

Footnote Four, and the burdens it imposed on government officials to justify their actions, did not emerge from a vacuum. One year before Justice Stone wrote the *Carolene Products* opinion, the Supreme Court went through the trauma of the "Constitutional Revolution" of 1937. The Court's invalidation of New Deal legislation in 1935 and 1936 helped President Roosevelt to win a smashing electoral victory in 1936, and then to propose his "court-packing" plan in February 1937. Suddenly aware of public opinion, the Court turned from preservation of property rights to protection of personal rights. What we might call the "Second Constitutional Revolution" began with Footnote Four, which reflected not only Roosevelt's electoral victory but also the civil-rights campaign of black Americans. Frustrated in their efforts to secure congressional legislation to punish lynching, black lawyers and white colleagues mapped an attack on segregation, aimed first at graduate schools in border states and ultimately at elementary schools in the Deep South.

Armed with the "terrible swift sword" of Footnote Four, the Supreme Court launched a crusade for justice. But the justices soon ran into World War Two, which subordinated justice to jingoism. The Supreme Court flunked Stone's constitutional exam in cases that involved religious and racial minorities. Once the war ended, the Court brushed the mothballs from Footnote Four and struck down most—but not all—laws that impinged on First Amendment rights or discriminated against minority groups. During the heyday of the Warren Court, from 1954 to 1969, the justices struck down virtually every law and regulation scrutinized under the Footnote Four test. One commentator called the test "strict in theory and fatal in fact." The years of the Burger Court, which ended in 1986, saw a cautious retreat from the "judicial activism" of its predecessor, but not the wholesale reversal of precedent that many had predicted and longed for. Indeed, by expanding "privacy" rights to include abortion, the Burger Court stretched the elastic phrases of the Constitution even wider.

The cases in this book reflect the impact of the Second Constitutional Revolution on American society. They also mirror some of the deepest and most enduring divisions among Americans— those of religion and race, protest and privacy. These four issues have given rise to many of the Supreme Court's most significant and controversial decisions. They have also stirred passions and even violence. Justice Hugo Black once wrote that "emotions bubble and tempers flare in racial and religious controversies." This is no less true for political protest and for controversies over privacy issues such as sexual behavior and abortion.

During the entire course of our nation's history, before and since the Constitution was adopted, Americans have written their prejudices into law. Colonial Massachusetts imposed the death penalty for blasphemy and adultery. "If any man lyeth with man-kinde as he lyeth with a woman," the same code provided, "both of them have committed abomination, they both shall surely be put to death." Most of these laws remained on the books after independence; as late as the 1970s, an effort to repeal the Bay State's blasphemy law died from ecclesiastical opposition. Even after ratification of the Bill of Rights, most states imposed restrictions on Catholics and Jews. No member of either religion could hold public office in New Hampshire until 1876. The most persecuted Americans were blacks, held in slavery until the Civil War and subjected to Jim Crow laws, the American form of apartheid, until the 1960s. Political dissenters were threatened with sedition laws as early as 1798, and during World War I an anti-war speech landed socialist leader Eugene Debs in Atlanta Penitentiary with a twenty-year sentence.

Religion and race, protest and privacy have remained as sources of conflict because of our heterogeneity. Americans are divided into hundreds of religious denominations; more than 30 million belong to racial minorities; political dissenters are small in number but vocal and often abrasive; and groups that fight discrimination on grounds of gender and sexual preference are increasingly militant. Much of the conflict over these issues is channeled into the political system. From city councils to Congress, lobbyists for public-interest groups—disparaged as "special interests" by President Reagan—seek legislation to protect their members from discrimination. They often fail: The legislative process is dominated by defenders of the status quo. Particularly at the local level, politicians do not pull out well-thumbed copies of the Constitution when they debate laws to ban picketers or abortion clinics, or refuse to approve zoning changes that would bring low-income housing (and blacks) into lily-white towns.

During this era of Footnote Four, more and more Americans who feel their rights have been violated have turned from legislators to judges for relief. The courts have not always welcomed these claims of constitutional rights. "For protection against abuses by legislatures," the Supreme Court lectured in 1877, "the people must resort to the polls, not to the courts." But if legislators have created the problem, by enacting laws which violate the Constitution, only judges can provide relief. The courts are inescapably part of the political system as it affects individual rights. A perceptive French visitor, Alexis de Tocqueville, noted in 1835, "Scarcely any political question arises in the United States that is not resolved, sooner or later, into a judicial question." A century later, Robert H. Jackson, who joined the Supreme Court in 1941, wrote of "government by lawsuit" and noted that "constitutional lawsuits are the stuff of power politics in America."

How can a single individual of modest income carry out the uniquely American threat, "I'll take my case to the Supreme Court"? The simple answer is that he or she can't, without the support of an organization with the resources to play the "power politics" of Supreme Court litigation. Today, the minimum cost of taking a constitutional case from trial to the Supreme Court would be $100,000. With hourly fees which go as high as $500, private lawyers have priced themselves out of cases brought by people of modest means. Some law firms do, however, provide *pro bono publico* representation of poor people. For example, the prestigious New York corporate firm of Skadden, Arps, Slate, Meagher & Flom donated more than $1 million of lawyers' time to the Arkansas "creationism" case in 1981.

More often, public-interest legal groups provide lawyers in civil-rights and liberties cases. The two most active and influential of these groups are the American Civil Liberties Union and the NAACP Legal Defense and Education Fund. Founded in 1920 and led for fifty years by Roger Baldwin, the ACLU defends the Bill of Rights for all Americans, regardless of their political position, from Communists to Nazis. This willingness to represent those whose views are feared and hated has cost the ACLU members and donations; defending the right of Nazis to picket city hall in Skokie, Illinois, a Chicago suburb with a large Jewish population, prompted some ACLU members to resign in protest. Only the federal government has appeared before the Supreme Court more often than the ACLU. During the years of the Warren Court, ACLU lawyers won 90 percent of their Supreme Court cases; during the Burger Court years, they lost about half. Significantly, the ACLU was involved in twelve of the sixteen cases in this book, although the cases were not selected for this reason. But these cases raised the kinds of civil-liberties issues that the ACLU exists to support.

The NAACP was founded in 1909 to protect black Americans from discrimination. Its legal arm was created in 1939 to take this crusade into courtrooms. The "Inc. Fund" was headed for more than two decades by Thurgood Marshall, who joined the Supreme Court in 1967. Marshall's legal team crafted a step-by-step legal assault on segregation which culminated in its greatest victory in 1954, when the Supreme Court struck down school segregation in the *Brown* case. Since that time, the Fund has separated from its parent group and moved into such conflicts as capital punishment and affirmative action. Although the NAACP was involved directly in only four of the cases in this book, its lawyers have appeared before the Supreme Court more than 200 times, and have the best victory record of any public-interest group.

The decade of the 1970s saw an explosion of public-interest law groups, many modeled on the NAACP legal arm and dedicated to defending members of other racial and ethnic groups. The Asian American Legal Defense and Education Fund and the Mexican American Legal Defense and Education Fund have the same focus and agenda of their progenitor. Feminist groups and defenders of abortion rights have established legal arms as well. The New Right has adopted the public-interest legal model; regional groups like the Pacific Legal Foundation, Mountain States Legal

Foundation, and Washington Legal Foundation defend "the precepts of individual liberties and the free enterprise system" with the financial backing of corporate sponsors.

Another form of involvement in rights litigation is the *amicus curiae* (Latin for "friend of the court") brief to the Supreme Court. Many religious, labor, and civic groups submit such briefs, in some cases to symbolize support and in others to press a novel legal point on the justices. In the *Shelley* case that attacked racial covenants in housing, *amicus* groups included the Grand Lodge of Elks, Protestant Council of New York City, American Federation of Labor, American Jewish Committee, American Association for the United Nations, and a half-dozen others. The *Bakke* case of 1978, which challenged racial quotas in medical schools, set an *amicus* record, with 120 groups joining in 58 briefs.

Not only is rights litigation costly, it is lengthy. The sixteen cases in this book took an average of four years between initial filing and Supreme Court decision. Elmer Gertz waited fourteen years for final action on his libel suit against the John Birch Society. All but one case, Gordon Hirabayashi's challenge to wartime internment, which went straight from trial court to Supreme Court, took at least three years to reach an end.

There is no guarantee, of course, that a constitutional case will even reach the Supreme Court. Since 1925, the Court has exercised almost complete discretion in choosing cases for argument and decision. For several decades, the nine justices have issued about 150 decisions each year. These cases are picked from a docket of four to five thousand requests for review, most often in the form of "petitions for certiorari." The chances, in other words, of gaining review are less than one in twenty. The figure is distorted by the federal government's success rate of more than 70 percent in petitions it files; the government participates, as a party or amicus, in about half of all the decided cases. The cases in this book, then, represent a minute fraction of some 8,000 decided since 1940. But they all raise issues of crucial importance: school prayer, racial covenants, loyalty oaths, abortion, school funding, gay rights, and others of equal significance.

Each case in this book has a person's name attached to the decision. But the Court has told us little more than last names— J.D. and Ethel Shelley are simply described as "Negroes" who "received from one Fitzgerald a warranty deed" to a house in

St. Louis. Barbara Elfbrandt is "a teacher and a Quaker" who refused to sign a loyalty oath in Arizona. Justice Byron White could not bring himself to use Michael Hardwick's name in his opinion which upheld Georgia's sodomy law; Michael was simply "respondent" to White. And so on.

There are faces behind the "masks of the law," voices behind the pages of the Court's opinions, people who speak to us in this book. Each face is distinctive, each voice is unique, each life is different. Backgrounds vary, motivations differ. But this chorus of sixteen harmonizes a common refrain: courage and conviction.

1

Lillian Gobitis
v. Minersville School
District

Walter Gobitis sued the Minersville, Pennsylvania school board
after his children, Lillian and William, were expelled in 1935
for refusing on religious grounds to salute the flag.
Courtesy of Lillian Gobitas Klose

I.
"We Live by Symbols"

Only one item appeared on the agenda of the Minersville, Pennsylvania school board at its meeting on November 6, 1935. Superintendent Charles E. Roudabush reported that three students had refused to join the daily ceremony of saluting the American flag that had been customary in Minersville schools since Roudabush arrived in 1914. The superintendent, who prided himself on firm discipline, was particularly annoyed at Walter Gobitis, whose children Lillian and William had first objected to the flag salute. Roudabush and Gobitis had argued about the issue over the past month, but heated debates had failed to resolve their dispute.

Walter Gobitis and his family belonged to Jehovah's Witnesses, a religious group whose energetic door-to-door preaching and hostility to Roman Catholicism combined to make Witnesses unpopular in towns such as Minersville, where close to 90 percent of the residents were Catholic. Gobitis was a Minersville native who was raised in the Catholic faith, and who took part in the flag-salute ceremony as a schoolboy. He and his family became Witnesses in 1931, when Lillian was eight and William was six, and the children saluted the flag every day until early October, 1935. (Although the family name was properly spelled "Gobitas," a court clerk's mistake perpetuated the spelling that the Supreme Court adopted and that persists to this day.)

The clash in Minersville, a town of ten thousand in the hilly anthracite coal region north of Philadelphia, was rooted in conflicting visions of patriotism and contrasting ideas of religious freedom.

15

Flag-salute ceremonies in public schools began during wartime: The New York legislature passed the first mandatory salute law in 1898, the day after the United States declared war on Spain. Only five states enacted flag-salute laws before World War I, but a national campaign began in 1919 as a project of the American Legion, founded that year by veterans to foster "one hundred per cent Americanism." During the next decade, the Legion campaign was joined by the Veterans of Foreign Wars, the Daughters of the American Revolution, and the Ku Klux Klan, the lattermost of which sought respectability in the 1920s through involvement in "patriotic" activities. By 1935, eighteen states had enacted flag-salute statutes, and hundreds of local school boards in other states had voted to compel all students to participate in the ceremony.

The Gobitis children were not the first objectors to the flag-salute ceremonies that began the school day in thousands of American communities. As early as 1918, when patriotic fervor and anti-German hostility swept the country during World War I, a handful of Mennonite children, members of a pacifist and largely German church, faced expulsion for refusal to salute the flag. Over the next fifteen years, the American Civil Liberties Union recorded a scattering of flag-salute cases around the country, but none had raised any constitutional challenge to compulsory participation in the ceremonies.

Beginning in 1935, Jehovah's Witnesses became the first religious group to promote a campaign of refusal to join classroom ceremonies, and to press their challenges in court on a constitutional basis. Ironically, in view of later claims that "unpatriotic" Witnesses were aiding Nazi propagandists, the sect's objections to compulsory flag-salute ceremonies began in Nazi Germany, which banned the Witnesses in 1933 on Hitler's orders. German Witnesses defied Nazi edicts to join the "raised-palm" Fascist salute in schools and at all public events, and ultimately more than ten thousand were imprisoned in concentration camps. In response to this persecution, the leader of American Witnesses, Joseph F. Rutherford, denounced compulsory flag-salute laws at the sect's national convention in 1935. Witnesses "do not 'Heil Hitler' nor any other creature," Rutherford told his followers.

Shortly after Rutherford's speech, his admonition was heeded by Carleton Nicholls, a third-grade student in Lynn, Massachusetts. Earlier that year, the Bay State had enacted a mandatory flag-salute law which required students to face the flag with a "raised-palm" salute, identical to the Nazi version. After Carleton's refusal to continue saluting, his father was arrested when he accompanied Carleton to school and they both refused to stand during the ceremony. This arrest prompted Rutherford, a lawyer whose followers called him "Judge," to praise Carleton in a national radio address for making a "wise choice" and to proclaim that other Witnesses "who act wisely will do the same thing."

Walter Gobitis and his family—along with every Witness who could—listened to Rutherford's speech on their radios, and within a few days Lillian and William, then in the seventh and fifth grades respectively, decided to emulate Carleton Nicholls. Their defiance upset Superintendent Roudabush, who knew he could not lawfully punish them. Neither the state legislature nor the local school board had made the salute mandatory or provided any penalties for refusal to participate. After his appeals to Walter Gobitis failed, Roudabush secured an opinion from the State Department of Public Instruction that the school board could enact a regulation to compel participation in the salute and to expel students who refused.

When the board met in November 1935, its members sat impatiently as Walter Gobitis and the mother of Edmund Wasliewski, a sixth-grader who had joined the objectors, explained the Witness position on the flag salute. "We are not desecrating the American flag," Gobitis said. "We show no disrespect for the flag, but we cannot salute it. The Bible tells us this, and we must obey." Gobitis pointed the board members to chapter 20 of Exodus, which warned believers not to "bow down" to any "graven image" which portrayed false gods. The flags of nations were images of Satan, who ruled the secular governments of the world, Gobitis told his unsympathetic listeners.

On the motion of Dr. Thomas J. McGurl, an Irish Catholic physician and influential Minersville resident, the board unanimously adopted a resolution requiring all students "to salute the flag of our Country as a part of the daily exercises" and providing that refusal to participate "shall be regarded as an act of insubordination and shall be dealt with accordingly." Roudabush immediately declared that "I hereby expel from the Minersville schools Lillian Gobitis, William Gobitis and Edmund Wasliewski for this act of insubordination, to wit, failure to salute the flag in our school exercises." Walter Gobitis left the meeting with a parting shot to Roudabush and the board: "I'm going to take you to court for this!"

Eighteen months passed before Gobitis made good his promise to sue the school board. During this time, Lillian and William attended a makeshift Witness school located thirty miles from Minersville. With the joint participation of Witness lawyers from the sect's Brooklyn headquarters, and the American Civil Liberties Union, Gobitis filed suit in the federal district court in Philadelphia on May 3, 1937. His complaint, brought as "next friend" of Lillian and William, argued that school-board members had acted "under color of state law" to deprive the children of rights to freedom of religion and speech guaranteed by the U.S. Constitution. The Due Process clause of the Fourteenth Amendment, stated the complaint, barred states and local governments from abridging any of the First Amendment rights that Congress could not deny to citizens.

As a group, federal judges in the 1930s were largely conservative, both in politics and in their approach to constitutional challenges to the actions of state and local officials. The political uproar over President Roosevelt's "court-packing" proposal, which reflected Roosevelt's frustration at the iron grip his Republican predecessors had fastened on the Supreme Court and the lower federal bench, through lifetime appointments of conservative judges, reached its peak shortly after Walter Gobitis filed his suit. Fortunately for Gobitis, his case was assigned to Judge Albert B. Maris, one of Roosevelt's first judicial appointments in Pennsylvania. Although Maris was a Quaker, from a small religious group noted for pacifism and tolerance, he had served with distinction in World War I.

The lawyers who defended the Minersville school board promptly urged Judge Maris to dismiss the suit, arguing that the flag-salute ceremony had no religious content and was simply a "secular regulation" of the curriculum, adopted for the "reasonable" purpose of "inculcating patriotism" in the students. The board had simply exercised its "police powers" to protect the "health, safety, welfare, and morals" of Minersville students, powers that courts traditionally protected against federal invasion. The board's lawyers argued that the U.S. Constitution did not restrict the powers of state and local officials, and they also pointed Judge Maris to several state court decisions which rejected flag-salute challenges, including the Massachusetts Supreme Court opinion dismissing the case brought by Carleton Nicholls.

After hearing the board's arguments, Judge Maris refused to dismiss the Gobitis suit and set the case for trial in February 1938. The judge's written opinion found the rights at issue not in the First Amendment, but in the Pennsylvania constitution, which protected "rights of conscience" against state and local abridgment. These rights were superior to the "police powers" claimed by the school board, and were included in the right to "liberty" protected by the Fourteenth Amendment. "In applying this principle," Judge Maris concluded, "the individual concerned must be the judge of the validity of his own religious beliefs."

When Judge Maris called the case to trial, Lillian and William Gobitis explained their religious beliefs and objections to the flag-salute ceremony in clear and convincing words. Superintendent Roudabush followed them to the witness stand, displaying his contempt for the children's stand. Asked by Judge Maris if he felt the children "sincerely held" their religious beliefs, Roudabush disagreed: "I feel that they were indoctrinated." The example of even a few objectors, he claimed, would be "demoralizing" and would spread "a disregard for our flag and country" among Minersville students, including "foreigners of every variety" who needed practice in patriotism to become good Americans.

In his final opinion, issued in June 1938, Judge Maris found it "clear from the evidence that the refusal of these two earnest Christian children to salute the flag cannot even remotely prejudice or imperil the safety, health, morals, property or personal rights of their fellows." He compared the "sincerity of conviction and devotion to principle" that Lillian and William Gobitis displayed with "that which brought our pioneer ancestors across the sea to seek liberty of conscience in a new land." Judge Maris ordered the Minersville school board to readmit the Gobitis children and to excuse them from participation in the flag-salute ceremony.

Lillian and William never returned to the Minersville schools. Judge Maris stayed his order, pending the board's appeal of his decision to the U.S. Court of Appeals in Philadelphia. Another eighteen months passed before the three-judge panel issued its decision, expressed in a unanimous opinion written by Judge William S. Clark. Although Clark was a Republican, first appointed to the federal district bench in 1925, President Roosevelt elevated him to the appellate court in 1938, rewarding Clark's judicial support of union organizers who faced local repression of their rights of speech and assembly. Victorious in the "Constitutional Revolution" that ended with Supreme Court approval in 1937 of New Deal laws to protect labor organizing, Roosevelt by 1938 had begun to reshape the entire federal judiciary, and he had appointed all three judges who decided the Gobitis case.

Judge Clark's opinion bristled with scorn for compulsory flag-salute laws. "Eighteen big states have seen fit to exert their power over a small number of little children," he began. The compulsory salute "happens to be abhorrent to the particular love of God of the little girl and boy now seeking our protection." After listing more than a hundred opinions upholding the "police powers" of the states, Judge Clark found them too light in balancing the judicial scale against the claims of religious dissenters.

After two judicial defeats, the Minersville school board first decided against a final appeal to the U.S. Supreme Court. But promises of financial support from "patriotic" groups overcame the board's initial reluctance. Asking the Supreme Court to hear the case did not guarantee a ruling; five times in recent years the justices had declined to review flag-salute cases decided by lower courts. All those cases, however, had upheld the state or local laws. Declining to hear an appeal from Judge Clark's opinion, on the other hand, would leave his decision in place. Along with this factor, it seems likely that the Supreme Court looked at the looming war clouds over Europe in deciding to hear a case that raised issues of patriotism and loyalty.

Joseph W. Henderson, the Philadelphia lawyer hired by the Minersville school board, repeated the arguments he had made without success in two lower courts when he appeared before the Supreme Court on April 25, 1940. The core of Henderson's argument was that the flag-salute ceremony "is not a religious rite" and was intended simply to inculcate "loyalty to the State and National Government." Two lawyers divided the time allotted to Walter Gobitis and his children. George K. Gardner, a professor at Harvard Law School, presented the position of the American Civil Liberties Union, stressing the primacy of the First Amendment in conflicts with state and local officials. Joseph Rutherford, who practiced law before he began leading the Witnesses, restated the theological objections of his followers to flag-salute laws.

When the nine justices met around their mahogany conference table to debate and decide the Gobitis case, the first to speak was Chief Justice Charles Evans Hughes, a former Secretary of State and Republican presidential candidate in 1916. Hughes assured his colleagues that the case had "nothing to do with religion" and involved only "a question of state power" to foster patriotism in the classroom. The only other justice to speak at length at the conference was Felix Frankfurter, who had arrived in New York City at the age of twelve, an Austrian Jew who spoke no English. Two years later, Frankfurter graduated from high school, his command of English polished by reciting Abraham Lincoln's wartime appeals to patriotism and national unity.

Impressed by Frankfurter's "moving statement at conference on the role of the public school in instilling love of country" in the children of immigrants, Chief Justice Hughes asked him to write the Court's opinion in the Gobitis case. Because none of the justices had objected at the conference, Hughes assumed that Frankfurter would write for a unanimous court.

Frankfurter's opinion began with a bow to the "grave responsibility" the Court faced in balancing "the conflicting claims of liberty and authority." The Gobitis case, he noted, forced the Court "to reconcile two rights in order to prevent either from destroying the other." America's historic role as a haven for religious dissenters required that "every possible leeway should be given to the claims of religious faith."

Despite these disclaimers, Frankfurter rejected claims that First Amendment rights deserved special protection against abridgment by legislative bodies. Religious belief, he wrote, "does not relieve the citizen from the discharge of political responsibilities." Frankfurter venerated the flag as a symbol that fostered "the binding tie of cohesive sentiment" among the citizens. "We live by symbols," he quoted from his judicial hero, Justice Oliver Wendell Holmes. Frankfurter also tied the flag-salute ceremony to growing concerns about defense preparedness: "National unity is the basis of national security." He ended his civics lesson with a warning that exempting Lillian and William Gobitis from the salute "might cast doubts in the minds of the other children" and weaken their American loyalty.

Frankfurter expected his opinion to gain unanimous support, and he was upset when Justice Harlan Fiske Stone circulated a dissenting opinion among his fellows. Stone took direct aim at Frankfurter's claim that "national security" interests could outweigh First Amendment rights. The flag-salute regulation forced the Gobitis children to deny "what they sincerely believe to be the higher commandments of God" and "violates their deepest religious convictions," Stone wrote. He noted that most laws which restricted personal liberties were aimed at "politically helpless minorities" such as Jehovah's Witnesses, who were treated with "little toleration" by those who resented their aggressive preaching.

Justice Frankfurter pleaded with Stone to withdraw his dissenting opinion in a private letter which expressed the "judicial restraint" position that Frankfurter had begun shaping. The Supreme Court should not "exercise our judicial power unduly" and thereby hold "too tight a rein" on state and local officials, he argued. Frankfurter bluntly raised the fears of global war that his published opinion skirted. Patriotic observances in preparing for wartime were "surely not irrelevant" in resolving the flag-salute debate, he told Stone. This exchange of letters expressed a basic conflict over judicial power which continues to divide members of the Supreme Court. Frankfurter would defer to "the organs of popular government" while Stone believed "the Constitution tips the balance" in favor of religion.

Frankfurter prevailed by an 8–1 vote in this battle of contending judicial philosophies, and the Supreme Court announced its decision in favor of the Minersville school board on June 3, 1940.

Supreme Court decisions often are criticized, and some are disobeyed, but few have ever provoked as violent a public reaction as the Gobitis opinion. Frankfurter's words unleashed a wave of attacks on Witnesses across the country. Within two weeks of the Court's decision, two federal officials later wrote, "hundreds of attacks upon the Witnesses were reported to the Department of Justice."

The Justice Department officials listed several of the most violent incidents. "At Kennebunk, Maine, the Kingdom Hall was burned. At Rockville, Maryland, the police assisted a mob in dispersing a Bible meeting. At Litchfield, Illinois, practically the entire town mobbed a company of some sixty Witnesses who were canvassing it, and it was necessary to call on the state troopers to protect the members of the sect." The federal officials were horrified by reports that the "chief of police and deputy sheriff had forced a group of Jehovah's Witnesses to drink large doses of castor oil and had paraded the victims through the streets of Richwood, West Virginia, tied together with police department rope." Equally horrifying, a Nebraska Witness was kidnapped, beaten, and castrated by vigilantes. The federal officials traced these terrorist acts directly to the Supreme Court's opinion in the Gobitis case. "In the two years following the decision," they wrote, "the files of the Department of Justice reflect an uninterrupted record of violence and persecution of the Witnesses. Almost without exception, the flag and the flag salute can be found as the percussion cap that sets off these acts."

Attacks on Witnesses fell off once the nation's attention shifted to wartime battlefields in Europe and the Pacific, but the widespread publicity they received damaged the Supreme Court's image as the ultimate arbiter of justice. Respected newspapers and scholars heaped criticism on the Court. In a 1942 opinion, three justices—William O. Douglas, Hugo Black, and Frank Murphy—declared that the Court had "wrongly decided" the Gobitis case and hinted broadly their eagerness to reverse that decision. When Douglas reported Black's change of mind, Justice Frankfurter scornfully asked if Black had been reading the Constitution. "No, but he has read the papers," Douglas replied.

Two new justices, Wiley Rutledge and Robert Jackson, joined the Court after the Gobitis decision. Their first votes indicated an intention to "tip the balance" toward the Witnesses in future cases. With a new majority in control, the Court agreed early in 1943 to decide a flag-salute case from West Virginia which was virtually identical in facts to the Gobitis case. The children of three Witnesses who lived near Charleston—Walter Barnette, Lucy McClure, and Paul Stull—had been expelled from school after the state board of education adopted a flag-salute regulation in 1942 which quoted liberally from Frankfurter's opinion in the Gobitis case.

Justice Jackson wrote a powerful opinion in the Barnette case which struck down the West Virginia law. Efforts to foster "national unity" through compulsion and coercion exposed religious dissenters like the Witnesses to the persecution of "village tyrants" and "evil men," Jackson warned. He cited "the Roman drive to stamp out Christianity" and "the fast-failing efforts of our present totalitarian enemies" as examples of the futility of compelled belief. "Those who begin coercive elimination of dissent soon find themselves exterminating dissenters. Compulsory unification of opinion achieves only the unanimity of the graveyard."

Justice Frankfurter had refused to protect First Amendment rights from limitation by local officials and electoral majorities. Justice Jackson took direct aim at this deferential position. "The very purpose of a Bill of Rights was to withdraw certain subjects from the vicissitudes of political controversy, to place them beyond the reach of majorities and officials," he wrote. "One's right to life, liberty, and property, to free speech, a free press, freedom of worship and assembly, and other fundamental rights may not be submitted to vote; they depend on the outcome of no elections."

Jackson ended with an eloquent affirmation of the libertarian ethic that found its first American expression in the Declaration of Independence. "If there is any fixed star in our constitutional constellation," he wrote, "it is that no official, high or petty, can prescribe what shall be orthodox in politics, nationalism, religion, or other matters of opinion, or force citizens to confess by word or act their faith therein."

In deciding the *Barnette* case, the Supreme Court expressly overruled its *Gobitis* decision, only three years after it was issued with only one dissent. Underscoring the symbolic impact of this reversal, the Court struck down the West Virginia flag-salute law on June 14, 1943—Flag Day.

II.
"Here Comes Jehovah!"

I was born in Minersville, Pennsylvania, in 1923. Both of my parents were also born in Minersville. Mother was Pennsylvania Dutch, and her family had been there more than two hundred years. Dad's family came straight to Minersville from a month-long trip from Lithuania. There are a lot of Lithuanians and Middle Europeans in Minersville. I think they must have known someone, and came straight to work in the coal mines, like my grandfather did. My grandmother was a self-made woman, who didn't even know how to read. She just bought property. Europeans believe in getting property. She opened up a bar, and she took in boarders. Later she opened a grocery store, which became my father's. As all of her children got married, she gave them a business, and she sent one of my uncles to college. For a little peasant woman, that was something.

We lived in a big house, over the store which was called the Economy Grocery. There were six of us finally, and I was the first. We had to work in the grocery store and we were very glad about that. The majority of the fathers worked in the coal mines, so having a grocery store was much nicer. Some children would lose their fathers with black damp, or a rock fall in the mine.

It was hard in Minersville during the Depression years. I remember Dad had a little account book for the bills that people ran up, all yellow and old. Some people never paid, but he never went after them. When the WPA and relief finally came along, it was quite a help. Those measures were very good. My uncle died on the WPA, from a heart attack, and my aunt was on relief. At least we had food. Everything else was do-it-yourself. We learned to sew, and make do with a lot of hand-me-downs. It was not awful. We were really a jolly family. While we worked we would listen to those old radio shows.

Dad was raised Catholic and Mother was Methodist, although her parents had been Jehovah's Witnesses since 1904. Mother and all the children were very active in the Methodist church. It was my father that first delved into being a Witness, when my grandparents came to live with us for a while. He started just out of curiosity. What takes so much of their time? When they were gone, he would look into their literature, because they didn't want to make him a captive audience. So we would come home from Sunday school and he would ask what we had learned, and he would say, Oh, look at this, look at that! Dad would enthusiastically call attention to Scriptures that indicated hell was man's common grave instead of torment, and also delightful verses from Isaiah that we felt would mean also a literal earthly paradise. Pretty soon we were having a Bible study in our home and not going to church.

In the summer of 1935, Judge Rutherford, the president of the Watchtower Society of Jehovah's Witnesses, gave this talk on the radio about what the Scriptures say on emblems. He said that he himself wouldn't give a salute to the flag, not because he didn't respect the flag as a symbol of the country but because of what the Scripture says about worshipping an image of the State.

We were all at different schools, but we liked them very much. I loved school, and I was with a nice group. I was actually kind of popular. I was class president in the seventh grade, and I had good grades. And I felt that, Oh, if I stop saluting the flag, I will blow all this! And I did. It sure worked out that way. I really was so fearful that, when the teacher would look my way, I would quick put out my hand and move my lips. We knew that Carleton Nicholls up in Lynn, Massachusetts, took a stand against the salute in school. He was expelled from school, and the story was in the newspapers.

My brother William was in the fifth grade at that time, the fall of 1935. The next day Bill came home and said, I stopped saluting the flag. So I knew this was the moment! This wasn't something my parents forced on us. They were very firm about that, that what you do is your decision, and you should understand what you're doing. I did a lot of reading and checking in the Bible and I really took my own stand.

I went first to my teacher, Miss Anna Shofstal, so I couldn't chicken out of it. She listened to my explanation and surprisingly, she just hugged me and said she thought it was very nice, to have courage like that. But the students were awful. I really should have explained to the whole class but I was fearful. I didn't know whether it was right to stand up or sit down. These days, we realize that the salute itself is the motions and the words. So I sat down and the whole room was aghast. After that, when I'd come to school, they would throw a hail of pebbles and yell things like, Here comes Jehovah! They were just jeering at me. Some of my girl friends would come and ask what it was about. That was nice. One-on-one is a lot easier.

They watched us for two weeks, my brother and I and Edmund Wasliewski, who was another Witness who wouldn't salute. With my brother, the teacher tried to force his arm up and he just held onto his pocket. After two weeks, they had the school-board meeting and Dad and Mom both went. They had grown up with these men on the school board and gone to school with them. The superintendent, Dr. Roudabush, was a very firm type of person, and Dr. McGurl, the board president, was also very firm. The others kind of followed suit.

Dad told the school board why we couldn't take part in the flag salute. Dad told us he was very nervous at the meeting. The board made its decision right then, without much discussion. The idea was that we were insubordinate, and there would be immediate expulsion. They said at the meeting, Don't even come to school tomorrow!

After we were expelled, we set up a school at home. There was a girl that helped out my mother in the house, about 16, and she taught us up on the third floor. They did permit us to have our books. Very shortly after that, we got an official letter and they said if you are not in a qualified school you will be sent to a reformatory. This was quite a problem. We didn't have a qualified teacher. But at that time there were so many children taking a stand, and there were all these newspaper articles about expulsions.

One day, Paul and Verna Jones telephoned us and said, We

are beginning a school in New Ringgold, Pennsylvania. They had a hundred-acre farm and it was real scratch. But they were a fine, fine family. They knocked out the wall between the dining room and living room and made it into a big country schoolhouse. There were forty of us all together, and three families boarded us. Twenty-two of us boarded with the Jones. We would sleep three to a bed, and there were beds in the hallways and people everywhere. We had to get up at 6 o'clock and do chores. But it was a lot of fun.

The farm was 30 miles from Minersville, and we had to stay there until the weekend. The roads were little two-lane highways, and it took a good while to make the 30 miles. Finally my father said, We need to have a school bus. We had a panel truck for the store and he put seats on both sides. We would start out at about 6 o'clock in the morning and all along the way we would pick up these *little* children and they'd be huddled in the winter cold and dark. It took about two hours to get to school, and we would have to go down dirt lanes to get to some of the houses. Dad drove the bus for two years. We didn't think our ordeal was pitiful. We had a good time. But when I look back, it *was* pitiful.

There was one girl named Eleanor in the Kingdom School who became a firm friend. We met earlier in 1935 in jail, when we were mobbed in the town of New Philadelphia and put into cells in the fire house. The churches there let out early on Sunday for the convenience of the mob. There were about forty of us that went into New Philadelphia to do witnessing from house to house. I remember being at a door, all alone, when this police car came up and the householder was kind of aghast at this little girl being taken away. I was eleven at that time. The police called me into the car and took me past the mob into the fire house. I remember one girl punched me and the mob was trying to break down the door of the fire house. There must have been close to a thousand people. We *did* expect trouble, we anticipated that. It was scary. But at the same time, you feel a certain calm when you're finally in the thick of it. Finally, at the end of the day the mob dispersed. The police kept the men, and the women and children could go home. They finally got out on bail and went back for a trial. I guess they had a few days in jail after that.

That was one of many attacks on Witnesses, like Mauch Chunk,

McAdoo, and Kulpmont in Pennsylvania; and Plainfield, Secaucus, and Perth Amboy in New Jersey. My father was in many of those, because we would all go as a group and try to witness, door to door. Many times, they were held a few days in jail. The main thing that made me hesitate about going along was thinking of my friends in the public school. But here were these *marvelous* friends in the Kingdom School, so it was certainly no loss.

One time when we did street work with our literature in Minersville, two girls passed by. They were my close friends in school, and I overheard them saying, Just think, we used to be friends with *her!* I remember knocking at a door and the girl inside said to her family, There's that Lillian Gobitis. But because we went to the Kingdom School we were kind of out of sight, out of mind. One girl in my school, who was really the smartest in the whole class, became a Witness and nine days ago I met her in Florida at one of our conventions. She told me that she asked her mother, Where are the Gobitises? Where's Lillian? They must have moved away! What happened to us really wasn't publicized until it got into the courts.

After we had been expelled, one of the Catholic churches in Minersville announced a boycott of our store, and it meant a great deal to us. More children had been born, and it was our living, so it was very important. Business fell off quite a lot. Sometimes my Dad sent my brother to my aunt's house next door for a loan, because it was kind of critical. After a while, though, time went by and the people felt that this was kind of ridiculous, that the priest would tell them where to buy their groceries. Dad was really well known and he made a go of it by making farmer sausage and kielbasi. People came from everywhere for these things and this is how we survived the boycott. So they came back.

The Kingdom School only went to eighth grade, so I had a problem after the two years. I still needed to go to school, and that's when I went to the business school in Pottsville, just four miles away, so I was living at home then. I just spent a year there. And after that we got a teacher who was able to teach high school. The teacher we had in New Ringgold was not a Witness but she felt so strongly about children getting expelled that she quit her position in Allentown and volunteered to teach us for a hundred dollars a month. All these families would just get up somehow and pay her. Her name was Erma Metzger, and she was a marvelous person. She became a Witness later. It was such a blessing. They got these school desks out of auctions for about thirty cents each, and books and everything just came out of the woodwork.

We wouldn't have done anything about our expulsion, but since the school board was so firm in our case, the Watchtower Society said they would like to use ours as a test case. Some schools were very kind and took the children back, but there were thousands that had hard, hard treatment, who were knocked against the wall and beaten and went home crying and almost hysterical.

I remember the trial in our case very vividly. It was in Philadelphia, at the federal court. Judge Maris was a quiet-looking person, a calm-looking person. He was a very agreeable person, not formidable at all. Bill and I had to go on the stand and testify. He explained that the Ten Commandments in Exodus 20 was our reason for not saluting the flag. When it was my turn I explained First John 5:21, "little children, keep yourselves from idols." I remember the school-board lawyer saying, I object! We have had one scripture and that's enough, he said. But he was overruled. Dr. Roudabush was very feisty on the stand, very angry and hostile. But we never felt any animosity on our part toward him. Like the Scriptures show, you hope that some day they'll change, and many do.

We felt completely optimistic about the case. Judge Maris had given such a marvelous opinion, and the three judges on the appellate court gave a favorable opinion. So when it went to Washington, my family went down to hear the argument in the Supreme Court. First there was a corporation case, and there was a lot of shuffling and noise and questions. Then they started our case with Mr. Gardner from the Civil Liberties Union. The justices still were not completely attentive to him. After that, Judge Rutherford argued our case. He did it a lot from a Biblical standpoint, like with Shadrach, Meshach, and Abednego, when they took a stand and wouldn't bow down to the image of Nebuchadnezzar. And of course he discussed legal things too. It was extremely arresting. You could really hear a pin drop! The justices listened so attentively.

With all this rapt attention, we felt very optimistic. And then, months later, we were in the kitchen with the radio on and it was time for the news, and they said, In Washington today, the

Supreme Court decided the flag case. It was against us, eight to one. Talk about a cold feeling! We absolutely did not expect that. That just set off a *wave* of persecution. It was like open season on Jehovah's Witnesses. That's when the mobs escalated. The Kingdom Hall in Litchfield, Illinois was totally destroyed by a mob, and there were more than three thousand Witnesses arrested every year for the next three years.

Sometimes a bunch of us teenagers would go out, calling on the homes in a town, and pretty soon a group starts to form, throwing tin cans and rocks at us. We would keep a car nearby and just go to another part of the territory. I remember on Wednesday nights we all did free family home Bible studies with people who wanted to learn more, and we would drop each other off along the road and the last one would pick us up. In this one place, I was driving to pick up Daddy, and a group came and started to let the air out of the tires and surround the car. I stepped on the gas and my father said, Don't you *ever* do that again! You could have hurt someone.

But that was such a common thing. Some of the Witnesses were attacked and badly hurt, like Rosco Jones, who went to the Supreme Court to challenge a licensing tax against Witnesses in Opelika, Alabama. He was a black Witness and his wife was arrested in La Grange, Georgia. He went to the local jail to see about her. They took him down in the basement and held him spread-eagled and hit him with an old bicycle tire, and kicked him in the ribs and stomach. Finally he fell unconscious and woke up in a cell. They released him after four or five days and pointed a pistol at him and said, If we *ever* see you with that black box— his book bag—you'll have had it! Some people had very hard ordeals, and some of them died later as a result of the injuries. And sometimes there were miraculous escapes.

After our case was decided, my brother Bill was called to the world headquarters of the Jehovah's Witnesses in Brooklyn. First he was doing what we call Pioneering, full-time service. We were in a bad situation at home, because the store always needed him, and he really was not able to make his quotas in home visits. So he had an opportunity to move to New York and live with a couple in the Bronx for a very nominal rent. Then he said, Lillian, why don't *you* come too. By that time, the husband was in prison in Danbury, Connecticut, because of the military. Hundreds of

Witnesses went to prison during the war because they were turned down for exemption as ministers. We consider all Witnesses to be ministers, and draft boards refused to recognize that.

So I moved there to the Bronx in New York. That was *very* interesting. And my partner was Eleanor, the girl that I had met in jail and had gone to Kingdom School with. We each had twenty home Bible studies. The world situation was so bad, the war was still on, and there was a lot of interest in Jehovah's Witnesses. We subsisted on donations in those days. You could go anywhere on the subway for five cents, and sometimes, when our little rent was due, we would get all worried, but some little old lady would say, Oh, I appreciate you girls coming! It was a free arrangement, but every once in a while they wanted to make a little donation and that took care of the rent for that month. We really had a wonderful time.

After a few months, I was called to the world headquarters in Brooklyn. This was a tremendous privilege, because there were people from all over the country and around the world who were giants of faith. They all had been in full-time service before they went there, and they were from all walks of life. There weren't many girls called to work there; it was mostly heavy work and we did mostly cleaning.

But we also had a radio station that served New York and Connecticut, and I was given a little part on the show after school every day. It was called Rachel and Uncle John. I was Rachel and Uncle John was played by an elderly gentleman, Mr. Macmillan, who would tell me Bible stories. Working with Brother Macmillan was no ordinary privilege. He had been one of the eight Watchtower officials who were incarcerated in Atlanta Penitentiary in 1919, and during the war years of the 'forties he visited a circuit of twenty-one prisons to encourage the men who were there for their Christian neutrality. Mr. Knorr, who became president of the Watchtower Society after Judge Rutherford died, said that the reason he chose me for the show was because of the flag salute case! So that opened doors.

After we lost our case, we thought that this is it and we'll just have to endure. Problems in the world were escalating, and we would get reports from Germany about hideous things. There were ten thousand Witnesses in the concentration camps and two thousand were finally killed. We just thought things would escalate until what the Scriptures call Armageddon and it would be the end of this system of things. We just need to endure, that was the feeling.

In 1943, we went back to Washington for the Supreme Court hearing in the Barnette case from West Virginia. This was a case that was almost the same as our flag-salute case. The people in that case were all cousins; the Stulls and McClures were cousins of the Barnettes. They were in the courtroom too, but no one thought to introduce us. A few years ago, we had a traveling minister down here in Atlanta named Dave McClure, and we went to a meeting where my husband told his experiences from the German concentration camps. And Erwin said, Dave, why don't you tell us your experiences from your case. And that was really an occasion, because it's like, you know this story but you really don't know how it ended. So he told about how on the school bus the kids were always picking fights with him. He was kind of a tough one and he'd battle his way out of the fights, and this was a daily thing. When their case went before the courts, the opposition lawyer didn't prepare because he thought it was an open-and-shut case. We'll just go by the Gobitis precedent and that's all!

In the Barnette case, we felt more optimistic this time, like there's a light at the end of the tunnel. We *never* thought it would come to court again. Already, there were rumors that Justices Murphy and Douglas and Black were changing their minds. We also knew that Justice Murphy was having his portrait done for the capitol in Michigan, where he had been governor, and the artist was one of Jehovah's Witnesses. He had long conversations with Justice Murphy while he was sitting for his portrait, and Murphy was expressing that he surely had second thoughts. And the newspapers, and Eleanor Roosevelt in her column, My Day, and Attorney General Biddle, all began to express sympathy for us. This was ridiculous, they said, treating us like Communists. These are little children, following their convictions. So the atmosphere changed, and the Court was won over on Flag Day—June 14, 1943. We really never thought that day would come.

Then our work took on a whole different nature. The missionary school, which was called the Gilead School, opened up right after that, in Ithaca, New York. We had people from all walks of life and countries. Nationalism is so foolish, and when we have ethnic or national or economic barriers, what richness of friendship we lose! Since Jehovah's Witnesses don't have that problem, we really made wonderful friends. Well, there were a series of conventions in Europe in 1951, and I was given a plane ticket by Mr. Macmillan. His son was in Europe in the military and had sent him a ticket, but he said, Rachel, I'm so old and tired and I've been in Europe so often with the Witnesses. You want to go so badly, so please use this ticket. And I surely did!

Since I was from the world headquarters I was allowed to stay at all the branches in Europe, and I met Erwin Klose at the branch in Wiesbaden, Germany. One evening they had a get-together and there was a concert pianist and violinist and singing. Erwin was a wonderful tenor, and when it was over I went up to tell him I thought he had a marvelous voice. He just kept smiling and I kept talking, and I found out later he did not understand one word of English! He had been arrested eleven times in Germany and occupied Holland and Belgium, and the Gestapo was always pursuing him.

After that Erwin took a crash course in English so he could attend the missionary school at Ithaca, and after he graduated we dated. He was sent to Austria and they permitted me to go through the Gilead School too. And in 1954 I sailed away to Vienna, Austria, and joined him in marriage and in missionary work. We just had a storybook life in Vienna. When I look back, I think that the very thing that caused me to lose my friends, the flag-salute case, was what caused Mr. Knorr to choose me for the service in which I had this storybook life.

After we came back to the United States, I went to work for a while and Erwin started a business in New York, representing a man we had met in Vienna who made tamping machines for railroad tracks. Erwin was very successful and later sold the business after it was a million-dollar business. Then we lived for six years in Canada and then we came to Atlanta in 1967. We were going where the need is greater. We had a beautiful home in New York and in Canada, but when we moved to Atlanta we decided to live in a mobile home, and we're still in the same mobile home twenty years later!

Our children did not have the problems my brother and I had in school as Jehovah's Witnesses. When we moved to Atlanta, Stephen was twelve and Judith was ten. They were granted exemptions from the flag salute in school, which had been the objective of all the court cases. One day Judith came home and said all the girls were waiting for her in the girls' room, and they shoved her to the floor and she had to battle her way out of it. Erwin asked me to go to the school counselor and he said, Mrs. Klose, they did that because she is one of Jehovah's Witnesses. That was during the miniskirt time and we didn't let her wear miniskirts. That was part of the ridicule, calling attention to her as a Witness. And the counselor said, I will not have that in my school, so he called the parents and everyone apologized.

It has been more than fifty years since I took a stand on the flag salute, but I would do it again in a second. Without reservations! Jehovah's Witnesses do feel that we're trying to follow the Scriptures, and Jesus said, They persecuted me, and they will persecute you also. We do expect that before the end there will be a tremendous, all-out wave of persecution. Jehovah's Witnesses are now banned in over forty countries. So we really try to build up our faith, to meet the apathy about religion that we meet from door to door. Still and all, the case affected our lives so much that Erwin and I would never have met each other without it, and we have passed its lessons on to our children.

2

Gordon Hirabayashi
v. United States

Gordon Hirabayashi was a University of
Washington senior in 1942 when he defied the
military curfew and exclusion orders that forced
Japanese Americans into wartime internment
camps. *Courtesy of Steven Okazaki, Mouchette Films,
San Francisco, CA*

I.
"A Jap's a Jap"

On the morning of May 16, 1942, Gordon Kiyoshi Hirabayashi arrived at the FBI office in Seattle, Washington. Somewhat formal in demeanor, the University of Washington senior shook hands with Special Agent Francis V. Manion and introduced his companion, Arthur Barnett, a young lawyer and fellow member of Seattle's Quaker community. Five days earlier, Gordon had defied a military order that required "all persons of Japanese ancestry" to register for evacuation to the state fairground at Puyallup, south of Seattle. From this temporary home, where Army troops herded them into cattle stalls and tents, the uprooted Japanese Americans would be shipped to "relocation centers" in desolate areas of desert or swampland, from California to Arkansas. Forced into exile, more than 120,000 Americans of Japanese ancestry endured wartime internment in America's concentration camps, housed in tarpaper barracks and guarded by armed soldiers.

After a few minutes of small talk, Gordon handed Agent Manion a neatly typed four-page document, headed "Why I refused to register for evacuation." Gordon's statement reflected his anguish as a Quaker volunteer over moving evacuees to the Puyallup fairground. "This order for the mass evacuation of all persons of Japanese descent denies them the right to live," he wrote. "It forces thousands of energetic, law-abiding individuals to exist in a miserable psychological, and a horrible physical, atmosphere." Gordon pointed out that native-born American citizens like himself constituted a majority of the evacuees, yet their rights "are denied on a wholesale scale without due process of law and civil liberties." His statement ended on a defiant note: "If I were to register and cooperate under those circumstances, I would be giving helpless consent to the denial of practically all of the things which give me incentive to live. I must maintain my Christian principles. I consider it my duty to maintain the democratic standards for which this nation lives. Therefore, I must refuse this order for evacuation."

After reading the statement, Manion reminded Gordon that he risked a year's imprisonment for his stand. Gordon remained adamant, even after Manion drove him to the registration center and offered a last chance to sign the forms. When they returned to the FBI office, Manion conferred with the U.S. attorney, who then filed criminal charges against Gordon for violating the evacuation order.

After placing his prisoner in the King County jail, Manion dug into Gordon's briefcase and discovered a diary that confessed his violation of the military curfew orders that kept Japanese Americans off the streets in the weeks before evacuation. "Peculiar, but I receive a lift—perhaps it is a release—when I consciously break the silly old curfew," Gordon wrote one night after escorting his friend Helen Blom to her home. Manion reported his find to the U.S. attorney, who promptly filed an additional criminal charge against Gordon for curfew violation.

The wartime internment of Japanese Americans began soon after the Japanese attack on Pearl Harbor of December 7, 1941. After an initial period of tolerance and press reminders that most residents of Japanese ancestry were "good Americans, born and educated as such," public pressure mounted for their mass removal from coastal states. Fueled by past decades of "Yellow Peril" agitation, and current fears of a follow-up "sneak attack" upon the American mainland, this campaign enlisted politicians and pundits. Los Angeles congressman Leland Ford urged in mid-January, 1942, that "all Japanese, whether citizens or not, be placed in inland concentration camps." The next month, right-wing columnist Westbrook Pegler demanded that Japanese Americans be placed "under armed guard to the last man and woman right now—and to hell with habeas corpus until the danger is over."

Despite these incendiary appeals, federal officials charged with protecting the Pacific coast from sabotage and espionage saw no reason for mass evacuation. Acting on orders from Attorney General Francis Biddle, FBI agents arrested more than two thousand Japanese aliens in the days after Pearl Harbor. Justice Department officers conducted individual loyalty hearings for this group; most were promptly released and returned to their families. The FBI also investigated hundreds of Army reports of signals to enemy submarines off the coast by lights or illicit radios, and dismissed each report as unfounded. FBI director J. Edgar Hoover reported that "the army was getting a bit hysterical" in blaming the phantom lights on Japanese Americans.

Attorney General Biddle, with Hoover's reports in hand, assured President Franklin Roosevelt on February 7 that Army officials had offered "no reasons for mass evacuation" as a military measure. Secretary of War Henry Stimson, a respected elder statesman in Roosevelt's wartime cabinet, shared Biddle's concerns: "We cannot discriminate among our citizens on the ground of racial origin," Stimson wrote in early February. Any forced removal of Japanese Americans, he noted, would tear "a tremendous hole in our constitutional system." Stimson felt that internment on racial grounds would conflict with the Due Process clause of the Fifth Amendment, which required formal charges and trial before any person could be deprived of "liberty" and confined by the government.

Within days of these statements, Biddle and Stimson capitulated to the advocates of internment. Three of Stimson's War Department subordinates combined to overcome his constitutional qualms. Stimson had asked his deputy, John J. McCloy, to frame a "final recommendation" on the treatment of Japanese Americans. McCloy, who scornfully dismissed the Constitution as "a piece of paper" which military officials could tear into shreds, later defended the internment as "retribution" for the Japanese attack on Pearl Harbor.

Colonel Karl Bendetsen, the young lawyer whom McCloy had delegated to draft the report to Stimson, exemplified the persistence of racial stereotypes: "The Japanese race is an enemy race," Bendetsen wrote over the signature of General John L. DeWitt, the West Coast Army commander. Even among those born in the United States, Bendetsen argued, "the racial strains are undiluted." General DeWitt hardly bothered to mask his racial prejudice. Regardless of citizenship, DeWitt bluntly told a congressional panel, "a Jap's a Jap."

The fate of Japanese Americans was sealed at a showdown meeting on February 17, 1942. McCloy and Bendetsen presented Attorney General Biddle with a proposed presidential order, providing that "any or all persons may be excluded" from their homes on military order. Biddle's deputy, Edward Ennis, heatedly opposed the War Department proposal on constitutional grounds, but arguments of "military necessity" finally persuaded the Attorney General. Two days later, President Roosevelt signed Executive Order 9066 and General DeWitt assigned Colonel Bendetsen to implement the evacuation and internment plans.

Gordon Hirabayashi languished in the King County jail for five months before his trial on October 20, 1942. Judge Lloyd Black, a former state prosecutor and American Legion post commander, had already dismissed the constitutional challenge filed by Gordon's trial lawyer, Frank Walters, who argued that the Constitution barred any form of racial discrimination. Rejecting this "technical interpretation" of the Fifth Amendment, Black answered that individual rights "should not be permitted to endanger all of the constitutional rights of the whole citizenry" during wartime. Judge Black added a large dose of racism to his opinion. Branding the Japanese as "unbelievably treacherous and wholly ruthless," he conjured up "suicide parachutists" who would drop from the skies onto Seattle's aircraft factories. Black predicted that these airborne invaders would seek "human camouflage and with uncanny skill discover and take advantage of any disloyalty among their kind." The military curfew and evacuation orders, he concluded, were reasonable protections against the "diabolically clever use of infiltration tactics" by potential Japanese saboteurs.

After this opinion, Gordon's trial became a perfunctory exercise. Gordon admitted his intentional violation of the curfew and evacuation orders, and explained to the all-male, elderly jurors his belief that "I should be given the privileges of a citizen" under the

Constitution, regardless of his race or ancestry. The government prosecutor, Allen Pomeroy, called Gordon's father as a prosecution witness, hoping that his halting English would remind the jurors of Gordon's ties to the Japanese enemy. Gordon's parents, brought to court from a California internment camp, spent two weeks in the King County jail on Judge Black's order.

After the trial testimony ended, Frank Walters told the jurors that "I am not representing a man who violated a valid law of the United States" and restated his attack on the racial basis of the military orders. Asking the jurors to convict Gordon, Allen Pomeroy reminded them of his Japanese ancestry and warned that "if we don't win this war with Japan there will be no trial by jury."

Judge Black sent the jurors to their deliberations with an instruction that the military orders were "valid and enforceable" laws. Whether Gordon had violated the orders was the only question for decision. Black answered for the jurors, telling them that "you are instructed to return a finding of guilty" on both criminal counts. The dutiful jurors returned in ten minutes with the proper verdicts, and Black sentenced Gordon to concurrent sentences of three months in jail for each conviction. Frank Walter stated his intention to appeal the convictions, and Gordon returned to jail after Judge Black denied his request for release on bail until the appeal was decided.

Before the U.S. Court of Appeals met in San Francisco to hear Gordon's appeal, two other internment challenges reached the appellate judges. Minoru Yasui, a young Oregon lawyer and Army reserve officer, had been convicted of curfew violation and sentenced to the maximum term of one year in jail. Before his trial, Yasui had spent nine months in solitary confinement. Fred Korematsu, a shipyard welder in the San Francisco area, had volunteered for Navy service before the Pearl Harbor attack but was rejected on medical grounds. Korematsu evaded the evacuation order for two months, hoping to remain with his Caucasian fiancee, but was caught and sentenced to a five-year probationary term in an internment camp.

The Court of Appeals met for argument on the three cases on February 19, 1943, the first anniversary of President Roosevelt's internment order. Five weeks later, the appellate judges sent the cases to the Supreme Court without decision, under the little-used procedure of "certification" of questions, over the protest of Judge William Denman, who denounced the "war-haste" with which the cases were being rushed to judgment. Denman's colleagues confessed that the question of "whether this exercise of the war power can be reconciled with traditional standards of personal liberty and freedom guaranteed by the Constitution, is most difficult."

Before the Supreme Court met to consider the cases, government lawyers fought a spirited, but unseen, battle over the evidence the justices should consider in making their decision. Solicitor General Charles Fahy delegated the task of preparing the government's briefs to Edward Ennis, who had earlier waged a futile battle against internment. During his preparation, Ennis discovered an official report of the Office of Naval Intelligence on the loyalty of Japanese Americans. Prepared by Kenneth Ringle, a Navy commander who spoke fluent Japanese, this lengthy report concluded that "less than three percent" of the entire group posed any potential threat and noted that FBI agents had already arrested most of these suspects. The Ringle report, circulated to Army officials before the evacuation began, urged that Japanese Americans be given individual loyalty hearings and that mass internment be avoided.

Ennis recognized the significance of this document and promptly informed Solicitor General Fahy that the government had "a duty to advise the Court of the existence of the Ringle memorandum" and the Army's knowledge of its conclusions. "It occurs to me that any other course of conduct might approximate the suppression of evidence," Ennis warned his superior. Fahy ignored this red-flag request.

When the Supreme Court convened on May 10, 1943, Fahy suggested that doubts about the loyalty of Japanese Americans had justified the military curfew and evacuation orders. These doubts made it "not unreasonable" for military officials "to fear that in case of an invasion there would be among this group of people a number of persons who might assist the enemy." Having planted the seed of genetic guilt, Fahy left it to germinate in the minds of the nine justices.

Just a week before meeting to decide the internment cases, the justices had issued bitterly divided opinions in the *Barnette* flag-salute case. Voiding the expulsion from public schools of Jehovah's Witnesses who objected on religious grounds to compulsory flag-salute laws, the Supreme Court majority had overturned its *Gobitis* decision, issued in 1940. Chief Justice Harlan Fiske Stone, who succeeded Charles Evans Hughes in 1941, hoped to heal the wounds of this fratricidal battle and urged his colleagues to join a unanimous opinion in the internment cases. The justices had earlier returned the Korematsu case to the court of appeals for decision on a technical issue, and the Yasui case was complicated by the trial judge's ruling that the defendant had lost his American citizenship. Gordon Hirabayashi's appeal thus became the vehicle for weighing "war powers" against "due process" in the constitutional scale.

Speaking first at the conference table, Stone placed a heavy thumb on the scale. Admitting that the military orders imposed "discrimination" on American citizens on racial grounds, he suggested that the Pearl Harbor attack showed the "earmarks of treachery" among Japanese Americans. Military officials had simply responded to the "grave danger" of sabotage and espionage by "disloyal members" of this minority. Stone also convinced his colleagues to leave the more troublesome evacuation issue for later decision. Only Justice Frank Murphy reserved his decision when Stone polled the court; every other justice voted to sustain Gordon's conviction for curfew violation.

The Chief Justice assumed the task of writing for the court, hoping to put his prestige behind the decision. Stone acknowledged that racial discrimination was "odious to a free people" and had "often been held to be a denial of equal protection" by the Supreme Court. During wartime, however, "the successful prosecution of the war" may justify measures which "place citizens of one ancestry in a different category from others." Stone suggested that Japanese Americans had failed to become "an integral part of the white population" and stressed their "attachments to Japan and its institutions." Stone's evidence for these assertions included "irritation" at laws that barred Japanese immigrants from American citizenship and the fact that many children attended "Japanese language schools" to maintain their cultural heritage. Military officials who feared a "fifth column" of disloyal Japanese

Americans were entitled, Stone concluded, to impose a curfew on "residents having ethnic affiliations with an invading enemy."

Before the Hirabayashi opinion was issued, Frank Murphy wrote a scathing dissent from Stone's racial assumptions. The court's only Catholic, Murphy noted that many immigrants sent their children to parochial and foreign-language schools, without any loss of loyalty. The issue to Murphy was not the curfew but "the gigantic round-up" of American citizens, in which he found "a melancholy resemblance to the treatment accorded to members of the Jewish race" by America's wartime enemies. This reference to Nazi concentration camps upset Justice Felix Frankfurter, who warned Murphy that any dissent would be "playing into the hands of the enemy." Faced with this appeal to patriotism, Murphy withdrew his dissent and filed a concurring opinion that placed the curfew order on "the very brink of constitutional power."

Eighteen months later, when the Supreme Court met to decide the Korematsu case, the tides of war had shifted and the continued detention of Japanese Americans struck many—including Army officials—as unnecessary. Nonetheless, Justice Hugo Black wrote for six members of the Court in upholding General DeWitt's evacuation orders. Black took pains to deny that Fred Korematsu's treatment reflected "hostility to him or his race," holding that it was based on "evidence of disloyalty" among Japanese Americans. One of the three dissenters, Justice Robert Jackson, disparaged Black's "evidence" as nothing more than the "self-serving statement" of General DeWitt, whose official report on the internment program had labeled Japanese Americans as members of an "enemy race." Justice Murphy revised his reluctant concurrence in the Hirabayashi case into an impassioned dissent in the Korematsu case. The forced exclusion of American citizens from their homes, Murphy wrote, "goes over 'the very brink of constitutional power' and falls into the ugly abyss of racism."

The surrender of Japan in 1945 did not end the internment of Japanese Americans: More than a year passed before the last concentration camp closed its gates. Slowly and fearfully, members of this "disloyal" minority returned to their homes, although many left the Pacific coast for new lives in the Midwest and East. Beginning in most cases from scratch, the former prisoners opened stores and farms, and sent their children to prestigious colleges and to success in business and professional careers. But the psychic scars of internment remained.

Four decades passed before Japanese Americans found a collective voice for their wartime trauma. Pressed by young people who joined the civil-rights and anti-war movements of the sixties and seventies, survivors of the concentration camps abandoned the Japanese tradition of "gaman"—"keep it inside"—and shared their feelings of hurt and shame. Moving from personal anguish to political action, Japanese Americans organized a "redress" movement and persuaded Congress in 1981 to establish a blue-ribbon panel to review the internment program and propose remedies for legal wrongs. After hearing testimony, often tearful, from 750 witnesses, and reviewing thousands of government documents, the Commission on Wartime Relocation and Internment of Civilians agreed that the internment "was not justified by military necessity" but had resulted from "race prejudice, war hysteria and a failure of political leadership." With only one dissent, the commissioners asked Congress to provide compensation of $20,000 for each internment survivor.

Another goal of the redress movement was to secure judicial reversal of the criminal convictions the Supreme Court had upheld in 1943 and 1944. Research by commission staff members and Peter Irons, a lawyer and legal historian, uncovered federal records that disclosed the "suppression of evidence" to the courts and the racist basis of the mass internment. After he showed these records to Gordon Hirabayashi, Minoru Yasui, and Fred Korematsu, Irons secured their agreement to reopen their cases through the little-used legal procedure of *coram nobis*, available only to criminal defendants whose trials had been tainted by "fundamental error" or "manifest injustice."

Aided by teams of volunteer lawyers, most of them children of former internees, Irons drafted *coram nobis* petitions which were filed in January 1983 with federal courts in Seattle, Portland, and San Francisco. Based entirely on government records, the lengthy petitions asked the courts to vacate the wartime convictions and make judicial findings on the government's misconduct. The government answered the petitions with a two-page response which labeled the internment as an "unfortunate episode" in

American history. Although government lawyers denied any misconduct, they did not challenge the charges of suppressing crucial evidence.

The Korematsu case became the first to reach decision, in October 1983. After hearing lawyers on both sides, Judge Marilyn Patel asked Fred Korematsu to address the court. "As long as my record stands in federal court," he quietly stated, "any American citizen can be held in prison or concentration camps without a trial or a hearing." Ruling from the bench, Judge Patel labeled the government's position as "tantamount to a confession of error" and erased Fred's conviction from the court's records. Ruling in January 1984, Judge Robert Belloni of the federal court in Portland, Oregon, vacated Minoru Yasui's conviction, although he declined to make findings on the petition's misconduct charges.

Gordon Hirabayashi waited until June 1985 for a hearing on his petition. By this time, government lawyers had decided to defend the wartime internment. Judge Donald Voorhees presided at the two-week hearing in the same Seattle courthouse in which Gordon was tried in 1942. Government lawyer Victor Stone called a parade of former FBI and intelligence officials to support claims that General DeWitt's wartime orders were "rational" responses to threats of espionage and sabotage. One official labeled Japanese Americans as "the most likely friends of the enemy" and another recalled "espionage nets" along the Pacific coast. Under examination by Gordon's lawyers, none of the government witnesses could point to a single documented instance of wartime espionage by Japanese Americans.

The star witness at Gordon's hearing was Edward Ennis, the former Justice Department lawyer who had objected to the "suppression of evidence" before the Supreme Court in 1943. Four decades later, Ennis repeated his objections and stated that John McCloy and Karl Bendetsen of the War Department had "deceived" him about the Army's false espionage charges. These wartime actions, Voorhees ruled in February 1986, constituted "error of the most fundamental character" and required vacation of Gordon's conviction for violating DeWitt's evacuation order. However, Voorhees described the curfew as a "relatively mild" restriction and upheld Gordon's conviction on this count.

Neither side was satisfied with this Solomonic outcome, the mirror image of the Supreme Court decisions of 1943, and both sets of lawyers filed appeals of Judge Voorhees' rulings. After hearing arguments and reading lengthy briefs, a three-judge panel of the Ninth Circuit Court of Appeals issued a unanimous opinion on September 24, 1987. Judge Mary Schroeder wrote for the court, concluding from the evidence presented to Judge Voorhees, that "General DeWitt was a racist" and that his military orders were "based upon racism rather than military necessity." Disagreeing with Judge Voorhees that "the curfew was a lesser restriction on freedom" than evacuation, the appellate judges vacated Gordon's remaining criminal conviction.

Government lawyers conceded defeat after this blunt rebuff and declined to file a final appeal with the Supreme Court. Gordon Hirabayashi, a college student in 1942 and now an emeritus professor, credited his victory to the new generation of Japanese Americans. "I was just one of the cogs" in the crusade for vindication, he reflected. "This was truly the people's case."

II.
"Am I an American?"

I was born in Seattle, Washington, on April 23, 1918. Both of my parents were born in Japan. My father came over to this country in 1907, when he was nineteen, and my mother came over in 1914, when she was also nineteen. They were married in this country, but their marriage was arranged in Japan by their families. I was the oldest of five kids in the family. My dad operated a fruit and vegetable store, more like a roadside stand, in Auburn, which was a rural farm community about twenty miles south of Seattle.

My parents had grown up in Buddhist homes in Japan, but they were both converted to Christianity when they were taking English lessons, preparatory to coming over to the United States. Although they took these lessons seven years apart, they both happened to have an English instructor who was a disciple of a unique Protestant movement which was known in Japan as Mukyo-kai. In English this would mean 'Non-Church Movement.' This was a small, unorthodox, nondenominational movement which had beliefs and values very much like the Quakers, with a strong emphasis on pacifism.

My parents did not allow Sunday sports or work, except during emergencies like harvest time. Their lives emphasized the oneness of belief and behavior. My father was sometimes accused of being *baka shōjiki*, which is roughly translated as stupidly honest. For example, while packing crates of lettuce, he would not make the usual spectacular selection of the outstanding heads for the top

50

row. If my father was the quiet and solid foundation of the family, my mother was the fire, providing warmth and sometimes intense heat. She was an activist—outgoing, articulate, feisty.

While I was a child, and through my teenage period, I often felt that our religious group was too rigid and restrictive. I also had to cope with the conflicts between Japanese and Western ideals and values. Growing up in a Japanese home created serious problems at school. The teacher would encourage me by saying, Speak up, Gordon! What do you think about that? Let's hear *your* view. The Japanese value system told me not to blurt out anything that was only half-baked, bringing shame to me and my family, and I frequently sat like a sphinx in school. But I was active in school activities and the Boy Scouts. I became a Life Scout and a senior patrol leader.

I entered the University of Washington in Seattle after I finished high school, and at first I was majoring in math. I wasn't very active politically at the university. I guess I still am not, in the formal political sense. But I was involved in a lot of issues. I belonged to the student YMCA, which was the main group around the so-called independents versus the Greek Row, with their 'for white gentiles only' policy, which was legal at that time. So when issues came up, we'd get into debates over certain positions, and I got involved in that sort of thing. Debates within the Y, Student Christian Movement, and conferences. Whenever issues came up, I always found myself taking the extreme liberal side, arguing those positions.

During one summer, I was sent to the Presidents' School; this was a training school of the YM and YWCA. This took place at Columbia University in New York City, and it overlapped with Union Theological Seminary, because they billeted us there and we worked for our meals on lunch shift. This was a liberal group, and we went to seminars with guys like A.J. Muste and Evan Thomas and Frank Olmstead, who were all advocates of social action and opposition to war and war preparation. I guess I was ready for that, because I was just eating that up. It all made sense to me, and after I returned to Seattle I applied to my draft board for conscientious objector status. I didn't get my CO right away, so I had to appeal. And I was prepared, if they didn't give it to me, to refuse military service.

The University of Washington has a quarter system, and I was working my way through school, so the first couple of years I went two quarters and then worked two quarters. Then I decided I'm missing too much, so I worked out a program where I worked full time and carried less than a full course load. So I was living on a shoestring. When I came back from New York, my roommate was in the same shoes, so the Y secretary put us up until we found a place to stay and found part-time jobs.

My roommate and I had been visiting different church groups, not belonging to any. We went to the University temple because they had an excellent choir, and we'd go to the Unitarian church once in a while because we liked what the minister said, and we'd drop in at the Quakers. And we liked that setting. That kind of appealed to us and we found ourselves gravitating over there more frequently, and after awhile we weren't shopping around. Sometime before the war we both applied for membership in the University Friends Meeting. My roommate was then sent down to a CO camp in California and after that I was fending for myself as a CO.

I remember that December 7, 1941 was a quiet Sunday morning in Seattle. We had just finished Meeting for Worship at the Friends Meeting and we drifted outside for visiting. Then, one of our members, who had stayed by the radio, broke the news. Japan has attacked Pearl Harbor in Hawaii! We are at war! It was unreal. The impact did not sink in for some time. My immediate worry was what would happen to my parents and their generation. Since they were legally ineligible for American citizenship, war with Japan instantly transformed them into 'enemy aliens.'

During the months between Pearl Harbor and the curfew order in March 1942, things were happening fast. I was a pretty naive, young country hick; my most serious problem was trying to earn enough to continue school. I didn't have any long-term plan. I had already been ordered to a Civilian Public Service camp in Oregon by my draft board, but the Selective Service had reclassified all draft-age persons of Japanese ancestry as aliens ineligible for conscription, so my order was canceled on the eve of my departure, after I had been treated to farewell parties with going-away gifts.

After the curfew order was announced, we knew there would be further orders to remove all persons of Japanese ancestry from the West Coast. When the exclusion orders specifying the deadline for forced removal from various districts of Seattle were posted on telephone poles, I was confronted with a dilemma: Do I stay out of trouble and succumb to the status of second-class citizen, or do I continue to live like other Americans and thus disobey the law?

When the curfew was imposed I obeyed for about a week. We had about twelve living in the Y dormitory, so it was a small group, and they all became my volunteer time-keepers. 'Hey, Gordy, it's five minutes to eight!' And I'd have to dash back from the library or from the coffee shop. One of those times, I stopped and I thought, Why the hell am I running back? Am I an American? And if I am, why am I running back and nobody else is? I think if the order said *all* civilians must obey the curfew, if it was just a nonessential restrictive move, I might not have objected. But I felt it was unfair, just to be referred to as a 'non-alien'—they never referred to me as a citizen. This was so pointedly, so obviously a violation of what the Constitution stood for, what citizenship meant. So I stopped and turned around and went back.

This shocked some of my friends. So I said, Well, *you're* here. What gives you any more right to stay here than me? And they couldn't answer that. After that, I just ignored the curfew. But nothing happened. And it became a kind of expression of freedom for me to make sure that I was out after eight. It wasn't hard in the University district; there were a lot of activities after eight.

When the exclusion order came, which was very close to that time, I was expecting to go along. I had dropped out of school at the end of the winter quarter, which was the end of March. I knew I wasn't going to be around very long, so I just didn't register for spring quarter and I volunteered for the fledgling, newly formed American Friends Service Committee. From time to time, districts of Seattle were on a deadline to move all the Japanese. So, with a car that was made available, I'd go and help—particularly families whose fathers were interned and there were a bunch of little kids, and I helped them to move. It really horrified me to help these families pack up their belongings and drive them down to the Puyallup fairground and leave them behind barbed wire.

I fully expected that when the University district deadline came up I would join them. Those who saw me waving them goodbye all expected to see me within a few weeks at the most. About two weeks before my time came up, I said to myself, If I am defying the curfew, how can I accept this thing? This is much worse, the same principle but much worse in terms of uprooting and denial of our rights, and the suffering. So that's when I began to mull it over and I kicked it around with my roommate, Bill Makino, and he agreed with me. So we said, Let's investigate this further and think about it. And we both decided we can't go along with it. It's an absolute denial of our rights.

I had no plans to bring a test case. Today, if I violate anything on the grounds of principle, I would spend some time thinking about the legal aspects, the court battles and so on. But at that time, I was just a student. I had read of World War I and constitutional cases, but I didn't give it very much thought. I did anticipate that I would be apprehended, but I didn't know very much about the legal procedures in these things. I just felt that something was going to happen to curtail my freedom.

I had met a lawyer named Arthur Barnett at the Friends Meeting. Bill and I met with Art and asked him some questions about the legal implications of the position we were contemplating. But there was no, Should we, or shouldn't we? Some people knew what I was thinking, but they didn't know what I was going to do.

Eventually, I wrote out a statement explaining the reasons I was refusing evacuation, and I planned to give it to the FBI when I turned myself in. By that time my roommate, Bill Makino, had to cope with his parents' request that he stick with them and go along to the camp. Bill was the only son of parents who were at least ten years older than my parents and the pressure was very strong on him. I didn't want to have someone who would be having remorse all the way through, because I figured that we'll run into serious problems. In the course of our discussions, I said, You should think this through carefully and, if there's any way you could persuade yourself to go with your family, you should do that. You should come with me *only* if you just can't go and you have to object. Then I welcome you. He thought about it and decided he'd have to stick with his family.

I didn't have the same moral pressure. Dad was physically able, so I didn't have that worry. My mother said that she gave me moral support but she wanted me to come with the family to the camp. I know you're right and I admire this stand of yours, she said, but we don't know if we'll ever see each other again. In that period, I didn't know what was going to happen to me, and I didn't know what was going to happen to them, where they were going, how far away and for how long. Everything was just a total blank, full of anxiety. So she said, It's a matter of life and death. Why stick to a principle? Stick with us. She used everything—tears and everything. And I couldn't do it.

So when I wrote my statement it was only me. When this got around, Mary Farquharson came to see me. Mary was the state senator for the University district and she was a regular resource person for the student Y. She said, I'm checking on a rumor that you are intending to defy the exclusion order. Is that true? And I said, Yes, I've already made a stand and written a statement. She said, Are you planning to make a test case of this? I said, I know that's a possibility, but I don't know very much about law and I don't have any money. I haven't talked to anybody about this. I don't know what's going to happen as a result of it and I've made no plans. And she said, Well, if you've made no plans, there's a group here that is very upset about what's happening to our liberties, the status of citizenship, and we'd like to battle it, but we haven't been able to find anyone yet. Do you have any objection to our group using your case as a vehicle to fight for citizens' rights?

Mary's group included some people I knew and respected—some Quakers, ministers, professors, businessmen in the University district. Our plan was to hire a constitutional lawyer, get the case started, and then the American Civil Liberties Union would take over. But we had to change these plans. Roger Baldwin, the national ACLU director, regretfully informed Mary that his national board had failed to back him. So Mary and the Seattle group organized a Gordon Hirabayashi Defense Committee and continued the fight.

The day after the University district deadline for evacuation, Art took me to the FBI office to turn myself in. At first, I was only charged with violating the exclusion order. They threw in the curfew count afterward. One of the FBI agents who interrogated me regarding the exclusion order refusal stopped at one point and said, Well, gee, if you feel this way about it, what would you do about curfew? And I said, Well, what were *you* doing the past few nights? Were you out after eight o'clock? He said, Yeah. And I said, So was I. Other Americans were ignoring it, and so did I. When they confiscated my journal from my briefcase, I had some events listed of violating the curfew, and they picked one of those and added it to the counts against me.

Shortly, Art left the FBI office and I was in their hands for most of that day. There was an initial attempt to get me to register for evacuation, and they drove me to the registration center in a Catholic church. But when I found there were no changes in the regulations from the time I had previously found it impossible to register, I refused their offer. They took me back to the car and I'm sitting there while they must have been mulling over what to do with me. And then they took me back to headquarters and promised to drop the charges and give me a ride to the fairgrounds in Puyallup, if I would just go in without registering. I told them that not only would I refuse that offer, but they were proposing to do something illegal.

At the end of the day I was checked into the federal tank of the King County jail in downtown Seattle. I had no notion of anything. I was so naive, I'd never even *seen* a jail. I was a sociology student but my class had never taken a field trip. After I was put in jail, within a couple of days I was brought into court for arraignment, and I was represented by a lawyer named John Geisness, with Art Barnett as advisor. We made a plea of not guilty to both counts and then they set bail. The original amount was five hundred dollars. So I said to Geisness, What if I put up that five hundred? Can I just walk out like anybody else? He raised this question and the judge, after consulting for a while, said, No, if he puts up bail he'll have to go to camp at Puyallup. Things would have been better physically in the camp. Emotionally, it would have been very difficult for me, because I had objected to the whole thing and then I'm there. I'd have to be subject to all sorts of regulations, many of which were objectionable. I just felt that I couldn't accept that, so I stayed on in jail.

In the course of my staying in jail from May to October, when my district court trial was set, there were two or three legal skirmishes during the summer. My lawyers filed motions requesting that the case be dropped because, as a citizen, I wasn't given due process and, in effect, I was subject to these orders only on the grounds of ancestry, which was outside of constitutional guarantees. Judge Black denied these challenges.

King County jail is a holding place, primarily for people to be arraigned or serve sentences of sixty days or less. So the stays are quite short, and when a guy like me is there for months, I'm the senior person. Eventually I became the 'mayor' of the tank and I was in that capacity when they brought my Dad in to testify at my trial.

My trial in October lasted just one day. It started in the morning and they took a noon recess and continued in the afternoon until my conviction. The government subpoenaed my parents and they put Dad on the stand. They only asked him a couple of questions, like, Were you born in Japan? Are you a Japanese citizen? The only point was to impress on the jury that this man was Japanese and didn't speak English well and that this defendant is his son.

I really objected to the government putting my parents in jail for ten days before my trial. They were brought up from the Tule Lake Concentration Camp in California and my Dad was placed in the federal tank with me. Mother was put in the only tank for women, with street walkers, petty thieves, embezzlers. The tank was cockroachy and the food was greasy. On the day of my trial, we had to wait ten minutes for her to come down. Six of the women had been working on her hair and fingernails. She came out looking like a queen. She told me that whatever the women were charged with, she had never met such warm-hearted people. But I'll *never* forgive the government for putting my parents in jail like that, just to prejudice the jury against me.

Judge Black's instructions to the jury before they retired were very succinct. You can forget all those legal arguments, he said. Here are the only questions that you must determine. I am instructing you that the curfew and exclusion orders of the Army are valid. You are to determine whether the defendant is of Japanese ancestry, and if he is, he's subject to this regulation. Then you are to determine whether he complied with it. Gee, there's no question! They go in and they were back in ten minutes. I was guilty on both counts. You could have a whole bunch of civil-liberties people on the jury and they are subject to the judge's instructions. They *had* to vote against me. It was cut and dried.

Judge Black sentenced me the next day. He said, Taking into consideration that you have already been five months in jail on a conviction with a maximum of twelve months, I'm going to sentence you to thirty days for the exclusion order conviction and thirty days for curfew order violation, to be served consecutively, or sixty days. Then he asked if the prisoner had anything to say, and I asked if he could add fifteen days to each count so that it would total ninety days. I'd been told by jailhouse friends that if my sentence was ninety days or longer, I could serve on a work camp and be outdoors instead of in jail behind bars. When Judge Black heard this he smiled and said, I could accommodate that. Why don't we make it three months on each count, to be served concurrently. Nobody saw any objection to that, and nobody realized that the Supreme Court would use that to avoid ruling on the exclusion order conviction.

Two days after I was sentenced, we appealed, and I continued to remain in jail because the judge and I couldn't agree on bail conditions. He said that if my backers put up the bail he would release me to one of the barbed-wire internment camps. And I said, If my backers put up the bail, I should be released out the front door like anybody else. He said, There's a law that says you're not allowed out in the streets, so I can't do that.

With that stalemate, I remained in jail until the end of the ninth month, four months into the appeal period. Then we worked out a compromise with Judge Black. By that time he was willing to get me out of jail. We'd become sort of like old friends in terms of his knowledge of me, and he said, We ought to get him out. We worked out a compromise that I would go to Spokane, which was outside the restricted area for Japanese. The American Friends Service Committee was setting up a branch in Spokane to work on the relocation of Japanese who might be able to come out of the camps if they had a place to live and a job. And my assignment would have been like a field officer working up places to stay and lining up jobs. Judge Black said, I want the prisoner's promise that he will not return to the restricted area for the duration of the appeal. That sounded acceptable to me, so I went out to the Spokane post.

When the Supreme Court decision in my case came down in June 1943, I expected I would have to serve my sentence. Around the middle of July a couple of FBI agents came after me in Spokane. I was living with a Japanese doctor at the time, and I was mowing the lawn when they came. What kept you so long? I said. I've been waiting for you. Can I go in and get my things? They took me to the federal attorney's office and booked me into custody. His name was Connolly and he said, Well, I guess you'll have to serve your sentence in the federal tank of the Spokane county jail. I said, Wait a minute! I've got ninety days to serve and that's too long for the county jail. So he said, The only federal work camp I can send you to is in Tucson, Arizona. But we don't have any money to send you there. You'll have to serve your time here.

I was wracking my brain. I said, What if I go on my own to Tucson? And Connolly said, If you want to do that, it's okay with me. In fact, I'll write a letter for you, in case somebody gives you problems. It was against my principles to pay my way to prison, so I hitchhiked. This is 1,600 miles away, down the middle of the mountain states, during gas rationing, so there's not many cars on the road, and traffic is slow. I stopped in Idaho to visit with my parents for a few days and then I stopped at Salt Lake City to visit friends, and finally got to Tucson after two weeks.

I went to the U.S. marshal's office and told them I was reporting to serve my sentence. This marshal looked in his papers and said, We don't have any record for you here. You might as well turn around and go back. You're free to go. I said, Look around, there must be something. If I go, someday you're going to find those papers and I'll have to interrupt what I'm doing and come back. So I might as well get this over with. It was a hot day, and he said, Why don't you go to an air-conditioned movie and come back tonight. Well, they found my papers at the bottom of the pile. So they took me to the work camp, which was like a CCC camp up in the mountains, and I did my sentence there. Most of the prisoners were there for selling liquor to Indians or as wetbacks, illegal aliens. It was actually a good experience, getting to know these people and working in the woods on conservation projects. The ironic thing was that the work camp was in the restricted area that I wasn't supposed to enter.

After my time was up, they gave me a bus ticket back to Spokane. I continued my work where I left off, with a feeling that I might as well settle in for the duration now. After one month, I got a special questionnaire from my draft board, which they had concocted for persons of Japanese ancestry. This one had the usual Selective Service questions that I had filled in already, plus these additional questions that demanded that you agree to serve in the military and renounce any loyalty to the emperor of Japan.

This was like, Have you stopped beating your wife? If you never had a loyalty to Japan, how could you renounce it? So I wrote to my draft board and asked if they were sending this to all sorts of Americans of various ancestries, or only to those of Japanese ancestry. I never got a response, and I waited for a reasonable time and put my response in. I told them the questions were a form of racial discrimination and that as an American citizen I can't support that. So I'm returning this unfilled.

Then I got an order to report for a physical. I ignored it, and then I got another order to report for induction in Oregon. When that date came, I didn't show up. Later on, when I went to prison for this for a year, I met some guys who had walked out of the CO camps. They said, When we were in the army base in Oregon we saw your name on the list of those who were reporting for induction. So we went down to the station that morning to welcome you, and when the train came in and you didn't get off, we let out a great cheer! I could have fought that case on appeal, because I was subject to the draft on the basis of ancestry, but by that time I was tired of court cases.

When I came out of prison, the war had just finished, and so I was released to Seattle. I had been married just before I went in, and my wife and twin daughters in their little baskets were waiting for me at the dock from McNeil Island, where the prison was. Although I had four mouths to feed by then, I thought I should first complete my bachelor's degree at the University of Washington, feeling that whatever I went into, a degree would come in handy. I completed my degree that year, and then I went on to graduate school in sociology and I finished my Ph.D. in 1952.

As my first appointment, I accepted an assistant professorship at the American University of Beirut in Lebanon. I had a strong feeling of wanting international experience and that was the first teaching job I could find. I was there for three years, and then I taught in Cairo until 1959, about four years. So for most of the 1950s I was in the Arab Middle East. I came back to North America for family reasons, primarily. My kids were getting to junior-high age, and I felt they should have continuity in high school, although we all appreciated the international schooling background for the early years. I finally accepted an offer at the University of Alberta, in Canada, since it was the most attractive offer. I have been there ever since, so I guess we have liked it personally and as a family. In 1983, the year during which I became 65, I retired at the end of the academic year and took an emeritus position.

After the Supreme Court decided my case in 1943, there was always a continuous hope and interest on my part that the case could be reviewed at some point. Not being a lawyer, I didn't know exactly what my options were. During the time I was overseas I didn't spend much time looking into that possibility, but during the latter part of the sixties and beginning of the seventies I had discussions with law professors at the University of California, but they couldn't find anything promising. And later I talked with a judge who suggested that I move to quash the charges in my case. The courts would have to look at that motion and in that process we might get a kind of hearing.

I shared that idea with a few others, but nothing came of it. I had certain feelings of finality about my case. You know, while I'm hoping as a layman that something can be done, well, the Supreme Court is the Supreme Court. That's the end, and when they have made a decision, there aren't many ways open to reverse it. It wasn't until Peter Irons called me from Boston in 1981, saying that he had discovered some documents that might present an opportunity under a rarely used legal device to petition for a rehearing, that I felt there was a chance. I said to him, I've been waiting over forty years for this kind of a phone call. So he arranged to fly out to Edmonton, and eventually we got a legal team organized that filed a petition in the federal court in Seattle to vacate my conviction.

My petition was filed in January 1983 and we had a two-week evidentiary hearing in June 1985. Judge Donald Voorhees, who presided over the case, impressed me as a very fair judge. He was obviously interested in the case and well-informed about the evidence. Naturally, I was delighted that he ruled that my exclusion order conviction had been tainted by government misconduct. But I was disappointed that he upheld the curfew conviction, and we appealed that. The government also appealed on the exclusion order. We had arguments before the appellate judges in March 1987, and they handed down a unanimous opinion in September, upholding Judge Voorhees on the exclusion order and also striking down the curfew conviction. So I finally got the vindication that I had wanted for forty years, although I'm a little disappointed that the Supreme Court didn't have a chance to overrule the decision they made in 1943.

When my case was before the Supreme Court in 1943, I fully expected that as a citizen the Constitution would protect me. Surprisingly, even though I lost, I did not abandon my beliefs and values. And I never look at my case as just my own, or just as a Japanese American case. It is an *American* case, with principles that affect the fundamental human rights of all Americans.

3

J.D. Shelley
v. Louis Kraemer

J.D. and Ethel Lee Shelley moved with their six children into a new home in St. Louis in 1945, only to face an eviction notice from white neighbors. *Photo by George Harris, courtesy of Life Picture Service*

I.
"This Contract
of Restrictions"

J.D. and Ethel Lee Shelley moved into their new home at 4600 Labadie Avenue, a tree-shaded street in the Grande Prairie neighborhood of St. Louis, Missouri, on September 11, 1945. With six active children to house, J.D. and Ethel were eager to leave their crowded apartment on North 9th Street, backed against the Mississippi River in a crime-ridden black ghetto. The Shelleys had arrived in St. Louis from rural Mississippi just before World War II, part of the growing black migration from the Deep South to northern cities, driven from fields to factories by Depression poverty. They asked their pastor, Robert Bishop, to help them, using savings from their wartime jobs, to find a more spacious residence. Elder Bishop, who combined ministry with real-estate sales, found a yellow-brick, two-apartment house on Labadie Avenue, and arranged its purchase from Geraldine Fitzgerald for $5,700. The Shelleys, who never met Mrs. Fitzgerald, were delighted to escape the ghetto with their children.

Just a few days later, an unexpected visitor knocked on the door and handed Ethel a summons to appear in court. Louis and Fern Kraemer, who lived ten blocks east on Labadie, had filed suit in the Circuit Court of St. Louis to evict J.D. and Ethel from their new home. According to the summons, the Shelleys had unlawfully purchased a building which was "covered" by a restrictive racial covenant. Recorded in 1911, the covenant was limited to the block on which the Shelleys lived, bounded by Cora Avenue on the west and Taylor Avenue on the east. "This contract of restrictions," the covenant read, was designed to prevent ownership or occupancy of the covered houses "by people of the Negro or Mongolian Race." Fern Kraemer's parents had been among the thirty property owners, of thirty-nine on the block, who signed the joint covenant, which purported to bind all future purchasers for a period of fifty years.

Behind the Kraemers stood the Marcus Avenue Improvement Association, founded in 1910 by white residents of the Grande Prairie neighborhood. Urging its members to adopt restrictive covenants, the group's officers promised that "in the event an attempt was made to sell to colored, the Association would back up the property owners to the fullest extent of the law." The use of such covenants to enforce residential segregation became widespread after 1917, when the U.S. Supreme Court struck down municipal laws which attempted to prevent blacks from purchasing or occupying property in "white" areas. Although cities were barred from adopting such laws, property owners could accomplish the same end through private agreements, under the "freedom of contract" doctrine the Court had constructed to block Progressive Era regulation of business and commerce.

During the first four decades of this century, the black population of northern cities tripled, while racial covenants helped to force this unwanted minority into crowded slums. Between 1910 and 1940, more than sixty thousand blacks arrived in St. Louis, with thousands more spilling across the Mississippi into East St. Louis, Illinois. During the mass migration of World War I, blacks pushed against their ghetto walls and met with resistance from the poor whites who competed for jobs and housing. Racial violence erupted in East St. Louis in June 1917. Carlos Hurd, reporting for the St. Louis *Post-Dispatch*, wrote that "a black skin was a death warrant" for those who faced white mobs. "I saw man after man, with his hands raised pleading for his life," Hurd wrote, executed by "the historic sentence of intolerance, death by stoning." More than one hundred blacks died in four days of rioting.

The growing use of racial covenants to maintain residential apartheid led the National Association for the Advancement of Colored People to begin, in 1922, a legal campaign against their enforcement. The first case to reach the U.S. Supreme Court began with a lawsuit between two white neighbors in the District of Columbia, who had both signed a racial covenant. One signer, Irene Corrigan, sold her property to a black woman named Helen Curtis and was sued by another signer, John Buckley, who sought to restrain the sale. Coming to the aid of Corrigan and Curtis, NAACP lawyers argued that judicial enforcement of such covenants placed the state behind a form of racial segregation which violated the "equal protection" clause of the Fourteenth Amendment. Ruling in 1926, the Supreme Court evaded a decision on this issue by dismissing the NAACP appeal in *Corrigan* v. *Buckley* as "insubstantial" and "frivolous." But the court issued an opinion holding that Fourteenth Amendment prohibitions "have reference to state action exclusively" and could not bar "private individuals from entering into contracts respecting the control and disposition of their own property." Judicial enforcement of the covenants did not constitute "state action" in such private suits.

Despite this setback, NAACP lawyers included legal attacks on racial covenants in their long-term campaign against all forms of state-enforced segregation. Members of other minorities joined the crusade against covenants. "The issue is much broader than that of simply preventing discrimination against Negroes," the NAACP noted in 1930, "for already such restrictive covenants have been used against Jews and Catholics." By the end of World War II, prospects for success in the Supreme Court seemed bright. The wartime migration of blacks to northern cities, pressure for access to decent housing, awareness of the horrors that Nazi racial ideology had created, and the dominance of "liberals" on the Supreme Court—all these factors encouraged NAACP lawyers and their allies.

Strategy for a renewed assault on racial covenants emerged from a two-day conference in Chicago in July 1945. Thurgood Marshall, NAACP special counsel, guided the attending lawyers toward a coordinated legal campaign in courts around the country, designed to force the Supreme Court to accept one or more cases for decision. One lawyer at the conference, George L. Vaughn of St. Louis, suggested that lawyers not ignore the "political angle" in selecting test cases: "Because the Negro vote played such an important part in the election of judges" in St. Louis, Vaughn predicted success in his city. The son of a slave, Vaughn held influential positions in both the NAACP and the Democratic party machine in St. Louis. He was also acquainted with Robert Bishop, who later sold the house on Labadie Avenue to J.D. and Ethel Shelley. Two months after the Chicago conference, the Shelleys presented George Vaughn with an ideal test case.

The suit brought by the Kraemers against the Shelleys proceeded rapidly to trial in October 1945. Fern Kraemer, nervous on the witness stand, testified briefly that she had inherited property covered by the racial covenant on Labadie Avenue from her parents, who had signed that document. Robert Bishop explained that Geraldine Fitzgerald, for whom he purchased the house from other signatories to the covenant, had been a "straw party" in the sale to the Shelleys. Judge William K. Koerner, who heard the case, recognized that Bishop had enlisted Mrs. Fitzgerald to shield the Shelleys from knowledge of the racial covenant.

Ethel Shelley told Judge Koerner from the witness stand that she knew nothing of the covenant until the Kraemers filed their suit. Judge Koerner asked if she knew "why you have been sued and why you are here?" Mrs. Shelley certainly did know. "Well, I understand the white people didn't want me back." George Vaughn came to trial with an arsenal of arguments against the covenant. He first claimed that the covenant had never been enforceable, because nine of the thirty-nine owners on the block in 1911 had failed to sign the document. Vaughn also pointed out that five houses on the block had been occupied by blacks, going back to 1882. The purpose of the covenant, to keep any blacks from living on the block, had never been met.

Vaughn also attacked the covenant on constitutional and social grounds, adopting material supplied by Thurgood Marshall and the NAACP staff. Judicial enforcement of the covenant, he claimed, would violate the federal Civil Rights Act of 1866, which extended to newly emancipated blacks the same right to buy and sell real property "as is enjoyed by white citizens." Vaughn blamed racial covenants for creating a ghetto that "narrowed, surrounded and circumscribed almost completely" the housing available to blacks in St. Louis. He also quoted from a report submitted to President Hoover in 1932, which found that residential segregation had confined blacks in slums that were "fatally unwholesome places, a menace to health, morals, and general decency of cities and plague spots for race exploitation, friction and riots."

Judge Koerner's ruling in the case justified Vaughn's prediction of judicial sympathy in St. Louis. Although he declined to address constitutional objections to the covenant, Koerner inferred from the document's wording that it was intended to bind property owners on Labadie Avenue only if "all the landowners should sign." Because nine of the initial owners had not signed, and black families had lived on the block for many years, Judge Koerner refused to enforce the covenant against the Shelleys.

Jubilation at this victory turned to gloom after the Missouri Supreme Court reversed Judge Koerner in December 1946. Gerald Seegers, counsel to the Marcus Avenue Improvement Association and nephew of its founder, convinced the appellate judges that the covenant had bound only the initial signatories and those who later purchased the covered property. Stressing the repeated use of "the undersigned" in the document, Judge James N. Douglas held that "the agreement by its terms intended to cover only the property of those owners who signed it." The signatories knew that blacks owned property on the block and "it must have been their intention to prevent greatly increased occupancy by negroes." Judge Douglas also cited the *Corrigan* ruling of the U.S. Supreme Court as precedent for holding that judicial enforcement of racial covenants did not constitute "state action" under the Fourteenth Amendment.

Defeat in the Shelley case, along with similar setbacks in Michigan and the District of Columbia, prompted Thurgood Marshall to call a second conference on racial covenants, held in January 1947 at Howard University in Washington, D.C. Urging the submission of appeals to the Supreme Court, Marshall noted two recent developments. First, although the Supreme Court had declined in 1945 to review the *Corrigan* ruling, two justices had voted to hear the challenge; only two more votes were needed to grant review in a new case. Second, President Harry Truman had appointed fifteen eminent citizens in December 1946 to the President's Committee on Civil Rights, and high on the panel's agenda was possible federal action against racial covenants.

The Howard conferees reviewed the available test cases and agreed that none presented an adequate trial record of evidence on "the effect of overcrowded slum conditions and black ghettos upon both the victims of discrimination and their fellow citizens." One NAACP lawyer reported the preparation of a Chicago case that would include testimony by economists and sociologists on the impact of restrictive covenants on racial tensions. Expert testimony on these issues, Marshall argued, might persuade the Supreme Court to accept a test case for argument. George Vaughn, who did not attend this conference, upset this cautious strategy when he filed an appeal for the Shelleys with the Supreme Court in April 1947. Marshall quickly arranged to rush the Michigan and the District of Columbia cases along, and the Supreme Court agreed to hear all the appeals in January 1948.

Preparing for these hearings, Marshall called a third strategy conference, which met in New York in September 1947. In place of trial testimony, Marshall suggested that legal briefs incorporate material on "the economic and social aspects of race restrictive covenants" from a study conducted by Dr. Robert Weaver, a noted black sociologist who directed the American Council on Race Relations. Weaver's study represented the first use in civil-rights cases of the "Brandeis brief" approach to litigation, named for Louis Brandeis, who defended minimum-wage laws for women with voluminous evidence from social and statistical studies, and who later served on the Supreme Court.

Thurgood Marshall also organized the preparation of *amicus curiae* briefs by fifteen organizations which joined the attack on racial covenants. These groups spanned the religious, ethnic, and political spectrums, and included the American Jewish Committee, Protestant Council of New York, Japanese American Citizens League, American Indian Council, American Civil Liberties Union, and Congress of Industrial Organizations. The *amicus* effort was designed to impress the Supreme Court with the broad coalition that opposed racial covenants.

Another influential voice, that of the federal government, joined the chorus in October 1947. The day after the President's Committee on Civil Rights issued its lengthy report, which recommended "intervention by the Department of Justice" in the campaign against racial covenants, Solicitor General Philip Perlman announced the government's intention to file a supporting *amicus* brief. The efforts of federal agencies to "clear and replace slum areas," the brief argued, were hindered by racial covenants, which deprived "minority racial groups" of access to decent housing. Several *amicus* briefs, including the government's, cited the Supreme Court holding in the *Hirabayashi* case that racial discrimination was "odious to a free people," an ironic reversal of the government's support for the wartime internment in that case.

Oral argument to the Supreme Court in the racial-covenant cases spanned two days in January 1948. When the court convened, spectators were surprised that only six justices took their seats behind the curved mahogany bench: Justices Stanley Reed, Robert Jackson, and Wiley Rutledge had decided not to hear or vote on the cases. Although no reasons were given, most likely these justices decided that ownership of restricted property might affect their judgment. Ten lawyers addressed the six remaining justices in four cases, including NAACP lawyers Charles Houston and Thurgood Marshall, and Solicitor General Perlman for the federal government.

George Vaughn began the argument for J.D. and Ethel Shelley on a personal note, telling the justices that his father was born into slavery and that Congress had enacted the Civil Rights Act of 1866 to ensure that former slaves could buy and sell property on an equal basis with white people. J.D. Shelley's occupation as a construction worker might have prompted Vaughn's statement of the black request to white neighbors: "Let me come in and sit by the fire. I helped build the house." Herman Willer, an influential white lawyer in St. Louis, had joined Vaughn in representing the Shelleys and concluded the argument with a review of the constitutional issues in the case.

The Supreme Court ruling in *Shelley* v. *Kraemer* swung a wrecker's ball against the legal fences that surrounded America's black ghettos. Chief Justice Fred Vinson wrote for all six justices who decided the racial covenant cases, in an opinion issued on May 3, 1948. Vinson's appointment by President Harry Truman in 1946, to replace Harlan Fiske Stone at the court's helm, came after six terms in Congress as a Kentucky Democrat and five years as a federal appellate judge. Vinson rewarded his close friend with unwavering support of Truman's policies on the Supreme Court, during seven years as Chief Justice.

Vinson's opinion identified J.D. and Ethel Shelley simply as "Negroes" who "received from one Fitzgerald a warranty deed to the parcel in question." After noting that the *Corrigan* case in

1926 had not decided "the validity of court enforcement" of racial covenants, Vinson moved to the arguments that George Vaughn and Herman Willer had raised. The central question was whether judicial enforcement of racial covenants involved state action. Vinson acknowledged that the Fourteenth Amendment "erects no shield against merely private conduct, however discriminatory or wrongful." But he also cited the Civil Rights Act of 1866 as protecting blacks from "discriminatory state action" in buying and selling property.

Vinson resolved the conflict between private rights and public interest in blunt terms. He first conceded that "restrictive covenants standing alone cannot be regarded as violative" of the Fourteenth Amendment rights of blacks. But Vinson saw the heavy hand of judicial power behind the covenants. "We have no doubt that there has been state action in these cases," he wrote. The involvement of state courts in enforcing racial covenants had placed "the full coercive power of government" behind the denial to blacks of rights "enjoyed as a matter of course by other citizens of different race or color." The courts were barred, Vinson concluded, from any role in denying the Shelleys and other blacks "the equal protection of the laws guaranteed by the Fourteenth Amendment."

The Supreme Court decision came during a time of Cold War tension and Dixiecrat defection from the Democratic coalition of black and white voters. Senator Strom Thurmond of South Carolina challenged President Truman in the 1948 election as the segregationist candidate. One of Thurmond's supporters, Mississippi congressman John Rankin, thundered on the House floor that "there must have been a celebration in Moscow" after the Supreme Court struck down racial covenants. Truman's position was stated by George Vaughn, who repeated his Supreme Court argument for the Shelleys in a spell-binding speech to the Democratic convention. The NAACP, primarily responsible for the legal victory, told its members that a "telling blow has been struck at segregation and inequality" and promised further attacks on American apartheid.

Ethel Lee Shelley, a deeply religious woman, expressed her feelings about her family's long struggle to keep their new home: "My little soul is overjoyed. Wait till I get by myself. I'll tell the Lord of my thankfulness."

II.
"I Ain't Moving Nowhere!"

I was born in Starkville, Mississippi, on Christmas Day in 1907. My folks worked on farms around there; they worked for white people. They named me J.D., but the initials don't stand for nothing. People call me J.D. or some people call me Shelley. Me and my wife, Ethel, got married on December 14, 1923. I wasn't quite sixteen and she was younger than me.

I been working all my life. When I was down South, I did sawmill work, railroad, construction, all like that. In Mississippi I did mostly construction work; just before I left they was building a highway in Starkville and I worked on that. After they completed that then I started doing construction work at the A & M college; they was building houses out there. That's where I was working when I left and came here to St. Louis.

There is a lot of reasons I left Mississippi and come up here. One of them is what happened to a colored girl that got in trouble with white people and the police. We was living in a place right out from the city that was owned by a white preacher who built some houses and rented to colored. My wife was working for these white people and she was going to quit and they asked her did she know anybody she could get to work there. She said, yes, she knowed a girl name of Sister Hon; she going to see her. So she sent this kid up there and before long this white lady claimed that she taken some jewelry from her.

So this particular Sunday my wife had went to church with the kids, but they come home after Sunday school. And the police come to the house that Sister Hon live in and we was all looking in it. The police they take Sister Hon away, and I told her father, who didn't say nothing, I say, Man, you let them take your kid, whyn't you go with your kid? And he say no. So they take Sister Hon up there to the lady's house and they beat her, they beat that child with a hose and then they brought her over to the colored quarter and throwed her in a ditch. And my kids come from church and they saw her, and they come running to the house and say, Dad, they done beat Sister Hon and she cain't walk.

I jumped up and got Hannah, another colored lady, and we tried to get the men and they wouldn't go. So Hannah said, Me and you get her, J.D. And we went up and got that child, she beat so bad she couldn't sit. And I said, It's time for me to leave here now. 'Cause, if they beat my kids like that, these white folks have to *lynch* me down here, so I'm going to leave. And I left, and come to St. Louis. That was in the fall of '39.

When I first come to St. Louis, my wife and kids they stayed in Mississippi and I stayed here for a year. When I first came here I was only making $17 a week. I was working at a medical place where they made pills, and I was paying $12 a month rent at that time. It was cheap; I didn't have to pay much for nothing. White people here was prejudiced against colored at that time. When I came to St. Louis, they had places like the Fox Theater, no colored could go there; and the baseball diamond up on Sportsman's Park, they don't allow no colored in there at one time. When they did open up Sportsman's Park for colored, onliest place they could sit was in the bleachers. That changed after the war. Down in South St. Louis, there's places now you can't go if you're colored.

After I was here for a year, I went back down to Mississippi and came back with my wife and kids. The first place I rented was on Francis Avenue and I moved from there to North 9th St. My wife was working at a baby-care company and during the war I was working out at the small-arms bullet plant, out on Goodfellow. They had women operating the machines that make bullets. The mechanics, they were all men, and they had to fix the machines when they broke down. The colored men, they had to fix the colored girls' machines; the white men, they fixed the white.

Some of the colored mechanics, they complained about this, they figure they should fix whatever machine is broke. So they had a meeting at the Kiel Auditorium downtown, which was called by the union. A union man come from up north somewhere, and the man say we got a war and colored is over there fighting for this country. And he say, There's got to be a change made; we going to fix it where the colored man going to be the mechanic on the machine for the white girl and the white men for the colored. And one white man get up and says he would rather work with a dog than work with a nigger. And they told him, You just have to work with a dog; if you want to stay out there you going to be a mechanic on the colored girls' machine. So they changed that.

With me having so many kids, they put me in 4F during the war. I had six kids, and it was hard fitting us all in the places we was living during the war. At that time it was hard for you to find a place when you had children, so every place we'd go they didn't want us. We had been wanting to buy us a house, but we thought we better save up some money while we was both working. I told my wife, I tell you what we'll do. My check is more than yours, and we'll just save my check and we'll use your check to take care of the family and the household.

So we had some money saved up, and I wanted to buy a new car. My wife says, J.D., no! We got these kids and it's hard for us to find a place. What we'll do, we'll take what money we got and buy us a home. And when we get it straight and I'm still working, then we'll buy us a car. I told her we couldn't pay for no home and she said we pay rent, so we can make the payments on a house.

I talked to my supervisor the next day when I got to work and he say, Shelley, you know what? Your wife is right. So I came home and told her, Well, we'll just go ahead and find a place. This was just about when the war was over in Japan. Ethel went to the Church of God in Christ and her pastor, Elder Robert Bishop, he was also in real estate. So we went and talked to him and he said, Yeah, I know a place on Labadie that's for sale. It's got two apartments, so you can rent one out. So we went and looked at it and decided we would buy it. The price of the house was five thousand, seven hundred.

The day we supposed to move, I got a fellow with a truck to move me. That evening when I got off work, I was riding the bus, and I got off at Cora. That's about two blocks from where my house was on Labadie. At that time, the police were walking the beat. This one police, he come up and he ask me what was my name and I told him, J.D. Shelley. He ask me what was I doing out here, and I told him I'm going home. He say, Home? Where you live? I say, 4600 Labadie. He say, Labadie? I say, I just moved; my family just moved today. I had a fellow to move me. I didn't take off from work, I just hired this fellow to move me. So the police, he followed me all the way to the house. He stopped on the sidewalk, and I went on up the steps and got my key out of my pocket and went on in the house. So he left.

Later on, it was just a few days later, I come home one evening and my wife, she says, J.D., we got to go to court. I said, Court for what? She say, This supposed to be a restricted area, no colored on this side of Taylor Avenue. We're not supposed to be living out here. A man just came here and gave me a summons when I got back from work. He'll be back to give you one. He got one for you too.

Around about seven o'clock the doorbell rang and I went to the door, and this man say, Are you Shelley? I say, yes. He say, I got some papers here for you. I say, Papers? For what? He say, It's just some papers. You going to take them? I say, I ain't going to take no papers unless you tell me what it's for. And he say, Mr. Shelley, I'm trying to help you. I say, I still ain't going to take no papers unless you tell me what's the papers for. Just like that. So he throwed the papers down on the floor and walked on out.

So I didn't have to go to court, because if you don't receive a summons in your hand, you don't got to go to court. But my wife had to go to court. Elder Bishop, he got lawyer Vaughn. George Vaughn was his name; he was a colored lawyer. I didn't know him, but I guess he was Elder Bishop's lawyer. A couple of weeks after this man come around with the papers, Ethel went to court. When we bought the house, there was a family living downstairs; he was a street-car motorman. When he saw the sign says the property was sold, he moved. So that's why I got to move in downstairs. The family that was living upstairs, they was renting from the real-estate agent and they stayed for a while. This man and his wife upstairs, they had to go to court too, and the judge wanted to know, how did we treat them. This white lady that lived upstairs, she say, They seem just like when the white were living downstairs. When I go down to the basement to wash, Miz Shelley, she come down and we laugh and talk. And she say, They treat us nice. We don't have no trouble.

What they say in court was that this was supposed to be a restricted area, no colored live on this side of Taylor Avenue. That's one or two blocks from where my house was on Labadie. This Jack Kraemer that sued us, he didn't even *own* no property on this block. I never even seen him around here. Nobody who lived on this block never say they want us to move. They say in court that they had restrictions on all the property on Labadie since 1911. I guess Elder Bishop knowed it, but I didn't know that when we bought the house. It was hard for me to hear a lot of what the judge and the lawyers say in court. You know how they do, they talk but you couldn't hear what they be saying.

I liked that house on Labadie. There was white on this side of me, and white on that side, and all the way down. I knowed all of them, and they treated us nice. None of the white never did say nothing about us living here. My supervisor say, Shelley, you might have to move, man. I says, Man, I ain't moving nowhere. Long as they don't mess with my kids. I ain't worried about them messing with me, but they better not mess with my kids. My kids was teenagers then.

There was some white boys that messed with my little daughter. She went to the store down on the corner and they messed with my daughter and throwed something at her, and my boy went out there and beat them. After that, the kids was all right. The white kids played with my kids, and their parents would have to come to the house sometimes to get them to come home.

After I moved out here, other colored started to buy and they started throwing stink bombs in their house. Every time they'd buy a house, they'd have trouble. They throw bricks in their window. But they never did bother me. My wife, she was going to church and praying. I'd go, but I wasn't like she was.

After the first time we went to court, the lawyers took the case up to the Supreme Court. They was having meetings at the churches about the case; the lawyers and all would be there. Lawyer Vaughn would talk, and this other lawyer, Mr. Willer, he would talk too. That was the Supreme lawyer. They'd be white there, and colored, and they'd be talking about this, and what it meant to colored to be able to buy a house where you wanted, long as you could afford it. They'd ask me questions, what did I think about it and I'd just tell them my opinion about it.

Lawyer Vaughn, he come to the house one night, he always come by and talk, and one night he say, Mr. Shelley, you know, I ain't never had a case this hard. This case getting on my nerves. This white lawyer, Mr. Willer, he was real nice, he come to the house a couple of times. But we still hadn't won the case. I didn't know whether we were going to win the case or not.

When they took it to the Supreme Court they passed a decision, they say it don't make no difference, white or colored, long as they was able to buy property, anywhere in the United States. When I got home that evening, my wife was sitting on the front porch reading the paper that says we won the case. That night, the photographer come, and we was sitting on the couch, with the kids sitting betwixt us, and some on the floor, and they had it in the newspaper.

When we won the case, we didn't sleep that night. People was calling me from overseas, congratulating me. Say they heard it on the news, they saw it in the paper. People called from everywhere. Every time we'd hang up, the phone rings.

We lived in that house on Labadie for maybe ten years. Then we moved over here to St. Louis Avenue, about two blocks, so we could have more room in the house. I sold that house on Labadie two years after I bought this house. People left owing two months rent, wouldn't pay, so I just got mad and sold it. I got nine-five when I sold it. I kept on working in construction long as I could, and my kids and their kids were all working too. Right now, I got five great-great-grandchildren. Ethel passed on September 15, 1984. We was married sixty years, and when we had our anniversary they had a big ceremony over to the church.

This neighborhood is almost all colored now. There was this one time, this was quite a few years after we won this case, I was down there at the tavern on the corner. And this boy says,

J.D. Shelley, you the one that caused us to be out here. A friend of mine was sitting there and he say, What you say? What you talking about? And this boy say, J.D., he's the first colored that bought out here. He made it possible for us. I ain't kidding you, Johnny. And Johnny say, I'll bet you five dollars. I say, Johnny, don't bet him no five dollars, because you going to *lose!* They had me holding the money. So this boy went up to his house and got this book and brought it back and he says, Now you read for yourself. And that book told about our case and it say that J.D. Shelley, he was the first one.

The way I see it, it was a good thing that we done this case. When all this happened, when I bought the property, I didn't think there was going to be anything about it. But I knowed it was important. We was the first ones to live where they said colored can't live.

4

Lloyd Barenblatt
v. United States

Lloyd Barenblatt was a college teacher and former
Communist who asserted his First Amendment
rights in 1954 against congressional inquisitors
of the McCarthy era. *Courtesy of Lloyd Barenblatt*

I.
"This Is Not a Court"

On the morning of June 28, 1954, Lloyd Barenblatt sat in the cavernous caucus room of the Old House Office Building in Washington, D.C. Earlier that month, he had been handed a subpoena to appear before the House Un-American Activities Committee. When he received the summons, Barenblatt was a psychology instructor at Vassar College in Poughkeepsie, New York. Vassar's president, Sarah Gibson Blandings, had earlier assured her trustees that faculty members who refused to answer questions before congressional committees could be fired. Barenblatt was not protected by tenure and, even before he testified, Vassar had declined to renew his teaching contract.

Precisely at 10:30, Representative Harold H. Velde rapped his gavel and began the hearing. Like Richard Nixon, his better-known predecessor on HUAC, Velde had won election to Congress after World War II by accusing the Democrats of softness on communism. "Get the Reds out of Washington" was the slogan that propelled the former FBI agent to a coveted seat on the Red-hunting panel. Unlike Nixon, whose dogged pursuit of Alger Hiss as an accused Soviet espionage agent won him headlines in 1948 and election as Vice President in 1952, Velde's targets were smaller fry, mostly teachers and ministers. After Velde became chairman in 1953, HUAC failed to unmask a single spy, real or imagined.

Velde had convened this routine hearing to "uncover" Communist party members who had taught in Michigan schools or universities. The committee intended "to demonstrate to the people of

Michigan" that Reds had infiltrated their state's schools and to expose "the identity of those individuals" who had acted as classroom commissars. Velde's first target was the University of Michigan, and his lead witness was Francis X. Crowley, a former university student and confessed party member. Crowley came before the committee as a repentant witness, eager to evade the contempt citation that Velde had threatened for refusing to identify former party colleagues at a prior hearing. After this hearing, Crowley had reportedly sought out a Catholic priest and experienced a religious conversion. Whether he feared punishment in the hereafter or prison in the here-and-now, Crowley became an informer, forced to "name names" and undergo the ritual of self-abasement that HUAC demanded as proof of patriotism.

When Crowley appeared at the second hearing, Velde had already extracted in executive session all the names of Communist party members that Crowley could recall from his years at the University of Michigan, between 1947 and 1950. Crowley's list of some thirty names included that of Lloyd Barenblatt, a graduate student in psychology who had joined the Haldane Club, the party group in the graduate school that was named after an eminent English scientist and fervent Communist. Crowley told Velde that the club was "mainly a discussion group" that read "pamphlets on Marxism" and debated "literature and cultures; the function of the artist in that respect." Crowley dashed Velde's vision of a Red "conspiracy" at the university, dedicated to the violent overthrow of the American system. Haldane Club members, Crowley said, were "mostly the intellectual type" and had never discussed "overthrowing anything."

Barenblatt sat quietly in the caucus room during Crowley's examination by Velde and the committee's counsel. Despite his agreement to "name names," Crowley resisted the demand that he brand Barenblatt a Communist party activist. Although he named his former roommate as a Haldane Club member, Crowley said that Barenblatt "was pretty much of the same opinion that I was about membership in the party." Recent visits with Barenblatt, Crowley told Velde, left him "convinced" that Barenblatt had left the Communist party and no longer advocated its doctrines.

Despite his clearance by Crowley, Barenblatt declined to cooperate with the committee when he took the witness stand. After outlining his education at the University of Michigan and his recently terminated position at Vassar College, Barenblatt began reading a lengthy statement of "my objections to the power and jurisdiction of this committee to inquire into my political beliefs, my religious beliefs, and any other personal and private affairs" the committee might ask him about. Before he completed this first sentence, HUAC member Clyde Doyle broke in to advise Barenblatt that it would be "a magnificent thing" to confess his party membership and "get out of that embarrassing situation."

"I appreciate your concern, sir," Barenblatt assured Doyle, but he refused to confess, and attempted to continue reading his statement. Velde grew impatient and demanded that Barenblatt answer the committee's rock-bottom question: "Are you now a member of the Communist party?" Barenblatt huddled with his lawyer, Philip Wittenberg, and then resumed his recitation. Velde's patience was now exhausted. "Now, Mr. Witness," he warned Barenblatt, "this is not a court of law." HUAC made the rules and the witness must comply. The only escape from a citation for contempt of Congress, Velde explained, was to claim the protection of the Fifth Amendment against self-incrimination. Velde was astounded when Barenblatt responded that his refusal to answer was grounded on the First Amendment and that the Fifth Amendment was "not included in my list of objections."

After lengthy and fruitless sparring over Barenblatt's political activities at the University of Michigan, Velde allowed his statement into the record. Richard L. Kunzig, the committee's counsel, asked a final question "so there can be no doubt in the written record at all." Barenblatt had not "in any way sought to invoke or raise the Fifth Amendment whatsoever," Kunzig inquired. "You are entirely correct, sir," Barenblatt assured him.

Under the existing rules of the game, Barenblatt could have left the hearing room without fear of prosecution. However, the label "Fifth Amendment Communist" would have trailed him like a sniffing dog. Claims that HUAC had no right under the First Amendment to inquire into political beliefs and associations were guaranteed to provoke a citation for criminal contempt and the risk of a year in jail. Sure enough, three weeks after Barenblatt's appearance, Velde asked the House of Representatives to approve a contempt citation. Not only had Barenblatt "refused to answer any questions concerning alleged Communist activities," the ungrammatical HUAC resolution read, but he had "failed to use his constitutional privilege under the Fifth Amendment" and had "used First Amendment (freedom of speech), which, up to the present time, has been held by the courts as inapplicable in this situation." The contempt resolution passed on a voice vote, without a single dissent.

Lloyd Barenblatt was far from alone as a target of the House Un-American Activities Committee. First created as a special committee in 1938, HUAC became a haven for Democratic party Dixiecrats and right-wing Republicans who ransacked New Deal agencies for Reds. America's wartime alliance with the Soviet Union blunted the search for subversives, but the first chilly winds of the Cold War revived the committee and its anti-Communist supporters such as the powerful American Legion. Complacency in the House leadership, which detested HUAC for attacking Roosevelt administration officials, proved costly. John E. Rankin, a Mississippi Democrat whose violent hatred of blacks and Jews was matched by his parliamentary cunning, squeezed out a surprise vote in January 1945 that made HUAC a standing House committee. Rankin's authorizing resolution gave HUAC broad power to investigate "the extent, character, and objects of un-American propaganda activities in the United States." What was "propaganda" to some, of course, struck others as protected expression of opinion under the First Amendment.

During the next dozen years, before the Supreme Court began to curb the committee's excesses, HUAC conducted some 230 public hearings and interrogated more than 3,000 witnesses, of whom 135 were cited for contempt. Two probes in particular brought the committee banner headlines. The search for Soviet spies, which sent Alger Hiss to prison for perjury, propelled Richard Nixon to national prominence. More exciting to the press and public was HUAC's 1947 investigation of the movie industry, which put Hollywood communists and fellow-travelers under the Klieg lights of exposure.

Witnesses who came before HUAC learned two painful lessons. One was that the committee's inquisitors had an insatiable appetite for names, demanding that witnesses list every Communist party member, past or present, they had ever encountered. During the Hollywood hearings, actor Larry Parks begged for escape from the committee's vice. "Don't present me with the choice of either being in contempt of the committee and going to jail or forcing me to really crawl through the mud to be an informer." Threatened with a contempt citation, Parks crawled, providing HUAC with twelve names, including that of Lee J. Cobb. Backing up the pain of exposure was the penalty of unemployment. The committee could not fire "unfriendly" witnesses or those named as Communists, but employers could and did. From Harlem to Hollywood, the "blacklist" of Reds cost thousands their jobs in factories, classrooms, and film studios. Even labor unions joined the crusade. The Screen Actors Guild, then headed by Ronald Reagan, barred Communists from membership and helped the studios enforce the Hollywood blacklist.

Lloyd Barenblatt's contempt citation was followed by a federal grand jury indictment for violation of an 1857 law which made it a crime for any person summoned before a congressional committee to "refuse to answer any question pertinent to the matter of inquiry" before the panel. His indictment had five separate counts, based on refusal to answer five questions, all related to Communist party activities. Conviction on all five counts could send Barenblatt to prison for five years. During the mid-1950s, contempt prosecutions clogged the federal courts; HUAC secured twenty-nine citations in 1954 alone.

What made Barenblatt's case unusual was that he declined to invoke his Fifth Amendment privilege, a guarantee of safe exit from HUAC's hearing room. The Supreme Court had grudgingly agreed that the right to avoid self-incrimination protected witnesses before Congress as well as courts. Barenblatt's insistence that the First Amendment barred the committee from *any* inquiry about political activities, Communist or otherwise, raised the legal stakes of his challenge. Ruling in 1951, the Supreme Court upheld the convictions of Communist party leaders for advocating the violent overthrow of the American government, holding that the party presented a "clear and present danger" to the country. The party's doctrines, and by implication its members, fell outside the First Amendment's protective mantle. Under this assumption, congressional inquiry into party membership was directed at a criminal conspiracy, not a peaceful debating club.

Barenblatt's challenge to HUAC took direct aim at the "clear and present danger" doctrine fashioned in 1919 by Justice Oliver Wendell Holmes. Before he testified, Barenblatt had read a short but powerful book by Alexander Meiklejohn, *Free Speech and Its Relation to Self-Government,* published in 1948. Then in his seventies, Meiklejohn had been president of Amherst College, and wrote his book in response to HUAC's assaults on free speech. Uncompromising in his First Amendment absolutism, Meiklejohn took on Holmes, arguing that action alone, and never the advocacy of ideas, could be suppressed by government. "No plan of action shall be outlawed because someone in control thinks it unwise, unfair, un-American," Meiklejohn wrote. The advocacy of ideas equally protects those who are "defending democracy or attacking it, planning a Communist reconstruction of our economy or criticizing it." These words so impressed Barenblatt that he decided to appear before HUAC armed only with the shield of the First Amendment.

Judge Alexander Holtzoff, who presided at Barenblatt's trial in March 1956, had no sympathy for Meiklejohn's argument. In fact, HUAC had no better friend than Holtzoff on the federal bench in Washington, D.C. Seventy years old, he had spent twenty years in the Justice Department, had acted as counsel to FBI director J. Edgar Hoover, and had served as an American Legion commander. Beginning in 1947, two years after he became a federal judge, Holtzoff began sending HUAC's victims to prison. Any witness who invoked the First Amendment before HUAC, he ruled that year, "acts at his peril." The same year, Holtzoff gave HUAC virtually unlimited scope in examining witnesses: "If the subject under scrutiny may have any possible relevancy and materiality, no matter how remote, to some possible legislation, it is within the power of Congress to investigate the matter."

Faced with this judicial Torquemada, Barenblatt's lawyer, Philip Wittenberg, abandoned the First Amendment argument and aimed his fire at the form of HUAC's questions to his client. Wittenberg, who first demanded that a jury be empaneled and then asked Judge Holtzoff to dismiss the jurors, argued that the committee had not told Barenblatt, before his testimony, just what legislation it might recommend to Congress to deal with "Communists in education." The questions Barenblatt had refused to answer thus lacked "pertinency" to any legitimate legislative purpose. Predictibly, Wittenberg got nowhere with this tack. Holtzoff listened with obvious impatience and immediately pronounced Barenblatt guilty of contempt. The sentence he imposed was imprisonment for six months and a fine of $250.

After his conviction, Barenblatt retained a new lawyer, David Scribner, to argue an appeal to the federal appellate court in Washington. All three judges on the panel that heard the appeal were conservative Republicans, including Warren Burger, a future Chief Justice of the Supreme Court. Their unanimous ruling, issued in January 1957, upheld Judge Holtzoff on every issue. Scribner had argued that HUAC's stated goal of "exposing" Communists in Michigan schools was not connected to any legislative purpose. The appellate panel refused to question HUAC's motives. "Courts must presume congressional investigations to have valid legislative purposes," Judge Walter Bastian wrote. "The fact that such an inquiry or investigation may reveal or 'expose' some facts embarrassing to someone is incidental and without effect upon the validity of the inquiry." Bastian also rejected Scribner's First Amendment argument, writing that the Supreme Court had "consistently rejected" such claims and that "Congress can inquire into 'private affairs' and, of course, political views and associations."

Scribner asked the Supreme Court to review this adverse ruling, and he won a momentary reprieve in June 1957. The justices returned Barenblatt's case to the Court of Appeals, based on the Supreme Court's decision in the case of John T. Watkins, a left-wing union official who had refused to identify former Communists at a HUAC hearing in 1954. The Court's opinion, written by Chief Justice Earl Warren, suggested that HUAC had no constitutional power to question citizens about their political beliefs and associations. "The mere summoning of a witness and compelling him to testify, against his will, about his beliefs, expressions or associations is a measure of governmental interference" with First Amendment rights, Warren wrote. The Chief Justice added a slap at HUAC's legislative domain: "It would be difficult to imagine a less explicit authorizing resolution" from Congress to a committee. Watkins won his freedom, however, not on First Amendment grounds but on the Court's narrower finding that HUAC had not advised him of the pertinency of its questions to its inquiry into labor unions.

Despite the opening Warren had offered, the appellate court

again upheld Barenblatt's conviction in January 1958. In this second round, all nine judges took part, and they divided five-to-four. Writing for the majority, Judge Bastian compared the Watkins and Barenblatt cases and found a "decisive distinction between the two." Admitting that Watkins had not been advised of the pertinency of the questions posed to him, Bastian considered the pertinency of HUAC's questions to Barenblatt "indubitably clear" and added that Barenblatt "came prepared to refuse to answer any questions of moment—pertinent or not." In two separate opinions, the dissenting judges read Warren's opinion as barring HUAC from investigating the "political activities and connections of university teachers."

Barenblatt returned to the Supreme Court in 1958 with two new lawyers and renewed hope for a reversal of his conviction. Edward J. Ennis and Nanette Dembitz of the American Civil Liberties Union joined David Scribner in defending Barenblatt. As a Justice Department lawyer, Ennis had asked the Supreme Court in 1943 to uphold Gordon Hirabayashi's conviction for violating the military orders against Japanese Americans. Ennis later became the ACLU's general counsel and revived the First Amendment argument of Alexander Meiklejohn when he appeared before the Supreme Court. Any congressional investigation into "what Communists are thinking about, what they're teaching," Ennis told the justices, "is plainly unconstitutional." Although he pressed the pertinency issue that Chief Justice Warren had opened in the Watkins case, Ennis rested his argument on the First Amendment so strongly that one justice commented, "Mr. Ennis, I'm greatly tempted to say: 'You're so good, why do you have to be so extreme?'"

The government's lawyer, Philip Monahan, matched Ennis in the extremity of his argument. Assuring the justices that HUAC's questions to Barenblatt were indeed pertinent to a legislative purpose, Monahan then struck a flame to Cold War kindling. The Supreme Court should acknowledge, he stated, the existence of a "world Communist movement" whose tactics included "treachery, deceit, infiltration, and any other means deemed necessary, to establish a Communist totalitarian dictatorship throughout the world." American Communists, Monahan claimed, worked "to foster in every way possible the political and other ends of the Soviet-based dictatorship to which it bears true allegiance." After fifteen minutes of Cold War rhetoric, Chief Justice Warren grew impatient: "Mr. Monahan, do we have to listen to all of that?"

When the Supreme Court voted to hear Barenblatt's appeal, only eight members took part and the justices were evenly split. When they gathered after the arguments to decide his fate, the decisive vote was cast by the Court's newest justice, Potter Stewart, a moderate Republican from Cincinnati. Speaking for the four who opposed HUAC's bully-boy tactics, Chief Justice Warren said the committee had not advised Barenblatt of the pertinency of its questions and that "*Watkins* requires reversal." Warren added that he considered HUAC's authorizing resolution "void" under the First Amendment. Justice Felix Frankfurter countered that "the ingredients of notice and pertinency were provided" to Barenblatt. Although he had recently assured Justice William Brennan that "there isn't a man on the Court who personally disapproves more than I do of the activities of all the Un-American Committees," Frankfurter's belief in "judicial restraint" led him to approve Barenblatt's conviction. Justice Stewart voted first at the conference table, and his vote sent Barenblatt to prison.

Justice John Marshall Harlan, a former Wall Street lawyer and grandson of an earlier Supreme Court justice, wrote the Court's majority opinion, issued on June 8, 1959. Holding that HUAC had given Barenblatt notice of the pertinency of its questions with "indisputable clarity," Harlan answered the First Amendment challenge with a Cold War rebuttal. The Court "recognized the close nexus between the Communist party and violent overthrow of government," Harlan wrote. Given this fact, the Court could not "blind itself to world affairs which have determined the whole course of our national policy since the end of World War II," he continued. The First Amendment did not make the college or university "a constitutional sanctuary from inquiry" into Communist activities.

Accusing the majority of judicial blindness, Justice Hugo Black wrote for the dissenters that "the Court today fails to see what is here for all to see—that exposure and punishment is the aim of this committee and the reason for its existence." Allowing HUAC "to try witnesses and punish them because they are or have been Communists or because they refuse to admit or deny Communist affiliations," Black wrote, substituted "drumhead courts" for "the right to a judicial trial" guaranteed by the Bill of Rights. Black ended his judicial sermon with the choice of perdition or perfection: "Ultimately all the questions in this case really boil down to one—whether we as a people will try fearfully and futilely to preserve democracy by adopting totalitarian methods, or whether in accordance with our traditions and our Constitution we will have the confidence and courage to be free."

Lloyd Barenblatt surrendered to begin his prison sentence after the Court's final ruling. The battle to abolish HUAC began in earnest the next year, led by Frank Wilkinson, another First Amendment challenger who served a one-year prison term for contempt. During the 1960s, Congress became increasingly embarrassed by the committee's abusive tactics and the disruptive antics of its New Left targets. Riots at HUAC hearings in San Francisco, Yippie witnesses who draped themselves in American flags, and the gradual thaw in Cold War attitudes finally persuaded Congress in 1975 to dismantle the committee. Thirty years after the House voted to hunt Reds by subpoena, Representative Robert Drinan rose to express gratitude that his colleagues had finally voted to excise "that self-inflicted wound called HUAC" from the body politic. Lloyd Barenblatt and thousands of other Americans, political prisoners and blacklist victims, still bear the scars of the American Inquisition.

II.
"All They Wanted
Were Names!"

I was born in New York City in 1923, very much a Depression-era child. I had one older sister, who is now a psychologist and not very much like me in my political orientation at all. My memories of the Depression are of living in slum tenements in the Bronx. We were evicted several times for not paying the rent.

My father was a garment worker of Russian–Jewish background. He worked as a cutter, and moved from shop to shop. He was active in the American Labor party, which was the party of Fiorello LaGuardia and which contained some people of radical orientation. Although he was unemployed much of the time, he was very intellectually oriented and somewhat radical, but he made it a principle *never* to try to indoctrinate me in any way. He was very careful about letting me develop my own opinions.

My schooling was entirely in the New York City public schools, of which I attended many because of our forced mobility. I went to DeWitt Clinton High School and City College. Although I was aware of politics in high school, I had a distaste for politics, although my inclinations were liberal. As a matter of fact, up through college I was very much of a patriot, although I had friends who were oriented to the Communists. They sort of repelled me, the Communist youth of the time. I was somewhat antagonistic to the American Communist party, which I saw as being doctrinaire and stupid and out of touch with the American people and American realities.

When I went to City College in 1940 I was in the Reserve Officers Training Corps. I believed in the war before the Russians got in. But I also had my shoulder hunched against that fashionable anticommunism. I studied zoology in college, and my last year I took a few psychology courses. After my third year I enlisted in the merchant marine but I came down with meningitis in training and was classified 4-F. While I was 4-F I applied for aviation cadet training in the army air force and I'm probably the only person who passed their supposedly rigid physical while I was 4-F.

I was in the army from March '44 to November '45. I was sent all over the South—Macon, Georgia; Fort Myers in Florida; Montgomery, Alabama. So I got a little tour of the Deep South. Serving in the South was good for me. I got to know about Americans; it was very educational. I had always prided myself on being more cosmopolitan. My mother had a saying from the old country: You can lead a donkey around the world but he'll come back to the same place still a jackass. One thing I came to realize, both from my experiences in merchant-marine training and the army, was that while I saw the war as somewhat ideological—a Good War against Fascism—I began to sense that the powers that were could not present this easily to the American public and the boys doing the fighting. They made it into a war to protect Our Way of Life. That's an interesting phenomenon. The same thing was going on in the Soviet Union. It became the Great Patriotic War for the Motherland.

I didn't get overseas during the war. Ironically, there were not enough air crew casualties. What they did was to establish this huge pool of prime-grade American beef in the training command, and they put the aviation cadet program on hold and had us doing various menial and clerical jobs on these air force posts. I was classified as a bombardier, but I worked in what they called special services as a disk jockey, playing a lot of jazz. For a while I was in the air inspector's office. My job there was to tear up obsolete air force manuals and regulations—we didn't have shredders then. I got strong hands from that job.

I got married while I was in the army and my then wife went to the University of Iowa and I went back to New York after my discharge. I got a boring job for a few months; couldn't stand it, so I went out to the University of Iowa and got accepted in their child psychology graduate program. The Cold War was in full swing then. I was active in the American Veterans Committee, which was set up after the war to support democratic and liberal issues, as an alternative to the blind patriotism of the American Legion. The local AVC chapter voted to condemn the coal miners' strike in '46 and the speech made in behalf of this motion was that it would look good, it would take away the leftist image of the AVC.

There was also an episode about this young man, Tom—apple-cheeked, blond, a typical midwestern young man in the Methodist Social Action Committee. He was put in jail because he put up posters protesting the fact that a black person could not get a haircut in Iowa City, even at the university barbershop. They had to travel forty miles to get their hair cut. The AVC decided not to do anything to help get Tom out of jail, which struck me as a disgusting cover-up for collaboration between the university and town officials.

I was not a Communist then, although I was accused of being a Communist because I opposed the motion made against the coal miners and because I called for support for getting this young man out of jail. I saw the full swing of the careerist executive committee of the AVC. I understand in retrospect that I was proposed for membership in the Communist party and *turned down!* I didn't know this at the time.

I did not do well during that year, that was '45 and '46. That was a chaotic period in my life. I was unhappy at Iowa, and they weren't too happy with me; understandably so. I did not perform well, I didn't get papers in on time. But I learned a hell of a lot. That's my personality. I think I learned twice as much as the other students from the best professors, who were great, even though I disagreed with their behavioristic approach, which I considered very parochial. But they knew their stuff and gave good accounts of opposing points of view.

Then I switched to the University of Michigan. Michigan had a very good reputation; it was becoming the number one psychology department in the country and I lucked out—they took me in, made me a teaching fellow. I think I was pretty highly regarded, and I was given a course to teach to the other graduate students in basic concepts of psychology.

I believed, by that time, in the imminent danger in this country of Fascism. There were many signs of repressive political legislation going onto the books. The bill of Hubert Humphrey and Herbert Lehman to set up concentration camps for political dissidents; becoming friendly with countries that backed the Fascists during the war, like Argentina; intervening in the civil war in Greece *against* the Partisans who fought the Nazis during the war—all these ominous events taking place, I really saw them as dangerous. They let the Fair Employment Practices Commission lapse after the war, and the protection of the poor from price-gouging was done away with by disarming the Office of Price Administration. The shame of it was that the liberals, as personified by the Americans for Democratic Action, swung right along with it! That was the most ominous of all.

And I also saw that the only real resistance to Fascist ideas was the stalwartness among the Communists. They also had the record of practically *being* the resistance in Europe during the war. So I decided to join the Communist party. Joining the party was very much like, I imagine, joining the Masons. You get to talking to someone, you see if they like you and you like them, and there's a really minimal exchange of profound ideas. Also, I could see that the tactic of the Communist party at that time was to put members into what they called mass organizations— terrible lingo!—to the liberal and civil-rights groups and unions; to have their people participate in those organizations. The Communists were the ones who were carrying things forward! They really had political courage and principle. They were the backbone of what I saw as the resistance to the ominous reaction taking place in our country at the time. They were the people that seemed to have the principles, the fortitude, and the courage to dedicate themselves and work in groups like the NAACP and the American Veterans Committee.

There was a lot of anger in me, going back to the army. I remember right after V–J Day I was in Fort Myers, Florida, and one of the sergeants took it upon himself to give a little speech to the assembled troops, about how we licked the Japs and the next thing we would do is work against the Russians! In my naiveté I said, What a fool! I thought we were going to march forward on this golden path of human rights and economic equality and political and social freedom, now that we'd licked the Fascists. But this semiliterate boob sergeant was right, and I was very wrong!

It turned out that being in the Communist party didn't involve much on my part. Most of it was attending meetings of the Haldane Club, which was the organization of Communists among the graduate students at Michigan. I got a reputation as being outspoken and obstructive at these meetings. Certainly, I was kind of a maverick thinker and I found a lot of the activities and pronouncements of the Communist party at best puzzling and at worst stupid and wrong. But in my mind, during that time, there was no place else to go. I certainly wasn't going to go along with the ADA, and I was fed up with the corruption in the American Veterans Committee. And there was no one else doing these things! The NAACP, which developed into a very active Negro protest movement during the Martin Luther King period, was looked upon as a more conservative organization. Then, if you were a white person and a member of the NAACP, you were a Communist! If you were not so in reality, you were labeled as such anyhow. And the only people who were actively, vociferously, dedicatedly working and talking on behalf of human rights for minorities, especially for blacks, were the Reds! A few liberals sort of chimed in when things were relatively safe, but when it wasn't, they weren't there.

When I was at Michigan in 1948, I was involved in the Progressive party campaign of Henry Wallace for president. I went around with a Wallace petition to small towns in Michigan. It was a very interesting experience. I remember one incident where I asked this guy who was tinkering with his car to sign the petition. He was very friendly and supportive, but he advised me not to go to this house or that house; to stay away from them. There was a not-too-subtle terrorism against Wallace supporters—an equation that to be for Wallace was to be a Red. The Red Scare atmosphere was pervasive, strong, ubiquitous. Of course, at that time many people like myself, democratic minded and well-intentioned people in the Communist party, as well as others, were not aware of the Stalinist horrors.

I got a job as an instructor in psychology at Vassar College in 1950, without a doctorate. My GI Bill benefits had run out and I heard about this job at Vassar, which is in Poughkeepsie, north of New York City. I was interviewed by the president, Sarah Gibson Blandings, who decided to hire me, I think, when I told her I was a jazz buff. It was very generous of them to keep me there for four years, without a doctorate. During my first two years at

Vassar I was still in the Communist party. At the time I was called before the House Un-American Activities Committee in 1954, I was *not* a Communist. I was in effect expelled or dropped from the Communist party, but I wasn't going to tell *them* that or, for a long time, anybody else. I didn't want to be involved in the 'separating the sheep from the goats' process. That would be counter to my stand. The irony of the thing was that, according to reports I got later on, the Communists in Poughkeepsie were going around, telling people not to support my case or contribute to my defense. When I first got the subpoena, they had offered to support my case, if I came under their wing and did what they said. And I told them I didn't need them, which they took very negatively and angrily!

My decision to leave the Communist party was not related to Stalinism in Russia. First of all, the comrades began to view me with more and more suspicion and discomfort, because of my outspoken feelings about their ploys and tactics. The final thing came around the Smith Act trials. First of all, I was opposed to the type of defense they put on in the Smith Act cases. They should have won that trial hands down! The defense was extremely peculiar.

In 1952 the party ironically asked a "loyalty oath" screening question of its members—would they help hide some people who were on trial on a Smith Act charge as leaders of the Communist party and who had skipped bail and gone underground? I told the person who asked me that I would not do this, that I thought the right of bail was a very precious American liberty and that if they accepted freedom on bail they should have honored that instead of running out and forfeiting the money that many poor people collected to put up bail for them in the first place. The fact that the party leaders skipped bail was an injustice to party members. I was very vocal in saying that this was very wrong. And I think this is one of the things that marked me as 'lousy' in their eyes.

When I was called to appear before the House Un-American Activities Committee in 1954, I was completely taken by surprise. They served me the subpoena as I was packing to leave Vassar in my little cabin in Pleasant Valley, near Poughkeepsie. After four years without a doctorate, Vassar had not renewed my contract and I had to leave. I was wondering why, all of a sudden, out of the clear blue, the committee would call *me!* It turned out that one of my very best friends, Francis X. Crowley, who had been called before the committee the year before and had taken an idiosyncratic stand, refusing to use any legal or constitutional reason for not testifying, subsequently was indicted and faced a year in prison. And he caved in.

None of us suspected Crowley. Francis had been one of my friends in the army. We sort of kept in contact after the war. Quite independently of me, he had become a Red. He came to see me when I was a graduate student at Michigan. He was down and out, disheveled, broke, hungry, dirty. I took him in, got him washed up, fed him, got him to enroll at Michigan, where he was an excellent student, became Phi Beta Kappa. Very smart guy, very erudite. His great bugaboo was informers! He was a great student of Irish literature and political history, and he was always raving against informers. That was the most pitiful thing, when they broke his spirit and made him an informer.

He petitioned to come before the committee again to purge himself of contempt. They required, of course, a conversion, an inquisitional reverse, which he performed. And he named, I guess, about forty names—anyone who had ever given him a break! There were times when, without much exaggeration, this had been life or death for him, because he had been severely depressed and wouldn't take care of himself for long periods of time. The Communist party at that time served as a familial and emotional support system for many people, for good or bad.

Well, I never suspected that Crowley could do anything like that until the day I appeared before the committee. They put him on stage with his back to the audience. When he mentioned my name, I was stunned! His betrayal was unimaginable to me. Looking back, I had many clues that he might be going this way, that I refused to believe. I myself was very critical of the Communist party, both from the standpoint of democratic principles and human rights and their lack of understanding of American equalitarian and democratic feelings. It was just plain stupidity! Dissidents in Europe at that time faced torture, faced death. People were running scared in this country—not only the fear of losing their job, but the greatest fear was the opprobrium of your neighbors, from your own family. That's what scared people more than anything else. I remember many conversations with Crowley about this, but it never occurred to me that he was preparing to use this to justify his informer act.

The treatment of the witnesses by the committee was, without any exaggeration, inquisitional. I was not allowed to make any preliminary statement, I was not allowed to expand or elaborate on any answers, I was not allowed to confer with my attorney on any matters except legal objections. All they wanted were names! And dates! It was an act of contrition to inform on others. It was transparently prosecutorial. There were very few hints even of gathering information for the purpose of legislation. The committee counsel asked me five questions, including whether I was or had been a member of the Communist party, and whether I knew Francis Crowley in the party. It was obvious that their purpose was to prepare me for a contempt citation and an indictment.

I knew that I would need a lawyer when I appeared before the committee. Corliss Lamont, who had been cited for contempt and was very wealthy, had established some sort of committee to help people called before HUAC and I went to see him. I was penniless, my salary at Vassar was between three and four thousand dollars, my parents had no money. How was I going to undertake this thing? I had imagined there were some people who would be willing to help, given my volunteering for this principled stand against the committee. My position was that the committee had no force or authority. I really based this on an argument that was presented by a grand old man of the academic world, Alexander Meiklejohn. He argued that legislative committees could only investigate activities that constituted action, such as espionage or sabotage or preparation for violence. But they had no power to ask questions that would abridge freedom of speech or association, even for members of the Communist party.

Two expressions in the Constitution, in very few words, supported my position. The beginning of the Preamble, "We, the people," and the word 'abridgment' in the First Amendment. Put together, what they mean is that the bodies of government, including Congress, derive their power from the larger governmental body, the people. There's nothing in the Constitution which explicitly gives the committee power to require testimony. It is a derived power for the purpose of legislating in knowledge and wisdom, and collecting information for that purpose. But the word 'abridgment' in the First Amendment proscribes any kind of what is now called a 'chilling effect' on free debate and discourse among the electorate. So the First Amendment is not primarily a freedom for the individual, it is a safeguard and necessary function of our primary body of government, the electorate. This was my argument. And I could get no lawyer to accept this!

First, I had trouble getting *any* kind of lawyer. They were all scared as hell. The lawyer I finally took on was Philip Wittenberg, who had handled Corliss Lamont's case and had written a piece in *The Nation,* 'How to Say No to the Demagogues.' His position with Lamont and the *Nation* article was not what I had in mind; it depended not on the First Amendment *per se* but on other legal technicalities. To Wittenberg's credit, he was not scared, provided the money was right. I heard him make a joke that was current among lawyers at that time. 'How did you do on your Red case?' 'Great! My client got five years, but I got off without any sentence at all.'

Wittenberg got me to go along with his position, looking for technicalities in the committee proceedings, but it was my own fault for going along. This obscured the primary principle on which I wished to make a stand. And the legal bills were tremendous! I did get some help from the Emergency Civil Liberties Committee, which was set up to defend 'Red' cases that the American Civil Liberties Union wouldn't touch. The proposition of the ECLC was that I was to be kind of a showpiece, a theatrical *cause célèbre* to raise money, and ECLC would take half. I bridled at that! Not as a squabble over money but as a matter of deception. By that time, there were several other First Amendment challenges to the House committee—Chandler Davis, John Gojack, some of the *New York Times* people—and they felt the same way I did. So we decided to form our own little committee to raise money for First Amendment people, which was not too successful. We didn't have the savvy, the know-how to do it.

My trial was in Washington, before Judge Holtzoff, who was terrible! He was notorious for being hard in 'Red' cases. Wittenberg would not put me on the stand; it appeared to me that he didn't want any political issues raised in my case. In fact, *nobody* testified at my trial! It was a question of law and not of evidence, and if it's only a matter of law, you don't need a jury. But Wittenberg asked for a jury trial, so we had a jury. It was rough. Holtzoff began by questioning whether there was any matter of evidence involved in this case at all. It was irrelevant as to whether I was or was not a Red. The only matter was whether I did indeed refuse to answer questions at a duly constituted committee proceeding. The questions of law were not a matter for a jury. Well, in the middle of the trial Wittenberg threw in the towel and agreed to dismiss the jury. He didn't consult me about a damn thing! I was stupid, I was callow, I was happy to get *any* kind of lawyer. And I was mystified by the priesthood of jurisprudence.

Well, we lost. I was sentenced to six months in jail, and then Wittenberg hit me with a tremendous bill and insisted I pay up before he would prepare an appeal. I said, Well, I'm going to have to look for another lawyer. Without asking me, he picked up the phone and called a very well-known and respected civil-liberties lawyer, and he said to him, How would you like to have the Barenblatt case? Then he said to me, This guy wants you to come see him. I went to see him, and I tried to explain to him first of all my position, which is the real reason I was miffed at Wittenberg, who really didn't want to reach the basic First Amendment argument. He looked at the ceiling and reflected and he said, That's interesting philosophy but it's not law. Then I heard through John Gojack of another lawyer, David Scribner, and he said he would take the case. He was broke, he didn't even have an office. And I got some money from friends, here and there. The only group that supported my case was the American Friends Service Committee.

Nobody wanted to be my lawyer when I was tried. By the time my case came up to the Supreme Court for the second time, after it had been remanded to the Circuit Court for another argument, *everybody* wanted to be my lawyer! So the second appeal was handled by the American Civil Liberties Union, which originally wouldn't touch the case. Where were they when I needed them?

I went down to the Supreme Court for the hearing in my case, after the appeals court decided against me for the second time. It was crowded; a lot of lawyers came. By that time, it was a big case, front page in the *Times*. Being in the Supreme Court was fascinating. One of my strongest impressions of the hearing in my case was the behavior of Felix Frankfurter. Hopping around, interrupting, screeching! I couldn't *believe* this; in fact, I thought maybe he was playing devil's advocate—but it was clear later that he came with his mind made up against me.

It was hard to tell about any of the other justices. Of course, my case had been to the court before and they had probably discussed it and exchanged opinions about the case previously. My feeling was that whatever their opinions were, and they were unknown to me, it was precast. Which direction, I did not know until I read the papers months later that I had lost, by a 5-to-4 vote. I was a little surprised, pleasantly, that it was as close as it was. What was historically important was the minority opinion written by Justice Black. No one reads the majority opinion anymore, but Black's opinion has become history.

During the time my case was on appeal, I was working in market research and advertising in New York. I was blacklisted in the academic world and went on Madison Avenue. I did that for about seven years, until I had to report to serve my jail term. I started out in the District of Columbia jail, which was a *horrible* place! Then they sent me to the D.C. workhouse, which is in Occoquan, Virginia. It looked like a small liberal-arts campus on the outside, but inside it was the pits.

I finally got transferred to the federal prison in Danbury, Connecticut. I had ten days in solitary in the Lewisburg penitentiary on the way. Lewisburg was a real prison, like in the Big House movies, but Danbury wasn't too bad. Of course, the overriding fear of political prisoners, of all prisoners, was of violence. That was always on my mind. The main fear about going to jail at that time was the righteous wrath of superpatriot inmates, to make some points in the eyes of their jailers by smashing a Red. One of the Smith Act defendants, a guy named Thompson, was hit over the head with a pipe, so it wasn't an idle fear. We also had the memory of the Remington affair. William Remington had been sent to prison for perjury after he denied being a Communist, and was murdered at the Lewisburg penitentiary by another inmate. But that kind of violence didn't happen to me.

I really got along pretty well with the other inmates. As a matter of fact, one day I was approached by what I presumed to be a Mafia member who said he had great admiration for me. What he wanted from me was the secrets of *my* organization. He said, You know, we take over this and we take over that, but you guys take over whole *countries!* I was also approached by a counterfeiter who wanted to make a deal with me. He said, I keep getting busted because I can't get the right paper. I bet the Russians can get me some good paper! That's the nearest thing I came to political questions among the inmates.

I came back to New York after I was released from Danbury, and finished my doctorate at Michigan in 1962. All I had left was my orals. Although my field was really psychology, I heard about this job in educational sociology at New York University. But they needed somebody in a hurry who could do quantitative research on this project that another professor had started and then left, so I applied for the job and I was interviewed by deans and department chairmen. The department chairman told me later, You had all these wonderful recommendations, but the dean didn't even look at them! He just said, Gee, this guy had a rough time. You ought to help him out! That dean died in a year or so, and he was replaced by somebody who viewed my criminal past with a great deal of opprobrium. There are still rumors, Is this guy a former Red; is he still a Red?

Would I do it over again? Yes, but I'd be better at it! Maybe I would do it myself this time. I really think that the American people didn't learn much of anything from the whole McCarthy era. They're still looking for Reds under the bed, and equating dissent with disloyalty. For myself, the experience was one that caused some damage and some enhancement to my life. I lost a lot of friends, and it cost me money and jobs. But I stood up at a time when many people kept quiet, or became informers, or left the country. I am *still* an American. I'm glad I took my stand, I don't regret it.

5

Daisy Bates
v. Little Rock

Daisy Bates headed the Arkansas NAACP during the 1957 showdown over Little Rock school integration, and stood firm against official demands for NAACP membership lists. *Courtesy of the* Arkansas Gazette, *© 1988*

I.
"Let's Pop 'Em!"

The city council of Little Rock, Arkansas, met in special session on October 31, 1957. On this Halloween evening, crowds of young pranksters swarmed along Main Street, squirting troops from the U.S. Army's elite 101st Airborne Division with shaving lather. The soldiers had patroled the streets of Little Rock for the past month, assigned by President Dwight D. Eisenhower to protect black students at Central High School from mob violence. Inside the City Hall chamber, the councilors had a trick in store for Daisy Bates, the young, outspoken president of the National Association for the Advancement of Colored People in Arkansas. The city's retaliation for her role in shepherding nine black teenagers through the howling mobs outside Central High was an arrest order, voted by the council without dissent.

The city ordinance that Daisy Bates refused to obey had been drafted by Bruce Bennett, the state's attorney general. An ambitious, forty-year-old lawyer from the segregationist stronghold of El Dorado in southern Arkansas, Bennett had taken office in January 1957 and moved quickly to forge legal shackles for the state NAACP. The Bennett Ordinance, as everyone called the Little Rock law, required "certain organizations" to file statements with the city clerk which included the names of all dues-paying members. These statements would be open for "the inspection of any interested party" as public records, available for copying and publication. Failure to comply would subject violators to criminal prosecution and fines. Although city officials would choose the covered groups, Bennett had boasted that the NAACP was his primary target and blamed the civil-rights group for the "turmoil and conflict between the races" in Arkansas. "When the public knows who the local officers of the NAACP are," he suggested, "I think it will materially reduce their activities."

The Little Rock ordinance was not the first legal weapon Bennett had aimed against the Arkansas NAACP. Earlier in 1957, the attorney general persuaded the state legislature to subject the NAACP to stringent registration and taxation regulations. Bennett modeled his statute on an Alabama law which had been dusted off in 1956 to punish the NAACP for backing the successful Birmingham bus boycott. Refusal to turn over membership lists resulted in a $100,000 fine and a judicial ban on NAACP activities which crippled the group's civil-rights campaign while it pursued costly and time-consuming appeals in federal courts.

Emboldened by the Alabama example, Bennett sued the Arkansas NAACP in state court for violating the registration law, after Daisy Bates had declined in August 1957 to submit the names of financial donors. Unlike Alabama's, the Arkansas case came before a "moderate" state judge who declined to issue the compliance orders that Bennett had requested. Meanwhile, NAACP lawyers asked a federal judge to intervene and strike down the state laws. After the state judge deferred to his federal colleague, Bennett lowered his sights to the municipal courts, assuming that local judges would share his desire to run the NAACP out of Arkansas. The attorney general had no trouble in convincing the city councils of Little Rock and its sister city, North Little Rock, to enact local versions of the state law on October 14, 1957.

The Little Rock city councilors invited Bennett to address their Halloween session before voting on the motion to arrest Daisy Bates and Rev. J.C. Crenchaw, president of the local NAACP chapter. "One of the troubles with the South," Bennett complained, "is that we have been letting the Negroes run to federal courts while we don't use the state courts to attack them." Describing the city ordinance as a defense against "NAACP–sponsored integration," the attorney general said the civil-rights group was "scared of losing its followers" if membership lists became public records. "Daisy Bates admits this in the NAACP suit in federal court," Bennett added. Alderman Bill Hood could not restrain his eagerness to arrest the defiant NAACP leaders. "Let's pop 'em!" Hood demanded.

The night the Little Rock council voted to "pop" the NAACP, Daisy Bates was speaking to the Cosmopolitan Club in New York City. Praising the courage of the black students at Central High, she described the daily gauntlet of insults and punches they endured in the school's corridors. During her speech Daisy told the audience that her husband, L.C. Bates, had called from Little Rock to tell her of the arrest order. (L.C. and Daisy had since 1941 published the state's leading black newspaper, *The State Press*.) Thurgood Marshall, the NAACP's legal director, assured reporters that Daisy would return home to contest the charges. "She is not the kind to run away from a fight," he added. Roy Wilkins, the group's executive secretary, told the press that the NAACP was determined to protect its members from "violence directed against them, their homes or their business establishments."

On Monday, November 4, accompanied by Rev. Crenchaw, Daisy Bates surrendered at the Little Rock police station. After the two civil-rights leaders were fingerprinted and photographed, they were released to await trial. Across the Arkansas River, Birdie Williams, president of the North Little Rock NAACP chapter, also submitted to arrest for refusing to comply with that city's Bennett Ordinance.

Behind the arrests of Daisy Bates and other NAACP officials stretched two centuries of slavery, another century of Jim Crow segregation, and three years of Southern resistance to judicial demands that public schools admit students without regard to race. The unanimous Supreme Court decision that school segregation violated the Constitution's "equal protection" guarantee, announced in *Brown* v. *Board of Education* on May 17, 1954, provoked outrage from Dixie defenders of American apartheid. But the Court's invitation to Southern states for further argument on implementation of the opinion deferred the battle over "race mixing" until the second *Brown* decision was issued on May 31, 1955. Ordering that school integration proceed "with all deliberate speed," the Court passed the buck to federal district judges, who were asked to assess the "good faith" efforts of local school boards to comply with this vague mandate.

The Supreme Court's refusal to set deadlines for desegregation invited Southern officials to invent foot-dragging tactics, and frustrated the NAACP lawyers who had struggled for years with cautious and often hostile federal judges, most of them closely tied to local power structures. The Court's faint-hearted approach was matched by the other branches of the federal government. Congress stayed away from involvement, although the Fourteenth Amendment—the basis of the *Brown* decision—authorized legislative enforcement of the "equal protection" guarantee. President Eisenhower refused to defend the Supreme Court's decision. "I think it makes no difference whether or not I endorse it," he said in 1956.

These evasions of responsibility had predictable results. Southern federal judges backed away from enforcing the *Brown* decision. "The Constitution," one judicial panel wrote, "does not require integration. It merely forbids discrimination." What this meant was that "no violation of the Constitution is involved even though the children of different races voluntarily attend different schools, as they attend different churches." The distinction between public and private institutions escaped these judges. The Dixie delegations in Congress invited defiance in the so-called Southern Manifesto, issued in March 1956 and signed by all but three members from the former Confederacy. Denouncing the *Brown* decision as "a clear abuse of judicial power," the lawmakers pledged "to use all lawful means to bring about a reversal" of the Supreme Court's ruling. And President Eisenhower failed to act in 1956 when Alabama officials defied federal court orders to admit a black student, Autherine Lucy, to the state university.

Outright defiance in Deep South states, and White House silence, encouraged die-hard segregationists in border states such as Tennessee and Arkansas to move against "moderates" who had agreed to token school integration. Arkansas in particular had taken a few small steps toward compliance with the *Brown* decision. The rural town of Hoxie, with just a handful of black students, ended its separate school system in June 1955. Governor Orval Faubus, elected as a racial "moderate" in 1954, added black members to state boards and Democratic party committees. Even before the Supreme Court issued its second *Brown* opinion, the Little Rock school board adopted the so-called Blossom Plan, named after school superintendent Virgil Blossom. What the plan called "phased" integration would begin with the admission of black students to prestigious Central High School in September

1957, with integration of other high schools, then junior highs, and finally elementary schools to proceed over a ten-year period.

The glacial pace of the Blossom Plan failed to satisfy the Arkansas NAACP. Led by Daisy Bates, elected to head the state organization in 1953 at the age of thirty, the Little Rock branch filed suit in federal court against the school board in February 1956. Six months later, Judge John E. Miller endorsed the Blossom Plan as a "good faith" effort to "ultimately bring about a school system not based on color distinctions." Although the NAACP appealed this decision, the federal appellate court in St. Louis upheld Judge Miller in April 1957, clearing a path for the first step of the Blossom Plan, the admission of nine black students to Central High on September 3, 1957.

During most of August, Daisy Bates helped to prepare the nine teenagers for the ordeal that awaited them. Her living room became a classroom, with lessons in learning to shrug off racial insults and stay out of fights. The night before the students were set to begin school, Daisy Bates answered her doorbell and faced a local reporter who said, "Mrs. Bates, do you know that national guardsmen are surrounding Central High?" Later that night, Governor Orval Faubus spoke to the state on television and explained that he had posted troops around the school in response to reports of heavy sales by Little Rock gun stores in recent weeks. Shedding his "moderate" mask, Faubus warned that "blood will run in the streets" if the black students tried to enter Central High.

Armed troops kept Central High closed the next day, while the school board's lawyers asked federal judge Ronald Davies— on temporary assignment to Little Rock from his North Dakota court—to rescind the integration order that Judge Miller had earlier issued. Judge Davies rejected the board's motion. The next morning, fifteen-year-old Elizabeth Eckford, dressed in bobby-sox gear and clutching a green school notebook, tried to enter Central High and was turned away by soldiers with bayonets. A menacing crowd surrounded Elizabeth and began yelling, "Get her! Lynch her!" "Get a rope and drag her over to this tree," someone hollered. Protected by Grace Lorch, a white NAACP member, Elizabeth finally escaped the mob on a city bus.

Americans across the country witnessed on television Elizabeth Eckford's dignity in the face of lynch-mob hysteria. Pressure mounted on President Eisenhower to put down the Arkansas insurrection. On Friday, September 20, Judge Davies enjoined Governor Faubus from using the guardsmen to keep black students from Central High. The following Monday, Little Rock police broke before a howling mob and the nine black students barely escaped from Central High. Faced with the prospect of televised lynchings, Eisenhower interrupted a golfing vacation and finally acted on Tuesday morning. His considerable patience with Faubus at last exhausted, the President ordered army paratroopers to escort Elizabeth Eckford and the other black students into Central High. Although the federal troops ended mob violence in the streets, a smaller mob of racist students roamed the Central High corridors and subjected the black students to verbal and physical assaults which school officials tolerated until the school year ended.

Daisy Bates became a national symbol of resistance to Orval Faubus; her picture appeared in *Life* magazine and the *New York Times* ran a sympathetic profile of the "Fighter for Integration." Her demand that President Eisenhower assure the safety of the black students at Central High gained national headlines. The price she paid in Little Rock for this publicity was fear and threats. "For the past three weeks she has been vilified, abused, threatened and intimidated," the *Times* reported after Eisenhower finally met her demand.

The price exacted from Daisy Bates by Little Rock's city council was arrest and trial for challenging the Bennett Ordinance. Judge Harry C. Robinson presided at the municipal court trial on December 3, 1957. Two weeks earlier, Judge Robinson had dismissed charges against thirteen white persons arrested for taking part in riots outside Central High. The judge denied the motion of NAACP lawyers to dismiss charges against Daisy Bates, although he dropped charges against Rev. Crenchaw when the city's lawyer could not produce any request that Crenchaw submit NAACP records. Judge Robinson did not want to hear constitutional objections to the Bennett Ordinance from the NAACP lawyer, Robert L. Carter. "I am going to hold that the ordinance is valid," Robinson said, finding Daisy Bates guilty and imposing a $100 fine.

Court rules allowed new trials in cases decided by municipal court judges, and Daisy Bates appeared before Judge William J.

Kirby of the Pulaski County Circuit Court on February 11, 1958. In the two months between the two trials, Robert Carter had appeared before the U.S. Supreme Court to defend the Alabama NAACP against the contempt citation and fines imposed for defying that state's demand for membership records. Described by one associate as "a partisan, a doer, a man deeply concerned with results," Carter was then forty and served as Thurgood Marshall's key assistant on the NAACP legal staff, which he joined in 1944.

Carter appeared before Judge Kirby with NAACP lawyer George Howard of Pine Bluff, Arkansas. Howard first argued that the charge should be dismissed because the Bennett Ordinance violated the First Amendment rights of free speech and assembly. Judge Kirby denied that "the ordinance is going to affect the right of freedom of speech or assembly either one." In his opinion, "the NAACP is a little too apprehensive about what will happen" if its membership list became public.

George Howard called Daisy Bates to the witness stand and asked if the NAACP had lost members in Little Rock after passage of the city ordinance. "Well, I will say it like this:" she replied. "For the past five years I have been collecting, I guess, 150 to 200 members each year—just renewals of the same people. This year, I guess I lost 100 or 150 of these same members because when I went back for renewals they said, 'Well, we will wait and see what happens with the Bennett Ordinance.'" She added that "professional people are afraid if their names are published they will be subjected to harrassment the same as I." Judge Kirby sustained the city lawyer's objection to this answer. The witness "has got no right to testify why she thinks they refused to join," he ruled.

Robert Carter took over and called a surprise witness, city councilor Lee H. Evans. Over the city's objection, Judge Kirby allowed the examination. "Up to now, you haven't violated the rules of evidence too bad," he told Carter. Why had the council enacted the ordinance, Carter inquired. Evans answered that the measure was designed to raise revenue. "We all knew that the city's finances were pretty low," he explained. Carter then called another councilor, Franklin Loy, who testified with a straight face that the city needed the names of NAACP members to determine if any were "guilty of a felony or possibly gambling or liquor violations." Loy did not believe that NAACP members would object to exposure of their names "if they had nothing to hide." Carter's obvious purpose in calling these witnesses was to build a record for appeal, because Judge Kirby—like the White Queen in *Alice in Wonderland*—had already convicted and fined Daisy Bates before he heard this testimony.

The Arkansas Supreme Court decided the appeal from this conviction in December 1958, along with a similar appeal from Birdie Williams of North Little Rock. The court's opinion, upholding both convictions, displayed a stubborn refusal to follow the U.S. Supreme Court's recent ruling in the Alabama case that Robert Carter had argued for the NAACP. The High Court had ruled without dissent in June 1958 that the First Amendment protected "freedom of association" from government intrusion and that past exposure of NAACP records had subjected members to "economic reprisal, loss of employment, threat of physical coercion, and other manifestations of public hostility." Noting that Robert Carter "laid great stress" on this precedent in his oral argument for Daisy Bates, the Arkansas judges ruled that the decision gave the NAACP "no protection in this case." Alabama had tried to "force the NAACP out of the state," wrote Judge Edward McFaddin, while Little Rock had enacted a "revenue measure" and sought only "to see if legal taxation is being evaded." Complaining that the NAACP wanted "immunity as though it were a favored child," McFaddin ignored the fact that Daisy Bates had submitted all the requested records except the membership list.

Almost a year elapsed between the ruling of the Arkansas judges and arguments before the U.S. Supreme Court in November 1959. This was a year of tumult and violence in Little Rock. Defying the direct order of the Supreme Court that he cease his "war against the Constitution," Governor Faubus closed the public schools for an entire year and robbed thousands of students, black and white, of education. Daisy Bates and her family survived the dynamite bombing of their home in July 1959, but *The State Press* died that year from an advertising boycott.

Oral argument before the Supreme Court lacked the drama

of recent battles between the NAACP and its Southern foes. Robert L. Carter, who would join the New York federal district bench in 1972, repeated the argument of his challenge to Alabama officials and stressed the Court's ruling in that case as precedent. Joseph C. Kemp represented Little Rock and conceded under tough questioning that he could not cite "any activity" of the NAACP that would require payment of the demanded license tax. The city of North Little Rock failed to send a lawyer or even file a brief to defend the conviction of Birdie Williams.

Not one justice defended Little Rock in the private conference that followed the argument. Chief Justice Earl Warren briskly disposed of the case, stating that the Bennett Ordinance "presents four questions: (1) Does this encroach on liberties? Yes; (2) Is it a legitimate ordinance? It is; (3) Is it enough to allow the encroachment? Sometimes; (4) But is it necessary here? I can't believe it was. I don't think the names are essential to accomplishing the purpose of the ordinance." Warren assigned Justice Potter Stewart to prepare the Court's unanimous opinion, handed down on February 23, 1960, three weeks after black college students began their sit-in challenge to segregation at the Woolworth's lunch counter in Greensboro, North Carolina.

Justice Stewart relied heavily on *NAACP* v. *Alabama,* which he cited six times in his brief opinion, for holding that forced disclosure of NAACP membership lists violated the Due Process clause of the Fourteenth Amendment and its protection of "freedom of association." The trials of Daisy Bates and Birdie Williams showed that disclosure of names "had been followed by harassment and threats of bodily harm." NAACP members "are protected not only against heavy-handed frontal attack" like Alabama's effort to ban the group, "but also from being stifled by more subtle governmental interference."

One irony of Stewart's opinion, written for a unanimous Court, was that it protected the names of black citizens from governmental inquiry, whereas, the year before, Stewart had joined a bare majority of a bitterly divided Court in rejecting Lloyd Barenblatt's refusal to disclose the names of Communist associates to an inquisitional committee. Daisy Bates may have gained more public sympathy than Lloyd Barenblatt for her courageous defense of civil rights, but the First Amendment was surely broad enough to cover both activists. That irony was noted by Justices Hugo Black and William

O. Douglas in their brief concurrence with Stewart's opinion, which stressed the First Amendment rights of speech and assembly and their protection against "harassment, humiliation, or exposure by government." Reds as well as blacks, the two justices suggested, were equally part of the spectrum of politics and color that the First Amendment spanned.

Thirty years after Orval Faubus declared war on the Constitution and Bruce Bennett declared war on Daisy Bates, the nine black teenagers who entered Central High in 1957 returned for an emotional reunion. Ernest Green, the first to graduate and now an investment banker in Washington, D.C., praised "the sacrifice of Mrs. Daisy Bates" in facing bayonets and bombs, in his baccalaureate address to Central High graduates of 1987. The symbolic reward for that sacrifice was that Daisy Bates could publish Green's speech in *The State Press*, which returned in 1983 as the conscience of Little Rock.

II.
"Stone This Time, Dynamite Next!"

I was born Daisy Lee Gatson in 1922, in the southern part of Arkansas, in the little sawmill town of Huttig. This is in Union County, near the Louisiana line. I always refer to Huttig as a sawmill plantation, where the pine trees were tall, not beautiful. My father worked in the sawmill, and they paid him in coupons, little slips of paper. So we would have to buy everything at the company store. He was a strong man, who had the most difficult and highest-paying job for a Negro at the sawmill.

The streets in Huttig were red clay, very muddy after it rained. There was very real segregation between white and black in Huttig, indeed there was. The grocery store and the post office on Main Street divided the white section of town from 'Nigra Town.' I was an only child, and I was always very inquisitive, observing everything and everybody around me. As I grew up in Huttig, I learned that the difference between the races was symbolized by the color of the buildings. Everything in the Negro community was painted a dull, drab red and everything in the white community was white.

I remember going to the store one time when I was about seven. My mother gave me a dollar one afternoon and told me to get a pound of center-cut pork chops from the butcher. There were several older white people at the meat counter when I arrived. After the butcher finished with them, I gave him my order. Before

117

he got me the pork chops, some more white adults came in and he filled their orders first. Since they were adults, I didn't mind waiting, although I was a little annoyed because I wanted to get home and help my mother with dinner.

A little white girl, about my age, came in and we chatted while the butcher was serving the adults. When he finished with them, he looked down from behind the counter and said, What can I get you, little girl? I thought he was talking to me and I told him again that I wanted a pound of pork chops. Then he snarled at me, I'm not talking to *you!* He asked the little white girl what she wanted and filled her order. When she left, the butcher grabbed my dollar, threw a pound of chops that were all fat onto some butcher paper, and he said, Niggers have to wait until I serve all the white people! Now get *out* of here!

I was so scared and ashamed that I ran all the way home crying. When I showed my mother the chops, I said, We should go back and make him give us some good meat. She just told me to stop crying. When my father came home, I told him what had happened and said we should go back to the market. He wouldn't talk to me then, but I asked him at bedtime why he wouldn't go see the butcher. He wouldn't talk at first, but my questions finally broke down his silence. He tried to explain that Negroes didn't have any rights that white people had to respect. I can't do anything about it, he said. If I went to the market, it would just cause trouble for the family. I'm not afraid for myself, but I *am* afraid for you and your mother. We never talked about it after that.

When I was about eight years old, I learned from a neighbor boy that my real mother had been murdered by a white man when I was just a baby. My father had been so hurt by this that he left me with his best friends, who were my Mother and Daddy, and he left town and never came back. It took me a long time to get over the hatred toward white people that I developed from that terrible knowledge. One time, I even slapped the face of a little white girl who had been my friend for a long time. She came up at the commissary on Main Street and offered me one of her two pennies to buy candy, and I just exploded with hurt and hostility.

When I was a teenager, still just a young girl, my Daddy died. The last time I saw him, in the hospital on the day he died, he told me a story that helped to sustain me in my life and to overcome my hatred for white people. The day of my Mother's funeral, he went to the post office to pick up his mail and he was blocked at the door by three white boys. There was a bucket of red paint by the door; the building foundations were being painted. Two of the boys blocked my father at the door and the third one picked up a paintbrush and painted a wide stripe down the back of his coat.

Daddy told me this story and said he knew that it was impossible to protest what they did to him. He wanted to wring their necks but he knew he would be lynched if he even touched them. And he told me, Hate can destroy you, Daisy. You should hate the humiliation, hate the insults, hate the discrimination. But try to do something, try to join with other blacks to change all this. Make your hate count for something, Daisy. And after that I discovered that I could be friendly with white people, and work with them to end discrimination.

I left Huttig and moved to Little Rock when I was married in 1941 to L.C. Bates. We met when I was fifteen and L.C. came to our house to sell insurance to my father. L.C. was in his thirties at the time, but he always treated me as an equal, despite the difference in our ages. He visited us frequently in the next three years, and he would bring me a little present and often he would take my family to the movies. I was attracted to him, but I was also attracted to his car. He was very soft-spoken, tall and thin, and a very gentle man, but very firm in what he believed. L.C. was born in Mississippi, his father was a minister, and his full name was Lucius Christopher, but everyone just called him L.C.

L.C. had been a journalist during the '30s, before he went into insurance sales. He had studied journalism at Wilberforce College in Ohio, and he worked in Colorado and several other states as a reporter. But black newspapers could barely survive the Depression, and L.C. lost his job. We moved to Little Rock right after we were married. Even though L.C. was successful in the insurance business, he was very eager to get back into journalism.

When L.C. told me he wanted to start a newspaper, I thought he was crazy! If I own the paper, he said, I can't lose my job. We didn't have much money, but my father had left me some and we decided to buy a church paper called *The Twin City Press*. They had a printing plant, which we needed to start a paper. We named our paper *The Arkansas State Press* and we published our first issue on May 9, 1941. My husband drew the masthead for the paper; it's the same one we have on this week's issue, right here. He drew a bull's head with these wide horns, and I looked at it and said, What does *this* mean? He stared at me, like the bull, and he said, That's *me!*

When I moved to Little Rock, there were 'good' relations between blacks and whites. But that meant that you stay in your place, that you know what the limits are for Daisy Bates. You couldn't stand up for your rights, because the police wouldn't protect you. I remember an incident during one of my trials. I went into the restroom in the courthouse, and there was a big sign by the door that said, White Women Only! I was mad, but I wasn't going to go to the basement and use the colored restroom. There was a lady in there who looked at me hard and then she said, Girl! You're in the wrong place! I was so angry, I could have pushed her head down in that toilet. But I just combed my hair and powdered my face, and then I turned around and smiled and walked out. But I hated that kind of treatment.

It was hard to keep the newspaper going during the war, although we built our circulation up to more than 10,000. Our major crusade was against police brutality toward blacks, which was rampant in Little Rock. The war brought thousands of soldiers to Camp Robinson, and they flocked into the city on weekend passes. Black soldiers became targets for the police, and things exploded in March 1942, when a city policeman shot and killed a popular black sergeant whose name was Thomas Foster. I wrote a story that accused the police of a 'bestial murder' and the Negro community was outraged.

Nothing was done about the murder of Sergeant Foster, but our stories cost the paper all the display advertising from the downtown stores. That crusade against police brutality almost closed the paper down, but we survived with advertising from smaller, independent merchants, and our circulation actually rose to 20,000. And police brutality began to decline, and eventually the city assigned Negro policemen to the Negro section of the city.

The first time I was arrested resulted from a story I wrote in *The State Press* in 1946. My husband was a hard worker, and he decided that he needed a vacation. He said, Daisy, I'm tired; you can put the paper out for a while. Well, I was looking forward to this chance to do the paper myself. At this time, the workers in the Southern Cotton Oil Mill went out on strike. They were black workers and belonged to the CIO. They were picketing the plant in shifts of four, and one of the scabs killed one of the strikers on the picket line. The scab was acquitted of murder, but the three other pickets were convicted of violating the state 'right-to-work' law and sentenced to a year's imprisonment. The law had a clause that said if there is *any* violence on a picket line, *any* striker who is present is guilty.

L.C. was gone when this happened, and I wrote a story that accused the judge of trying the case to a 'hand-picked' jury that was all white, and telling them they *had* to convict the strikers. When my husband returned from his vacation, before we printed the story, he cautioned me that the judge was a powerful man in the state. That may be, I said, but the real intent of this law is to destroy organized labor in Arkansas.

We published this story in *The State Press,* and a few days later two sheriff's deputies knocked on the door to our house, with warrants to arrest me and my husband for contempt of court. We were taken to the jail, booked, fingerprinted, and they took mug shots with jail numbers. After we posted bond, we had trouble finding any lawyers who would represent us. Finally, two of the CIO lawyers who worked with the strikers took our case. Our hearing was before the judge we had criticized. He told us that he didn't like the implication that the strikers had been railroaded to the penitentiary, and he sentenced me and L.C. to ten days in prison.

We only spent seven hours in jail before our lawyers got one of the state supreme court judges to order our release on appeal. The supreme court finally dismissed the case, and their opinion said that the expression of opinion, even about judges, didn't threaten the administration of justice. But the judge and his political friends really wanted to put our paper out of business.

My husband and I had been members of the NAACP since the time we moved to Little Rock. It wasn't a very large organization, just a couple of hundred members, and it didn't get involved in demonstrations or anything very public. *The State Press* had always supported the NAACP and its positions, although L.C. and I sometimes thought they weren't aggressive enough in fighting against police brutality and the intimidation of Negroes who tried to vote and use public facilities. But I believed in the NAACP and its role as a national voice for Negroes, and when I was asked in 1952 to become the president of the Arkansas state conference of NAACP chapters, I agreed to serve. I was only thirty years old at this time, but Rev. Marcus Taylor, a very wise man who headed the branch in Little Rock, told me the NAACP needed younger leadership for the struggles ahead.

The real struggle in the South was to end segregation in the schools. The schools I had attended in Huttig got their textbooks from the white schools, after they were all tattered and worn out, and I knew how important an equal education was for Negroes, to get jobs and take part in politics. And the legal campaign against school segregation became the main focus of the NAACP at the time I became the state president. When the Supreme Court ruled in 1954 that school segregation was unconstitutional, we were initially somewhat optimistic in Arkansas that the state and the local schools boards would comply with the law of the land. A couple of smaller towns, Fayetteville and Charleston, announced that they were going to admit Negro students to the public schools.

At first, the school board in Little Rock said that it really wanted to integrate the schools. The superintendent was a man named Virgil Blossom, and he wanted to run for governor. And he started going back and forth. After the Supreme Court ruling came down, Blossom spent the next two years talking about integration plans that were vague and didn't have any deadlines. Nothing really happened, and when a group of Negro parents asked the NAACP to give them some legal assistance in pushing for a realistic plan for integration, I helped them file a suit in the federal court in Little Rock that asked that all grades be integrated, starting immediately.

That suit didn't achieve what we wanted. We had to wait more than a year for a decision, until just a few weeks before schools would open in the fall of 1957. When the federal judge finally ruled, he said that the Little Rock school board had acted in good faith when it adopted an integration plan that started with the high schools and would end with the elementary schools after several years.

By the time the judge ruled on our suit, I didn't expect that integration would begin at Central High School without some kind of opposition. I had gone around to visit the homes of Negro parents who had children in high school, to ask if they would request that their children be assigned to Central. And I found nine parents who agreed. We spent a lot of time in my home, preparing these children for what might happen in school, like being spit on and shoved and called names. They were all very brave children, but they were also typical teenagers. Some of them were noisy and outgoing, and some were quiet and shy. But they were all determined to go to Central and endure anything that happened to them. They told me, Mrs. Bates, we are *going* to that school and we want you to help us!

I really didn't expect that anything would happen to me for getting involved in the integration battle. One night, about two weeks before the schools were going to open, I was watching the eleven o'clock news on television, and I heard that the governor of Georgia had come to Little Rock and had praised the 'patriots' who were fighting for states' rights and opposing school integration. I took my dog, Skippy, out for a walk after the news and when I got back I was sitting on the divan, looking at the newspaper. Suddenly, there was this loud crash and something came right through the living room window. My husband came rushing into the room and he found me on the floor, covered with broken glass. After he found out that I wasn't hurt, we picked up the large rock that had come through the window and read the note that was tied to it. It said, Stone This Time, Dynamite Next! That was really the first time I realized that we were at war in Little Rock. At that time, I think I hated everything this country stood for. I didn't think I *had* a country!

The schools in Little Rock were scheduled to open on September 3, 1957, the day after Labor Day. About seven o'clock on Labor Day, a newspaper reporter came by our house and told me and L.C. that Central High was surrounded by National Guard troops. We were astounded by this news, and we drove down to the school to see what was happening. There were hundreds of troops getting out of army trucks, lining up in front of the school. They were in full uniform, with helmets, rifles, and bayonets. Someone told us that Governor Faubus was going to speak on television that evening, and we went home to watch the broadcast. I was horrified by his speech. Faubus said that he had called out the National Guard because of reports that white supremacists were headed toward Little Rock in caravans of cars. Then he said that 'blood will run in the streets' if the Negro students tried to enter Central High the next day.

I spent most of that night on the telephone, calling parents of the nine children and telling them to be at my house the next morning. The children were going to walk to Central with ministers in front of them and behind. But when they were supposed to start, one of them—Elizabeth Eckford—wasn't there. We were in a panic, and then we heard over a car radio that a Negro girl was being mobbed at Central. L.C. drove off to find her, and we were all relieved when he returned with news that she had escaped from the mob on a city bus.

Elizabeth had walked alone through that screaming mob up to the bayonets of the National Guard troops, with people yelling that she should be lynched, just a little girl of fifteen. The TV and news pictures of Elizabeth walking bravely through that mob went around the world and made her into a national heroine. But she was terribly hurt by that experience. She stayed at my house for a few nights after that, and she woke up screaming in the middle of the night, just shaking with terror.

The National Guard kept the school closed for a couple of weeks, and the federal government wouldn't intervene. I went to see the United States attorney, Mr. Cobb, and all he said was, Go see the FBI and give them a report. Well, the FBI knew who all the mob leaders were, but they never did anything to prevent them from terrorizing the children.

After Faubus withdrew the National Guard troops, the children went to Central High on September 23. But the mob was so big, and so bent on murder, that the city police couldn't stop them from storming the school, and they took the children out after a couple of hours. Two days later, President Eisenhower put the National Guard under federal control and the children returned to school. They stayed in school the rest of that year, but they were continually harassed by a small group of white children.

The mob's hatred was particularly directed at me and my husband. There were three KKK crosses burned on our lawn, and shots were fired into the house from cars that drove by. L.C. would stay up at night with a .45 automatic pistol, sometimes until dawn. We put floodlights around the house, and some of our friends organized a volunteer guard patrol.

The school crisis went on for another two years in Little Rock. Governor Faubus put bills through the state legislature that closed the schools in 1958, and it wasn't until the Supreme Court finally ruled that was unconstitutional that the schools opened and the mob violence stopped. During that whole time, L.C. and I were being attacked, physically and otherwise. Just before the schools were set to reopen in July 1959, somebody threw a dynamite bomb from a car onto our lawn. The bomb didn't hit the house, but it blew a hole in the lawn and really rocked the whole neighborhood. I sent a telegram to the Attorney General in Washington, telling him what happened and that nobody had ever been arrested for any of the attacks on us. But he just answered that there was no federal jurisdiction over the bombing and he said I should go to the local police. Of course *that* wasn't going to protect us!

The way my Supreme Court case got started goes back to the attacks on me in 1957 as president of the state NAACP conference. The state attorney general then was Bruce Bennett, and he had been behind a law the state legislature had passed to force the NAACP to disclose its membership lists and contributors. The first thing he did was to file suits against me and Rev. J.C. Crenchaw under the state law. But we got that suit blocked in court; that was in September 1957. What Bennett wanted to do was tie us up in court, so he tried another tactic. He got the Little Rock city council to pass another bill that required the NAACP to turn over its membership and financial records to the city. Of course, once they were turned over, the newspapers could copy them and print the lists. That was the whole purpose of these laws.

As soon as the city council passed the bill, they sent me a letter, demanding that I turn over all the NAACP records to the city clerk. They set a deadline, I think, of two weeks for me to comply. I sent them a letter and told them that they could have the financial information, but I wasn't going to turn over the membership records. When the deadline expired, I was in New York for a meeting with NAACP lawyers about the situation in Little Rock. I remember I was at a reception that was hosted by Governor Harriman when someone told me that the Little Rock city council had ordered the police to arrest me and Rev. Crenchaw. Thurgood Marshall was at this reception and he said, Daisy, they can arrest you but they can't destroy the NAACP!

When I got back to Little Rock, Rev. Crenchaw and I went down to the police station and turned ourselves in. Then we were booked and released on bail. We had two trials in the case, first in the municipal court and then in the district court. At the first trial, the city attorney couldn't prove that Rev. Crenchaw was ever sent a letter to turn over the Little Rock branch records, so his case was dismissed. The judge said he knew I was the head of *something* in the NAACP, so he would hold me responsible for the records. He said, This ordinance is valid and Mrs. Bates has refused to comply. So he found me guilty and fined me $100. Birdie Williams was the president of the North Little Rock branch, and she was also convicted in another trial.

My second trial in the district court came out the same way, although the judge reduced the fine to $25. I testified and told the judge that many of the NAACP members in Little Rock, maybe half of them, would not renew their membership because they were afraid of exposure under the Bennett Ordinance and harassment. The city attorney asked me whether I had been in New York recently. My attorney was Robert Carter, who was from the NAACP legal office in New York, and he objected to this question. What the city attorney was trying to do, obviously, was to link me with 'outside agitators' and suggest that we took all our orders in Little Rock from New York.

Both of the cases, Birdie Williams' and mine, were appealed to the state supreme court, where we lost, and then to the U.S. Supreme Court. By the time the cases were decided in our favor, L.C. and I had lost *The State Press* in 1959. Over the past two years, ever since the school crisis started, we had been losing some of our biggest advertisers—the power company, the gas company, the telephone company. And many of the smaller advertisers pulled out from the paper when they were threatened with bombings. L.C. and I had received hundreds of letters of support for the paper, and people had contributed money, but we just couldn't pay the bills and the staff. It was a painful, heart-rending decision, but there just wasn't any alternative.

After we closed *The State Press*, L.C. became a field representative for the NAACP in 1960. He started right after the sit-in movement began in the South, and he traveled all around Arkansas, and other parts of the South, during the most dangerous times for civil-rights workers. There were times when he had to call in to the office every two hours, just to let them know he was still alive!

L.C. retired in 1971 from the NAACP, and he passed away in 1980. I spent most of my time, after we closed the paper, on projects to help black communities in Arkansas—self-help projects. During the 1960s, I worked for the Office of Economic Opportunity, the 'War on Poverty,' to help some of these communities develop industries and jobs and housing. One of these was the town of Mitchellville, which is in the southeastern part of Arkansas. That was my project, helping the people in Mitchellville, and I still go down and visit the people there, who have done wonderful things to build up their town.

Even though I was very active in all kinds of activities to build up and strengthen the black communities in Arkansas, I never gave up hope that one day *The State Press* could reopen. And in 1983 we finally raised the money and organized the support to start the paper up again. You can see the picture of L.C. on the office wall over there; this paper is really a tribute to him and his dedication. This paper still has the bull he drew on its masthead. He *was* a bull, and he never stopped fighting against racism and discrimination. I love putting out the paper.

Arkansas is still a racist state, and Little Rock is still a racist city. I know that we have made some progress; the city even has a black woman as the mayor. But whites still have the upper hand—they control the jobs and the government. And black people still don't have all the protections of the Constitution. We were considered *property* and not human beings when the Constitution was adopted. The courts can't change how white people think about blacks. They have to change themselves. I'm still not sure they *can* change.

6

Robert Mack Bell
v. Maryland

Robert Mack Bell was a high-school class president in Baltimore when he was arrested during the 1960 "sit-in" movement to protest lunch-counter segregation. *Courtesy of Morgan State University*

I.
"I'm at the Mercy of My Customers"

At 4:15 on the afternoon of Friday, June 17, 1960, a group of neatly dressed black students entered the lobby of Hooper's restaurant in downtown Baltimore, Maryland. Located one block from the city courthouse, Hooper's had a large dining room and a lounge that was popular with lawyers and judges. Rather, it was popular with *white* lawyers and judges, because Hooper's, along with 90 percent of Baltimore restaurants at the time, refused to serve black patrons. A century after the Civil War, Baltimore remained Southern in atmosphere and attitude, with Jim Crow schools, colleges, hospitals, and restaurants.

The black youngsters who entered Hooper's lobby, about eighteen in number, were met by the hostess on duty, Ella Mae Dunlop. Apprehensive but still polite, she asked the first person who approached her, "May I help you?" The answer was also polite: "Yes, I'd like to be seated." The hostess was prepared for this request. "I'm sorry, but we haven't integrated yet." This exchange turned from civility to confrontation as the youngster replied, "Well, aren't you ashamed of yourselves!" Ella Mae Dunlop was unfazed by this retort: "Well, no, I'm not. That's Mr. Hooper's orders. It's the preference of the customers." She obviously did not mean the prospective customers who crowded into the lobby. "Well, you mean you're not going to seat us?" one student asked. "That's right," she answered.

Attracted by the commotion, the restaurant manager, Albert Warfel, hastened to the lobby and confronted John R. Quarles, who stood out from the group as older and more assertive. Quarles was twenty-eight years old, a student at all-black Morgan State College and a leader in the Civic Action Group, which spearheaded the "sit-in" movement against segregation in Baltimore. "We have not integrated the restaurant," Warfel informed Quarles, blocking his path to the dining area. His words had no effect, as the students pushed past Warfel and spread out through the restaurant, each one occupying a separate table. The handful of white diners watched as the students opened books and began to study, while waitresses huddled in nervous groups.

Within minutes, the restaurant's owner, G. Carroll Hooper, came into the dining area from the lounge. After a quick conference with Warfel, Hooper approached John Quarles and sat down at the table he occupied. Informing Quarles for a third time that the restaurant did not serve blacks, Hooper appealed for sympathy. He personally considered segregation "an insult to human dignity" and sympathized with the goals of the black students, he said. But he could not change his policy. "I'm at the mercy of my customers," Hooper explained to Quarles. "I'm trying to do what they want. If they fail to come in, these people are not paying my expenses, and my bills." Hooper said that he employed one hundred black workers in his kitchens. "Go back and talk to them," Hooper urged Quarles, to discover that they were "in sympathy with me" on the segregation policy. Quarles answered that the black students had not entered Hooper's restaurant to "destroy his business" but were "simply there seeking service as humans and also as citizens of the United States of America."

During this diningroom debate over property rights and human rights, Warfel hustled outside the restaurant and found two Baltimore police officers, Sgt. Sauer and Lt. Redding. With the officers in tow, Warfel returned to the dining room and recited the Maryland trespass law to the unwanted patrons: "Any person or persons who shall enter upon or cross over the land, premises or private property of any person or persons in this State after having been duly notified by the owner or his agent not to do so shall be deemed guilty of a misdemeanor," Warfel read from the statute, which he kept handy for just such an occasion. After this warning, about six of the students left the restaurant, picking up picket signs outside and conducting a sidewalk vigil. Among the twelve who refused to leave was Robert Mack Bell, the sixteen-year-old student-body president at all-black Dunbar High School. Bell had recruited a busload of Dunbar students to join the sit-in with students from Morgan State.

The police made no move to arrest the remaining students or drag them out of the restaurant. This was a civil sit-in, with both sides anxious to avoid violence. Baltimore was not part of the Deep South, where hostile crowds often poured catsup on sit-in students, spit on them, or burned them with cigarettes. Albert Warfel simply took down the names and addresses of those who refused to leave, while Carroll Hooper went down the block to the courthouse and swore out warrants in the magistrate's office against the twelve who remained. Robert Mack Bell was first on the alphabetical list, and thus lent his name to the case that later reached the Supreme Court. Monday morning, Bell and the other students returned to the downtown police station, where they were fingerprinted, photographed, booked, and released to their parents' custody until their trial for trespass.

Robert Mack Bell was only one of thousands of students, black and white, who joined the sit-in movement to end segregation in public accommodations. The campaign began on February 1, 1960, when four freshmen at a black college in Greensboro, North Carolina, sat down at a Woolworth's lunch-counter and asked for service. They were refused and the counter was closed. The students returned the next day and were again denied service. On the third day, they were arrested for trespass. Within weeks, the sit-in movement swept across the South and enlisted an army of northern supporters, who picketed Woolworth's and other drug-store chains which refused to serve blacks in their Dixie outlets. Religious, civic, and political leaders rushed to join the students. Eleanor Roosevelt defended the sit-ins against former President Harry Truman's charges of Communist instigation, and jazz great Duke Ellington marched on a Baltimore picket line. Daisy Bates, who headed the Arkansas NAACP and battled school segregation in Little Rock, organized black students to protest lunch-counter discrimination.

The Greensboro students who sat down at the Woolworth's counter were not the first to use the sit-in tactic. Sit-ins actually began in May 1942, at Jack Spratt's restaurant in Chicago, organized by members of the Congress of Racial Equality, an interracial group which followed the Gandhian principle of nonviolent action against oppression. During the late 1940s, CORE activists began the first Freedom Rides in the South, which ended with arrests at bus stations in North Carolina. Fear of violent reaction in the Deep South, and the lack of federal support and protection, cut short this early civil-rights campaign. During the early 1950s, CORE activists in Baltimore launched a sit-in campaign which ended lunch-counter segregation in several drugstore chains, and began an effort to integrate the popular Gwynn Oak Amusement Park which lasted another decade.

None of these earlier actions generated the resulting mass movement that began in Greensboro and quickly led to formation of the Student Nonviolent Coordinating Committee. Several factors help to explain this new militance and its popular support. For one, students were attacking segregation in its Deep South bastion, as sit-ins spread to states like Alabama and Mississippi. Millions of Americans viewed on television the violent attacks on peaceful students by mobs which local police and FBI agents often did nothing to restrain. The independence struggles of black Africans, and shock at the Sharpeville massacre in March 1960, in which South African police killed hundreds of demonstrators against apartheid, also fueled the fervor of students who risked arrest and expulsion from school to join the movement.

By the end of 1960, close to 5,000 students had been jailed in sit-in demonstrations. Most often based on local trespass laws, these arrests swamped the jails and courts. Virtually all the demonstrators were convicted in summary trials, and dozens of appeals from these convictions began the slow journey through the judicial system. Early in the sit-in movement, experienced lawyers of the NAACP Legal Defense and Education Fund took the lead in guiding these appeals from state courts to the Supreme Court in Washington, D.C. Thurgood Marshall, the NAACP legal director, was a courtroom veteran of landmark civil-rights litigation.

Six weeks after the initial Greensboro sit-in, Marshall convened a meeting of civil-rights lawyers in Washington. Linking the sit-in movement and the struggle "against apartheid in South Africa" to "the cry for freedom" around the world, Marshall said that American students "are just simply sick and tired of waiting patiently without protest for the rights they know to be theirs." The lawyers at the meeting, he reported, were "handling the sit-in cases from Delaware to the Gulf of Mexico. We have compared notes. We have shared our legal thoughts, our legal briefs and legal procedures. We are going to give to those young people the best legal defense available to them." Marshall noted that the Southern strategy of mass arrests and trials was designed "in the hope our wearing our legal staff and our pocketbook down." Marshall promised his adversaries a protracted struggle. "We are prepared to stay in court after court, in city after city and state after state as long as they can stay there."

Among the hundreds of sit-in cases that came before judges in 1960 was the trial of Robert Mack Bell and eleven other black students in Baltimore. Judge Joseph R. Byrnes heard the case in criminal court without a jury on November 10. James W. Murphy, who prosecuted the students, first called Ella Mae Dunlop, the Hooper's restaurant hostess. She recounted her refusal to seat the black students, who then "broke through the line and seated themselves." The students' lawyer, Robert Watts, asked the hostess if the students had behaved in an orderly manner. "Well, I wouldn't say they were mannerly," she responded. Good manners were important in Baltimore. Watts continued his questions. "Had they been white people they would have been seated, is that correct?" The hostess agreed. Skin color was more important than manners in Baltimore, it seemed. Watts had one last important question. "Now, you refused them admission to this restaurant solely on the basis of their color, is that correct?" "Yes, sir."

After restaurant manager Albert Warfel testified that he contacted the police and read the trespass act to the students, owner Carroll Hooper took the stand and recalled his debate with John Quarles. "I set at the table with him," Hooper said, "and talked to him why my policy was not yet one of integration." Hooper tried to convince the students that his policy was simply a business decision. "I wanted to prove to them it wasn't *my* policy, my personal prejudice. I told them that as long as my customers were deciding who they want to eat with, I'm at the mercy of my customers." Caught between sympathy and segregation, Hooper lashed out at the teen-age defendants: "They are trying to legislate by terror, going to force me to either serve or close." Judge Byrnes admonished Hooper that "it would be more helpful if you didn't get too emotional."

Robert Mack Bell did not take the stand, and John Quarles testified as the group's leader, dressed in his college ROTC uniform. The Hooper's sit-in began, Quarles said, when Bell approached him at a civil-rights meeting and volunteered to recruit Dunbar students to join those from Morgan State College. Asked by prosecutor Murphy why the students refused to leave Hooper's, Quarles answered that "we were in hopes that Mr. Hooper would change his policy and serve us." Robert Watts asked why the students risked arrest when their appeal to conscience failed. "I think arrest is a small price to pay for your freedom as a human being," Quarles responded.

Robert Watts and the other lawyers who represented the students, Tucker Dearing and Juanita Jackson Mitchell, filed with Judge Byrnes a motion asking for dismissal of the trespass charges. State support of private segregation through enforcement of trespass laws violated the Fourteenth Amendment guarantee of "equal protection of the laws," they argued. Judge Byrnes denied the motion, found Robert Mack Bell and the other students guilty, fined them $10 each, and suspended the fine. The lack of penalty reflected Byrnes' belief that the students "are not law-breaking people." Their protest "was one of principle rather than any intentional attempt to violate the law," he wrote in his opinion.

Maryland's highest court, upholding the convictions in January 1962, stated the legal question as whether the state could "use its judicial process to enforce the racially discriminatory practices of a private owner, once that owner has opened his property to the general public." Because the law in Maryland did not either require or prohibit restaurant segregation, enforcement of trespass laws was neutral and did not constitute "state action" that took sides between Carroll Hooper and the black students. Protesters could not "invade or remain upon the property of private citizens, so long as private citizens retain the right to choose their guests or customers," the judges concluded.

The appeal from this decision reached the Supreme Court for argument on October 14, 1963, along with sit-in cases from four other states. During the past three years, the civil-rights struggle had convulsed the Deep South and challenged a reluctant federal government to act. The Freedom Riders of 1961, organized by CORE to challenge bus-station segregation, drove past North Carolina, where they ended in 1947, into Alabama and Mississippi. A mob in Anniston, Alabama, set a bus afire, dragged its occupants out, and beat them with iron bars while police and FBI agents stood by. Police chief "Bull" Connor answered mass rallies and marches of Birmingham blacks in 1963 with dogs, tear gas, and high-powered fire hoses.

Responding to police terrorism with peaceful resolve, more than 200,000 Americans, black and white, gathered in Washington in August 1963 before the Lincoln monument and stirred to Martin Luther King's "dream" that his children would grow up in a nation free of racism. Eighteen days later, this dream became a nightmare in Birmingham when four little black girls died in their Sunday-school dresses, victims of a church bombing by Klansmen.

Heavy curtains keep the noise of the outside world from the Supreme Court chamber, but the cries of pain from Birmingham found echoes in lawyerly language during the sit-in arguments. Congress had been considering a civil-rights bill which would outlaw segregation in public accommodations, and the church bombing spurred lawmakers to overcome Dixiecrat delaying tactics. Jack Greenberg of the NAACP legal staff appeared for Robert Mack Bell. His argument was rooted in the Supreme Court's 1948 decision in *Shelley* v. *Kraemer,* striking down judicial enforcement of racial covenants as "state action" that violated the Fourteenth Amendment's "equal protection" clause. The *Shelley* case meant that "property rights must be created and enforced subject to the Fourteenth Amendment," Greenberg stated. Hooper's restaurant was not a private club for white members but a place of public accommodation. The issue before the Supreme Court was whether Carroll Hooper could "invoke the full machinery of the state police, the prosecutor, the courts and so forth, to impose criminal sanctions on the Negro citizens who seek services in places of public accommodation open to all except Negroes." State enforcement of trespass laws to protect vestiges of the "slave system" could not be squared with the Constitution, Greenberg concluded.

Maryland's lawyer, Loring Hawes, claimed that the state remained neutral in the dispute between Carroll Hooper and the students. Hawes reminded the justices that the police "took no part whatsoever in the goings-on in the restaurant itself." The state's brief also argued that the *Shelley* decision "has no application" to the sit-in case; J.D. and Ethel Shelley had a "property right" in their home but the students had no such right to service at Hooper's. State enforcement of trespass laws was available to every property owner, Hawes concluded.

Ralph Spritzer, appearing for the federal government as "friend of the court," brought the outside world into the Court's chamber. He asked the justices to recognize that "the Congress is considering legislation" which would prohibit restaurant segregation throughout the nation. Spritzer also noted that the students had engaged in a "peaceful and orderly protest against discrimination" and were protected by the First Amendment. Looking beyond the dry words of the trespass law, Spritzer urged that "something should depend on the moral quality of the conduct."

Moral issues took a back seat to politics when the justices met to decide the sit-in cases on October 18, 1963. During the previous year the Court had reversed convictions in several sit-in cases on narrow grounds, unwilling to deal with difficult constitutional issues. The justices again reversed three of the pending cases at their conference, but found no narrow path through the Bell case and another from Florida. In most previous civil-rights cases, including *Shelley, Brown,* and *Bates,* the Court had issued unanimous decisions. Confronted with private property rights and claims of state neutrality, divisions among the justices now surfaced in heated debate.

Chief Justice Earl Warren, always sensitive to moral claims, urged his colleagues to "get to the 'raw' of the problem and reach the basic questions." The owner of a public restaurant "abandons private choice" in selecting customers, Warren said. Citing the *Shelley* case, he added that as long as prospective patrons "behave themselves, the owner can't have police to help to throw them out. The state then unconstitutionally enforces discrimination." Justice Hugo Black presented the case for property rights. Speaking emotionally of his "Pappy," who ran a rural Alabama general store, Black said "I don't think the Constitution forbids the owner of a store to keep people out."

During the conference debate, Chief Justice Warren and Justice William J. Brennan stressed that Congress was then considering a civil-rights bill with a strong public accommodations section.

Voting to uphold the sit-in convictions, they argued, might cripple the bill's chances to survive a Southern filibuster. Several justices vowed to delay the sit-in decisions as long as possible, hoping that Congress would pass the bill before the Court ruled. Persuasion and threat both failed. When the debate ended, Black prevailed by a one-vote margin and the Court voted to uphold Robert Mack Bell's conviction.

The Court's minority refused to concede and finally convinced Justice Potter Stewart to join in asking the U.S. Solicitor General to file an additional brief expressing the government's views of "the broader constitutional issues" in the cases. This delaying tactic outraged Black, but it put off final decision for several months. During this time, the assassination of President John F. Kennedy shocked the nation and placed Lyndon B. Johnson in the White House. Johnson adopted the civil-rights slogan of "We Shall Overcome" in asking Congress to pass the bill. While lawmakers debated, slowed by Southern tactics, members of the Supreme Court traded draft opinions in the sit-in cases and thought about the broader issues. The Court's delicate balance was upset on May 15, 1964, when Justice Tom C. Clark, like President Johnson a Texan, told an "exceedingly tense" conference that his mind had changed.

Clark's defection from the majority not only changed the vote; it also disrupted the alignment of justices on the legal issues before the Court. Justice Brennan, hoping to add Justice Stewart to the new majority, proposed that the Court base its decision on a recently enacted Maryland law which banned restaurant discrimination in Baltimore. Brennan wanted to return the Bell case to the Maryland courts for decision under the new state law. Chief Justice Warren and Justices Douglas and Goldberg considered this tactic an evasion of basic issues and refused to agree. But Brennan's invitation to Stewart worked. On June 15, five days after the Senate ended the Southern filibuster against the civil-rights bill, Stewart joined Brennan. Justice Black, now supported only by Justices Harlan and White, stubbornly defended the sit-in convictions.

Eight months after the cases were argued, the Court was split into three equal factions. Six members agreed that the trespass convictions should be reversed, but they differed on the legal grounds. With this patched-together majority in control, the Court finally issued its decision on June 22, 1964, three days after the Senate passed the civil-rights bill and sent it to President Johnson. Brennan wrote the "opinion of the Court" and noted that Maryland had substituted "a right for a crime" in the Bell case. Speaking only for Clark and Stewart, Brennan reversed the convictions and returned the case to the state court.

In his angry opinion, Justice Douglas accused his colleagues of cowardice. Congress and the nation were consumed by the civil-rights question, "Yet we stand mute, avoiding decision of the basic issue by an obvious pretense." The basic issue to Douglas was "apartheid" in America, a "relic of slavery" and "badge of second-class citizenship." The property rights of corporations could not prevail over the Constitution, Douglas concluded. Justice Black's dissent, first drafted as a majority opinion, was equally angry. The Fourteenth Amendment "does not prohibit privately owned restaurants from choosing their own customers," Black asserted. Writing that the Court's decision would "destroy" the "right of a man who owns a business to run the business in his own way," Black must have had his "Pappy" in mind.

The Supreme Court waited too long to decide whether Robert Mack Bell and other black Americans had a constitutional right to sit with whites at restaurants. Congress answered the question for the Court, while the civil-rights struggle moved from lunch counters to voting booths. The most significant footnote to the sit-in decisions was written in Philadelphia, Mississippi, on the day they were issued: Three SNCC workers in a voting-rights campaign—Michael Schwerner, James Chaney, and Andrew Goodman—were murdered by Klansmen, their bodies buried under an earthen dam.

Their struggle continues to this day.

II.
"Baptism by Fire"

I was born in North Carolina back in 1943, one of three boys, to Thomas Bell and Rosa Lee Bell. I was the youngest of the three boys. I was born in Edgecomb County, in the northeastern part of the state, in a place called Rocky Mount. Didn't stay there very long. My mother moved with the three boys to Baltimore when I was about two years old, after my parents separated. So I was raised by my mother, and all of my schooling occurred here in Baltimore.

My mother was from the old school. In those days everybody in the rural South got married early and had as many children as they could, to work on the farm. My mother was really uneducated. Back in those days they didn't do much in the way of schooling for blacks in North Carolina. Having married early and begun a family early, she had to leave school. I think the farthest she went was to the third grade, and even then it was on a part-time basis. My mother's prime occupation was housework; she was a domestic. She was, however, very interested in the three boys' getting an education and she pushed with strength and vigor our getting into school and staying in school and finishing school. Finishing school, to her, meant finishing high school. She was very strong about that. She didn't have formal education herself, but she knew the ABCs and she taught me the ABCs before I went to school and she taught me how to write my name.

My mother was a very strong individual who had a firm set of ideals. She knew what was right and wrong; she told us about

141

that, and if you didn't toe the line you heard about it and felt it as well. She was an active church person, sometimes a bit too active for my taste. She made certain that we were off to Sunday school, and when we began to read well enough, part of our chores was to read segments of the Bible to her. She listened very actively to the Sunday church services on the radio and she went herself. She also went to the evangelism meetings. Her primary interest in religion was on the hereafter, as opposed to the here-and-now. She was not herself an activist, in the sense of church people who marched in demonstrations. But that's not to say she was not interested in progress or wasn't happy to see it come.

I had no difficulties throughout my early years, except that I used to fight a lot. We lived in a ghetto-type neighborhood in Baltimore. Going to school, coming from school, I used to fight virtually every day. It was just a macho kind of thing. You'd run into somebody and get into a little fight with these kids. Nothing serious. We'd wait for each other every day. I thought I was being picked on, but I wouldn't pass up the challenge and neither would anybody else. All the way through school, from kindergarten to high school, I didn't encounter any problems. In fact, I rather enjoyed school. I was rather active in school, from safety patrol to yard patrol, and I got involved in various clubs. I was interested in history and the newspaper and that kind of thing.

My experience in the sit-ins began just after I was elected student-government president at the end of my junior year at Dunbar High School. I was still sixteen, just about to turn seventeen. This was the spring of 1960. At about that time, the big civil-rights push was going around Baltimore, headed up by the Civic Interest Group. The NAACP and Student Nonviolent Coordinating Committee were involved as well in the civil-rights movement in Baltimore, but the group I was involved in was the CIG. Sometime in the early part of June, someone contacted me from CIG and asked me, as president of the student government, if I would be interested in organizing a group of Dunbar students to participate in sit-in demonstrations downtown. They would supply the buses; they would have one of their members on the bus who would be more or less the leader for that bus, to keep us primed as to what would be done, who would make sure we got to the places we were supposed to be. In other words, he would give overall direction. My job was to put together the group.

I was able to get together enough Dunbar students to fill a bus and go downtown for the sit-ins. We didn't know where we were going at the time we got on the bus. We knew we were going downtown and we were going to do some picketing and possibly some sit-ins. I had no idea about the targets. One of my responsibilities was to tell everyone that wanted to go and signed up what the drill was, and that was that we were *not* to be talking back, yelling and screaming at folks, spitting back, or hitting people. I was told to make sure that they all understood that. I knew something about nonviolence from reading about some of the things that had already occurred, but I had never been involved in it and certainly had no idea what it was like in actual practice. I was also told to have the students from Dunbar get permission from their parents before signing up to go on the bus. This was not done with the cooperation of the school administration at all. This was the last day of school, so we didn't have to get their permission. So I got a list together and we filled the bus, although we split up once we got downtown.

This was my first sit-in, my first involvement with civil rights as an activist. I guess it was baptism by fire. Not only for me, but for everybody from my high school that went. And Baltimore was just getting started around that time. So we got on the bus and went downtown. The first thing that we did was to picket the Reed's Drug Store, and we did that for a time. Quite frankly, it was an amazing experience. You never really can understand, from having somebody tell you, exactly what it's like, people looking at you with open and overt hatred. People were spitting and yelling and screaming at us; the epithets were ones that you would imagine they would be in the context of that situation. Some people on the picket line were hit, although there was not as much physical violence as I thought there might be. The police were standing about, watching, but they didn't intervene to protect us from getting hit and they didn't arrest anyone.

I don't know how long we stayed on the picket line at Reed's, but some of us then moved down the street to Hooper's Restaurant, where we went in. Hooper's was a fairly large place, with a lobby and a main dining room up some steps and a cafeteria on the lower level. There must have been sixteen or seventeen of us that went in. Before going in, we were briefed that we were to go in, sit at the tables, and demand to be served. The person who was our adult leader from the Civic Interest Group was named

John Quarles. He was a veteran of these demonstrations, although I didn't know him before he got on our bus that morning. Part of our drill was that everyone who went had to have some money. If we were served, it would be rather embarrassing not to be able to pay. Nobody expected that we *would* be served, but we had money just in case.

This was my first experience, and I was not particularly brave at that point. I knew I would be faced with the prospect of someone ordering me out of there and eventually the police ordering me out. I was not the bravest of persons, but I was also pretty secure in knowing that I would do exactly what they had instructed me to do. I was *not* going to get up and leave, I was going to sit there. The only thing I had to say was that I want to be served. And when they asked me to leave, I would refuse. That's exactly what I did. I was a little bit nervous; I think all the youngsters were nervous, particularly when the policemen came in and read us the trespass ordinance and demanded that we leave.

The people at Hooper's were trying to get us to leave, and telling us that they didn't serve blacks. They shut off all of the services and indicated that they couldn't serve us, and then they told us they were going to call the police. John Quarles was the one who talked with the hostess and the restaurant manager and told them that we just wanted to be served like anyone else. While he was talking with them, the rest of us went in and sat at the tables in the dining room and cafeteria. And then the police came and read us the trespass ordinance and we all refused. A few of the students left the restaurant and went outside to picket with signs that told people why we were there—to be treated just like any other American.

Actually, nobody really got arrested at Hooper's. John Quarles worked out a deal with the police. It was clear that we were going to be quote arrested unquote, but they arranged that we wouldn't be arrested on the spot. We would have to report the next morning for processing at the police station. They did not cart us away in the paddy wagons and take us to jail. I think part of that was that we were high-school students. In Baltimore City at that time, if you were sixteen you were treated as an adult. I suspect that because of our age they decided they would not take us down in the paddy wagon; they would process us later. Once that arrangement was made, we were told to go home and report to the old Central District station the next morning. Everybody went down and we were all fingerprinted and processed, charges were lodged against us for trespass, and we were allowed to leave. We did not actually spend any time in jail. We *saw* the jail—we were right back there where everybody was—but we never had to stay there. Then pictures were taken on the Central District steps and there were stories in the paper about us. For a day or so, I was a celebrity.

We had already arranged through CIG for counsel, and we had Juanita Jackson Mitchell, Tucker Dearing, and Robert Watts; those were the three lawyers. Tucker Dearing did the bulk of the work on the case. Our trial took place in the old courthouse, on the second floor. It's sort of interesting that I later sat on the bench as a judge with a lot of the folk that were involved in my case in some way or another. Robert Watts became a judge on the municipal court and later on the supreme bench, which is the court in which I was convicted. The prosecutor was a gentleman by the name of James Murphy. He later was elected a judge of the supreme bench. When I came to the supreme bench, Murphy and Watts were both judges on the court.

There were twelve of us that were tried for trespass at Hooper's restaurant. And we lost. Interestingly, they kept us outside during most of the trial. Only about three or four of us were called to testify. I was not one. I don't know why. The lawyers were handling it, and they weren't discussing much with us. The police testified, the people from the restaurant testified, some of us testified. The judge, whose name was Byrnes, found us all guilty and imposed a fine of $10, which he suspended. Judge Byrnes made this little statement when we were sentenced, saying that he recognized we were not lawbreakers and that we had acted on principle.

Interestingly, I was never involved in another sit-in or any kind of demonstration. This one experience had a lasting effect on me. I made up my mind after that day that I just didn't have that business in me. I couldn't go through that same kind of situation again. I was convinced that I could not walk a picket line and have this kind of yelling and screaming and spitting and hitting occur to me or around me without some kind of response that I would want to make. So I made up my mind immediately thereafter that I would not participate actively in another one. I *knew* that I was not a good candidate for nonviolence. One thing I did know was that I would never jeopardize the effort of those who did take part in sit-ins and pickets. But I also knew that if I went back again it would become more and more difficult. It was my impression that my best bet was just not to do it on an active basis. Now I would do anything else that I could do, but I would never walk another picket line again.

I finished high school in '61, and I entered Morgan State College in Baltimore that fall. During my first year at Morgan State, there was a long effort to integrate the Gwynn Oaks amusement park near Baltimore. Hundreds of people took part in pickets and sit-ins at Gwynn Oaks and there was a lot of violence directed at them, and hundreds of arrests. A lot of Morgan State students were involved at Gwynn Oaks, but I *never* walked the picket line out there. I never went out and I never went near it. I lent whatever other support I could, helping them write things, but never did I go anywhere near Gwynn Oaks.

We lost our case in the state court of appeals and then we appealed to the Supreme Court. I wasn't really involved in the case after the trial. Once we lost, the lawyers were more concerned with the case rather than the individuals involved. They took it to the Supreme Court; I don't even know that we were asked about the appeal. I remember right after the decision being announced at our trial, and despite the fact that the $10 fine was suspended, I recall Tucker Dearing saying that he was going to take an appeal. After that, there was no contact, nobody called us up and said, Do you want us to appeal the case any further? It was just done.

I suppose it sounds odd that I didn't attend the Supreme Court hearing in my case. It's interesting that I didn't even know when it was. Nobody kept us posted on it or anything else. And I didn't inquire about it, either. Kind of strange behavior for someone who wanted to become a lawyer, but that's just the way it happened. I *was* aware when the case was decided, and I even read the decisions, as long as the damn things were. I was disappointed in the Supreme Court, quite frankly. I would have been more satisfied had they gone one way or the other. They did reverse our convictions, but they didn't rule on any of the constitutional issues. What they did was to send the case back to the Maryland court of appeals, which is our highest court, with instructions to decide whether the public-accommodations law that was enacted in Baltimore after our convictions was a ground for reversal. I didn't realize at the time what was going on, but it was clearly a political decision.

Justice Brennan, who wrote the opinion for the Supreme Court, probably recognized that he couldn't get a majority for reversal on the constitutional issues. This is hindsight, but I now realize that he was trying to obtain a result that would not set an adverse precedent by sending the case back and letting the state court of appeals take him off the hook. I rather liked the view of Justice Goldberg, who wrote an opinion that *did* reach the constitutional issues; and I was totally disappointed in Black, who wrote a dissent that defended the right to discriminate. I recall having gone through constitutional law in college and talking about how forward-looking Black was, and I was surprised that Black took the position he did. I would have assumed that Black would have gone the other way. At that time, I had not yet learned to appreciate Brennan.

I had decided to go to law school years before I decided to get involved in sit-ins. This is going to sound strange, but I used to read a lot of Perry Mason novels and I became very interested in the law. The whole point was that you can help people—a very simplified view, but it turns out that I think that's probably correct. What I was doing at Morgan was basically preparing myself to become a lawyer. I was a history major in college, and I took enough courses in political science to have a major in that as well. I was also very active in campus politics at Morgan: faculty–student committees and student organizations. I was out for a year with tuberculosis, and I stayed for an extra year, taking courses in English and philosophy, courses which I find now were of inestimable value to me.

The truth of the matter is that I had always entertained the idea that *maybe* I could attend Harvard Law School, but I had also been somewhat realistic about having to go someplace else. One factor was that I didn't have any money at that time. During my junior year at Morgan I met Senator Paul Sarbanes, who was at that time running for House of Delegates from my district. So I helped him and we had a discussion about law school. It was he who told me about how good Harvard was, from his perspective of having gone himself. So I credit him with my going to Harvard. Harvard accepted me; I got a full scholarship for the first year and I was on part-loan, part-scholarship for the rest of the time.

I became a little bit concerned about having a conviction, the closer it got to the time I applied to law school. In fact, when I applied I wrote a rather long essay about this experience with the idea of finding out whether it would affect my going to law school. The second rationale was to explain what the situation was. I realized after I had written this thing that I needn't have bothered, because nobody was concerned about it at all. In fact, one of my professors in constitutional law thought it was the greatest thing in the world and spent some time talking about the case. That was Dean Sacks. In fact, the whole hour was devoted to my case and I carried most of it. He called on me and asked me to give the background information. We discussed the merits of the case to some extent, and I don't remember anybody who supported the dissenting opinion. This was a rather small seminar, and I suspect that if anybody felt the dissent was correct they were a little too nice to take that position.

The question of what to do after law school was always a problem for most black students coming out when I did, which was '69. What I really wanted to do was to become involved, quote-unquote, go back to the community, and help folk. I was leaning toward legal aid, public-interest types of law, having volunteered with Community Legal Services in Boston, having worked on the Civil Rights–Civil Liberties Law Review. I always had this thing about coming back to Baltimore and trying to improve the lot of the black community.

As it turns out, I ended up going to work for Piper & Marbury, the biggest firm in Baltimore. But you can probably understand what followed. Piper had at that time begun a neighborhood legal office in the black ghetto, and they staffed it with two lawyers. I knew from having worked at Piper during the summer, while I was in law school, that they encouraged volunteer hours being given for poor people. So, coming to Piper, I could kill two birds with one stone. I would have the opportunity to do the volunteer legal work and help folk that way, and I'd also be able to obtain the experience and grounding in the law that one can get from a large law firm if one handles it correctly. So that was my motivation. And I became the first black associate they hired at Piper.

I did a lot of things when I first got to Piper. I started in public and municipal financing, and I ended up in real-estate financing and development. This was during the time when the new-town craze was on. I was doing some union work for Provident Hospital and I worked for the Salvation Army. Eventually I spent a year heading up the community legal office, just before I went on the bench in 1975. We would be available to provide legal services to people who had need of them but who didn't have the money to pay. I had a varied practice down there. Aside from that office, I was doing volunteer work at the Echo House Foundation, which was a multipurpose center in West Baltimore that had a drug rehabilitation component, a housing component, all kinds of things.

I can tell you unequivocally that I never wanted to be a judge. But Baltimore has a population of close to 60 percent black, and it turned the corner back in 1974. Unfortunately, we had maybe four black judges on the circuit court and we had three or four on the district court, out of twenty-two on each bench. But we also had a situation wherein we had black people who were interested in becoming judges but we didn't have anybody who the powers-that-be thought could achieve it. Most of the people had applied before and had been turned down. We wanted to increase the number of blacks on the bench but, being realistic, we knew there would be some difficulties with some people who aspired.

So I had a discussion with a couple of judges who, recognizing from my background that I could possibly make the list and be appointed, suggested that maybe I should apply. This was rather an unusual situation, since at that time I was only thirty-one. But I took up the challenge and I applied, although I did not make the list the first time because they told me I was a bit too young. The second time I did make the list and I was appointed by the governor. I had some help in that regard because my former college history teacher was married to one of the judges, who was rather influential. And I had been representing a drug program for youth and we were trying to relocate the facility from one place to another place within the council district of Victorine Adams, who happens to be the wife of one of the more influential political figures in Baltimore, Little Willie Adams. So I had to go through her as a councilperson to get her to introduce an ordinance, and we had a set-to about that and she refused to do it. She didn't want her people giving her a hard time about putting a drug program in their midst, but she could understand what I was trying to do. I didn't yell and scream and make a big issue out of it, so I made a friend and she also went to bat for me, because she was impressed by the fact that I was able to disagree with her and do my job without being disagreeable. Also Piper helped. I had explained to the managing partner early on that I wasn't really interested in becoming a partner. He told me that whatever I wanted to do he would help. That's how I got started.

I'm on my third court now. I started on the district court, then I went to the circuit court, and now I'm on the court of special appeals. This is the intermediate appellate court in Maryland. I would prefer, as I always did, being involved in the fight itself, rather than refereeing. But the longer I've stayed the more I've become convinced that the role I play is a worthwhile one. The toughest job I have had is sending folk to jail, but I've always liked the challenge of being able to resolve tough issues. The toughest decision I ever had to make was a death penalty case, when I was on the circuit court. The sentence in that case was life in prison. I don't like playing God. I can do it much more easily if it stops short of the ultimate; the closer it gets to the ultimate the more difficult it becomes. Right now, I don't have to worry about that, because all the death penalty cases go to another court.

Intellectually, this job is probably more challenging than any of the other courts I've been on. I write roughly a hundred opinions a year, of which a certain percentage are published. The numbers up here are a little more than on lower courts and make it a little more difficult. And the issues now can be somewhat taxing and tough. But I enjoy something that you can get your teeth into. I've found myself really interested in subject matter I had really never thought about before, if the cases raise interesting issues. I don't mind zoning cases any more, which are rather tough cases. I don't mind the domestic equity cases, child custody, and the new Maryland Marital Property Act. You can get your teeth into those things.

I also find that I do a lot of dissenting on this court, particularly in criminal cases, where civil liberties are an issue—Fourth Amendment primarily in search-and-seizure cases. I see a retrenchment in that area and it really troubles me. I think the principle that courts should follow precedent is something we have all got to respect and you have to apply. Otherwise you have no way of predicting what's going to happen from one case to the next. But when you get to a case where the rationale just doesn't make *any* sense whatsoever, I feel less inclined to pay deference to precedent. And in the Fourth Amendment area, it's hard to find a case on all fours with precedent. The closer the facts are to the case I have before me, you can really box me in with precedent.

Fortunately, I can also argue from the standpoint of the Maryland constitution as opposed to the federal constitution. This is something that I think lawyers should start to focus on, because state constitutions can be construed more liberally than can the federal constitution. This is where the action is, meaning if properly used we can be assured of greater protection. Our problem is that lawyers have not yet picked this up, so when you get a case which presents a Fourth Amendment issue, rather than presenting the question in terms of the federal constitution *and* the state constitution, they generally limit their argument to the former. And we're constrained only to decide questions raised and decided below. Consequently, if the feds don't help them, that's the end of the case.

I think the courts are really at the heart of this whole thing. In this arena the focus may be on schools or housing or economic issues, but the courts are going to continue to play a great role in it. And the courts on the state level are going to have to be brought into the process, because that's where it's going to happen.

Looking back on my case and the experience of the civil-rights movement since that time, I think it had to change from demonstrations to litigation and legislation, simply because you can only appeal to conscience so often. That can only work so long. That's what the sit-in movement was intended to do: to work on the conscience of the country. Having done that, I think it was time to move to another vehicle. And the civil-rights movement was more than the sit-ins. Rap Brown, Stokely Carmichael, Roy Wilkins, Martin Luther King—it took all kinds of people and all kinds of approaches to make the gains we have seen in civil rights.

How did my case and that experience affect me? I suspect that without it I would not have become as involved in certain community activities as I did. I try to keep myself very much involved and I try to keep my thinking fresh on issues. I tell young people as often as I can not only about what things *used* to be like but how they can ensure that things never get back to that position again. Moving into the area of excellence is what I'm focusing on.

I spoke last year to the bar association, on the one-hundredth anniversary of the admission of the first black lawyer in Maryland, and I recalled in that speech what it must have been like to be the first black lawyer in an all-white society. I tried to say to them that while we have made some progress, we certainly have not reached the point where it is secondary that this person is black, or that we can take it for granted that I can do the exact same things you can do. But that progress gives us something to build on and it also gives us a point of reference so that we can avoid ever returning to where we used to be.

I think my case has given me that point of reference, and it also makes me appreciate the extent of progress that has been made. And it also made me able to gauge the extent of the progress which has yet to be made. I think, not just about that case, but about that era in that fashion. The unfortunate thing is that younger people don't remember it. They don't *know* what happened. And therefore you're finding a different kind of attitude and a complacency which I think is more dangerous than anything else. So our job is pretty hard.

7

Daniel Seeger
v. United States

Dan Seeger, standing before the Supreme Court
with his lawyer, challenged in 1957 the draft
law that forced conscientious objectors to swear
belief in a Supreme Being. *Courtesy of Daniel A.
Seeger*

I.
"A Truthful, Decent Young Citizen"

On July 15, 1957, Daniel A. Seeger composed a brief, polite letter to his local draft board in Queens, New York. "As a result of the resolution of a number of problems of conscience with which I have been preoccupied for the past months," he wrote, "I am bound to declare myself unwilling to participate in any violent military conflict, or in activities made in preparation for such an undertaking." In this serious, somewhat pedantic tone, Dan Seeger informed the board members that he would refuse military service. He was then 21, having recently completed his third year at Queens College as a physics major.

Dan based his stand against military service on concerns about "the welfare of humanity and the preservation of the democratic values which we in the United States are struggling to maintain." He added that "I have concluded that war, from the practical standpoint, is futile and self-defeating, and that from the more important moral standpoint, it is unethical."

Dan's draft board interpreted this letter as a request for exemption from service as a conscientious objector, although the letter did not use this term. Under the draft law, young men with sincere objections to participation in war could be assigned either to non-combatant service in the army or to alternative civilian service, usually in hospitals. The law limited exemption to those whose pacifism was based on "religious training and belief." Dan's letter used the word "moral" to describe the basis of his objection and did not mention religion. Nonetheless, the board promptly sent him a copy of Form 150, the special form for conscientious objectors, generally known by the shorthand term "CO's."

Within a week, Dan returned the completed Form 150. However, he slightly altered the form and vastly expanded its length. One question asked whether he believed in a "Supreme Being" and offered two boxes for an answer, one labeled "yes" and the other "no." Dan added a neatly drawn and checked third box and the words, "Please see attached sheets." In seven single-spaced, typed pages which he appended to the form, Dan explained why he couldn't squeeze into the yes and no boxes. His statement displayed much thought and exposure to philosophers who had wrestled with the question of God's existence. "Of course, the existence of God cannot be proven or disproven," Dan wrote, "and the essence of his nature cannot be determined." The capital letter for "God" and the lower-case for "his" hinted at Dan's agnostic position. Although he declined to answer the "Supreme Being" question, Dan assured the board members that "skepticism or disbelief in the existence of God does not necessarily mean lack of faith in anything whatsoever. Such personages as Plato, Aristotle and Spinoza evolved comprehensive ethical systems of intellectual and moral integrity without belief in God, except in the remotest sense."

Another question asked the names of persons who influenced the objector's stand, and Dan listed Leo Tolstoy, Bertrand Russell, Mahatma Gandhi, and a Quaker pamphlet entitled *Speak Truth to Power*. Unlike Dan's first letter, this response to Form 150 asserted his "religious faith in a purely ethical creed." But the draft law excluded those whose pacifism reflected "essentially political, sociological, or philosophical views or a merely personal moral code." Although Dan was untutored in law, his statement was perfectly designed to provoke a constitutional test of the government's demand that CO's profess a belief in a Supreme Being as the price of exemption.

Conscientious objectors to war have always been a small, and most often a persecuted, minority. Although the scriptures of many religions preach nonresistance to evil, most also counsel obedience to state commands. Early Christians rejected military service, not only for scriptural reasons but from revulsion at emperor worship as well. After Constantine's conversion in the fourth century, the Catholic church excommunicated those who refused military service, and religious objectors often were tortured. The Protestant Reformation brought a revival of pacifism among dozens of Anabaptist sects which emulated the early Christians, including "peace churches" like the Quakers, Mennonites, and Brethren. Members of these churches joined the flood of European immigrants to America, before and after the Revolution, who sought escape from military conscription. Napoleon swept more than 2 million conscripts into his army between 1800 and 1812, and Americans responded with revulsion. During the War of 1812, Daniel Webster opposed any military draft as "despotism."

The American experience with conscription began during the Civil War and provoked widespread resistance. Ten thousand Union troops were diverted from the Gettysburg campaign to battle New York draft rioters, mostly Irish immigrants, who denounced the draft as slavery imposed on those who could not afford to buy exemptions which were offered to the wealthy. Congress enacted a draft law during World War I over vehement opposition: "Must we Prussianize ourselves," asked Rep. James Byrnes of South Carolina, "in order to win democracy for the people of the world?"

Pressure from pacifist and liberal groups secured exemption from combatant service for members of "a well-recognized religious sect" which opposed war on creedal grounds. Local draft boards approved more than 50,000 claims of conscientious objection by members of peace churches. But CO's were inducted into noncombatant service and forced to wear army uniforms. Nearly 4,000 in this group refused to serve; some 500 were tried at courts-martial and tossed into military prisons. Sentences were harsh: Seventeen were sentenced to death (although none was executed) and 142 to life imprisonment. The Rockefeller Foundation sponsored a study concluding that "objectors were often subjected to indignities and physical cruelty. Some were beaten; others were hung by their fingers to the doors of their cells in such a way that their feet barely touched the floor."

Two decades after the Armistice ended conscription, Europe

was again engulfed in war and the advocates of American "preparedness" urged Congress to revive the draft. Fears that CO's might again be tortured in military prisons led pacifists and civil libertarians (the American Civil Liberties Union grew out of efforts to protect World War I objectors) to press Congress for broader grounds for exemption and alternative civilian service. The 1940 Selective Training and Service Act provided that a draft registrant "who, by reason of religious training and belief, is conscientiously opposed to participation in war in any form" could be exempted from combatant service to perform "work of national importance under civilian direction."

The "good war" against the Nazis was unquestionably more popular than the earlier war against the "Huns." The 100,000 religious objectors during World War II constituted only a tiny fraction of the 34 million men who registered with local draft boards. Most CO's performed noncombatant military service, usually in the medical corps, or worked on conservation projects in Civilian Public Service camps. Only 6,000 objectors, most of them Jehovah's Witnesses, went to federal prison. Conditions behind bars improved: Guards did sometimes beat objectors, but official torture was rare. Imprisoned CO's conducted sporadic but often successful hunger and work strikes to protest racial segregation and brutality.

The wartime draft law expired when World War II ended. But the nation's first peacetime draft began in 1948, as Cold War tension mounted over the Soviet invasion of Eastern Europe and the formation of NATO in response. Congress adopted the Universal Military Training and Service Act, adding to the 1940 law a requirement that CO's profess "belief in a relation to a Supreme Being involving duties superior to those arising from any human relation." This new clause was added without committee discussion or floor debate, and its author was not identified. Over the next decade, even during the Korean War, the number of CO's dwindled to a handful. And none of them challenged the "Supreme Being" clause until Dan Seeger submitted his Form 150 in 1957.

The Queens draft board filed Dan's form and took no action on his CO application. A year later, when Dan became a part-time student, the board revoked his student deferment and placed him in the 1-A group, eligible for immediate army induction. Dan then asked for a personal hearing to appeal this classification and entered the labyrinth of Selective Service proceedings. The local board denied his appeal in October 1958 and ordered Dan to report for a preinduction physical examination. The district appeals board upheld this decision several months later. Dan next appeared in September 1959 before John M. Lockwood, an examiner of the Selective Service Hearing Board. For the first time, the government gave Dan a sympathetic ear.

Lockwood had before him at the hearing an exhaustive FBI report on Daniel A. Seeger. Agents had inquired at every school Dan had ever attended and every business which had employed him. Not one person uttered a derogatory word about Dan. The FBI learned from Bayside High School officials that Dan was active in the Newman Club of Catholic students, sang in the school choir, belonged to the Arista honor society, and received the Pi Mu Epsilon award for excellence in mathematics. One former teacher said that Dan was "very intelligent" and had been "interested in human welfare" in high school. Agents also interviewed a Queens College official who described Dan as a "very intelligent person of high moral character" who was active in the Outdoor Club, editor of the college newspaper, and Chief Justice of the Student Court. Supervisors at the Marine Midland Trust Company, where Dan worked as a clerk from 5 P.M. to 1 A.M. for $60 a week, praised him as a diligent employee. During the summer of '57, Dan worked as a bellhop and bartender at the exclusive Corinthian Yacht Club, where his boss considered him "completely trustworthy" and a "very gentle" person. Agents also talked with neighbors of Dan's parents, reporting their view of a "very fine, exceptionally religious family."

Dan appeared at the hearing with two friends, one of them a Queens College professor, Dwight Durling. John Lockwood first asked Dan to explain the basis of his objection to military service. According to Lockwood's report, Dan answered that research and reading in religious teachings had convinced him "that peace throughout the world could only be accomplished by the laying down of arms by all." Dan told Lockwood that service in the army medical corps would simply be "patching them up to put them back at firing again" but that he could accept alternative civilian service. Lockwood also reported that Dan had "strong sympathetic support for the Quaker movement." Dwight Durling told Lockwood that he disagreed with Dan's pacifist views but considered him "completely sincere."

Lockwood's report to the Justice Department described Dan as "a truthful, decent young citizen who conscientiously objects to joining in any manner" the nation's military forces. Lockwood added the caution that if Dan were drafted into the army his "extreme intelligence and lucidity would create a problem" by "preaching nonviolent subversion" of the army's missions. Conceding that Dan's views, although religious in basis, were "not responsive" to the Supreme Being requirement, Lockwood still recommended that he be granted CO status and assigned to alternative service.

Lockwood's report failed to impress T. Oscar Smith, chief of the Justice Department's Conscientious Objector Section. Smith issued a brief order in May 1960 which rejected Dan's claim. Dan then took the final step in the Selective Service bureaucracy and asked the Presidential Appeal Board to reverse Smith's decision. He lost again in August 1960. Two months later, Dan's draft board ordered him to report to the Whitehall Induction Center in Manhattan for army induction. Dan showed up on October 20 but refused to take the symbolic step forward into military service. Sent home by army officials, Dan waited two more years, until November 13, 1962, for his indictment by a federal grand jury. Under the draft law, Dan faced five years in prison for his challenge to the Supreme Being clause.

District Judge Richard H. Levet presided at Dan Seeger's trial on March 26, 1963, at the federal courthouse in Manhattan. Levet was almost seventy, a former Republican official in wealthy Westchester county whom President Dwight Eisenhower had placed on the bench in 1956. Kenneth Greenawalt, whose corporate law clients included the Woolworth Company, represented Dan as a volunteer for the Central Committee for Conscientious Objectors. The trial began on a sour note for Dan. Greenawalt asked Judge Levet for a brief trial delay in order to present "a very distinguished theologian" as an expert witness. The witness, who was out of town for a few weeks, would testify that "religious belief is not confined to a belief in a Supreme Being" and that a person could be genuinely religious without "belief in a Divine Being." Judge Levet curtly denied the request: "I cannot very well hold this case up for weeks and weeks in order for somebody to come back from a long, long trip. You either have to fish or cut bait."

Forced to proceed, Greenawalt stipulated that Dan's religious beliefs were "not based on a supernatural person or a Supreme Being known as God." He argued, however, that the First Amendment barred the government from conditioning draft exemption on belief in a Supreme Being. Greenawalt cited the recent Supreme Court decision in the *Torcaso* case. The Court held in 1961 that Maryland must give a notary-public commission to Roy Torcaso, who refused to swear his belief in God to secure the public post. Government could not, the Court stated, place its power "on the side of one particular sort of believers—those who are willing to say that they believe in 'the existence of God.' " The *Torcaso* case, Greenawalt argued, made the draft law's Supreme Being clause unconstitutional. Dan Seeger needed only to show that his pacifism was based on "religious training and belief" to gain exemption. Ezra Friedman, who prosecuted the case, stipulated that Dan would merit exemption under this standard.

Greenawalt's argument did not impress Judge Levet. His written opinion noted that military service was not a public office and derided reliance on *Torcaso* as "specious." Levet wrote that draft exemption "is a matter of legislative grace and not a matter of right." If Congress could withhold *all* exemptions, it "has a clear right to limit such exemptions" to those who met the Supreme Being test. Levet found Dan Seeger guilty of refusing the draft board's induction order and sentenced him to a year and a day in prison.

Judge Levet's opinion did not impress the judges of the U.S. Court of Appeals in New York. Judge Irving Kaufman wrote for a unanimous three-judge panel which reversed Dan's conviction in January 1964. Kaufman had gained judicial notoriety in 1950 when he sentenced Julius and Ethel Rosenberg to death for passing atom-bomb secrets to the Soviets; his later career was marked by sensitivity to First Amendment claims. Unlike Levet, whose hostility to Dan was obvious, Kaufman praised his "unquestioned integrity and sincerity." Kaufman also differed with Levet on the *Torcaso* case, holding that it rested on "far broader grounds" than whether the religious test involved a public office. Kaufman located the proper exemption standard in the *Kauten* draft case, decided by his court in 1943 and cited by the Supreme Court in other significant cases. The *Kauten* standard rested on religious sincerity and not on supernatural belief. Judge Kaufman cited *Kauten* in writing that "for many in today's 'skeptical generation,' just as for Daniel Seeger, the stern and moral voice of conscience occupies that hallowed place in the hearts and minds of men which was traditionally reserved for the commandments of God." Kaufman's opinion concluded that the Supreme Being clause violated the First Amendment and was flatly unlawful.

Dan's victory in the appellate court did not end his case. The government asked the Supreme Court to reverse Judge Kaufman and to review two other draft cases. Arno Sascha Jakobson in New York and Forrest Britt Peter in California had been convicted after their draft boards turned down CO applications. These men differed from Dan Seeger in claiming they *had* met the Supreme Being test. Solicitor General Archibald Cox, who later gained fame when he was fired as Watergate special counsel by President Richard Nixon, argued all three draft cases before the Supreme Court in November 1964.

Cox first told the justices that Dan Seeger's case presented "the basic constitutional issue" on the Supreme Being clause and was "the one with which we are most concerned." His argument was both disarming and unyielding. "I'm impressed with him as quite a fellow," Cox said of Seeger. The rest of Cox's argument belied this concession. He portrayed Seeger's pacifism as "overwhelmingly political" in motivation. "Now, in saying that Seeger's views are not religious," Cox added, "I don't mean to denigrate them." Cox then painted an apocalyptic picture of military threats to "democratic values, Western civilization, the ideals of American life." He claimed that the "life and death" of an "entire nation" depended on the draft. Accordingly, "the community has the right to set its judgment" on conditions for draft exemption. Conceding that religious definitions involved "fine shadings of belief," Cox argued that the "national understanding of what constitutes religion" was based on belief in a Supreme Being.

Archibald Cox's argument did not impress the Supreme Court. The justices listened respectfully to Cox and peppered Kenneth Greenawalt with questions, but their vote to reverse Dan Seeger's conviction was unanimous. Chief Justice Earl Warren set the tone in the Court's conference room: "I don't know how to define 'Supreme Being' and judges perhaps ought not to do so." Both liberals and conservatives lined up behind Warren. Justice Hugo Black, the Court's "absolutist" on First Amendment issues, said that if a religious objection to war was "honest, conscientious, that's enough." Justice John M. Harlan, who most often deferred to legislators, agreed that Congress could not "pick and choose between religious beliefs."

Guiding the conference discussion, Chief Justice Warren urged his colleagues to frame a narrow opinion which would duck the constitutional issue and allow Dan Seeger to squeeze into the Supreme Being box on Form 150. The sole opponent of this disposition was Justice Arthur Goldberg, who argued that Judge Kaufman had correctly answered the First Amendment question. Goldberg found no converts on the Court and Warren assigned the opinion to Justice Tom Clark, who generally took a crabbed view of First Amendment claims.

The opinion that Clark wrote for the Court, issued on March 8, 1965, held that Dan Seeger "did not disavow any belief" in a Supreme Being in his answers to Form 150. Clark noted Seeger's statement that "the cosmic order does, perhaps, suggest a creative intelligence." Clark ignored Seeger's doubt that "this intelligence is informed with a moral purpose." What impressed Clark, more than any quibble over words, was that Seeger's beliefs "occupy the same place in his life as the belief in a traditional deity holds in the lives of his friends, the Quakers." The Court's opinion freed Dan Seeger from a prison term, but it also allowed the Selective Service System to impose a religious test on war objectors.

The timing of the Court's opinion reveals a great deal about the impact of politics on law. One month later, 20,000 marchers, many of them students facing the draft, gathered at the Washington Monument to protest American bombing of North Vietnam. Paul Potter, president of Students for a Democratic Society, spoke of "increasing numbers of young men who are unwilling to and will not fight in Vietnam." The SDS promised "massive civil disobedience" against the draft. The militant End The Draft movement organized acts of draft-card returning and burning that provoked Congress to make card-burning a federal crime. The Supreme Court upheld this law in 1965 in the *O'Brien* case.

Five years later, ruling on a "Supreme Being" case which was virtually identical to Dan Seeger's, Justice Harlan confessed his "mistake" in joining that earlier opinion. Three other justices argued that "purely ethical or moral" objections to military service, even those that reflected religious views, should not qualify for draft exemption. The Court's resolve in the Seeger case buckled under wartime pressures, much as the Court had backed the wartime internment of Japanese Americans in the *Hirabayashi* and *Korematsu* cases. America's defeat in Vietnam ended the draft, but the revival of Selective Service "registration" has sent CO's to prison once again. Those who "speak truth to power" as war objectors remain a small minority in an increasingly militarized society. But the conflict between conscience and conscription has not ended.

II.
"Check Box Yes,
Check Box No"

I was born here in New York City in 1935, the oldest of four children. Just before the Second World War my parents bought a small house in Queens. At that time our neighborhood, where they still live, was in an undeveloped area. It was almost like the country, even though it was right within New York City. It was very rural-looking, and there was a large amount of vacant land in the neighborhood that was semiforested. It was like living in a small town.

My father is the son of German immigrants. He worked as a compositor in a print shop, and he remained in the same small firm for more than fifty years. He gradually became part of the management. My mother was the daughter of Welsh and English immigrants.

My father was the oldest of eight children. He had to help support this family at a very early age, so he only went to grammar school. He's a very centered and calm, serene, wise person, not formally educated but widely read. So it wasn't as if I was brought up in a home where learning was not esteemed. My mother did go to high school, but not to college. Both my parents were readers and were interested in what went on in the world. They tended to be conservative in their views. I remember their strong opposition to the policies of Franklin Delano Roosevelt. But they were not uninvolved or disinterested in the world.

Both of my parents are sincere and devout Roman Catholics. My mother's side of the family was Protestant, but she became a Catholic when she married my father. I associate them with the Catholicism of Pius XII rather than Vatican II. Two of my father's brothers are priests and one of his sisters was a Dominican nun.

I went to school at St. Kevin's Roman Catholic School in Queens. I started school at just about the time we got into World War II. My memories of those years are pretty vivid. We frequently had air-raid drills in first and second grade, so I was certainly aware the war was going on. It was also in the movies a lot. My father used to send us to the movies every Saturday afternoon so he could listen to the opera in peace. So I used to see the war in newsreels, and the comic books we read were all full of 'Japs' and 'Huns' and that kind of propaganda. There was very good reason to be concerned with what was going on in the world, but a lot of what came my way as a child was not, I suppose, very informed or sensitive. The war was a big part of our home life, because we would stamp on tin cans and save them, shopping was difficult because we had to have ration stamps, and there were food shortages. Sometimes there wasn't any meat in the stores. So I had a vivid impression that the war was going on.

I went to St. Kevin's School for eight years and then to a public high school, Bayside High School, and then to Queens College, the local branch of what is now the City University. My attitude toward my religious upbringing has changed with time. At one time, I was almost anti-Catholic because I rebelled against what had gone on in St. Kevin's in the '40s. I say I've mellowed because I've gotten a much greater appreciation for the diversity of Roman Catholicism and for the sweep and depth of different Roman Catholic schools of thought. What I rebelled against was an unresilient, parish-level Roman Catholicism as taught by certain nuns that really wasn't adequate for understanding or dealing with life as I experienced it.

I don't want to criticise my parochial-school education too harshly—the people who were teaching were doing the best they knew how. But it was mainly fear and guilt that we were taught, and a sense of our own depravity, which is really the wrong thing to be teaching small children, as far as I'm concerned. I didn't rebel in grammar school. I was somewhat pious and very devoted to all this. It was only when I got into the environment of public school at the high-school level that it began to erode. By the time I was in college I had dropped out of Roman Catholicism, much to my parents' dismay.

There was no choice about my going to Queens College. My parents couldn't afford any kind of tuition. The City University was actually free in those days, although you did have to pay for your textbooks. We were all 'day-hop' students; I lived with my parents and took two buses to get to the campus. Queens was a marvelous, fine college—it wasn't Harvard or Yale but it was an excellent educational institution with many fine faculty. I don't know how many of them were celebrated in the world of scholarship, but they were conscientious people who loved their subjects and who were able to transmit their enthusiasm. I especially remember one professor, Dwight Durling, who helped me out with my draft case.

I was a physics major in college. I can't recall how I was attracted to physics. It was just assumed I would be in some branch of the sciences. My parents laid on me the necessity of studying something practical, something that would enable me to make a living. Although I had drifted away from the church, I always remained interested in philosophical and spiritual questions, and I tried to take as many liberal-arts courses as the rather stringent mathematics and physics curriculum would allow, in addition to the required literature and contemporary civilization courses. I wasn't disinterested in physics, by any means. I still remain very interested in science, in figuring out how the world works. Nowadays, we all get very mystical about science and see religious insights creeping out of it everywhere, but that wasn't true in those days. I was just very interested in the way things worked.

One of my required courses at Queens was called Contemporary Civilization, a rigorous and good course that lasted four semesters. We had to read primary source materials, everything from the Magna Carta, excerpts from St. Augustine, Thomas Hobbes, and John Locke—a little taste of this and a little taste of that. For some reason that will probably never be explainable, when we read Gandhi something stuck. I was touched in a very profound way. Not that things didn't stick with me from these other people, but something moved me very deeply about Gandhi's writings, even on the basis of the few little excerpts we were given. It was in one of those textbooks over there, on my bookshelf. I haven't looked at it in a long time. Let me get it down. Here it is, *Man in Contemporary Society,* which would certainly be an unacceptable title nowadays.

Here's the selection I remembered: Mohandas Gandhi, page 753, 'Indian Home Rule.' The other person in here who was very important was John Dewey. Here is his essay, 'A Common Faith.' Gandhi and Dewey and Henry David Thoreau, for some reason, had more of an impact on me than any others. I'm sure I read more of Gandhi than what appeared in this book, but somehow that got me started. At a certain point I decided, as a result of this course work and this reading, that I wasn't going to serve in the army.

I can't quite believe this in retrospect, but the truth of the matter is that I came to the decision that I wasn't going to serve in the army in a very solitary way, a way that I think these things hardly ever happen. Usually, people are socialized into a point of view. They meet people, and pick things up from the people they associate with. I'm quite positive that my views on military service came from reading. I was bookish in college. I had friends, but I was also introspective. On campus, in those days, conscientious objection was unheard of. It just wasn't part of the atmosphere at all. Those were the days of the McCarthy era, and the big liberal crusade was working to end McCarthyism.

In those days, everyone over the age of eighteen had to register for the draft. I had registered with my local board in Queens in a perfunctory way, without thinking about it very much, when I was eighteen, and then I went off to college. We all had to carry draft cards, and we all got classification cards periodically, that let us know our standing with respect to the possibility of being drafted. The upshot of all this was that at a certain point in college, when I got my periodic card telling me I once again had a 2-S classification, which is a student deferment, I said to myself that I better let them know I didn't intend to serve in the army.

So I wrote a very brief letter to my draft board. I said something like: Dear Sirs, I have given this a lot of reflection and I have decided I am not going to serve in your army and I think you ought to know. It was decently phrased, I suppose—a little sophomoric, I'm sure, but there it was. And I sent it off. I had never heard of a conscientious objector. I didn't know if anyone else had done this or not.

I wasn't aware of the consequences in the least. You know how students are. I couldn't think much beyond the next day. Anyway, I sent this letter off and the draft board did what was suitable; they ignored the letter, because as long as I was qualified for a student deferment the conscientious-objector classification didn't fit. So they kept sending these cards and I just put them in my wallet and went on my merry way.

At the end of my college career I had to finish a few courses, and I lost my student deferment because I was on a part-time program. My draft board began ordering me to preinduction physicals. And I said to myself, Hey, they must have overlooked my letter. What are they trying to do? So I wrote them another letter, reminding them of my earlier letter. And in response, they did the correct thing again, which was they sent me Form 150, the form for conscientious objectors.

Now this was very astonishing to me. It was the first hint I had that other people had this concern also, because this form was printed, and it was obviously produced by the thousands. So I had my first hint—it sounds incredible nowadays, after the Vietnam War and everything connected with that—that there were other people who did this.

The second thing that quite astonished me was that under the letterhead of an agency of the United States government, I was asked, Do you believe in a Supreme Being? Check box yes, check box no. This surprised me, because I didn't make any particular connection between my theological beliefs and my determination not to fight in the army. I didn't quite see them as connected, and everything I had been led to believe about the American way of life was that the government doesn't meddle with people's private religious convictions. So I was startled to get this form.

In my naiveté I thought: I have nothing to hide. I didn't think of the philosophical ramifications of cooperating with them. I was completely unschooled and untutored and uncounseled in any way. So I filled out their form. When I reached the question about belief in a Supreme Being, it said, Check box yes, check box no. So I drew in a third check box, and I wrote, Please see attached sheets. And I then wrote pages and pages of speculative philosophy, expressing a kind of agnostic position about what human beings could or could not know about ultimate reality. I sent the form and my answers back to my local board. Then the draft board once again did what was appropriate, according to their regulations. Since I had placed myself outside the law with my theological lack of conviction, they continued to order me to preinduction physicals. So I was once again saying to myself, What's going on here?

Then one of my friends at college said, Why don't you look up the Quakers? They might be able to help you. So I looked up the Quakers in the Yellow Pages, and I found my way to the American Friends Service Committee regional office in Manhattan, where I now serve as head of staff. The AFSC was then located in a walkup above a barber shop on Third Avenue. When I got there, I was asked to fill out a form while I was waiting to be counseled by the executive secretary, Robert Gilmore. The office manager, Joyce Mertz, noticed that I had an interesting handwriting. So while I was sitting and waiting she put me to work lettering the bindings of the books in which are kept the minutes of the regional office's governing body. These books, which represented my first volunteer job for the AFSC, are now sitting in my office to remind me of that day when I walked in as a client. We now have a staff of approximately thirty people, so it is a much bigger operation.

Back in those days, Friends would get their 1-O classification as conscientious objectors fairly automatically if they followed procedures, although some Friends refused to cooperate with the system and went to jail. The Quakers were also counseling people who were not Friends, many of whom were conscientious people like themselves, but who were getting sent to jail on theological grounds. This was very painful for the Friends. So when I came along and Robert Gilmore looked at my material, he saw something that was unusual. Usually, spiritually unorthodox objectors had renounced religion as well as war and the draft, whereas I was claiming to be religious.

The crucial thing about my position was that I followed John Dewey, who insisted that one could be religious without necessarily believing in a Supreme Being. Dewey himself was an atheist, which I was not, but he nevertheless had a spiritual approach to life, and he insisted that one could be religious without being theistic. Even though I was waffling on theological questions, I claimed in no uncertain terms that my conscientious objection was a religious conviction. So I had wrapped myself in the mantle of the

First Amendment, without any conscious strategy for doing so, by claiming to have a religious conviction.

Eventually Robert Gilmore asked if I would mind being a test case. He was following advice from the Central Committee for Conscientious Objectors in Philadelphia with respect to my situation, which was nonroutine. I really didn't know what I was doing; I was just a naive student at the time. So I just said, Oh sure, and the whole process of starting a test case began. My initial documentation, on which everything depended, had been developed completely in isolation, but thereafter I had the highest-quality counseling. Everything from there on was done in a very meticulous, legal, careful way.

After deciding to begin a case to test whether the Supreme Being clause, which was section 6(j) of the Selective Service law, was constitutional, I went through all the procedures, from a local board hearing all the way up to President Kennedy. All these hierarchies basically came to the conclusion that I did not qualify under section 6(j), which was a reasonable conclusion for them to reach, given the language of the law.

Once my conscientious-objector application was turned down at the presidential level, I was drafted. My local board sent me the usual induction form and a subway token, instructing me to report to the Whitehall Street Induction Center in lower Manhattan.

This was a very critical point. I had to show up in order to make this a test case. If you don't go through the preinduction process to the very last moment, just before you take the symbolic step forward, they will throw your case out of court because you didn't give the system every chance to make the right decision. At the same time, if you go too far and take the step forward, you wind up in the army, and if you refuse to serve you're given a court-martial rather than having a civilian trial, so no precedent could be established.

So I was educated very carefully, before I went to the Whitehall Center, about this symbolic step forward. I was also told that in previous cases, when one person in a roomful of recruits and draftees had not stepped forward, he simply wound up in a different row. No one believed he had refused to step forward, and so he faced a court-martial anyway. So I was instructed to tell them as soon as I arrived that I wasn't going to take the step.

I showed up at 6 A.M. at Whitehall Induction Center, and there's this cranky sergeant drinking his coffee and all these confused young people coming in. I arrived and announced that I wasn't going to take one step forward. Even though these legal precedents had been established, this sergeant apparently had no idea that anyone could refuse induction and he couldn't believe his ears. He started an incredible tirade. There was a rather bad scene, where I was belittled and maligned and barked at. This was the first opportunity for the military to show these new guys who's boss. There was only verbal abuse, fortunately. I still had to go through the preinduction physical. Then they decided they would separate me out from everyone else so they wouldn't spoil the induction ceremony for the other people.

At the end of the day, all these guys were back in the same waiting room, ready to climb on the bus to Fort Dix. Meanwhile, the Whitehall induction officials had called Washington and learned that this was going to be a test case, and suddenly everything became very proper. I was no longer barked at. I was dealt with by a superior officer, and treated very nicely. At the end of the day, the officer, with all his brass buttons, came to me in front of all the other draftees, shook my hand, and sent me on my way. These guys who had seen me barked at in the morning were utterly bewildered, I suppose, by this whole process. So then I just walked away.

The Central Committee for Conscientious Objectors had established a defense fund, and had gotten a very distinguished lawyer, Kenneth Greenawalt, to be ready to defend me. Mr. Greenawalt was a very able attorney who worked mostly for corporations. I don't believe he was particularly interested in peace issues, as such, but he had a special interest in church–state cases. He was a Congregationalist, a very kind person, but also sharp and clear.

Much to my surprise, the government did not immediately prosecute me. I went home from the Whitehall Center and two years ground by. Everything was in place, and we were all ready to go with this ambitious constitutional test of section 6(j) of the draft law, and we never heard a thing from the government. We were about to fold up the defense committee, send back the contributions, and forget the whole thing, when my indictment finally came in the mail. We quickly went back into action, preparing for my trial in the federal district court in Manhattan.

In the district court, we had a cranky old judge named Levet, who was very unsympathetic, barking all around the place like the sergeant at the Whitehall Center. I was amazed to find the judge acting like a character in a grade-B movie. Judge Levet found against us, as everyone expected. The big issue, as far as Mr. Greenawalt was concerned, was whether we would get certiorari in the Supreme Court. I was just learning about these things, but apparently the Supreme Court picks and chooses the cases it wants to hear; and he was afraid we would have two negative decisions in the lower courts and the Supreme Court would conveniently decide not to hear us, and let the lower-court decisions stand.

We then went to the Circuit Court of Appeals, also in Manhattan. The three-judge panel that heard my appeal was presided over by Judge Irving Kaufman, who had sentenced the Rosenbergs to death. I was not thrilled at all to find him on my case, but it turned out that he wrote a *wonderful* opinion. I attended all the hearings. It was quite a different cut of business than the district court had been. Judge Kaufman wrote a decision that astounded everybody, because the three-judge panel unanimously came out in my favor.

The decision was a marvel, cutting right to the core of the issue and declaring section 6(j) patently unconstitutional. That was wonderful for us, because it meant we were guaranteed a Supreme Court hearing. It was hardly likely the Supreme Court would let one of the circuit courts do this without reviewing the case. So we were suddenly not only given a brilliant and wonderful decision in our favor, but we also knew we would get to the Supreme Court, although the government was now the losing party in the case.

The Court of Appeals decision created a stir. I became one of these celebrities-of-the-moment, and I was on TV talk shows with Basil Rathbone and Phyllis Diller, trotting around to all the studios. The story about my case, with my picture, appeared on the front page of *The New York Times*.

I remember being astounded by my visit to the Supreme Court when my case was argued. My parents, a few friends, Mr. Greenawalt and his family, all went to the Supreme Court with me. The Court was hearing several cases that morning, and we listened to those arguments. One case before mine had to do with the

Musicians Union, and one of the justices disqualified himself because he used to play the flute and belonged to the union. Another case had to do with banking and overseas investment and it was dull, dull, dull. Everyone in the courtroom was going to sleep.

When my case came up, there was a certain stirring of the atmosphere in the courtroom. It was clear that this was going to be more interesting to everyone, including the justices. I was astonished by several things. I was being tried for my religious convictions in a place that was made to resemble a 'pagan' temple, and I couldn't figure out why I was being pilloried for my views in a place like this, although it was lovely architecture. The second thing I noticed was that I was being tried for my convictions in a procedure which began with the words, Oyez, oyez, oyez, followed by an appeal for God's blessing on the honorable court. I felt immediately that the cards were stacked against me.

The hearing proceeded and it turned out that Archibald Cox, who argued for the government as the Solicitor General, was wearing a cutaway with striped pants. My lawyer only had a dark blue suit on, and I again felt a little bit at a disadvantage. As it turned out, it was a very fair and good hearing, and there was some very sharp questioning of Mr. Greenawalt by some of the justices. It wasn't hostile, but close questioning, and he was very adept and brilliant, I thought, in his responses. I remember that Justice Goldberg was on the court and he had one of the pages bring a Bible, from which he read passages into the record. He was clearly on my side, and he used Scripture to make his points. I was very pleased at the quality of the justices' grappling with the issues, and I was spectacularly pleased with the fine defense Mr. Greenawalt made.

I had finished college at the time my case was argued in 1964. I knew I didn't want to work in defense, but physics in those days was almost all defense, so I worked first for Sloan–Kettering Institute for Cancer Research, and then for Columbia University, assisting in research. Part of this research was at Los Alamos National Laboratory, where the atomic bomb was invented. I actually only worked in physics for three or four years, and then I joined the AFSC staff in the New York office as the college secretary. At the AFSC, where I was given the volunteer calligraphy job when I first walked in, I undertook more volunteer assignments while I was being counseled about my draft case. I worked for

AFSC in mental hospitals, leading groups of college students in work camps. Then I was put on the youth committee, and then on the executive committee, and then I was invited to join the staff. My draft case took eight years to resolve, I think, and I was working for the AFSC for most of that time.

The Supreme Court decision in my case was a disappointment. We were pleased to win, and it was a unanimous decision, but we would have preferred Judge Kaufman's decision. What the court held was that if the conscientious convictions in the life of a religiously unorthodox objector to military service parallel the place that belief in a Supreme Being holds in the life of a conventionally religious person, then the exemption from service should be granted. This business of construing the Supreme Being clause to be constitutional in this labored way, by reinterpreting its language, seemed very artificial to me, very geometric and forced. Nevertheless, it did have the result that Form 150 was revised and the Supreme Being question, with its checkboxes, was removed from the form. So it had the practical result we had sought, but it didn't have the philosophical neatness of just declaring the law unconstitutional.

After the Supreme Court decision, I thought I would be given an order to do alternative service, but by that time I was well over draft age. In a sense, I got off scot-free from the draft. But the kind of work I had been doing at the AFSC would have been readily recognized as alternative service, so in another sense I had been doing alternative service for many more years than was required. So that was the end of it. As a matter of fact, when my case was over, I more or less forgot about it. It had not been a sole preoccupation in my life for all those eight years, in any case.

I could not by any stretch of the imagination claim to be a martyr. When we consider our own century and what people have had to endure in these times, I appear to be the beneficiary of the American justice system in its most pristine and beautiful form, the way we *expect* it to perform. I am not deluded into thinking this is the way the American justice system *always* works, but I experienced it as it *should* work, administered by people who were conscious of doing something important and who were at their best throughout. So I have absolutely nothing to complain about.

As soon as my case was over, I wanted to move on to other things. I was still fairly young, and I just wanted to get on with the future. So I haven't thought about it that much since then. Of course, many people have been through the Selective Service system in the shadow of my case and have used it. I often meet people who say, Oh, *you're* Dan Seeger, and they seem thrilled because my case was crucial to the government's recognition of their conscientious-objector claim. I don't regret being a test case, but I certainly don't want to live my life as the Seeger case.

I never doubted that my case accomplished something, once it had been won. But I didn't want to dwell on it; I wanted to get on with the next thing. I was just becoming executive secretary of the New York AFSC office, so I had a very challenging job on my hands. The office was growing and needed a lot of management, and I was mainly trying to raise money and offer supervisory support for the staff. During the Vietnam War, we had a huge draft-counseling program, although the issues had moved beyond the Supreme Being clause of the draft law to selective conscientious objection. We counseled many young men who were not opposed to war in every circumstance, but who nevertheless had deep conscientious scruples about fighting in a war like that in Vietnam. The office also encompassed a lot of work in domestic social-justice issues, so I had to give much attention to those important matters also, and I became much more of a generalist.

I eventually joined the Religious Society of Friends, so I am now a Quaker, and a lot of my energy has gone into trying to find ways to understand, articulate, and project the spiritual underpinnings of peace activism and social justice work. I am concerned because a lot of people are in anti-war work for the very sensible and obvious reason that we're going to incinerate ourselves eventually unless we change the course of events. They perceive the corrupting character of this war preparation, which is ruining everything. Even if the war doesn't occur, we're going to fatally undermine our values. What I feel isn't quite clear enough for us to grasp is how we sustain the work for peace and sustain its spiritual quality in spite of years of frustration. The movement for peace and justice suffers repeated bouts of individual and collective burnout.

You and I have seen several sourings of good things—the civil-rights movement, the peace movement too, and a lot of anti-

Vietnam War work. So there's something missing. We went through the anti-Vietnam War movement, and when the war was over there was no peace movement left either. People's peace convictions weren't really rooted in a place that lasted. The Iran hostage crisis occurred, and all of a sudden the mood of the country changed and Reagan was elected. My concern has been to try to find something which holds through thick and thin and doesn't depend on a war to keep people going. That's a dead end, to need a war with its television images to keep you in a state of elevated indignation. That's a horrible way to keep a movement going, a movement that hopes to build a bright new future in a world of peace. Will an era of harmony and peace grow out of perpetual outrage?

I've never stopped trying to winnow out these issues, throwing off and discarding things that might have been suitable for a six-year-old in parochial school but that weren't capable of sustaining growth beyond that stage. Although a lot of my subsequent inner explorations weren't directly connected with my draft case as such, they've been going on pretty constantly since it began.

The philosophical and spiritual position I defined in the material I filed with the Selective Service system hasn't been overruled, it's been deepened and extended. I don't feel I'm in a different place than I was then. But rather, that beginning has taken on a richer and more meaningful coloration as time goes on. It was a little flat at the beginning, and it's a little more three-dimensional now.

We are promised that if we seek we shall find. I've found this to be true. Some people have what might be called conversion experiences, like St. Paul's on the road to Damascus, and they suddenly see a whole new vision of life. But any spiritual growth that has been given to me has come only little by little. But I do think it accumulates, in response to whatever inner stillness I have been able to cultivate, to allow the larger harmonies of the Creation to be heard within my heart. These harmonies can indeed be heard, and occasionally I even resonate to them. Such experiences leave one with a great feeling of hope and optimism. I am certain that a great spiritual reawakening is in the offing. The very tragedies and contradictions all about us are alerting people to the deeper implications of what is occurring, stimulating a questioning about the significance of human life, about the proper relationship among families, neighbors, and nations, and about the role and responsibility and destiny of humankind in the Creation.

We may be generations away from a shared vision about the things upon which we can build a harmonious, secure, and just future for all of humankind. But if we survive at all, it will come, I really believe. And I think it is fitting that the survival question must remain, for the time, unanswerable. If we knew for sure of an optimistic answer we might be tempted to sloth. If we knew for certain that disaster was inevitable, we would be paralyzed with despair. The fact that human survival is truly hanging in the balance keeps us striving. I can't conceive of a more enlivening and worthwhile thing to do with one's days and energies than to grapple with these great questions.

8

Barbara Elfbrandt
v. Imogene Russell

Barbara and Vern Elfbrandt were
junior-high teachers in Tucson, Arizona,
who refused in 1960 to sign "loyalty" oaths
that violated their Quaker principles.
Courtesy of Barbara Elfbrandt

I.
"Those Whose Scruples Are the Most Sensitive"

The teachers at Amphitheater Junior High School in Tucson, Arizona, were instructed by school officials to comply with a newly enacted state law on May 1, 1961. The symbolism of that date provides an ironic footnote to what later happened to Barbara Elfbrandt, an eighth-grade English and social-studies teacher at the school on Tucson's north side. In Communist countries, "May Day" is marked by parades of military might. By official proclamation, May 1 is "Law Day" in the United States; the choice of date for this celebration is a Cold War artifact. The timing of the notice to the Amphitheater teachers was coincidental, but the loyalty oath they were asked to sign bore the stamp of Cold War hysteria.

Barbara Elfbrandt was the only teacher in her school who did not sign the oath in the principal's office. Instead, she took the form home and talked about it with her husband. Vern Elfbrandt was then working as a union organizer, on leave from his teaching position at a high school in the Hispanic area of Tucson's south side. Barbara and Vern had talked many times over the past few months about the possible consequences of refusing to sign the loyalty oath. The oath itself was fairly innocuous. Signers were sworn to defend the United States and Arizona "against all enemies, foreign and domestic," and to "faithfully and impartially discharge the duties" of public office. The Elfbrandts were more concerned about a warning on the form that any teacher who signed the oath and who "knowingly and wilfully" joined the Communist party or "any other organization having for one of its purposes" the overthrow of the Arizona government could be sent to prison for perjury.

Barbara and Vern had joined a small group of Tucson teachers and social activists who lobbied the legislature in Phoenix against the Arizona Communist Control Act, which imposed the loyalty oath on teachers and outlawed the Communist party. Their amateur efforts proved no match for the professionals of the Radical Right, more powerful in Arizona than in almost any other state. By 1961, the tide of McCarthyism had receded across much of the country. The political career of Senator Joe McCarthy, whose attacks on "Fifth Amendment Communists" first excited and later embarrassed his Republican colleagues, was crippled by his censure in 1954. But Arizona's junior Senator, Barry Goldwater, voted against the censure motion and continued McCarthy's crusade against "subversives" in government. Goldwater's backing helped to secure passage of the Arizona loyalty oath. His political ally and fellow Republican, Governor Paul J. Fannin, signed the law on March 30, 1961.

Despite their high positions, Goldwater and Fannin had less influence in pushing the loyalty oath through the Arizona legislature than did Dr. Fred C. Schwarz, an Australian physician who abandoned his country and profession in the 1950s to become an impresario of Americanism. Schwarz had arrived in Phoenix in February 1961 to conduct rallies and "schools" for his Christian Anti-Communism Crusade. His itinerary during that year spanned America from the Hollywood Bowl to Madison Square Garden. "Hollywood's Answer to Communism," televised every night for a week, featured stars like Roy Rogers, Jane Russell, James Stewart, and Ronald Reagan, who vowed that Reds had no place on the silver screen. After members of the U.S. Senate and House warmed up the crowd, Schwarz delivered an apocalyptic warning that "unless America wakes up within the next ten years, she will be dictated to by the Communist dictatorship."

The anti-Communist "school" that Schwarz conducted in Phoenix and twenty other cities offered a math lesson with a political answer. In this simple equation, liberal equaled socialist and socialist equaled Communist. Schwarz's instructor in this class was W.

Cleon Skousen, who attacked the fledgling administration of President John F. Kennedy. Arguing that Kennedy's liberal advisor, Arthur Schlesinger, Jr., was really a "democratic socialist," Skousen concluded that the address of Marxist communism "is the White House." The conservative mayor of Salt Lake City had earlier fired Skousen as police chief and denounced him as a "little Hitler" for abusing citizens, but Fred Schwarz hired Skousen for his oratorical talents, not his peace-keeping abilities. Schwarz stirred thousands of Arizonans into a frenzy and sent them to the state capitol, where they ringed the building with pickets and demanded that legislators vote for the Communist Control Act as the price of passage into the chamber. The new law's preamble, which cited "recent events in the neighboring country of Cuba" to support the oath provision, reflected Schwarz's call for American action against the Castro regime.

Loyalty oaths as a condition of public employment were hardly new when the Arizona legislature voted to require one of all teachers. The kings of England had required oaths as a pledge of fealty for centuries, binding their subjects to temporal and heavenly kingdom alike. James I described kings as the "breathing images of God upon earth," and Blackstone's famous *Commentaries* on English law stated that the oath "strengthens the *social* tie by uniting it with that of *religion*." Loyalty oaths in the United States had traditionally exacted a positive pledge of commitment to the state. The Red Scare that followed World War I prompted twenty-one states to require loyalty oaths of teachers, but these were phrased in positive terms of patriotism.

The negative oath, which required public employees to swear that they did not advocate the government's overthrow or belong to subversive groups, stemmed from the swift change in American foreign policy toward the Soviet Union that followed World War II. The Cold War abroad was matched by a domestic crusade against American Communists and their "front–group" sympathizers. President Harry Truman launched the Anti-Communist crusade against the Soviets in his "Truman Doctrine" speech of March 12, 1947. Ten days later, Truman signed an executive order which established a Loyalty Review Board to screen more

than 2 million federal employees and to remove "subversive ele-
ments" from government offices. The loyalty mania reached far
beyond concern with Communist party membership: Interroga-
tors asked federal employees whether they entertained members
of other races in their homes, their views on the draft, and whether
they supported the Truman Doctrine. By the end of 1952, after
some 6.6 million Americans had been subjected to loyalty-security
review, the Administration admitted that only one Communist
had been uncovered in federal employment.

Loyalty enforcers singled out teachers for special scrutiny, both
in universities and public schools. Fears that Communist teachers
would subvert their students had less importance in the loyalty
craze than suspicion that liberal teachers would not preach the
Cold War gospel with sufficient fervor. Between 1948 and 1954,
a majority of states required that high-school students be instructed
in "Democracy versus Communism" courses. Most teachers assigned to these classes had no qualms about their ideological content; those who did usually swallowed their objections and plodded
through the simple-minded lessons. The state of Maryland was
first to add a non-Communist disclaimer to the loyalty oath required of teachers. Named after the lawyer who drafted the law
in 1948, Maryland's "Ober Act" outlawed "subversive" groups
and barred their members from public employment.

Other states quickly emulated Maryland and modeled new laws
after the Ober Act. Most demanded that teachers swear they were
not subversive. University of California faculty were ordered in
1949 to swear that "I am not a member of the Communist party."
Widespread resistance to signing this oath, which applied only
to teachers, soon wilted under pressure from the University's regents. Many professors considered the oath an infringement on
principles of academic freedom; others objected to being singled
out for suspicion. Less than half of the faculty signed the initial
form, but threats to fire those who declined to comply reduced
the "refuseniks" to thirty-one after a year. Significantly, even the
most right-wing regents agreed that there were no Communists
among the objectors. California's governor, Earl Warren, opposed
the decision to fire the nonsigners but the regents ignored him.
Warren then convinced the state legislature to impose a loyalty
oath on *all* state employees. Eventually, about half of the fired
professors signed the new oath and returned to the classroom.

But several of those who took a stand of conscience and lost their jobs at the University of California never returned to academic life. The conformity crusade took a toll across the country: Professor Arval Morris of the University of Washington Law School estimated that approximately 500 teachers lost their jobs between 1948 and 1958 for refusing to sign oaths or answer the questions of loyalty boards.

The scattered resistance to loyalty oaths was centered in universities. Elementary and high-school teachers had far less protection from dismissal, faced more direct pressure from principals and parents to conform, and rarely asserted claims to academic freedom in the classroom. Local school boards, conservative in outlook and shy of controversy, exercised almost total control over curriculum, textbooks, and teaching assignments. With the exception of New York City, whose purge of Communist teachers in city high schools was upheld by the U.S. Supreme Court in 1951, few public-school teachers challenged loyalty programs during the Cold War years.

Barbara Elfbrandt took the initiative on June 1, 1961. Four weeks before the deadline for signing the form she had been given on May 1, she filed suit in Pima County Superior Court against Imogene Russell, who chaired the Amphitheater Elementary School District, and a host of local and state officials, including Gov. Fannin and Arizona's attorney general, Robert Pickrell. Drafted by Tucson lawyer W. Edward Morgan and filed on behalf of all Arizona teachers, the suit asked for an injunction against enforcement of the loyalty oath and a judicial declaration that it violated the state and federal constitutions. Morgan added a bushel of objections to the oath, but he centered the suit on First and Fifth Amendment claims. The law infringed on freedoms of speech and assembly, Morgan asserted, and its failure to provide hearings at which objectors could explain their reasons deprived them of due-process guarantees. The suit also noted that Barbara Elfbrandt was a Quaker and also refused to sign the oath on religious grounds. Oddly, the legislature had provided that "continuing employees" could not be fired if they refused to sign the oath; the only penalty was the withholding of any salary.

The first round in the case ended quickly. Judge Timothy Mahoney, on temporary assignment from rural Pinal county, decided the case on the basis of stipulations of fact by Morgan and government lawyers who represented the long list of official defendants. Both sides agreed that Barbara "refused and will continue to refuse" to sign the loyalty oath and was a "continuing employee" and protected against discharge for her stand. Barbara did not appear in court, and Judge Mahoney ruled against her after a brief hearing, without a written opinion on the issues. Judicial rules in Arizona permitted a direct appeal to the state Supreme Court, and Morgan promptly asked for review.

The second round in the case dragged on for almost two years. Vern Elfbrandt returned to teaching after Judge Mahoney's decision and refused to sign the oath. While the Supreme Court sat on the case, both Barbara and Vern worked without pay, scraping by with modest contributions from friends. Two other Tucson teachers, Clyde Appleton and Jerry Dolgoff, also refused to sign and joined the suit. Again by coincidence, the court's ruling was issued on "Law Day," May 1, 1963.

Writing for the court, Justice Fred C. Struckmeyer first noted that the suit had raised "nearly every conceivable constitutional aspect" of the oath; he then dismissed every objection. Struckmeyer had no doubt that Arizona could bar "its enemies from seeking or holding public employment." He reached the constitutional issues, it appeared, only because Barbara Elfbrandt was a Quaker and the oath "weighs most heavily on those whose scruples are the most sensitive." With this concession to conscience, Justice Struckmeyer addressed the argument that the bar on membership in groups that had both legal and illegal aims infringed on First Amendment rights of speech and association. The risk that teachers who joined such groups might spread the "insidious poison" of Communism "is not one the people of the state are willing to accept," Struckmeyer wrote. Balanced against Arizona's interest in protecting its citizens against enemies "who have publicly vowed to 'bury' us," the oath "only minimally and incidentally conflicts with the First Amendment." The justice offered a prediction that the Soviet Union only waited for an "opportune time" to deliver a "thermonuclear first strike" on the United States. This Cold War rhetoric showed that loyalty remained a hot issue in Arizona.

Edward Morgan answered the state court's decision with a petition to the U.S. Supreme Court for review. More than a year later, at the very end of the term in June 1964, the justices returned the case to the Arizona court for rehearing. The justices had recently struck down a loyalty oath required of faculty at the University of Washington, in a case called *Baggett* v. *Bullitt.* This oath demanded that professors swear they did not belong to the Communist party or "any other subversive organization." Washington included "advocacy" of unlawful acts in defining subversion. The Supreme Court held that states could not require employees "to choose between subscribing to any unduly vague and broad oath, thereby incurring the likelihood of prosecution, and conscientiously refusing to take the oath with the consequent loss of employment" and perhaps of their careers.

Asked to reconsider their first decision in light of the *Baggett* opinion, all but one of the Arizona justices stuck to their guns. Justice Struckmeyer, again writing for the court, found a "vital distinction" between the Washington and Arizona laws. "Arizona does not seek to punish" the advocates of revolution, he wrote, but only those who actually commit revolutionary acts. The justice ignored the fact that the law proscribed membership in organizations, not the commission of violent acts. This intentional oversight bothered Chief Justice Charles C. Bernstein, whose solitary dissent stressed the "troublesome" issue of membership in *any* group, such as international scientific agencies, which might include Communist members. An Arizona university professor could not know whether such membership might bring "honors from his university" or a prison term for perjury, Justice Bernstein wryly noted.

After losing three rounds in Arizona, Edward Morgan once again asked the High Court for review. Barbara and Vern Elfbrandt had worked four years without pay by the time Morgan filed his second petition in May 1965. The petition reflected frustration and anger. Morgan wrote that teachers who opposed the loyalty oath faced prosecution "before an unknown jury in a State whipped by Barry Goldwater right-wing Birchite 'hard-core' Americanism." Noting that "hysterical legislators" had passed the law during picketing by Fred Schwarz's followers, Morgan wrote that Arizona gained nothing from the oath except "red-baiting" of those who refused to sign. Morgan also denounced the law for failing to provide hearings to objectors.

Answering for Arizona, Philip M. Haggerty of the state attorney general's office chided Morgan for citing "the presence of pickets" at the state capitol, and his "scandalous" attack on Senator Goldwater. Haggerty then echoed Justice Struckmeyer in arguing that state employees "bear a heavy primary responsibility for defensive procedures in the event of enemy attack." Disloyal teachers might disrupt the "national defense system" in Arizona's military industries and bases. Haggerty branded the Elfbrandts' religious objections to the oath as "utterly immaterial" and answered Morgan's claim that hearings for objectors were required with the rejoinder that the law "contains no provisions for excuse." Arizona presumed that those who refused to sign the oath admitted their disloyalty. No further inquiry was necessary.

The case finally came before the Supreme Court for argument on February 24, 1966. Before the bench, Morgan and Haggerty toned down the rhetorical excesses of their briefs. Morgan stressed that Barbara Elfbrandt was a Quaker and belittled the loyalty oath as pointless. "The State of Arizona hasn't had one prosecution," he noted. "There hasn't been one person turned up as a subversive." Morgan spent much of his half-hour of argument trying to wrap the *Baggett* decision around his case.

Haggerty answered that the Washington law struck down in the *Baggett* case "is simply not the same law" that Arizona passed. "It doesn't say the same things," he stated. According to Haggerty, the difference lay in Arizona's requirement that members of banned organizations commit "actual acts" of violence rather than advocate them. Haggerty was asked how someone could sign the oath if they belonged to a group that had been cited by the House Un-American Activities Committee but never found by a court to be subversive. "He could resign from the organization and then sign the oath," he advised. The inquiring justice remained skeptical. Haggerty confessed that any objector to the oath would risk "convincing the jury" that she did not know the group had any unlawful aims. In his final two minutes of rebuttal, Edward Morgan cast scorn on Haggerty's advice to teachers. "What type of organization" did Arizona mean to ban? "What type of membership" was unlawful? Morgan's questions hung in the air as Chief Justice Warren adjourned the argument.

Warren answered these questions the next day in the Court's conference room. Surprisingly, he had earlier voted against hearing Barbara Elfbrandt's appeal, which would have left her forever without pay if she remained a teacher. The Chief Justice now supported her position. He told his colleagues that the Arizona law was too vague to enforce and limited rights of association. When the justices voted, Warren joined a bare majority for reversing the Arizona court, and asked Justice William O. Douglas to write the Court's opinion.

Douglas framed his opinion around Chief Justice Bernstein's dissent to the second decision of the Arizona Supreme Court. The Arizona law failed to protect innocent members of groups which might include subversives and contained "a conclusive presumption that the member shares the unlawful aims of the organization." Douglas also touched on Edward Morgan's fear of placing Barbara Elfbrandt at the mercy of Arizona jurors in a perjury trial. "People often label as 'communist' ideas which they oppose," Douglas wrote, "and they often make up our juries." Although his opinion rested on the vagueness issue, Douglas took a parting shot at Arizona's effort to convict a Quaker of "guilt by association" with subversion.

The four dissenters spoke through Justice Byron R. White, who formerly headed the Justice Department's criminal division and consistently supported governments in loyalty cases. White could see no reason why Arizona needed teachers "who insist on holding membership in and lending their name and influence to those organizations aiming at violent overthrow" of the state government. Arizona barred from public employment only those who held "knowing membership" in subversive groups, White stressed. Despite the law's failure to provide hearings for objectors, White felt that innocent members of organizations with unlawful aims could sign the oath in good conscience. White left unanswered the question of what constituted "knowledge" of an organization's subversive aims. The dissenters were content to give Arizona "the power to treat such false swearing as perjury."

Barbara and Vern Elfbrandt learned of their narrow victory on April 18, 1966. They had worked for almost five years without salary, teaching in a state which demanded conformity for a check. Their loyalty could not be bought, but their conscience exacted the price of genteel poverty. Even after the Supreme Court's ruling, the Tucson school boards refused to give the Elfbrandts the pay they had been denied for their stand. Several more years passed before Edward Morgan pressured the boards into paying the missing checks. In their example, Barbara and Vern Elfbrandt gave teachers across the country a priceless lesson in the rewards of conscience and conviction.

II.
"What We Were
All About"

I was born in Medford, Oregon, in 1933 in the depths of the
Depression. I was an only child. My family left Medford when I
was quite small and I don't remember anything about it. I grew
up until I was school age in Portland. Jobs were very hard to
find at that time. My father was one of those who were hit pretty
hard by the Depression, and he did anything and everything he
could. He got a job in Portland in a nursery by claiming that he
knew how to grow roses, which he did not. But he learned quickly.
It was those kind of years where you did anything to get a job.

About 1939 we moved on to Spokane, Washington, where my
father had another job in a nursery. After his work in the nurseries
he became an auto mechanic and later a shop foreman at an
auto dealership. So he was essentially a working man. Mother
worked on and off outside the home, in nurseries with my father
and as a clerk, to get me through college, but she really preferred
staying home. We stayed in Spokane all through my school years.

I don't know where to say my ideals came from. I think they
really did come from my home, without my realizing it. Neither
my father nor my mother preached very much about anything,
but they were strong supporters of Roosevelt and the New Deal,
and I no doubt heard a good deal of that at home. I smile now,
because many things that I learned about my background, I
learned after I had done something like refuse to sign a loyalty

oath. Then my father would casually say, Well, you know your grandfather was a Wobbly. I didn't know that. My father had been involved in unions in his early working days.

My mother came from a Seventh-Day Adventist background that she was not very happy about. She sort of escaped when she was a teenager by leaving home and working for a family. There had always been problems with religious questions in her family because her father was not an Adventist and her mother was very devout. She had this ideal that her daughter ought to be able to make those decisions for herself. Neither of my parents was active in churches, but whenever I showed any curiosity in the local church my parents always saw that I got there, so I went to a number of churches when I was small. When I was a teenager I joined a Baptist church and was quite active in it until I graduated from college. My father mentioned to me after I joined the church that his mother had been a Baptist, which I did not know.

Neither of my parents finished high school, but they had dreams that their daughter would not only finish high school but go to college, and I was always going to go to college as long as I can remember. I went to Whitworth College in Spokane, which is a small, private, Presbyterian school. Whitworth was a fairly conservative school, and I went there during the Eisenhower years. I remember that in 1952 I was one of only two students who wore a Stevenson button. As soon as I graduated in 1955 I went back to the high school I had graduated from, Lewis and Clark, and became a history teacher for a couple of years. I was really delighted to be teaching there. I was teaching everything, American history and world history and the beginning social-studies course for freshmen, and even some geography.

When I got the job at Lewis and Clark High School, right after I finished at Whitworth, I was one of two women in the history department. The other one was Katherine Hunt, who chaired the department and had been a teacher of mine when I was a student there. She had been involved in the institute on international affairs that was sponsored every spring by the American Friends Service Committee and Washington State College. It was about the only event that happened in Spokane in relation to international affairs, and she told me about it and encouraged me to take part. I was immediately enchanted by the Service Committee and all the people I met.

Then I met Vern Elfbrandt, who became my husband and who died five years ago. Vern was born and grew up in Spokane. His mother died when he was young and he lived with his father, who was a school custodian, and his brother, in a succession of rooming houses. Vern was just finishing college although he was older than I. He had been a union organizer for several different unions around Spokane. Vern was an asthmatic and we always had to consider his health. It was important for him to finish school and get at least a B.A. degree, and perhaps he could sustain a job if he became a teacher. He graduated from Eastern Washington College of Education in 1956, but I don't think he was nearly as idealistic about teaching as I was. I had decided when I was sixteen to become a teacher and I was dedicated to that.

Vern was a real social activist. He had given a great part of his life and his thought to social change. And I was interested in the same thing. A great deal of what we were all about had to do with that. We married the day before we came to Tucson in 1957. Vern had been here earlier, thinking that living here would be easier for him because of the milder winters and dry climate. The problem was that he hadn't finished his education. So he came back to Spokane and graduated with a degree in education at about the time we met. After another year in Spokane, Vern decided that winters were too difficult and that he would like to try Arizona again.

I read a lot in the paper and listened a lot during the McCarthy era, and there was something in me that just told me that was all wrong. But I didn't really understand what that meant on a personal level until Vern and I got to Tucson in 1957. We immediately became politically active in one thing and another. Vern told me something about the political climate here, because he had spent time in Tucson. As a union organizer, he was particularly concerned about the fact that unions were rather weak here; this is a right-to-work state with lots of cheap labor. We're almost a colony of some of the more industrial states like California.

One of the first things we learned here was that Arizona had no public-accommodations law, and there are a lot of minorities here. If you were black or Mexican American, you could not sit down at Woolworth's lunch counter and get a cup of coffee. There were only two places in Tucson where you could rent a motel room, and they were the most expensive places in town. A black person could rent a room at the Arizona Inn or the Ghost Ranch Lodge, but he wasn't likely to have the money to afford it.

Vern already knew some Quakers in the community, and we rented an apartment from the clerk of the Tucson Friends Meeting. So we met the people in Tucson who were socially active and very quickly got involved. There is another factor that was important for what later happened to us: Vern had gotten a teaching job in social studies at a junior high on the south side of Tucson, where the majority of students came from Spanish-speaking backgrounds.

Vern became known a bit as a troublemaker, because he was outspoken, but he got along with people fairly well. But you *did* get the impression that people either liked Vernon Elfbrandt a great deal or disliked him. The people who disliked him, I think it was their perception of what he stood for and not because they knew him. He would speak his mind no matter where he was or what the circumstances were. One aspect of his personality was that he never had a sense of hierarchy. He always met his principal or his superintendant on an equal basis; he called them both by their first name, which other teachers didn't. Vern dressed casually and acted casually. I admired that, but I never really understood where it came from.

One of Vern's colleagues was a man named Clyde Appleton, who was a music teacher and taught in the same building as Vern. They immediately became fast friends because they were both union teachers, members of the American Federation of Teachers. The Pima County teachers union was a small group of the disgruntled in those days. Clyde was one of two other teachers besides Vern and myself who refused to sign the loyalty oath.

Clyde was into folk music that had to do with social themes. He had organized a little group called the Tucson Folk Singers, who got together once a month and sang. Many of these people had been active during the McCarthy era and had been burned for one reason or another. This was a social way that many of them could get together and sing and talk about the old days, but they weren't currently active. As time went on, I would meet people who were socially active, through the Friends Service Committee, and then I would meet people at the sings who knew as much or more about social issues, but who weren't generally active.

Stories began to come out from these people, and I began to realize what the McCarthy era did, and that all these people had scars of various kinds. Many of them had lost a job. They were almost like a group of refugees. They were the most interesting and fascinating people, with lots of experiences and great ideas. But you couldn't get them to a meeting about anything in town, for two reasons. One, what had happened to them; but also their feeling that, If I show up at your meeting and get active, it's going to taint whatever you're doing.

After Vern and I had been here about a year, and had met a lot of people and become active, rumor had it that Vern and I and some others were the newest Communist cell in town. It's difficult to say where it started. It was interesting to see the shock waves in the community and how various people reacted to it. It never really bothered me that much, although perhaps it should have. There was a group of people fairly close to us who weren't impressed or affected by that. But a lot of people who knew us were really quite threatened and afraid.

I was working on a master's degree in history the first two years we were in Tucson. Vern and I had agreed that only one of us would work at a time, and we would live on one salary, and this was my opportunity to go to school. In addition to history, I took labor relations and economics and geography, and some advanced political theory. I was having a good time and didn't work very hard on finishing my thesis for the master's. The rumors did affect some people at the university. My political-science professor was a little upset by it. We had a small class with only twelve people, and he never looked my way and never called on me.

We found out some of the people who were passing the rumors around that we were Communists, and we confronted some of them. For those people who had been burned and lost jobs, or who had jobs and didn't want to lose them, it was understandable that they would be susceptible to these rumors and pass them around. We worked it out quite well, and in subsequent years some of those people were good friends.

I began teaching in the fall of 1960 at a junior high in one of the smaller districts, in the north part of Tucson. I was teaching what was called a core curriculum in social studies and English. The loyalty oath became a factor in the state legislature the next spring, in 1961. The rodeo is a big activity here, and it is customary in Tucson for the schools to be out for a couple of days for rodeo vacation in late February. Vern had made arrangements to take a bus to Phoenix with some students to see the state legislature in action, and I took three students with me in my automobile.

We were on some list that got us copies of all the bills before the state legislature every year, and we knew there were bills this year that would establish an Un-American Activities Committee in Arizona, and one about a state sedition law, and a third bill about a loyalty oath. It was quite accidental that we were there the same day the legislature debated the loyalty oath bill. There were pickets outside the House of Representatives with 'Minutemen' on their posters, and they were passing out leaflets that supported all these bills. The import of the flyers was that there were organizations that were basically Communist inspired. Some of them were the ACLU, the NAACP, the Congress of Racial Equality, and SNCC. This was at the beginning of the civil-rights movement in the South. I was concerned, because I had been active with some of those organizations. The committee and the sedition law and the oath were supposed to protect us from communism.

During this time, one of Fred Schwarz's anti-Communist crusades was going on in Phoenix, and they were having big rallies every night in one of the stadiums. This was 1961, and it's generally considered to be a little after the high point of the McCarthy era. But there was still a McCarthy atmosphere in Arizona.

One of the legislators from Tucson told us that members of the legislature, in order to get through the crowd of pickets into the chamber, would have to take an oath to support these bills. The flyers they were passing out became meaningful to me as I sat in the gallery and heard the debate on the floor.

I was disturbed by what I heard in the legislature. We were on the verge of making major changes in Arizona in civil rights, and we particularly needed a public-accommodations law. This legislation was a signal to all those people who wanted to support those changes that this was dangerous stuff to be fooling around with. I resented that. I was very active in the civil-rights movement and the peace movement. We had a lot of picketing and boycotting, and we never got a public-accommodations law until after the Civil Rights Act of 1964. We had already had a peace march in Tucson in which we supported a test-ban treaty. I immediately saw all this as very dangerous. My proof of this was all the great people I met in Tucson who were not active in anything because of the McCarthy era and their fears of being active. So I didn't see this legislation as some kind of idle threat.

The reason I was upset as I listened to the debate is that it wasn't really a debate. I learned later that those people who had spoken against the bills in the Democratic party caucus were afraid to speak on the floor, because of the atmosphere of intimidation, and because the legislation was being pushed by the chairman of the appropriations committee. There were three people in the state who had publicly opposed the loyalty oath legislation, and they were the presidents of the two state universities and the editor of *The Arizona Daily Star,* the morning paper in Tucson. The debate was really a condemnation of these three people who had *dared* to speak out against this legislation. The day I was there with my students there was not a dissenting vote against the loyalty oath on an important preliminary vote. I felt the intimidation very strongly, and I felt how dangerous this was. Both Vern and I came away from the session that day very pensive about the whole thing.

The part of the loyalty oath bill that concerned me the most was a paragraph that said, in short, that in signing the oath you were not a member of the Communist party *or* any other organization having as one of its purposes the forceful overthrow of the state of Arizona or the United States. That language I objected to.

When I taught in Spokane, I had signed the Washington state loyalty oath that was later declared unconstitutional. That oath was even more horrendous because it had the attorney general's list of 'subversive' organizations on it. That was when I was much less politically aware and hadn't had all my experiences in the civil-rights and peace movements. I did have a long talk with a teacher at Lewis and Clark that I admired, telling her all the reasons I didn't think this was legitimate. But I didn't know a soul in those days who knew about oaths at all. So I signed it. But I had learned enough in Arizona to have a basic distrust of this loyalty oath and to know that it was dangerous legislation.

After that day in the legislature, Vern and I came back to Tucson and spoke to friends, and helped to organize a group to meet and talk about our concerns that these bills would pass. We began making calls, speaking to legislators, actively lobbying against the bills. It was all kind of *ad hoc* and put together very rapidly. The House finally passed the sedition bill and the loyalty oath, and after more debate the Senate passed the bills in March of 1961 and the governor signed them the same day. The maximum penalty for perjuring the oath was a $20,000 fine or twenty years in prison.

All the teachers were asked to sign the oath within a matter of days. The school administrators wanted everyone to sign it right then so they could get them all notarized and sent off. Most people didn't read it and just signed right away. I didn't say a word. I quietly took it away and brought it home.

Vern and I continued to talk about it. He wasn't confronted with signing the oath at the time, because he was going on leave for the next year. It was his turn, now that I had a job, to go back to school. I had this extra pressure of feeling it was my job to bring in the income and here I was, considering not signing this oath. And I expected to be fired on the spot if I told them I would not sign this piece of paper to keep my job.

We had already had a meeting with a larger group of teachers and some lawyers. Well, we fought it and we lost; are we going to do anything? Nothing was decided, but one of the lawyers said that he was willing to consider taking a case. He was not saying anything about whether he thought it was a winnable case, but he thought it was something worthy of the time and effort to fight in court. This was W. Edward Morgan, who later became my lawyer. Ed had been at the original meetings when we tried to lobby against the oath, and he was part of the group around town that you met at meetings about public accommodations or peace. In those days there was no public defender in Tucson, and Ed represented most of the people in town who didn't have money, or the labor unions, or the NAACP, or whatever the good cause was.

I went to see Ed and said I had come to the conclusion that I was not going to sign the oath. I said, I don't know what that means for me or for Vern, but I think it means I have to go out and look for a job. But if you're looking for a plaintiff, I'm willing to consider it. Ed was very realistic, as I look back now. He said,

This is not a winnable case in Arizona; it's too politically hot and we're not going to get any relief here. The only place we can go for relief is the U.S. Supreme Court. Ed explained to me how few cases, one percent or less, are taken by the U.S. Supreme Court. But he felt this was a worthy case and he would like to handle it, if I wanted to do it.

We filed the suit on June 1, 1961. The first defendant was a woman named Imogene Russell, who was chair of the school board. My school district was a little shocked. Here's this new teacher, in her first year, and suddenly she's on the front page of the paper and she didn't sign a loyalty oath. A photographer ran out to the school and took my picture, and I was nervous. Reporters and newspapers always frightened me a little bit. I was never prepared for the idea that this would be front-page news. I've had the experience of driving down the street and seeing my name in a banner headline. But I never got hate mail and midnight phone-calls. At the very beginning, Ed Morgan had told a reporter that I was a Quaker. So it seemed to be viewed in Tucson as a religious thing, and we don't bother people much about their religion, even if we think it's a little strange. I was just this nice little Quaker lady.

I really expected to be fired, but school was almost out for that year and I had my contract for the next year. During the summer a deputy attorney general came down from Phoenix and met with me and Ed Morgan. I didn't know all that his conversation meant, but the import was, Are you really serious about carrying this through? He said that lawyers had gone over the oath and they didn't think we had any chance of winning. One of his arguments was, Look, Mrs. Elfbrandt, we're never going to prosecute anybody under that law. I looked at him, and I said, Who's going to say what's going to happen in this state politically ten or twenty years down the line? That's what the McCarthy era was all about.

The lawyer said something else that turned out to be significant. Do you know, Mrs. Elfbrandt, that you cannot be fired for not signing the oath? This was interesting. The way the bill was worded, if you were a new employee and refused to sign the oath, you couldn't be hired. But for a continuing employee like me, you just couldn't be paid. You could be fired for some other reason, such as incompetence, but not for refusing to sign that piece of paper.

My school district evidently made the decision to stick with me. In the flurry of being called by reporters out of the blue about this teacher you've got, they said I was a good teacher. So it was in the paper that I was a good teacher, and to announce later that a good teacher had been fired might have been difficult. But I'm sure they weren't prepared for the fact that I would be teaching at their school for the next five years without any pay, because that's what eventually happened.

There were a couple of teachers in my school who were good friends and very sympathetic and supportive. There were other people on the faculty who couldn't understand who this strange woman was, and it couldn't be any further from their experience or concern. When we sat around in the teachers' lounge, nobody spoke about the loyalty oath. The principals played everything very straight, although there was one administrator who was active in the American Legion and who resented me and the notoriety that had come to the school district because of me.

With my students, my custom was not to say anything about the case. I didn't have to. Two or three months into the semester there would be some screaming headline and the next day I'd walk into my classroom and the class would be bedlam and everybody would be asking at once, What is this? And I would quiet them down and spend one period, two periods, maybe the whole week if it took that, answering every question they had, telling them everything they wanted to know. By that time they knew me, and they knew I was a pretty ordinary teacher.

When the case first came up in Superior Court in Tucson, I never appeared. I sat in Ed Morgan's office all day, waiting to be called, while the lawyers in court stipulated to all the facts. It turned out that was a stroke of genius, because Ed had all the facts the way he wanted them. But the facts were fairly simple. There was an oath, I was a teacher, I had refused to sign this thing. So there was never a trial. We were asking for an injunction, and we were ruled against. We went right to the state Supreme Court, but we had to cool our heels for two years before the case was decided.

By that time, I had taught another year and I had a new contract. After that first year, Vern went to work part-time as an organizer for the State, County and Municipal Workers union, organizing custodians in the school district. We had a small group, called the Emergency Committee, which tried to raise funds to support us. Clyde Appleton and Jerry Dolgoff also hadn't signed, and they did not receive any pay, either.

Somehow we struggled through that year. We finally got ourselves pretty well organized, to where we could live on the money the committee raised. Our landlady contributed the rent for five years. She didn't want us to leave, so she excused the rent. That was nice but it embarrassed me a bit, the thought that we were living on charity. Our friends also got together and we had permanent invitations to dinner at least four nights a week. It was like living in a continuous party atmosphere. And these people stuck with us for five years. Ed Morgan had said at the beginning, You know, the Supreme Court is a five-year proposition, so I knew we were in for the long haul. We learned to live day-by-day.

After Vern's leave of absence was over, his school took him back, although he didn't get paid because he wouldn't sign the oath. Clyde went off to North Carolina and taught at Shaw University and sent money back to us. By prior agreement, Jerry Dolgoff stuck with us through the state supreme court and then decided to sign and support us by having an income.

We were turned down by the state supreme court in 1963. It was a 5-to-0 vote against us. A reporter called me at school for a comment, and he couldn't understand why I seemed so happy! But we had waited around for two years, and now we could go to the U.S. Supreme Court. Ed Morgan was correct: There was no remedy here in Arizona. So we filed our petition for certiorari with the U.S. Supreme Court. They sent us back to the state supreme court, and asked them to reconsider in light of the Washington case, Baggett v. Bullitt, which had thrown out the more horrendous loyalty oath that I had once signed. So we submitted briefs and we argued it all over again. We got one vote the second time around, and then we went back to the U.S. Supreme Court.

Some people generously donated money so that Vern and I could go to Washington for the argument, which was in February 1966. I had never been in the Supreme Court, and we sat through some other arguments to get a feel of what the Court was about. They don't make any special arrangements for plaintiffs, and in order to get a seat you have to be there early. One of the interesting interchanges during the argument was in reaction to a remark by the state's lawyer that the law had some relationship to those Wobblies in the Arizona hills. This went back fifty years to the copper strikers at Bisbee, who had been put on a train and dumped in the desert. Abe Fortas was on the Court and he just could not let that go by. He leaned down over the bench and peered at the state's lawyer and wanted to know more about these Wobblies in the hills. Justice Black wanted to know if the state of Arizona was in any imminent danger of being overthrown by the Wobblies. I'm sure the lawyer was sorry he said anything about Wobblies. So there were some light moments during the argument.

This was a 5-to-4 decision when it came down, so it was a very close case, even in the Warren Court. We could easily have lost it. The day the case was decided, the administrator who belonged to the American Legion called all the students together and told them there had been some strange decisions from the Supreme Court. I'm sure they didn't know what he meant, but I knew what he meant!

During this whole loyalty oath case, I never thought of doing anything else than teaching for the rest of my life. But after teaching another year, and learning that I would probably never get another social-studies position and would be stuck in English, I decided to leave teaching and went to the university in community development work. The courses were interesting, but I already knew how to work with minority people. I was a social activist, and I had all this experience with the AFSC.

So I took a bunch of vocational preference tests. It was like starting over! I was going to wipe the slate clean. I remember being depressed for two weeks when it turned out that what I wanted *most* in life was to be a social-studies teacher! But the next profession I tested high in was law. This was the first time the possibility of law had ever struck me. And it didn't have much to do with my case. Vern and I hashed it out and decided that's what I would do. When I told Ed Morgan, his reaction was real shock! I had never talked to him about it. He just stared at me, and sputtered a bit, and spent a few minutes trying to talk me out of it. Then he said, Be down here at 9 A.M. on Monday morning. And I worked for him from then on, all the way through law school, and practiced in his office for nine years.

My idea was to be helpful to community groups, and I could be useful if I had a skill. I went to law school feeling that law would be part of a bag of tricks in community development. When I was practicing law, it didn't make any difference what I was doing, I always ended up doing community organizing, just as Vern was doing in his own way. That's what our life together was about, and that's what I still consider I *am* about.

I helped to organize the AFSC office here about nine years ago, and I decided to apply for the job as director because I always ended up doing that kind of work, and it's nice to get paid for what you want to do. I still pay my bar dues, and just last night I was getting out a pleading. It's not part of my job description, but it's a tremendous advantage to be a member of the bar and have that license and have that *in* with the legal community. I have made use of that a great deal in my community organizing work.

Would I do it again? I think I would. I was lucky to have the right issue at the right time in the right place. There is a real possibility that if I took the same case back to the Supreme Court in this political setting I would *lose* that case. After all, it was only won by one vote in the Warren years.

I have talked with other people who have been through what you might call ordeals like mine. Unlike them, mine turned out not to be an ordeal. For all your intellectual ideals that you're getting a chance to live out, you really need a lot of emotional support. I got a lot of support, not only from the Friends Meeting but from the group of people who stood by us for a long time.

And the loyalty oath case was not the most important thing in my life at that time. I think that's important. I've known people for whom a case has become an obsession. For me, life went on every day. I could go for weeks without thinking about the case. And that helped me to keep a perspective. It was a very busy time in my life. I had to get up and go to school. Yeah, I was different because I didn't get paid. But I learned that I didn't go to school because I got paid. For me, the case was a real lesson in who I was and what my life was about.

9

Susan Epperson
v. Arkansas

Susan Epperson taught high-school biology
in Little Rock, Arkansas, when she challenged
in 1965 the state "Scopes" law that barred
the teaching of human evolution. *Courtesy of
the* Arkansas Gazette, © *1988*

I.
"Somewhere in Heaven, John Scopes Is Smiling"

"Teacher at Central High Challenges Constitutionality of Evolution Law." This front-page headline jolted readers of *The Arkansas Gazette* on December 7, 1965. During the previous decade, Little Rock's prestigious Central High School had dominated headlines in Arkansas and the nation during the pitched battles, in both courts and streets, over school integration. After two years of turmoil, quiet returned to Central High in 1959 as the school admitted a token number of black students.

On the surface, this new headline about Central High had nothing to do with racial integration. But the evolution controversy tapped the deep roots of Southern racism: Those who called black people "monkeys" recoiled at the notion that humans had evolved from apes. And for those Fundamentalists who mixed racism with religion, the Genesis account of creation allowed a separate origin for blacks and whites. Not all opponents of evolution also fought school integration, but the groups had considerable overlap in the South. For many in the Bible Belt, banning evolution from the schools was part of the crusade to protect the "Southern Way of Life" from "atheists" and "race mixers," equally evil in Dixie demonology.

The *Gazette* headline framed a picture of Susan Epperson, the Central High teacher whose lawsuit challenged an Arkansas law enacted in 1928 which imposed criminal penalties for teaching that "mankind ascended or descended from a lower order of animals." The 24-year-old biology teacher hardly fit the image of the Yankee carpetbagger, intent on imposing a new Reconstruction on the old South. The *Gazette* reported that Susan Epperson was a graduate of The College of the Ozarks in Clarksville, Arkansas, where her father, Dr. T.L. Smith, had taught biology since 1919. The story quoted Susan as saying that her parents "both are dedicated Christians who see no conflict between their belief in God and the scientific search for truth. I share this belief." Susan held a master's degree from the University of Illinois, the article noted, and was "married to First Lt. Jon O. Epperson, who is a member of a missile crew stationed at the Little Rock Air Force Base."

The newspaper picture of the smiling young teacher may have disarmed some Arkansas residents who in the Sputnik era considered the law against teaching evolution an embarrassing anachronism. Science became king of the curriculum in American high schools as the nation scrambled to catch the Soviets in space. Biology as well as physics and math prospered in the new pedagogy, and high-school textbooks discarded the caution of past decades and returned Charles Darwin and his theory of natural selection to its central place in human evolution. Susan Epperson, who began her second year of teaching at Central High in 1965, had selected a brand-new edition of an old textbook, *Modern Biology* by James Otto and Albert Towle, for her tenth-grade students. Evolution had vanished from this text in 1926, but the new edition stated that evidence of "changes in plants and animals" over time indicated that humans and apes "may have had a common, generalized ancestor in the remote past." Cautious and qualified, this statement still clashed with the Arkansas law and confronted Susan Epperson with the risks of firing and fines.

Susan told the sympathetic *Gazette* reporter that Forrest Rozzell, director of the Arkansas Education Association, had asked her to bring the suit; she had agreed "because of my concept of my responsibilities both as a teacher of biology and as an American citizen." Susan's careful selection as a test-case plaintiff emerged between the story's lines. Rozzell had in fact planned his attack on the Arkansas law for several months. The first step began with a move by State Representative Nathan Schoenfeld, a member of the state's small Jewish community, to repeal the 1928 statute.

Introduced in January 1965, Schoenfeld's bill prompted the liberal *Gazette* to praise his effort at "rectifying the ancient error." But it never reached a vote.

Rozzell decided that a legal attack on the law was more likely to succeed than legislative action, and he consulted Eugene R. Warren, counsel to the teacher's association. The two men then approached Arch Ford, the state's Commissioner of Education, who issued a supportive statement that "the law was a dead issue and there was no reason for keeping it on the statute books." Opposition quickly emerged from Ford's superior, Governor Orval Faubus, who had ringed Central High with armed troops in 1957 to keep out black students. Faubus now wanted to keep out evolution, and he supported the law "as a safeguard to keep way-out teachers in line." With the lines drawn, Rozzell and Warren began searching for a plaintiff, and approached Virginia Minor, a Central High teacher who was active in the AEA and also headed the Little Rock chapter of the American Association of University Women. She immediately identified Susan Epperson as a perfect plaintiff; a church-going Arkansas native with a husband in Air Force blue.

Rozzell worked on organizing public support for the case while Warren drafted a legal complaint. Filed in Pulaski County Chancery Court on December 6, 1965, the suit claimed that the ban on teaching evolution violated two clauses of the First Amendment, those that protected free speech and barred any "establishment of religion" by government. Warren also charged the law with impeding the "free communication of thoughts and opinions" that the Arkansas constitution protected. The suit, seeking an injunction against the law's enforcement, was assigned to Chancellor Murray O. Reed for hearing and decision without a jury.

The crusade against teaching evolution in public schools began some fifty years after the publication in 1859 of Darwin's seminal book *The Origin of Species*. Before the twentieth century, only a handful of American youngsters, most from affluent families, attended public high schools, and evolution was the reigning orthodoxy in biology. The new century brought with it a rapid expansion of public school education; the number of high schools doubled in the first decade. This period also saw rapid growth in cities, factories, and immigration from Southern and Eastern Europe. The new Americans were mostly Jews and Catholics. Leaders of the mainstream churches adapted to change and welcomed Darwin's theory to the Social Gospel movement, which preached an "onward and upward" brand of theology.

Protestant, conservative, rural America viewed these social changes with suspicion, and denounced the Social Gospel as heresy. Evangelical leaders responded between 1909 and 1912 with "The Fundamentals," a pamphlet series which proclaimed biblical literalism as the antidote to "modernism." Few of the Fundamentalists, as they soon called themselves, were Bible-thumping bookburners; many joined Progressive campaigns against child labor and sweatshops, seen as the evil spawn of secular greed. The two religious camps agreed on many social reforms but parted ways over evolution, which Fundamentalists could not square with the Genesis account of creation. The issue quickly moved from pamphlets to pulpits and then to political rallies.

The Progressive era died in World War I, and the Social Gospel was badly wounded in the postwar Red Scare. Fundamentalists took the offensive in midwestern and southern states and made evolution a leading target of legislative restriction. Between 1920 and 1926, eight southern states barred the teaching of evolution in public schools, and local school boards in many other states told their teachers not to present Darwin's theory to students. The growing movement gained a leader in William Jennings Bryan, three-time Democratic presidential candidate and a spellbinding orator. "All the ills from which America suffers can be traced back to the teaching of evolution," Bryan thundered in 1924. "It would be better to destroy every other book ever written, and just save the first three verses of Genesis."

Tennessee became the battleground for the first courtroom war over evolution. Bryan's support had prompted the passage in March 1925 of the first state law against teaching evolution. Several weeks later, the American Civil Liberties Union placed an ad in a Chattanooga newspaper: "We are looking for a Tennessee teacher who is willing to accept our services in testing this law in the courts." John T. Scopes, a 24-year-old biology teacher in rural Dayton, volunteered as a test-case plaintiff and wired the ACLU for help. Meeting the same day in Memphis, the World's

Christian Fundamentals Association denounced "the teaching of the unscientific, anti-Christian, atheistic, anarchistic, pagan rationalistic evolutionary theory," and delegates voted to ask Bryan to prosecute Scopes for the Dayton school board. Vowing to wage "a battle royal between the Christian people of Tennessee and the so-called scientists," Bryan agreed and the board hired him without salary.

The "Monkey Trial" in Dayton pitted Bryan against Clarence Darrow, the legendary lawyer for underdogs. Conducted in a carnival atmosphere for two humid weeks, the trial ended with the anticlimax of Scopes' conviction. The main act was Bryan's duel on the witness stand—as an expert on the Bible—with Darrow, who jumped his opponent through the hoops of biblical literalism until he collapsed. Those who followed the trial, broadcast by radio and covered by the press like summer sweat, either grinned or winced at Bryan's humiliation by the master of cross-examination. Two weeks later, Bryan collapsed and died of a heart attack. The loss of its leader slowed the crusade against evolution to a crawl. And the Tennessee Supreme Court reversed Scopes' conviction on a technicality, preventing the U.S. Supreme Court from reviewing the case.

Following the Dayton debacle, only two southern states—Arkansas and Mississippi—enacted laws against evolution. The Arkansas legislature declined in 1927 to pass a bill which Fundamentalists pushed; mainstream church leaders opposed the bill at the cost of vilification and heresy trials. The bill's main sponsor then gathered enough signatures to place the measure on the statewide ballot in 1928. Civic and academic leaders, including a former governor, leading ministers, and the presidents of the University of Arkansas and other colleges, pleaded with voters to protect "our schools from foolish and futile legislation and the good name of our state from ridicule." Supporters of Act No. 1 countered with an effective newspaper ad, titled "The Bible or Atheism, Which?" The choice was simple: "If you agree with atheism, vote against Act No. 1. If you agree with the Bible, vote for Act No. 1." Atheists were scarce in Arkansas, and voters approved the law by a 63 percent margin.

After this final electoral victory, the crusade against evolution lost its zeal and became dormant for three decades. The economic collapse of 1929 and the Great Depression took people's minds off the issue, and southern support of Franklin Roosevelt's liberal New Deal blunted the Fundamentalist movement. But in fact the evolutionists had retreated in the face of public hostility; timid textbook editors snipped out any mention of Darwin, and fearful high-school biology teachers avoided conflict with parents and school boards. Only after the Cold War eased and the Science War began did another biology teacher dare to risk the legal defeat that John Scopes had suffered.

Thirty years separated the Scopes trial and the hearing on Susan Epperson's case, but light-years separated their atmosphere. The first dragged on for two weeks; the second was briskly halted after two hours on April 1, 1966. Witnesses paraded to the stand in Dayton to declaim on religion and biology; Judge Murray O. Reed in Little Rock barred testimony on either topic, limiting the case to constitutional issues. Unlike Clarence Darrow, whose questions were sharp as rapiers, Eugene Warren gently examined Susan for just ten minutes and hardly questioned the state's four witnesses, all of them school officials. Susan's testimony was directed to just one point: "I brought this law suit because I have a text book which includes the theory about the origin or the descent or the ascent of man from a lower form of animals. This seemed to be a widely accepted theory and I feel it is my responsibility to acquaint my students with it."

The most striking contrast between Dayton and Little Rock was that Arkansas Attorney General Bruce Bennett, who defended the state law, was no William Jennings Bryan. Bennett took personal charge of the Epperson trial, as he had in the 1957 trial of Daisy Bates for refusing to give Bennett the NAACP's membership list. Although he swaggered into court with Bryan's bombast and braggadocio, Bennett was cut down by Warren's objections when he tried to put evolution on trial. Judge Reed sustained every one of Warren's objections. Bennett was so poorly prepared, so obviously ignorant of science, that the audience frequently tittered. "This is a serious matter," Judge Reed admonished. "The only question here is a constitutional question of law and it is a serious one." Bennett left the courtroom in a pique, his play to the galleries frustrated.

Judge Reed did not reject "Creation" in his written opinion, issued two months later, but he rejected the law against teaching evolution: "This Court is of the opinion that a chapter in a biology book, adopted by the school administrative authorities, stating that a specific theory has been advanced by an individual that man ascended or descended from a lower form of animal life, does not constitute such a hazard to the safety, health and morals of the community that the constitutional freedoms may justifiably be suppressed by the state." Two decades of Supreme Court opinions which raised the "wall of separation" between church and school convinced Reed that "the unconstitutionality of the statute under consideration is not subject to doubt."

Attorney General Bennett's appeal of this ruling went to the Arkansas Supreme Court without oral argument; the justices and both lawyers saw the court as a quick whistle stop on the road to Washington, D.C. The court's opinion, issued on June 5, 1967, set a two-sentence record for brevity. The first sentence ruled that the state law "is a valid exercise of the state's power to specify the curriculum in its public schools." No precedent was cited, no issues discussed. The second sentence left lawyers and judges scratching their heads in puzzlement. "The court expresses no opinion on the question whether the Act prohibits any explanation of the theory of evolution or merely prohibits teaching that the theory is true," the judges wrote. Whether Susan Epperson could assign chapter 39 of *Modern Biology* to her students was a question the justices left unanswered.

The U.S. Supreme Court heard arguments in the case more than a year later, on October 16, 1968. Eugene Warren was so confident of victory that he used only ten minutes of the half-hour allotted to him, and did not even discuss the free-speech and establishment-of-religion issues that his brief addressed. Warren aimed his fire at the law's vagueness, citing the Arkansas Supreme Court opinion as evidence. Both the law and the opinion left Arkansas teachers "genuinely confused and concerned" about what and how they could teach, Warren said. The consequence of "a lot of uncertainty and a lot of fright" was that "biology is not even taught" in many Arkansas schools, he added.

Attorney General Bennett did not make the state's argument, because the state's voters had sent him back to private practice in the 1966 election. Don Langston, a young assistant to the new attorney general, displayed an obvious distaste for his task and spent only a few more minutes than Warren at the podium. He blamed Bennett and the Arkansas Supreme Court for his plight, complaining that the state justices failed to provide any reasoning for their opinion. Langston only smiled when Justice Thurgood Marshall asked whether, since the state court disposed of the case in two sentences, he would "object to us disposing of that in one sentence?" After Langston defended the law as a "neutrality act" which equally proscribed Darwin's and "opposing theories" of human origins, he was forced to admit that the law did not prohibit "the literal reading of Genesis" in biology classes. His argument in tatters, Langston abruptly sat down.

The question at the Court's conference, two days later, was not whether to strike down the law but what grounds to use. Chief Justice Earl Warren agreed with Eugene Warren that "the Act is too vague to stand." Hugo Black and William O. Douglas agreed. "I don't think establishment of religion is really in the case," Douglas stated. Potter Stewart said the law "prohibits freedom of speech" by teachers. The remaining five justices felt the law violated the First Amendment's "establishment of religion" clause; Don Langston had virtually conceded this point at oral argument. Justice Abe Fortas, one of the majority on this issue, volunteered to write the Court's opinion. Fortas had vivid memories of the Scopes trial, which he followed as a fifteen-year-old Jewish boy in Memphis, Tennessee. He had always admired John Scopes, and felt that striking down the Arkansas law would also erase the blot on Tennessee's history.

Fortas began his opinion, issued on November 12, 1968, by noting "the celebrated Scopes case" and linking both the Tennessee and Arkansas laws against evolution to "the upsurge of 'fundamentalist' fervor of the twenties." The opinion dripped with scorn for those who banned a scientific theory from schools because it conflicted with their "fundamentalist sectarian conviction" that evolution was un-Christian. Fortas bowed to the power of state and local school boards to shape curriculum, but limited that power in areas that "directly and sharply implicate basic constitutional values." Arkansas could not "prevent its teachers from discussing the theory of evolution because it is contrary to the belief of some that the Book of Genesis must be the exclusive source of doctrine as to the origins of man." Referring in his conclusion to "the sensational publicity attendant upon the Scopes trial," Fortas left no doubt that he, a Jew from Tennessee, had answered Bryan's claim to represent "the Christian people of Tennessee" against "the so-called scientists." John Scopes and Susan Epperson, both scientists and both teachers, both won in the opinion that Fortas wrote.

Acclaim for the Court's opinion in the press was virtually unanimous, but one person refused to dance on Bryan's grave. John T. Scopes, living in retirement in Shreveport, Louisiana, sounded a note of caution. "The fight will go on with other actors and other plays," he said. "You don't protect any of your individual liberties by lying down and going to sleep." Savoring victory and disregarding Scopes, evolutionists spent the next decade in slumber. But their opponents burned the midnight oil, devising new legal and legislative strategies which sought to return the Bible to biology. In 1978, a Yale Law School student and fervent creationist, Wendell Bird, published a lengthy student note in *The Yale Law Journal*, "Freedom of Religion and Science Instruction in Public Schools." Bird built his "equal time" case for "scientific creationism" in schools on Supreme Court decisions which recognized the rights of religious minorities like Jehovah's Witnesses and the Amish to practice their beliefs without state interference. The student who rejected evolution, Bird argued, was little different from the Gobitis children who rejected the flag-salute ceremony on religious grounds or the Yoder children who rejected compulsory education after the eighth grade.

Bird's article impressed leaders of the Institute for Creation Research and Creation Science Research Center, separate but sympathetic groups based near San Diego, California. Fueled by the national growth of the Religious Right in the 1970s, which demanded that prayer be returned to schools and abortion banned, the creationist movement took new aim at evolution. After his graduation from Yale, Bird joined the Institute for Creation Research and drafted "equal time" laws which sought an end-run around the Epperson decision. Beginning in 1980, the creationist effort gained support from an increasingly conservative public. Ronald Reagan, who had encouraged the creationists as California's governor, stated during his successful presidential campaign that he had "a great many questions" about evolution. A national opinion poll in 1981 revealed that 76 percent of the public favored "equal time" for evolution and creationism in the schools. The same year, the legislatures of Arkansas and Louisiana adopted the "equal time" laws that Bird had drafted.

The American Civil Liberties Union immediately challenged the Arkansas law. Rather than biology teachers like John Scopes and Susan Epperson, the ACLU recruited Little Rock ministers as plaintiffs, led by Rev. Bill McLean and including Methodist, Episcopal, Catholic, and Presbyterian pastors. Lawyers from a powerhouse New York firm (Skadden, Arps) joined as volunteer counsel and overwhelmed the Arkansas attorney general in resources. Judge William R. Overton, placed on the Arkansas federal bench by President Jimmy Carter, differed from Judge Reed in the Epperson case by allowing both sides to present a parade of expert witnesses on religion and biology.

Stephen Jay Gould of Harvard, the nation's leading evolutionary theorist, testified for the ACLU and defended natural selection as a "fact" and not simply speculation. Although he rejected Wendell Bird's offer to participate as Bryan had done in Tennessee, Arkansas Attorney General Steve Clark based his defense on Bird's outline. But Clark could not find any credible scientists who accepted creationist arguments, or creationists with scientific credentials. He wound up with witnesses who testified that they believed life on Earth began from "cometary seeding," and biblical literalists who denied that contrary evidence could shake their beliefs. Bird and other creationists, including TV evangelists Pat Robertson and Jerry Falwell, responded by denouncing Clark as an ACLU stooge.

Judge Overton expanded on Justice Fortas' opinion in throwing out the new Arkansas law in January 1982. Citing the Epperson opinion, he wrote that "Arkansas, like a number of states whose citizens have relatively homogeneous religious beliefs, has a long history of official opposition to evolution which is motivated by adherence to Fundamentalist beliefs in the inerrancy of the Book of Genesis." Overton relied on testimony by Stephen Jay Gould and other scientists in sending "creation science" to perdition. The view of human origins based on Genesis "has no scientific factual basis or legitimate education purpose," Overton concluded.

Attorney General Clark, who spent almost a half-million dollars defending the law, cut his losses and declined to appeal the decision.

Only the Louisiana "equal time" law remained on the books after this creationist defeat. The courts moved slowly, and the Supreme Court did not rule until June 1987 on the case brought by Donald Aguillard, a high-school biology teacher in LaFayette. Writing for a 7–2 majority, Justice William Brennan struck down the statute on Establishment Clause grounds: "The preeminant purpose of the Louisiana legislature was clearly to advance the religious viewpoint that a supernatural being created humankind," Brennan wrote.

For the first time, however, creationists found allies on the Supreme Court. Speaking for himself and Chief Justice William Rehnquist, Justice Antonin Scalia wrote that "Christian fundamentalists" were entitled "to have whatever scientific evidence there may be against evolution presented in their schools, just as Mr. Scopes was entitled to present whatever scientific evidence there was for it." Scalia then referred to "ample uncontradicted testimony that 'creation science' is a body of scientific knowledge rather than revealed belief." But he did not cite any such testimony, and ignored the brief presented by seventy-two Nobel laureates who argued that "creationism is not based on scientific research" and failed to meet basic tests of evidence.

Responses to the Supreme Court decision reflected the sharp divisions that remained after sixty years of conflict between creationists and evolutionists. Wendell Bird expressed optimism that the Supreme Court would someday reverse itself. "With four justices approaching age 80, the Court won't stay the same forever," he predicted. Ira Glasser, the ACLU's executive director, savored his group's ultimate victory: "Somewhere in heaven, John Scopes is smiling."

II.
"Teaching in the Bible Belt"

I was born in 1941 in Little Rock, Arkansas. My parents lived in Clarksville, Arkansas, near the Ozark mountains, about a hundred miles west of Little Rock. My dad was a biology professor at a small Presbyterian college, The College of the Ozarks. I spent my entire childhood in Clarksville, which, compared to my married life traveling a lot, is a completely different thing.

My father was born in Alabama in 1890, so he was in his fifties when I was born. He was in the First World War; and after the war he went back to Wooster College in Ohio, where he had received his bachelor's degree, to see about job possibilities. They said, There's a small Presbyterian college in Arkansas that needs a biology teacher, and so he went down. The school was very small, not many facilities, but he ended up being there fifty years, with times off to go back for further degrees.

Fairly early on, Daddy wanted to be a missionary. He just felt he wanted to do something in the way of the Lord's work. He wanted to be a doctor, he was interested in science, but that didn't work out—I don't know if he didn't make it into medical school, or the war came along. But he looked at his teaching at The College of the Ozarks as a mission. Many of the students who went there did not have much money for a college education. Most of them were from the Ozarks, but they also have students from all over the world. One of the efforts of the school is to provide a college education for local young people, and he felt very devoted to that and really gave his life to it.

So, early on, I had the inspiration of service, of working for other people and not for money. Certainly my dad was never a wealthy man by any means, and that was just not important to him, and it wasn't important to my mother. And by-and-large it's not important to me. I'm sure it's because of them, and I'm glad. Daddy took time off from teaching for graduate work. He went to the University of Chicago for a master's, and later to Columbia University for a doctorate.

My parents were at first not able to have children, and so they adopted my brother, David, in 1939 as an infant. Then a couple of years later mother got pregnant and I came along. About the time I was born, when my brother was about two, they discovered he had muscular dystrophy. David lived until he was a junior in college. He was a wonderful brother, and you learn many lessons when you live in a situation like that.

I grew up right across the street from the college chapel. My mother still lives in the same house. I have wonderful memories of going over in the late afternoons to the science building where my dad taught. Classes would be over, it would be about time for him to come home, so I would go over and meet him. And usually the janitor would be buffing the floors to a high shine, and the late-afternoon sun would be hitting that newly waxed, shiny floor, and I would smell the wax. It's amazing how those things stick with you. I'd walk into the lab and there was the big swordfish snout and skeletons and specimens on the shelves, and beautiful rocks in the rock collection. I really have lots of nice memories of the science lab.

I think my going into science was sort of predisposition, because of being so crazy about my dad. He was the kind of teacher who was fascinated with what he was doing. A lot of students came to the college with a business major, or history major, in mind, and ended up majoring in biology, because they had courses with my dad. By the time I got to college in 1958, he'd been teaching there for forty years and he was still just as excited about what he was doing, which is wonderful.

I went to The College of the Ozarks, right there at home. Because my math test scores were very good, it seemed that mathematics was what I should major in, so I began with that. The mathematics didn't work out, and then I considered English. I still enjoy English, I still entertain thoughts of going back and getting a master's degree in English for the pure fun of it, because I like to read and I like literature. But the more I took courses in biology, which I enjoyed, and talked with my folks about what to major in, I decided to major in biology.

Taking courses from my dad was interesting. He'd been teaching for so many years that it was just second nature to him, and there was no difficulty adjusting to having a daughter in class. I remember wondering, Should I call him Daddy or Prof? A lot of students called him Prof—after many years at a place, things like that come along and stick, and he didn't mind it at all. But when I had occasion to call him by name, I would just say Daddy.

Like everyone else, I found him a fascinating teacher, and I loved his courses. I had him for my freshman general-science class, which had some biology and some botany. I also had him later on for a geology course. We went on some interesting field trips—there are some interesting caves around Arkansas that we visited, and there's some interesting uplift in the Ozark mountains, and we studied that.

I had a histology course from him, the study of tissues of the body; and an embryology course, which was very interesting. We grew chick embryos and made slides. Being at a school without a lot of excess money, he had learned to improvise. To make slides of these chick embryos we had to embed them in wax and then slice them very thin with a fine instrument so you get cross sections of what you're going to look at. He had devised a method of taking heavy paper and folding these tiny little boxes. Then we melted wax and filled them half full and put in the embryos and then more wax. When I see the money that is spent in some school labs, I'm appalled—to me, some of it's a waste. Maybe what we did took more time, but it wasn't much more.

Evolution was certainly dealt with in our courses. Because of where he was teaching, in the Bible Belt, Daddy often referred to 'progressive change' rather than using the word evolution, since the word can get people excited. Yet he certainly talked about evolution, about change, and the evidence in the rocks. By the time I came along, he had received a doctorate from Columbia University and he did drosophila research with Theodosius Dobzhansky. Because of an accident with his fruit-fly stock, Daddy wound up doing his dissertation on a species of moth, and he was invited to an international genetics congress in Edinburgh to give a paper based on his dissertation. That was his and my mother's one trip to Europe.

I think when you have studied with people like Dobzhansky and others, and when you see the kind of thing you can do with insects in just a few generations, the kind of genetic changes that occur, you understand the mechanisms of evolution better, although it's extended over a much greater length of time. So the idea of accepting it is not difficult. I was raised with the idea that you could certainly be a Christian, which both of my parents were, and still accept the evidence for evolution that we see in the rocks. It's not just the rocks—there's a lot of biochemical evidence and serological evidence—and it's just not a problem. It never has been for me.

I received my bachelor's degree in 1962 and went away that next fall to graduate school at the University of Illinois in Champaign-Urbana. I lived there for two years and got my masters in zoology. I worked half-time during those two years, in a mosquito genetics lab where they were studying DDT resistance in various strains of mosquitos—which is another evidence for the kinds of changes that can bring about evolutionary change.

Teaching was always an option for me, something I wanted to consider. Of course, with my dad being a teacher, that was certainly an inspiration, the fact that he seemed to enjoy it so much. My mother was also a teacher, being a high-school librarian for ten years. And as I grew up, I taught Sunday school and was involved in teaching that way. My graduate professor at Illinois encouraged me to go ahead for a doctorate, and my parents would have supported me.

But I had already met Jon, who's now my husband, at that time. In fact, I met him in the summertime right after I graduated from college. He had come to Little Rock with the Air Force, and we met and liked each other a lot. I'm sure that's a question a lot of women face: Do I move ahead in this career or profession, or do I marry? I knew I wanted a home and children, and I can remember walking back from the lab at Illinois to the house where I was living, and going by houses and seeing the warm light shining out through the windows. I used to think, I'd really like a home, and sooner or later do more grad work. Jon has always encouraged me to go on, if I wanted to do anything like that.

Jon's being at Little Rock Air Force Base had a good deal to do with the places I applied for teaching jobs. Of course, Arkansas was home, too. I applied a few places in Arkansas, including Little Rock Central; went down and interviewed, and got the job. I was teaching tenth-grade biology, with a straight schedule of biology classes. I feel very fortunate to have taught at that school, and for that to have been my first teaching experience. It was a very rewarding, enjoyable experience. This was after all of the integration problems. Still, at that time—I went there in '64—we only had token integration. In most of my classes there would be maybe four or five black kids. But it was moving in that direction.

When I started teaching at Central, I knew there was some kind of evolution law in Arkansas. I hadn't really heard it talked about a whole lot, but I knew there was some kind of restriction on teaching evolution. There had been some articles in *The Arkansas Gazette,* in Little Rock, about 'Let's get rid of this old law, there's a problem here.' And there were letters back and forth—people who were very much opposed to trying to get rid of it, and others who thought that it was old and antiquated and being ignored, and should be taken off the books. So there was already some controversy. I also knew the law was disregarded by-and-large. Certainly the courses at the University of Arkansas would teach evolution concepts, in contradiction to the law. So it was sort of in the back of my mind.

In the fall of my second year at Central, in 1965, Mrs. Virginia Minor came to see me one afternoon. She was a fellow teacher and a friend; she taught home economics and ran the kindergarten program at Central. Mrs. Minor told me that the Arkansas Education Association was considering a lawsuit to try to have the evolution law declared unconstitutional. She asked me, Do you think you'd be interested?

I was terrified at the prospect. But I thought, Well, it sounds interesting. I told my husband about it, and he really got excited. He said, Oh, go and talk to them! They had to have a teacher who was under threat of the law. The executive secretary of the AEA, a man named Mr. Forrest Rozzell, had gone to The College of the Ozarks and had science under my dad, and he knew my folks quite well. He knew a good bit about my background: He knew I had a Christian background, he knew I was a native of the state. Those things were good, to have a plaintiff be in that situation, to avoid criticism about outside agitators. Of course, there would be criticism anyway!

I agreed to talk with Mr. Rozzell and Mrs. Minor and the lawyer for the AEA, Mr. Eugene Warren, who was a super fellow, a marvelous lawyer. One afternoon that fall we met after school in Mrs. Minor's kindergarten room, and we sat in little, tiny chairs at little, tiny tables. It was sort of funny. Mr. Warren had prepared a five-page complaint to file in court. All of it, the idea of courts and lawsuits, was really foreign to me. I wasn't familiar with the process at all. But he was very good, and explained the case to me and told me how it compared with the Scopes case. Scopes supposedly taught evolution in Tennessee, where they had a similar law, and he was arrested and taken to court and had that famous trial in the 1920s. They were hoping to get his case to the Supreme Court, but it was thrown out on a technicality in the lower court, so they couldn't carry it further.

As I read the complaint, even though I hadn't carefully thought about the law, it expressed very clearly the kind of things that I really did think, when it was actually put into words. One, that the law was being disregarded. So in that sense, a message was being sent to students that if you don't like a law, then just go ahead and break it. Which, of course, is civil disobedience, a wonderful thing that we can do in America; but I also thought that maybe that wasn't the best way to try to handle it. I felt very strongly, and still do, that a teacher is someone who should set an example and *be* an example to students. So this presented a dilemma.

The other dilemma was, I'm a science teacher and if you've studied some science, and the more you study, you understand that evolution is a very unifying principle in the understanding of all kinds of biology. To leave it out, to not be able to say anything about it, is really shortchanging your students, not giving them the full picture. And also not giving them something that helps to tie the whole discipline together. So there was this dilemma—do I not teach this, which I feel is important to teach? This dilemma was presented in the complaint that Mr. Warren showed me. It really expressed what I thought about the situation. Another concern was just how backward it made Arkansas look to have a law like this on the books.

I went home from this meeting and talked about it with my

husband, with the thought of not getting involved if he weren't behind me, but he certainly was. My only real reason for not doing it, since ideologically I agreed with what they were trying to do, was just that I was afraid. Afraid there would be people who would hate me, and people who would say nasty things, people who would say that I wasn't a Christian. But I decided that that wasn't sufficient reason to say no.

I was assured in that first meeting in Mrs. Minor's office that this is just going to be a plain constitutional matter; the judges are going to settle it in chambers; it's never going to go to court; we're going to avoid the kind of hubbub that surrounded the Scopes trial; you probably won't have to testify. It sounded real easygoing. Little did I know! So I said yes.

Mr. Warren told me the day he'd go down to the courthouse to file the complaint and said it would probably be in the morning paper. All these interesting things you learn along the way! Reporters go every day to the courthouse to see what kind of suits have been filed, so you knew that would get into the paper. Somewhere they got ahold of a picture of me, and that was on the front page of the *Gazette* the next day, with an article, 'Teacher Challenges Evolution Law.'

I hadn't consulted with my principal or anybody about this. I do believe we as American citizens have the right to file a suit like this. We're really blessed in America. But I thought I should at least let the principal know what we were doing. I wanted him to be slightly forewarned, so I went to his office after school the day before I knew Mr. Warren would be filing the suit, and I had a copy of the complaint with me. He was a very, very nice man, named Harry Carter, just a wonderful fellow.

I said, I have some news that may not make you very happy. And he said, You're leaving! Which was kind of nice to hear, that that might be bad news. I said, No, not yet. I knew that we'd probably be moving the next summer. I said, I've taken part in a lawsuit and I wanted you to hear about it. I handed him the complaint and he read it, and then he said, Good, it's about time this was done; I admire you for getting involved. If you have any difficulty with anyone here in the building, just let me know. I was *so* relieved! He was so supportive, it was wonderful. A couple of people in the building said things, but nothing really big.

The next day it was in the paper, and several of my students came and waved the clipping. Oh, Mrs. Epperson, look! Your picture's in the paper! Are you for it or against it? I thought, That's typical—they see the picture but they don't read the article to find out what's happening. I spent a little time in each class that day, briefly telling them what we were doing and how I was involved.

Every once in a while after that, I'd meet with Mr. Warren and he'd tell me what was happening. I really was not involved a lot in the mechanics of it. The AEA was handling it—their lawyer was handling the legal aspects—and I was very involved with teaching, which is a very full-time job. At some point, they said that the state attorney general, Mr. Bruce Bennett, who was also running for reelection that year, wanted to go to court. Of course, he wanted to call a bunch of ministers and really make a lot of hay out of it. He wanted it to be another Scopes trial, to go on a long time and be sensational. We really didn't want that. I was assured from the very beginning that every effort would be made to keep it respectable. That was one of my fears about getting involved. I didn't want to get involved in some kind of fiasco.

But they told me that the attorney general has made it such that we *have* to go to court, and you'll *have* to testify. Oh, panic! We went to court the first of April, and a lot of people joked about April Fools Day. The case was tried in the chancery court in Little Rock, before Judge Murray O. Reed. I thought he was a good judge. Of course, when someone decides in your favor, you'll think they were a good judge.

Mr. Warren put me on the witness stand, and he asked about my educational background; how I happened to be teaching at Central; would I teach evolution as a fact or a theory. It seems to be reassuring to people if you say, I'm only going to teach it as a theory. There are different uses of the word 'theory,' and to someone like Stephen Jay Gould, those educated in science, a scientific theory is something with a great deal of support. Mr. Warren established that I was under some kind of threat from this law and that I thought it should be declared unconstitutional.

Bennett was a little bit flamboyant; I think he wanted to have a show. We had a lot of friends out at the Air Force base who had been Jon's bachelor friends before we married, and they were getting a big kick out of this. One of them had gone into a restaurant that had a bar, and Bruce Bennett was in the bar talking with someone, before the trial came up, and he overheard him saying, She's too pretty to come from a monkey! I don't know why she wants to teach this! I thought that was really funny.

Mr. Bennett asked if I believed the theory of evolution, and questions about did I believe in God. Most of these Warren objected to, and Warren had told me beforehand, Give me time to object. Another instruction he gave me was to just answer the question; a good witness answers just the question. I tried to do that, and he told me later I was a good witness, although I was really terrified on the stand. Fortunately, I was on the stand less than two hours.

The *Gazette* published a bit of dialogue from the trial the next day that sort of captured the atmosphere of the trial. Bennett asked me, Have you heard of Nitsky's theory of evolution? I asked him to spell it for me—I thought he meant Friedrich Nietzsche, but I wasn't sure, and I wasn't about to go on the assumption that that's what he meant. I didn't know that Nietzsche *had* a theory of evolution. But it's amazing how Darwin's ideas get grabbed up by different groups. So I asked him to spell it and he couldn't spell it and he didn't have it right there in his folder. The next day, the *Gazette* published this and wrote, Do you think he meant Green Bay linebacker Ray Nitschke?

Most of that day, I recall him shuffling through papers, because many of the objections by Warren were sustained by Judge Reed. Bennett kept trying to introduce things that, as far as we were concerned, were irrelevant to the case. Whether I believed in evolution or whether I was a Christian were really not relevant to the case. The point was that this was a law which supported one particular religious viewpoint in state-supported schools. And also that as a teacher I felt this was something I needed to teach. I can recall Bruce Bennett leafing through his files trying to find some other way he could come at this. He also asked me if I believed in the 'infinite protozoan.' And I said, I think of them as finite. I can recall some laughter in the court at that time.

In late May, Judge Reed handed down his decision in our favor. School was out soon after that, and my husband was sent by the Air Force to the University of Missouri to get his masters in math, so we moved that summer to Missouri. I worked at an immunology lab at the medical school, which was very interesting. Bruce Bennett appealed the case right away to the Arkansas Supreme Court, and the court took no action for about a year. So for a year it was legal, at least on the books, to teach evolution in Arkansas.

Then in June of '67, they handed down what's called a *per curiam* order, simply stating, We reverse the decision of the lower court. There were some questions Mr. Warren had come up with—one was the vagueness of the wording in the law. It says, You may not teach. Well, what does 'teach' mean? You can go on for days about what it means to teach. Does it mean to be dogmatic? Does it mean to present information? Supposedly it is unconstitutional to make something a crime when the wording of the law is vague. And the Arkansas Supreme Court said, Basically, we find the law perfectly appropriate and we reverse Judge Reed's decision, without clarifying anything about the law's vagueness. The court didn't give any comfort to teachers, so that they know what is the guideline; how much can they say or not say; what's allowed.

So right on the heels of that, Mr. Warren appealed to the U.S. Supreme Court. There again, we didn't know if they would agree to hear it. Many people considered the case sort of ridiculous. The law was being broken anyway, so why bother? It did affect two other states, because Tennessee and Mississippi had laws. I think in '67 the Tennessee legislature repealed their law; maybe they saw what was about to happen and decided they might as well clean up their own house. There had been efforts in the Arkansas legislature before our case to repeal it, but there seemed to be just enough voter sentiment for some people that they didn't vote to eliminate the law. Now it was up to the Supreme Court to decide the issue, and they did hear our case in the fall of 1968.

After my husband finished his masters at Missouri, he was assigned to the Pentagon, and we were living in Maryland, in the D.C. area. So we went to the Supreme Court hearing. Mr. Warren told me it would probably be heard this certain morning in October. There was some kind of civil-rights case being heard before mine. So we got there and we heard a little bit of this other case and then our case was discussed. I remember sitting there and hoping that I looked very anonymous. But it was very interesting.

Bruce Bennett did not win the election in '66, so the state of Arkansas had a new attorney general. One of his assistants, Don

Langston, argued the case for the state. I knew Don, not really well: He'd been a little ahead of me at The College of the Ozarks. Before the hearing, I saw Don and we chatted a minute or two, and we were joking and laughing about being there. It became quite apparent in the arguments in the Supreme Court that the state of Arkansas would be happy to be rid of this law. One of the justices commented to Don, It sounds as if you're not really too excited about defending this law.

I remember Thurgood Marshall and Earl Warren and Potter Stewart and Byron White. Abe Fortas was a name I had heard before, and I noticed him. It was fascinating to see people you had seen in the paper and read about. One of them asked, Is Mrs. Epperson still teaching in Arkansas anymore? She apparently isn't under threat from this law anymore, so why should we be so concerned? This *was* the case; I had moved away. But I looked at it as an effort for *all* Arkansas biology teachers, certainly not just for me. If nothing else, it would clarify the issue. Whether I was there or not was not so important.

I think I first learned the Supreme Court had ruled in our favor from newspaper reporters who called. *Time* magazine came out to our house in Maryland and took a picture of me and little Mark—he's six-two now. Mark thinks that's so great he got into *Time* magazine.

One interesting aspect of the case was that I got to meet John Scopes through Jerry Tompkins, a Presbyterian minister who had written a book about the Scopes trial. Jerry had interviewed John Scopes, who was a very quiet, retiring kind of person. Jerry said he'd really like for us to meet John Scopes, that it would be historic. Scopes was living in Shreveport, Louisiana, and at Christmas one year we were going to southern Arkansas to see my grandmother. Jon and I drove down with Jerry one day to Shreveport and we all met at a Holiday Inn and had lunch in a private room with Mr. Scopes and his wife. We had a nice, quiet visit and a friendly chat. As we were leaving, he made a point of letting me know that he was really supportive of me. He had wanted to come to our trial and show his support, but he knew it would just create a furor, which it probably would have. But he assured me that his absence didn't mean that he didn't support what we had done.

We left D.C. in early '71 for Jon to come to the math faculty at the Air Force Academy. Jon taught there for two years; then the academy sent him for a doctorate in statistics to Texas A&M. We went back in '76 and in '81 Jon was ready for a sabbatical, and that's when we went to Holland for two years. From there he was assigned to the Pentagon again, so we were back in D.C. from '83 to '86; and last summer we moved back here to Colorado.

I'd always envisioned going back to teaching. I look at it like my dad did—as a calling, as something I can do to make a contribution. Since we came to Colorado, I took a couple of courses and got my certificate, and I've been substitute-teaching in the middle school and high school. I've just filled in a full-time subbing position but I don't have a position for next year. It's not nearly the amount of work that's involved in full-time teaching, and yet I can keep in touch with the schools and keep up-to-date in my field, and still be at home when my kids were home. I felt it was important to be with my children and I enjoyed that.

Since my case was decided, the so-called creationism movement has come to the forefront. I'm really opposed to how they're trying to put religion into biology classes. I heard from the Creation Research Society when my case came about, a letter saying I was wrong and shouldn't be doing this, and there's just as much scientific evidence for creation as there is for evolution. I remember thinking, What kind of fly-by-night group is this? They were saying the earth is much younger than the paleontological evidence shows and that carbon dating is bunk, and that God just put all the fossil evidence there to make the earth *look* old! Why, I don't know. This doesn't sound like the omnipotent God that I worship, it just sounds cockeyed to me.

They say they're scientific, but I do not see evidence of the scientific method and the kind of investigative approach that has given us the evidence we have for evolution. As far as I understand it, creationism is not science. Therefore, it does not belong in a science classroom. If they want to teach these ideas in a history course or philosophy course, I'm not opposed to their talking about their ideas. This is not just an effort to get rid of evolution in the schools, it's an effort to debunk a lot of science—techniques like carbon dating. The scientific method as such is under fire. It's kind of like, Let's go back to medieval days and let's not account for what we see.

I don't think creationism is good science, and I don't think it's good religion. They say they're not coming from the Bible, but of course they are. They're trying to equate the creation of the world with an established scientific theory. I believe God made the world, although I can't explain how He did it. And there are gaps in the evolutionary record, there are things we just don't know, and I'm willing to live with that. But there is a preponderance of evidence for evolutionary change.

The creationists say, you can't *show* evolution. Well, you can show it in insects, in things that have a faster generation time than humans. To me, there's an awful lot of evidence to support it. One of the basic differences between creationism and science is that a scientist looks at things, just like Darwin did when he went sailing on the Beagle. He hadn't even thought of coming up with the theory of evolution, but he saw all these life forms and these islands and he thought, Hmmm, how does this fit together? A scientist sees mold growing on something and puts it on a plate and it kills bacteria, and he says, Hmmm, what's happening here? You *see* things and observe, and you draw conclusions and try to make some kind of unity out of that, and then you come up with a theory about bactericides or whatever. The creationists, on the other hand, already have a conclusion, and they eliminate whatever evidence they don't want. It's just not science to start with a foregone conclusion and then try to find evidence to support it.

I was very happy to read that the Supreme Court declared that the Louisiana 'equal time' creationism law was unconstitutional. It was obviously a correct decision. Of course I'm opposed to such laws because of the confusion they would cause for science teachers and students. I really believe young people need to study the Bible and learn about God—but these are not for public schools to teach, and certainly not for science teachers!

10

Mary Beth Tinker
v. Des Moines

Mary Beth Tinker was 13 when she was suspended in 1965 from school in Des Moines, Iowa, for wearing a black armband to protest American bombing in Vietnam. *Courtesy of the* Des Moines Register, © *1988*

I.
"Take a Stand! That's What You're Here For!"

On the morning of December 16, 1965, Mary Beth Tinker wore a black armband to her eighth-grade classes at Warren Harding Junior High School in Des Moines, Iowa. Her morning classes passed without incident, and she had lunch in the school cafeteria with friends who discussed the armband and topics more typical of conversation among thirteen-year-olds. Mary went from lunch to her algebra class. Before the bell rang, she was summoned to the office of Chester Pratt, the Harding principal. He demanded that Mary remove the armband, and she complied. Pratt did not allow Mary to return to algebra class, but suspended her from school and sent her home for violating a school-board edict which banned armbands from all Des Moines schools.

Mary wore her black armband to school in the American heartland as a symbol of mourning for those who were dying 10,000 miles from Des Moines, in Vietnam. The armband also expressed support for a Christmas truce and cease-fire in Vietnam. Mary's act of symbolic protest put her on the front page of *The Des Moines Register* the next morning. "Wear Black Arm Bands, Two Students Sent Home," the paper reported. Chris Eckhardt, a sophomore at Roosevelt High School, had also been suspended for defying the armband edict. Don Blackman, the Roosevelt vice-principal who suspended Chris, told the *Register* that "no commotion or disturbance" had taken place in the school. The school-board president, Ora Niffenegger, defended the ban on armbands as a "disciplinary measure" against any "disturbing influence" in Des Moines schools. Niffenegger pounded a patriotic drum: "Our country's leaders have decided on a course of action and we should support them." Mary and Chris followed a different drummer and found themselves out of school; they could return when they removed their armbands and rejoined the parade.

That same Thursday night, about twenty-five students and parents met to discuss the armband issue and decide on a response to the suspensions. The meeting was called by Mary's father, Rev. Leonard Tinker, a Methodist minister who worked as peace education director of the American Friends Service Committee regional office in Des Moines. The group issued a statement expressing "deep concern" that students were being "deprived of an important opportunity to participate in this form of expression" about the war. Earlier that day, students had asked the school board for an "emergency meeting" on the ban. Ora Niffenegger refused, saying the issue "wasn't important enough" to warrant review before the next scheduled meeting. Friday morning, three more students were suspended, including Mary's brother John, a tenth-grade student at North High School.

Following the five suspensions, the battle over the armband issue began with moderate words on both sides. Craig Sawyer, a Drake University law professor, spoke for the Iowa Civil Liberties Union in asking the school board to rescind its edict. The Union's statement recognized the need to protect "the educational atmosphere of the school" from disruption, but also recognized "the students' right to freely express themselves" on controversial issues. School superintendent Dwight Davis disavowed any intent to ban the expression of student views on Vietnam: "There should be an opportunity to discuss controversial issues in school," he said. "You have to draw the line somewhere," Davis added. The board drew the line at armbands because they threatened "a disruptive influence at the school." The board's policy had been adopted two days before Mary Tinker was suspended, and the front-page *Register* story about the ban appeared under an editorial cartoon of an American soldier stabbed in the back with a knife that read "Viet Cong Propaganda."

Calls for a truce had no more impact in Des Moines than in Vietnam, although one battle was largely rhetorical and the other was fought with bombs and bullets. Despite the cease-fire campaign, fighting in Vietnam continued as Christmas approached. More than 250 American troops died in combat that week, the war's highest toll yet. One of those casualties was Pvt. James Flagg of Des Moines, a nineteen-year-old black paratrooper and graduate of John Tinker's school, North High. Flagg's picture and the report of his death appeared on the *Register*'s front page, next to a story about fighting in the Des Moines schools over the armband issue. Ross Peterson, a Roosevelt High Senior who wore black clothes to school but not an armband, was "slugged in the mouth" at the lunch break on Friday. Bruce Clark, a suspended Roosevelt senior, claimed that football coach Donald Prior called those who wore armbands "Communists" and encouraged students in gym class to shout "Beat the Viet Cong" during jumping-jack exercises. Prior supported the shouters: "They are proving their Americanism. They are on the side of President Johnson."

Over the past century, pacifism and patriotism have been equally strong currents in traditionally Republican Midwest states like Iowa. On one side, many of Iowa's German immigrants had opposed American involvement in World War I. On the other, sixteen antiwar activists were arrested in Des Moines during the "Red Scare" that swept the nation after the Armistice. Pacifism prevailed in the 1964 election, when President Lyndon Johnson campaigned on a pledge of "no wider war" in Vietnam and trounced Barry Goldwater in Des Moines. But Johnson abandoned his pledge early in 1965, after South Vietnamese troops fled from Viet Cong attacks throughout the country. By year's end, 200,000 American troops occupied South Vietnam and 250,000 pounds of bombs had rained from B-52s onto North Vietnam. The tradition of Midwest patriotism rallied many in Des Moines to Johnson's side against the "Nervous Nellies" who opposed his massive escalation of the Vietnam War. Others in Des Moines risked the tarbrush of "treason" to support Mary Tinker's symbolic act of protest against the war.

On December 21, 1965, a State Department spokesman said the United States was considering the Viet Cong's proposal for a Christmas truce. American agreement was announced the next day. The Des Moines school board also met on December 21, but no truce was reached on the armband issue. More than 200 people jammed the meeting room for a two-hour debate. Craig Sawyer, speaking for the Iowa Civil Liberties Union and parents of the five suspended students, asked for their immediate reinstatement and repeal of the armband edict. Board member George Caudill asked Sawyer if he also supported a student's right to wear an armband with a Nazi swastika. "Yes," Sawyer replied, "and the Jewish Star of David and the Cross of the Catholic Church and an armband saying 'Down with the School Board.'"

In the best tradition of American town meetings, the Des Moines school-board debate exposed the roots of the conflict between free expression and public order. One board member, Rev. Robert Keck of St. John's Methodist Church, supported the suspended students. "Controversy is at the heart of education," he said, "and the disturbance of set thinking is the catalyst." Referring to physical attacks on students who wore armbands or black clothing, Rev. Keck said the board had let "the ruffian element dictate educational policy." George Caudill, a pediatric physician, responded that classrooms "should not and cannot be used for demonstrations" on any issue. "Regardless of the type of demonstration," he said, "it will be disruptive to some degree." Speaking from the audience, an elderly citizen asked the board to "maintain law and order in the schools" and recalled his school days: "If we did something wrong, we got the stick" from teachers and parents alike.

Bruce Clark, one of the suspended students, reminded the board that black armbands had been allowed in 1963 to mourn the four black girls killed in a church bombing in Birmingham, Alabama. Lorena Tinker, Mary and John's mother, assured the board that she and her husband had "not encouraged our children to be defiant." Mary and John, and the four other Tinker children, were raised "to be responsible citizens in a democracy," their mother said. "Our children have been raised in a home where we've held certain values. They are, in their way, witnessing to the values we believe in." After one board member moved to postpone any action on the issue, Craig Sawyer burst out, "I am demanding that you decide it. Take a stand! That's what you're here for." The board finally took a stand, voting 4–3 to continue the ban on armbands. Speaking for the Iowa Civil Liberties Union, Sawyer suggested that the board would soon meet Mary Beth Tinker in court.

Arguments over armbands took up only a small portion of America's debate over Vietnam. Protest against the war began indoors, through "teach-ins" that were conducted with academic decorum in early 1965. Bouyed by a five-day bombing halt in May, protesters held back from mass rallies and marches, successful tactics of the civil-rights movement. The resumption of bombing, and growing American casualties, pushed the protesters into the streets, where they faced hostility and violent attacks. Members of the Hell's Angels motorcycle gang beat antiwar marchers in Berkeley, California. Marchers in New York City became targets for eggs and red paint. Charges that demonstrators were disloyal mounted. One World War II veteran carried a sign at the New York rally in October: "Support Our Men in Vietnam—Don't Stab Them in the Back." FBI director J. Edgar Hoover belittled war opponents as "halfway citizens who are neither morally, mentally nor emotionally mature."

As casualties mounted in Vietnam, protest took new forms, both symbolic and tragic. In October 1965, Catholic pacifist David Miller burned his draft card outside the Whitehall Street army induction center in Manhattan, where Dan Seeger had refused induction in 1960. And on November 2 a young Quaker, Norman Morrison, sat on the Pentagon steps, poured a gallon of gasoline over his body, struck a match, and burned to death. Buddhist monks in Vietnam had horrified Americans with similar acts of protest, but Morrison's sacrifice of life brought the war home to many Americans.

The antiwar movement exploded in size as Christmas approached in 1965. Dr. Benjamin Spock, the noted baby doctor who headed the Doctors for Johnson Committee in 1964, spoke to a massive rally in Washington in November 1965 and deplored "the virtual absence of debate in Congress" over the war. Among the 25,000 people who gathered at the Washington Monument to hear Dr. Spock and other speakers were Maggie Eckhardt and her son Chris, who returned to Des Moines eager to fill Dr. Spock's antiwar prescription. When Chris met at his home with Mary and John Tinker and a few other Des Moines teenagers, they decided that symbolic black armbands would let their fellow students know of their concern for peace in Vietnam.

Following the suspensions in December 1965, the armband issue moved from the classroom to the courtroom. Mary and the other students returned to school after Christmas without their armbands, while the Iowa Civil Liberties Union filed suit in federal court against the Des Moines school board, seeking an injunction against the armband policy. Dan L. Johnston, a twenty-eight-year-old graduate of Drake Law School in Des Moines, represented the students. The board's lawyer was Allan A. Herrick, seventy-year-old partner in one of the city's largest firms, whose practice was centered on defending insurance companies against claimants. The case was assigned to Chief District Judge Roy L. Stephenson, who had been awarded the Bronze and Silver stars during World War II combat duty and who remained in the Iowa National Guard as a Lt. Colonel. An active Republican, Stephenson was named to the federal bench in 1960 by President Eisenhower.

The hearing before Judge Stephenson was brief, and Johnston and Herrick directed their legal arguments solely at the First Amendment and its limits. Mary and John Tinker and Chris Eckhardt each testified, Stephenson wrote in his opinion, "that their purpose in wearing the armbands was to mourn those who had died in the Vietnam war and to support Senator Robert F. Kennedy's proposal that the truce proposed for Christmas Day, 1965, be extended indefinitely." None of the school officials who testified cited any actual disruption of school activities by the armband protest.

Stephenson's opinion, issued on September 1, 1966, made clear his belief that students left their First Amendment rights at the school door. He admitted—citing the Supreme Court's decision in the *Barnette* case of 1943, striking down the school expulsion of Jehovah's Witnesses who refused to join flag-salute ceremonies—that wearing an armband "is a symbolic act and falls within the protection of the first amendment's free speech clause." But he countered that precedent with the Supreme Court's 1951 decision that Communist party leaders presented a "clear and present danger" to American society and that free speech protections "are not absolute."

Judge Stephenson's opinion reached beyond Mary, John, and Chris to put all Vietnam War protesters on trial. He noted that the school-board's armband edict was adopted when "debate over the Vietnam war had become vehement in many localities. A protest march against the war had been recently held in Washington, D.C. A wave of draft card burning incidents protesting the war had swept the country." Stephenson also noted that supporters and opponents of the war "were quite vocal in expressing their views" at the board meeting to debate the armband policy. "It is against this background that the Court must review the reasonableness of the regulation."

Stephenson bowed to the First Amendment in writing that an issue "should never be excluded from the classroom merely because it is controversial." But the board's concern for "the disciplined atmosphere of the classroom" took first prize in this balancing test. Stephenson allowed the "heckler's veto" to prevail over the lack of evidence of any actual classroom disruption. "While the armbands themselves may not be disruptive," he wrote, "the reactions and comments from other students as a result of the armbands would be likely to disturb the disciplined atmosphere required for any classroom." What the judge considered "likely" had not in fact happened, as school officials conceded. But Stephenson considered the armband policy "reasonable" and denied the injunction request.

More than 20,000 Americans died in Vietnam, and many more Vietnamese perished, before the U.S. Supreme Court met to hear arguments in the armband case on November 12, 1968. The federal appeals court in St. Louis had considered the case the previous year, but the judges split evenly and sent the case to Washington without an opinion. The nation had been profoundly shaken during the past two years: Vietnam had driven President Johnson from office; Martin Luther King and Robert Kennedy had fallen from assassins' bullets; Richard Nixon had been elected president with a "secret plan" to end the war. After fifteen years of judicial activism, the Warren Court neared its end: Earl Warren announced his retirement as Chief Justice, but stayed on after Lyndon Johnson failed in a lame-duck move to elevate Justice Abe Fortas to Warren's center seat on the bench. Meanwhile, the war continued as arguments began over Mary Tinker's armband.

Dan Johnston had barely completed his opening statement when Justice Hugo Black fired a barrage of hostile questions at him. Black had misread the trial record and somehow assumed that Mary's armband had disrupted her algebra class. Mary had in fact been called to Principal Pratt's office before the class began. Johnston pointed out that the trial record included "no testimony" by anyone that armbands had disrupted classroom activities. Black, as firm a disciplinarian in schools as he was tolerant of dissent outside them, ignored Johnston's citation to the record. Johnston also noted that school officials had allowed students to wear political buttons and even the German Iron Cross, a symbol to many of the Nazi regime. Schools should tolerate symbolic statements which did not disrupt school activities, Johnston argued. "Marching in the hallway or standing up in the class and making a speech about the war in Vietnam during mathematics class; that kind of thing I think the Court can prohibit."

Allan Herrick took the offensive from the outset of his argument for the Des Moines school board. School officials should not "wait until violence, disorder and disruption break out" before they ban a controversial message. A little latter-day McCarthyism crept into Herrick's argument when he tried to link the Des Moines students with a controversial group which none of them had joined, Students for a Democratic Society. Chris Eckhardt and his mother had attended an antiwar demonstration in Washington "which I am sure this Court is familiar with," Herrick said, referring to the November 1965 march that SDS and many other groups had sponsored. Herrick obviously hoped the justices were also familiar with the violence that erupted in Chicago at the Democratic convention in 1968, prompting the indictment of several SDS leaders on riot charges.

Herrick repeatedly claimed that Des Moines had been "inflamed" by antiwar protests and that an "explosive" situation had prompted the armband policy. Stating that the protesters had "exploited" the press, Herrick then exploited the death of Pvt. James Flagg. "A former student of one of our high schools was killed in Vietnam," he told the justices. "It was felt that if any kind of demonstration existed it might evolve into something which would be difficult to control." One justice responded with a question: "Do we have a city in this country that hasn't had someone killed in Vietnam?" Herrick confessed that he knew of none, but repeated that antiwar protests "could be explosive."

Chief Justice Warren argued at the Court's conference on the armband case that school officials had picked out only one message to censor and thus violated the "equal protection" clause of the Fourteenth Amendment. If schools "allowed wearing of Fascist crosses" and political campaign buttons, they could not outlaw Mary Tinker's armband, Warren said. Justice Byron White urged that the decision rest on the First Amendment, agreeing with Dan Johnston that "there's no evidence" of disruption in the classrooms. White's position prevailed and the justices voted 7–2 to reverse Judge Stephenson; only Hugo Black and John Harlan dissented.

Justice Abe Fortas agreed to write the Court's opinion, even though he had voted against hearing the case, which would have upheld Judge Stephenson and the Des Moines school board. This would be the last major First Amendment decision of the Warren Court, issued on February 24, 1969. Looking forward to an uncertain future, Fortas took a long look back at fifty years of Supreme Court precedent and concluded that neither students nor teachers "shed their constitutional rights to freedom of expression or speech at the schoolhouse gate." Fortas adopted Warren's argument that Des Moines school officials had tolerated political buttons and even the Iron Cross, "traditionally a symbol of Nazism." Mary Tinker and four other students had been suspended for "wearing on their sleeve a band of black cloth, not more than two inches wide." Their protest caused "no interference with work and no disorder." With the nation engulfed in an unpopular war, Fortas bluntly stated that schools "may not be enclaves of totalitarianism." His opinion rang with echoes of the *Barnette* opinion of Justice Robert Jackson, who supported the rights of students to express their views during a popular war.

Justice Hugo Black had become increasingly crotchety in his eighties and had lost his patience with the younger generation. His dissenting opinion denied that the Des Moines students could "use the schools at their whim as a platform" for their antiwar views. Citing his long record of opposition to censorship of political opinion, Black noted: that "I have never believed that any person has a right to give speeches or engage in demonstrations where he pleases and when he pleases." Black again ignored the trial record and cited "evidence that a teacher of mathematics had his lesson period practically 'wrecked' chiefly by disputes with Mary Beth Tinker" over her armband. Black's opinion conjured up an octogenarian's nightmare of teen-age riot and rampage: "Students all over the land are already running loose, conducting break-ins, sit-ins, lie-ins, and smash-ins." Endorsing "the old-fashioned slogan that 'children are to be seen not heard'," Black saw in Mary Tinker's armband "the beginning of a new revolutionary era of permissiveness in this country" that would end with "rioting, property seizures, and destruction."

The *Tinker* decision represented the high-water mark of Warren Court rulings in First Amendment cases. After chipping away at rights of student expression for the next two decades, the Supreme Court finally adopted Hugo Black's dissent, ruling in January 1988 that school officials could censor the contents of student newspapers. Justice Byron White, who had grudgingly joined the *Tinker* majority in 1969, wrote in *Hazlewood School District* v. *Kuhlmeier* that students had no right to publish material which was "ungrammatical, poorly written, inadequately researched, vulgar or profane, or unsuitable for immature audiences." White wrote for a 5–4 majority in holding that the principal of Hazlewood East High School in suburban St. Louis acted properly in cutting two articles from the school paper. One dealt with the impact of divorce on students at Hazlewood East; the other described the experiences of three students involving pregnancy. White, now in his seventies, concluded that "the standard articulated in *Tinker* for determining when a school may punish student expression need not also be the standard for determining when a school may refuse to lend its name and resources to the dissemination of student expression." White concluded by quoting Black's denial that the Constitution compels officials "to surrender control of the American public school system to public school students." Kathy Kuhlmeier, one of the censored student journalists, responded that school officials might now limit reporting to "school proms, football games and piddly stuff."

Writing for the four dissenters, Justice William J. Brennan accused the majority of "abandoning *Tinker* in this case." His prose heated by outrage, Brennan wrote that the lesson of *Tinker* was that teachers and school boards had no "general warrant to act as 'thought police' stifling discussion of all but state-approved topics and advocacy of all but the official position." Brennan concluded on a rueful note: "The young men and women of Hazlewood East expected a civics lesson, but not the one the Court teaches them today." Abortion had replaced armbands as the issue, and another generation of students had replaced Mary Tinker. When her son Lenny reaches high school, he will read these conflicting Supreme Court civics lessons—and decide for himself which best reflected the spirit of the First Amendment.

II.
"I'm Going to *Kill* You!"

I was born in Burlington, Iowa, in 1952. My father was a Methodist minister at the time I was born. He was raised in Hudson, New York, but he was making the circuit of small Iowa towns as a Methodist minister. We lived in Burlington, and we lived in Atlantic, Iowa, and eventually when I was about five or six we moved to Des Moines, Iowa. My father was assigned to a fairly big church there, Epworth Methodist Church. My mother was pretty much a housewife at that time. There were six kids in the family, three girls and three boys, and I was the fourth. I had an older sister and two older brothers, and a younger sister and brother.

My parents met in seminary school, at Scarritt College, which was in Nashville, Tennessee. My mother was interested in the ministry also, although only my father got ordained as a minister. They both had very strong views about racial equality, and that's what caused most of the problems my family had when I was young. I think going to seminary in Tennessee in the 1940s, when the South was still segregated, had a lot to do with their feelings about the evils of racism.

My mother is very unusual. She's very outspoken and has a lot of courage, and she has kind of paid a price for that, in terms of employment. She was strong, and believed in standing up for what you think is right. My father was much more quiet, strong in a sort of quiet way. He was very religious and taught us this love of life, and a higher meaning in life, and a love of nature. My father died several years ago, and my mother now lives in Corpus Christi, Texas.

Their controversial life started in Atlantic, before we moved to Des Moines, when they had some trouble with integrating a swimming pool there. That must have been in the late fifties, and that's when swimming pools were really hot, because you didn't want to get contaminated with black people's skin or germs or whatever. I was five when we moved from Atlantic to Des Moines, and I didn't understand a lot of what was going on when I was so young. But I do remember about the swimming pool, and I certainly couldn't understand why people couldn't all go to the same swimming pool.

After we moved to Des Moines, my mother started getting more involved in civil-rights things and my father did, too. I remember there were a lot of civil-rights demonstrations that we all took part in, my parents and all the kids who could hold picket signs. We would go to the courthouse in Des Moines and picket around housing issues and voting rights. This was around the time when the southern civil-rights movement was becoming active and the freedom rides were going on. I remember there was a call by the Southern Christian Leadership Conference for ministers in the north to come down to the South to witness what was going on there and help protect the freedom riders, because they'd be under less attack if the news was focusing on these northern ministers coming down. So my parents went to Mississippi for a few weeks.

Since we lived in a mixed neighborhood in Des Moines, I went to school with a lot of black kids and played with them and had no problems. So, when the civil-rights movement got started, it just seemed kind of natural to get involved with it. A lot of my parents' adult friends were involved in it, and their kids joined in and picked up their values. Actually, it was kind of inspiring and I still have that feeling now of being part of some kind of a struggle, people standing together to speak up for themselves or to make life better for themselves and their kids.

A very important incident happened when I was about ten. It was in about '62, I guess, when my father was removed from the Methodist church. He was not allowed to preach any more, because they were trying to integrate the Epworth Church where he was the minister. We lived in a racially mixed, kind of working-class neighborhood, where Epworth was, on the east side of town. The board of directors of the church was mad at him and gave him all kinds of hell, so he was basically put out of the Methodist church. They kept him as a Methodist minister, technically, but he didn't have anywhere to preach and he couldn't find another church. That was hard on him, because he really enjoyed preaching.

After that, we looked around at different churches. I remember my parents were shopping for churches, going to different ones, and thinking where would they fit in. About a year later, in about '64, he went to work for the Quakers. They took him on as a peace education coordinator for the American Friends Service Committee, which had a regional office in Des Moines. His job was to do a lot of education around a five-state area in the midwest. He'd stop at places, mostly churches, and talk to them about the Vietnam War, which was his job with the Friends. He'd take all kinds of literature and leaflets and movies, to promote the idea of resolving the Vietnam War and having peace in Vietnam.

I used to travel around with my father on his trips. It was kind of fun. I remember going to Kansas with him sometimes. For a treat, he'd take us with him to Chicago once or twice. I guess that affected me as far as the Vietnam War was concerned. And taking part in civil-rights demonstrations with my parents must have affected me personally about what happened to *them* as a result of being involved in integration issues.

My parents really had a lot of employment problems because of their involvement in controversial things. They were both punished for their views and what they did. Back then, my mother had a masters degree in psychology, and she was teaching at this small Lutheran college, Grand View College. She started organizing against the Vietnam War at the college. So she got fired from her job at Grand View. But my mother kept it up. She was removed from four or five colleges, like Drake University. Slowly she'd get pushed out because she was really mouthy, plus she had these six kids. Everybody thought she had no business being involved in a career like that. She finally decided that in order to ensure her employment she would have to go on in school if she was going to be outspoken and still be organizing. After a lot of work, she completed her Ph.D. in psychology at Iowa State in 1969, and now she does counseling on her own.

After the Vietnam War started to escalate and became controversial, we were going to these various demonstrations and pickets

against the war. There was a teen group also that had its own
activities. I was kind of a hanger-on because I was a little young.
I remember sitting at Bill and Maggie Eckhardt's house one night—
their son, Chris, was also involved in our group, along with my
older brother, John—and we decided to wear these black armbands
to school. I think the idea came nationally from something that
Bobby Kennedy started. It was part of a call for a Christmas
truce in '65, when there was this tremendous bombing of North
Vietnam.

By then the movement against the Vietnam War was beginning
to grow. It wasn't nearly what it became later, but there were
quite a few people involved nationally. I remember it all being
very exciting; everyone was joining together with this great idea,
and our meetings had a lot of creativity and enthusiasm. I was a
young kid, but I could still be part of it and still be important.
It wasn't just for the adults, and the kids were respected: When
we had something to say, people would listen.

So then we just planned this little thing of wearing these armbands to school. It was moving forward and we didn't think it
was going to be that big of a deal. We had no idea it was going
to be such a big thing because we were already doing these other
little demonstrations and nothing much came of them. All the
kids at this meeting went to different schools. The one I went to
was Warren Harding Junior High School; I was in eighth grade.

Kids at my school must have already had some opinion about
me, because I remember one boy, when I told him that we were
planning to wear armbands, he said, Oh, there you go again! I
think I was already speaking out. I remember one incident where
I raised something in a history class about the war, and the teacher
said, Mary, there's a pep rally this Friday—don't you *ever* think
of having fun?

That kind of hurt my feelings, to think I was no fun. I had a
big social life and a lot of friends. I ran around and got in trouble
and went to the movie shows at night and snuck around with
boys, like all the other kids. My best friend's dad owned a tavern;
we used to spend all our weekends together and think up little
plots and plans and run around like that. I remember another
kid in our friendship group whose father owned a fruit stand.
One time, I had this little date with this black boy who I'd known

since I was a child, and that weekend I went by her father's fruit stand and she said, Oh, you're a nigger lover! I guess there was some fallout from that.

After we had our meeting at the Eckhardt's and decided to wear the black armbands, we were all going to do it on the same day. I told this kid at school about it, and the day before we were going to wear the armbands it came up somehow in my algebra class. The teacher got really mad and he said, If anybody in this class wears an armband to school they'll get kicked out of my class. I went back and told the group and the next thing we knew, the school board made this policy against wearing armbands. They had a special meeting and decided that any student who wore an armband would be suspended from school.

The next day I went to school and I wore the armband all morning. The kids were kind of talking, but it was all friendly, nothing hostile. Then I got to my algebra class, right after lunch, and sat down. The teacher came in, and everyone was kind of whispering; they didn't know what was going to happen. Then this guy came to the door of the class and he said, Mary Tinker, you're wanted out here in the hall. Then they called me down to the principal's office.

The girls' counselor was there in the office. She was real nice. She said, Mary, you know we're going to have to suspend you from school unless you take off that armband. Oddly enough, I took it off. I took off the armband because I was intimidated. I was in this office with these people, the principal was there, and they were giving me these threats and I didn't know what was going to happen, so I took it off. The principal was pretty hostile. Then they suspended me anyway. That's the ironic thing about it. There was a moment there where I thought, This is the *end* of it.

The principal sent me home and called my parents. I went home, and everyone was getting a little bit hysterical. It was getting to be a big deal. Everyone was sort of milling around the house. My brother John, who was in the eleventh grade at another school, didn't wear an armband until the next day, and he got suspended right after he got to school. The two little kids in the family, Hope and Paul, were in elementary school. Hope was in the fifth grade and Paul was in the second grade. They wore black armbands too, but nothing happened to them. I don't think the schools thought people would support suspending *little* kids for something like that.

We got suspended about a week before the Christmas holiday started. We were out of school that week, and every day there was a lot of activity. We were going to meetings, discussing this, figuring out what was going on. The school board had a meeting after we were suspended that hundreds of people went to, and there was a lot of argument and coverage in the newspapers and television. We all went there, wearing these armbands, and they decided to maintain their policy.

After the Christmas holiday, we went back to school but we didn't wear armbands. What we did was to wear black clothes every day for a long time, I think until school ended for the year. We wore all black because there was nothing they could do about that, but it was still this statement. It was our way of fighting back. By then, I think some of the kids were thinking, That's just the nutty Tinker kids. But they got used to it real quick.

After all the publicity about what we did, we got a lot of repercussions. People threw red paint at our house, and we got lots of calls. We got all kinds of threats to our family, even death threats. They even threatened my little brothers and sisters, which was *really* sick. People called our house on Christmas Eve and said the house would be blown up by morning. There was a radio talk-show host in Des Moines who was a right-wing war hawk, and he would always start in on our family, the Tinker family. My mother used to listen to this all the time. I couldn't stand to listen to it, but she loved to tune in and see what they were saying. One night he said that if anyone wanted to use a shotgun on my father he would pay for the court costs if anything happened.

I was leaving for school one morning, on my way out the door, and the phone rang and I picked it up. This woman said, Is this Mary Tinker? And I said yes. And she said, I'm going to *kill* you! At that time, I started a policy I still have today; it's a habit. When anyone calls, I always find out who it is before I talk to them, because of that happening that one morning. It's made me a lot more hardened in certain ways, when you learn in a personal way what the repercussions are for doing unpopular things.

It was around that time when the ACLU stepped in and offered to support a lawsuit against the school board. My parents didn't have any money and no one else did—these weren't rich people. My parents were always broke. We had to make these depositions for the court, but I don't remember too much about what happened in court. But we did have to appeal to the circuit court in St. Louis, because the judge in Des Moines dismissed our case.

By the time the Supreme Court decided our case in 1969, we had moved from Des Moines to St. Louis. My father transferred to St. Louis with the AFSC, in the fall of '68. By that time, he was doing a lot of draft counseling. We had just moved to St. Louis. I was a junior in high school by then, sixteen years old. I was new in town, and I didn't know anyone. When you're that age, your friends are so important. I was like a fish out of water; I was kind of scared and shy.

When the Supreme Court decided the case, in our favor, suddenly it was mass hysteria. All these national papers and magazines wrote articles when the case broke. *Time* magazine came and did this whole photo session at the school. They came to my chemistry class; it was really crazy. I was trying to make sense of it all. Where does this all fit in with my personal life? I was trying to make new friends and here I am, this maniac who's all over the news. All the kids were talking about it. I think in a way I just wanted to put it out of my mind. I didn't want to be a big star, because I was a teen-ager. Teen-agers never want to stand out in a crowd. They just want to blend in. It was kind of a rough time when it broke. I was without as much personal support as when it happened, when I had a lot of my own friends around, and my parents' friends. My parents didn't really know anyone here in St. Louis either, outside of the people at the Service Committee.

After I recovered from all the shock when this hit the fan, and not having any friends, we started this little group, and I started being known a little better. Our group was called the Student Mobilization Committee, which was part of the antiwar movement going on in high schools and colleges around the country. It was a peace group, and we worked hand-in-hand with the black student union in the high school, at University City High School. We would go to demonstrations at the colleges and write articles, but I was getting cynical about the armband decision.

I remember being invited to take part in a walk from Columbia, Missouri, to Jefferson City, which is the state capital, because some kids from Columbia were writing an article for a school newspaper about the war, and they were censored—they couldn't write this article. So this huge group of kids and some adults walked about thirty miles, and they invited me to come and speak in Jefferson City when we got to the end of our march. And I said at the rally, Big deal—this armband case really doesn't mean *anything* because you still can't write an article in the paper; you still get ostracized; the war's still going on; these civil-rights cases that are fought through the courts are really just on paper and don't mean that much.

When I got older I became involved in women's rights and black-power groups that were active in St. Louis. Then I started getting real cynical about it. I felt like these legal decisions are really not going to make that much difference. Where it's going to be decided is through political pressure in the streets. I saw the improvements in black rights happening more through people rising up together than these legal decisions. Since then I've changed. I think it's really both that are necessary to change things; it all goes in together.

I didn't go to college when I finished high school. I was getting kind of rebellious about all this professionalism. My parents had lost their jobs; they had this problem with employment—my mother was working on her Ph.D., which wasn't helping her to get employed at all. When she *did* get her Ph.D. she was sort of blacklisted, and she couldn't get a job. I just decided this is not where it's at. I had been raised in kind of a lower-middle-class family; they were professional but they were broke. But they still had these professional values, and I felt like I wanted to be a traitor to my class in terms of these middle-class professional values.

I was also getting more class awareness, becoming more aware of working-class issues and how these working-class kids had been forced into the Vietnam War because they didn't have any alternatives. For a lot of the middle-class peaceniks, like me, it was easy to protest. It wasn't always easy, but you couldn't really blame the working-class soldiers and the black kids who were snatched up and sent off to Vietnam just because they couldn't afford the price of going to Harvard.

I started out being an apprentice to a piano technician and I learned to repair and tune pianos. From my parents' experience I thought that your job shouldn't be controversial or political at all. That's why I went into piano tuning. I thought, I'll do these political things on the side. In that way, they can never fire me—which through history is actually not true: Millions of trades people have been punished and fired for their political activities and protest.

I was also curious about other ways of organizing the world for a more humane government, so I went to Cuba in 1970. That was quite an experience. Very few people in this country know how much the Cubans have improved their health care and education since their revolution. During most of the '70s I was angry with organized religion. I wouldn't be involved with any church. It seemed to me that most churches were just supporting the status quo and weren't concerned with social issues. But I recently started going to the Unitarian church. I have a lot of friends who are Jewish, who kind of made me an honorary Jew, and I celebrate Passover seders and Hanukah.

I was real angry about the atrocities that happen to people here in this country—kids getting sick, heat being switched off, people trying to keep warm with twenty-five coats. I just get really fuming about that stuff, the fact that our society doesn't provide any support services for families. The result is that we don't raise adults who are adequately functioning individuals and they can't raise their children, so they destroy their kids and beat on their wives. I get real emotional about that kind of stuff.

I liked piano tuning, but I felt like I needed to have another skill, and nursing seemed like a good practical skill. I thought nursing would be closer to what my real heart interests are, which is more trying to support families and make life more decent for them. I got a scholarship from the Veterans Administration and they put me through the last two years of nursing school. Then I had an obligation to work for the VA. I told them on the application, and I really believe it, that it would be a privilege to work with our veterans who have sacrificed part of their lives. And I believe that. I think the veterans should have good services and I am happy to be working in the VA.

The VA is one of the only public hospital systems left in this country; they're destroying all the other public hospitals. Of course, Reagan has tried to destroy the VA, too. A lot of the vets are very much antiwar, and anti-Vietnam War for sure. A lot of the guys I meet in the hospital actually were involved in antiwar protests before they got snatched up and sent off to Vietnam.

Even though I went through a period of being cynical about the armband case, I'm not at all sorry I did it. I'm glad that it all happened. I feel it was a privilege to be part of that whole time period and I'm really proud that we had a part in ending the crazy Vietnam War. Especially today, when I get to talk to a lot of Vietnam vets and their families, it makes me even more sure that what we did was right and that the war was really a painful mistake. I work with a lot of paraplegics and quadriplegics, and some of them were injured in the Vietnam War. One guy I worked with today was amputated from the trunk down; his spine was shot up in the war. So I don't have any regrets about it at all. I'm proud to have been part of anything that stopped the war.

11

Dr. Jane Hodgson
v. Minnesota

Dr. Jane Hodgson's challenge in 1970 to a
Minnesota law against abortions resulted in her
criminal conviction and the Supreme Court's
refusal to consider her appeal. *Photo by Joe Oden,
St. Paul Pioneer Press Dispatch, © 1988*

I.
"I Couldn't Make a Child Suffer"

On April 29, 1970, Dr. Jane Hodgson performed an abortion on Nancy Kay Widmyer in the Charles T. Miller Hospital, St. Paul, Minnesota. Nancy was a twenty-three-year-old mother of three children—six, three, and two years old—and the wife of a construction worker. She and her children had recently gone through a bout of rubella, which most people call German measles. Because she knew that women who contract rubella early in pregnancy suffer a great risk of having a deformed child, Nancy consulted Dr. Hodgson, her obstetrician, for advice. The doctor and her patient agreed that terminating the pregnancy was the best choice for Nancy. The abortion was uncomplicated and Nancy left the hospital in good health.

The abortion was also illegal under Minnesota law. If Dr. Hodgson had declined to perform the abortion, Nancy would be forced to choose from limited and unpleasant alternatives. Carrying the fetus to term risked a badly deformed child, an enormous emotional and financial burden on a young family with three children and a modest income. Nancy could visit a back-alley abortionist like Elmer Hultgren, convicted three times in Minnesota for criminal abortions. Hultgren had recently aborted a pregnant college student who developed a serious infection; he was arrested under the same law Dr. Hodgson violated and was sentenced to prison, where he had already spent nearly three years. Nancy could finally have tried one of the dangerous methods of self-abortion that desperate women use, such as Lysol or knitting needles. At least 400 women died in the United States every year from illegal or self-induced abortions.

Dr. Jane Hodgson was an unlikely crusader against Minnesota's criminal abortion law, which banned all abortions except those required to save a pregnant woman's life. She could have performed the abortion on Nancy Widmyer quietly, without risking a prison term or loss of her medical license. Dr. Hodgson was no back-alley abortionist—she was in fact a founding Fellow of the American College of Obstetrics and Gynecology, and past president of the Minnesota Society of Obstetricians and Gynecologists, the first woman elected to that office. Dr. Hodgson was fifty-five years old in 1970, a 1940 graduate of the University of Minnesota Medical School and former resident at the prestigious Mayo Clinic in Rochester, Minnesota. In thirty years of practice, she had delivered more than four thousand babies and performed fewer than a dozen abortions. Much of her practice and research was aimed at improving fertility and helping her patients have healthy, wanted children.

When she decided to challenge the law, Dr. Hodgson's first step was to file suit in federal district court in St. Paul, seeking both a judicial declaration that the law violated the U.S. Constitution and an injunction against its enforcement by state officials. Stewart R. Perry, a young Minneapolis lawyer and American Civil Liberties Union volunteer, filed the complaint on April 16, 1970, asking for an emergency hearing and ruling before an abortion on Nancy Widmyer—disguised as "Jane Doe" in court papers— became more risky. This petition was denied, the first judicial rebuff to Dr. Hodgson, who performed the abortion several days later.

Perry then amended the complaint to ask for federal protection against Dr. Hodgson's prosecution by William Randall, the Ramsey County attorney in St. Paul. Under rules which governed challenges to state laws, the case came before a three-judge federal panel, which dismissed the complaint on May 19, the second judicial rebuff. Chief Judge Edward J. Devitt wrote for the panel, which split 2–1 on the case. Devitt, a former Republican congressman and state judge, was placed on the federal bench in 1954 by President Dwight Eisenhower. Like most officials and judges in St. Paul, Devitt was an active Roman Catholic; the city of 310,000 housed sixty-seven Catholic churches, and the clergy strongly backed the state's ban on abortions. However much Devitt may have tried to separate his religious views and judicial duties, he was born and raised in an overwhelmingly Catholic city and culture, in which abortion was anathema.

Devitt's brief opinion rested on the "abstention" doctrine that cautioned federal judges against interfering with state criminal prosecutions, particularly before any indictment was issued. "No indictment has been returned," he wrote, and thus Dr. Hodgson was "in the wrong court." Supreme Court rulings allowed federal intervention before state prosecution which might have a "chilling effect" on constitutional rights, but Devitt denied that the prospect of prosecution would chill Dr. Hodgson's actions. Senior Circuit Judge Charles J. Vogel dissented but did not write an opinion. Judge Philip Neville filed a grudging concurrence, writing that "the entire medical profession and innumerable pregnant women live under the sword of Damocles." Referring to both doctors and patients, Neville said their "freedom of choice is 'chilled' by the cloud of a statute which renders their actions illegal" and threatens criminal penalties.

Encouraged by the dissent and concurrence, Stewart Perry asked the panel to reconsider the case after Dr. Hodgson's criminal indictment on May 21, 1970. Before the federal judges ruled, the case received a third judicial rebuff from state judge Ronald E. Hachey, who denied Perry's motion to dismiss the indictment on constitutional grounds. Hachey's written opinion leaned heavily on morality to defend the state law, writing that "the ultimate source of law is from the ultimate Lawgiver Himself." The judge had harsh words for those who accept "the philosophy of excuse" and "become instruments of their own damnation." Hachey arranged to have his opinion printed in *The Catholic Bulletin,* the weekly paper for Minnesota Catholics. Two days after this ruling, on July 1, the federal panel issued the fourth rebuff, this time without dissent. The judges decided, in an opinion issued without an author, to adopt "a hands-off policy as to pending state court proceedings."

Before the case reached trial, Stewart Perry was joined as counsel by Roy Lucas, a young New York lawyer who had become a specialist and crusader in abortion cases across the country. Dr.

Hodgson learned of his work and traveled to New York to recruit him to represent her; Lucas assumed the major role in the trial. The lawyers made two efforts in November to block the criminal trial. Perry first asked Judge Hachey to step down from the case, citing the publication of Hachey's opinion in the Catholic weekly, and newspaper reports that Hachey had voiced objections to abortion to a Catholic group. These activities suggested to Perry that the judge would use the trial "as a forum to air his personal views on the morality of abortion." Furious at this attack on his impartiality, Hachey told Perry that his charge "borders on contemptuous conduct." Judicial rules, however, entitled Perry to request another judge. Hachey stepped down and was replaced by Judge J. Jerome Plunkett, who had attended a Catholic military academy and served as a municipal and state judge in St. Paul since 1954. Plunkett set the case for trial on November 12.

The final move against Dr. Hodgson's prosecution ended with a fifth judicial rebuff, this time from the U.S. Supreme Court. Lucas filed an application to stay the trial with Justice Harry A. Blackmun, who ruled on emergency motions from the federal circuit that included Minnesota. Blackmun was the Court's newest member, having been confirmed on May 12, 1970—the third nominee of President Richard Nixon to fill the seat vacated by Justice Abe Fortas, who resigned after the media trumpeted charges of financial impropriety. Blackmun practiced and taught law in St. Paul and Minneapolis before joining the federal circuit court in 1959; for twenty years he represented the Mayo Clinic, at which Dr. Hodgson had earlier practiced. Acting for the first time on an abortion case, Blackmun referred Lucas' motion to his colleagues, who voted without dissent on November 6 to allow the trial to proceed. The Supreme Court rarely grants such motions, but the justices were obviously unwilling to enter the debate over abortion.

The trial of Dr. Jane Hodgson began in a packed courtroom on Thursday, November 12, 1970. Reporters flocked to the first trial on record of a physician for performing a hospital abortion. Dr. Hodgson seemed eager to explain her stand. "I was beginning to feel like a criminal anyway," she told Seth King of *The New York Times*. "I've always had a proper respect for the law, and

I've performed very few of even the so-called 'legal' abortions," she added. "But they aren't the ones that bother me. It's the ones I've refused to perform that haunt me."

Dan Hollihan, a young lawyer from the county attorney's office, called Nancy Widmyer as the first prosecution witness. She had consulted Dr. Hodgson on April 14 and learned that women who contracted rubella early in pregnancy had a 60 percent risk of bearing a deformed child. "If there was any way I didn't have to go through with the pregnancy," she told Hollihan, "I didn't want the child." She then discussed the options with her husband and returned to Dr. Hodgson's office. "Dr. Hodgson asked me if I would agree to be a test case and I agreed," Nancy said. Hollihan's only other witness was Dr. Robert Woodburn, the Miller Hospital pathologist, who related that Dr. Hodgson had submitted the fetus to him for routine examination.

Roy Lucas did not contest the prosecution's facts, and presented witnesses only to challenge the law's validity under constitutional standards. He first brought Nancy Widmyer back to the stand and asked her feelings about the prospects of raising a deformed children. "I felt it would be cruel to the baby," Nancy replied. "I couldn't make a child suffer, and I couldn't live with myself knowing I could have done something about it." Nancy also considered her three young children: "I didn't feel I could give them the care all children need, and still properly care for a deformed child."

Lucas next called Dr. Elizabeth Jerome, a Minneapolis pediatrician and medical professor. She had treated the Widmyer children for rubella, and she related that children born to women with rubella often suffered from eye defects, nerve deafness, mental retardation, congenital heart defects, and failure to develop physically. She was followed by Dr. Louis Z. Cooper, who directed the Rubella Project at New York University. With the courtroom darkened, Dr. Cooper provided dramatic evidence of the effects of maternal rubella on infants, through slides and movies of affected children. Lucas then called his best-known medical witness, Dr. Christopher Tietze, who had conducted numerous studies of abortion in the United States and abroad. Viennese-born and bearded, Dr. Tietze testified that legal abortions, performed by doctors, were among the safest medical procedures.

Dr. Jane Hodgson took the stand as the final defense witness in the five-day trial. The overflow audience listened in "church-like silence," reported *The St. Paul Pioneer Press,* as the defendant addressed the moral aspects of abortion. Looking directly at Judge Plunkett, the father of eight children, Dr. Hodgson expressed her concern "for the living generation as opposed to the generation represented by the sperm or ovum." During the early years of her practice she never performed abortions. "But as time went on and I saw the problems involved, my attitude changed." She had seen unwanted pregnancies lead to disgrace, forced marriages, criminal abortions, and even death. "I became more and more frustrated as I became aware of the hypocrisies surrounding the problem."

Roy Lucas directed his questions at the most sensitive issues in the abortion question. Did she favor "abortion on demand" in unwanted pregnancies, he asked Dr. Hodgson. "Any ethical doctor resents the expression 'abortion on demand.' I always consider the best interests of my patient, and if the law was repealed I still would do so. 'Abortion on demand' is a form of name-calling by the opposition—an inflammatory expression."

Lucas asked a final, crucial question: "Do you regard the fertilized ovum as equivalent to a human person?" Dr. Hodgson answered as both a woman and a physician: "No, and most women wouldn't. We are more pragmatic than men, more concerned with reality. I'm concerned about the sacredness of life, but this is only a few embryonic cells. I have to consider the person standing before me. We, as physicians, should be concerned with the quality of life as it develops, not merely with its preservation."

Emotions ran high during the trial, and anger erupted when Dan Hollihan called his final rebuttal witness, Dr. Bart T. Heffernan, an Illinois specialist in cardiology. Active in the antiabortion movement, Dr. Heffernan did not treat pregnant women. Hollihan told Judge Plunkett that his witness would show slides on the development of fetal life and abortion techniques. Roy Lucas promptly objected, and Judge Plunkett ruled that Dr. Heffernan would be an incompetent witness, because he lacked medical experience in obstetrics. Dr. Heffernan left the stand and lashed out at Lucas: "You believe that life can be taken for personal gain. That is your religious belief and you are trying to shove it down the throats of others."

Following the testimony, Perry and Lucas renewed their motion to dismiss the indictment, and Judge Plunkett listened to several hours of lawyers' arguments on constitutional issues. Stating that he had carefully reviewed the trial testimony and the decisions of ten other courts, the judge denied the motion without further comment and pronounced Dr. Hodgson guilty.

Judge Plunkett then called Dr. Hodgson to the bench for sentencing. He imposed a thirty-day jail term, which he suspended, and placed the defendant on unsupervised probation for a year. The judge then said he wished to add some personal remarks to the court record. "You are to be commended for your forthrightness," he told Dr. Hodgson. "It has not been an easy position for you to take in this matter—not easy at all—but you can take solace, if you can call it such, in the esteem of your colleagues. I say frankly you are a credit to yourself. Some will condemn and some will praise, but the right decision by anyone in a professional capacity is not always the easy one and not always popular, as I think you have learned and as I have learned in this trial." Dr. Hodgson won Judge Plunkett's respect, but her challenge was rebuffed for a sixth time.

Following her conviction and sentence, Dr. Hodgson pursued two avenues of legal redress. She appealed her conviction to the Minnesota Supreme Court, and she also asked the U.S. Supreme Court to review the federal judicial panel's dismissal of her first complaint against the state law. Once again, the Supreme Court in Washington evaded the abortion issue, the seventh rebuff to the case. Only Justice William O. Douglas voted to hear the federal case, in a ruling issued on May 17, 1971. Meanwhile, the Minnesota court simply sat on the criminal appeal for more than two years. Dr. Hodgson's determined effort to bring the abortion issue before the appellate courts, even at the cost of her medical license, proved futile.

It took another case, another determined woman, and more than two years for the Supreme Court to confront the abortion issue. Even the nine justices, insulated from direct public pressure, can remain deaf to the clamor outside their marble temple only so long. Black Americans had shouted their protests against segregation until the Court heard their cries in the 1950s. America's women, a majority treated by lawmakers like a minority, took up the tocsin in the next decade. Political pressure from the feminist movement in the 1960s finally persuaded the two most populous states, New York and California, to grant abortion rights beginning in 1970. Ironically, New York's liberal new law took effect only weeks after Dr. Jane Hodgson committed an abortion crime in Minnesota. By 1972, twenty-eight states had removed some barriers to legal abortions and the yearly number of deaths from abortion complications dropped more than 90 percent, from four hundred to thirty-nine.

But women in many states, mostly in the Midwest and South, still confronted barriers to abortion which few could scale. Poor women, white and black alike, faced the highest walls. One of these women, Norma McCorvey of Texas, finally persuaded the Supreme Court to listen. The justices accepted her case—in which she was disguised as "Jane Roe"—for argument, in part because the lower federal court had left both sides in a quandary: The court declared the Texas law unconstitutional, but declined to enjoin its enforcement. Roy Lucas, who had represented Dr. Hodgson, joined Sarah Weddington, a young Texas lawyer, in asking the Supreme Court to untangle the case and strike down the Texas law.

Justice Harry Blackmun did not shrink from deciding this second abortion case, issued as *Roe* v. *Wade* in January 1973. Well acquainted with doctors at the Mayo Clinic, Blackmun volunteered to write the Court's opinion, which included citations to *Dorland's Illustrated Medical Dictionary* and other treatises. The heart of Blackmun's opinion was his holding that the Constitution envisioned a "right of privacy" that was "broad enough to encompass a woman's decision whether or not to terminate her pregnancy."

One immediate consequence of Blackmun's opinion was the reversal of Dr. Hodgson's criminal conviction by the Minnesota Supreme Court. Ruling on February 2, 1973, the court held that Nancy Widmyer's abortion "was a medical decision based on the doctor's professional judgment." The court also grudgingly struck down Elmer Hultgren's last conviction, urging the state legislature to outlaw abortions by persons who were not physicians.

Another, more divisive, consequence of the *Roe* decision came in the "right to life" movement, first centered among Catholics but soon broadened to fundamentalist Protestants and some conservative Jews. Adopted by the Religious Right, this campaign took on overtly political tones. Speaking in 1980, one of the Religious Rights's political leaders, Paul Weyrich, linked feminists and the "antifamily movement" with Communists, whose goal "has always been to break down the traditional family." Weyrich also denounced "economic opportunists who profit by the decline in traditional values, through pornography, abortion clinics, the contraceptive mentality, drug sales." Linking people like Dr. Hodgson with dealers in pornography and drugs sounds extreme, but some extremist opponents of abortion have bombed clinics and terrorized their patients. Fueled by frustration, this backlash movement has gained legislative victories and persuaded the Supreme Court to cut back the *Roe* decision's guarantees to poor and young women.

The "right to life" movement won its first significant victory in 1976 when Congress first barred the use of Medicaid funding for abortions. The Hyde Amendment, named after its House sponsor, an Illinois Republican and fervent abortion opponent, reached the Supreme Court in 1980 in a suit sponsored by the ACLU. Dr. Hodgson joined as a plaintiff and testified for two days as an expert witness in *Harris* v. *McRae*, the case's name in the Supreme Court.

Dr. Hodgson's second effort to defend abortion rights was rebuffed by the Supreme Court. Justice Potter Stewart, writing for a 6–3 majority, left the *Roe* decision alive only for women with financial means. Stewart wrote that "although government may not place obstacles in the path of a woman's exercise of her freedom of choice, it need not remove those not of its own creation. Indigency falls in the latter category." Stewart preferred the antiseptic term "indigency" to the more descriptive "poverty." His defense of the Hyde Amendment was a classic of circular argument. The "indigent woman's" inability to afford an abortion was the product not of governmental action "but rather of her indigency." Justice Blackmun, one of three dissenters, scorned the "condescension" in the Court's opinion and predicted that "the cancer of poverty will continue to grow" in America's body politic.

During the five years after the *Roe* decision, Dr. Hodgson filed several suits in Minnesota federal courts against state efforts to restrict abortion rights. The courts generally struck down legislative moves to place legal handcuffs on doctors, but Dr. Hodgson's challenge to Medicaid restrictions in Minnesota fell with the *McRae* decision of the Supreme Court.

Dr. Hodgson returned to federal court in 1981 to challenge a Minnesota law that required a pregnant woman under eighteen to notify both of her parents at least forty-eight hours before an abortion. Testifying as both plaintiff and physician, Dr. Hodgson convinced both a federal district judge and an appellate panel to strike the law down. Ruling in August 1987, Senior Circuit Judge Max Rosenn wrote, for a unanimous appellate panel, that compelled parental notice of an abortion decision "is almost always disastrous" to young women and their families. "Clinic counselors with extensive experience" in Minnesota provided evidence "that the law did not promote family integrity or communication; on the contrary, it disrupted and damaged family relationships." Lacking one member after the June 1987 resignation of Justice Lewis Powell, the Supreme Court split 4–4 in January 1988 on a similar Illinois parental-notification law. The state of Minnesota persuaded the full appellate court to reconsider Judge Rosenn's decision. Dr. Hodgson's case was argued on February 12, 1988, before all ten circuit judges, six of them appointed by President Ronald Reagan. The Senate confirmation of Justice Anthony Kennedy in February 1988 brought the Supreme Court to full strength and promised an ultimate decision on state efforts to draw an "age line" between pregnant women who want to exercise their abortion rights.

Very few Americans have gone to court as often as Dr. Jane Hodgson. Both as defendant and plaintiff, citizen and physician, she has defended freedom of choice on abortion for two decades. Her efforts have been rebuffed by many judges—but she has never conceded defeat to the Religious Right. Polls show that the public supports her position. A bipartisan polling effort in 1988 found that 88 percent of Americans support the principle of abortion rights, while only 10 percent oppose abortion under all circumstances. But abortion opponents are vocal and politically astute, and both legislators and judges read newspapers and watch television. As long as political and legal decisions are influenced by decibles, the abortion debate will continue. And as long as Dr. Hodgson remains active, she will raise her voice to support women's rights to control their bodies.

II.
"This Was Lousy Medicine"

I was born in Crookston, Minnesota, in 1915. Crookston is close to North Dakota and the Canadian border; it's a town of about 8,000 now and it was smaller then. My mother was a school teacher and my father was a doctor. My father was born in Toronto and his father was a Methodist minister, so they were poor as church mice. He'd lived in a number of different places in Canada, because they'd go from assignment to assignment. He was a high-school dropout who came back and went to night school and then to the University of Toronto, so he was older when he went to medical school.

My father graduated from medical school along about 1890 and migrated to this country and became a practitioner in a small town. My parents were married about the turn of the century. They were older when I was born; my mother was near forty and my father was older than that. I had a sister who was eight years older. I was very fortunate as a child. We weren't wealthy by any means, but we had a comfortable living. My childhood was very happy.

My father was really a feminist if there ever was one. He'd always wanted a son, but he never made me feel inadequate because I wasn't a boy. I took it for granted that I could do anything a boy could do. My mother was a feminist too, in a way. She was ahead of her time. I remember she was so incensed about the situation in the South and the treatment of blacks, even though she was born and raised in northern Minnesota and we had no blacks at all. She was very liberal in her views, considering she came from the Victorian period.

My parents were very strict in some ways. We never had any liquor in the house. My father was a very religious man, but he was not a churchgoer; he was seeing patients all the time. There were things he carried over from his fundamentalist father. He'd been disciplined as a child and couldn't play cards on Sunday. He did not really approve of dancing and he would frown when I went to a dance; he'd let me know he wasn't too happy. And I couldn't go to movies on Sunday.

My father made a lot of calls out in the country. I loved to go with him. When we'd go to the hospital I'd sit and wait for him or even go with him on rounds. He was also a prison physician, and I'd go with him to the prison a lot. I was never conscious of wanting to study medicine then; it was just something a girl didn't do. But I'm sure that his being a doctor and taking me with him made a difference.

My years in school were very happy, because I was an achiever and I enjoyed school. Back in those days it was the vogue to push kids—I only spent half a year in each of the first four grades, which was not good. I didn't mind it, it was fine with me. By the time I got to high school, I think most people forgot the age difference. I had a lot of friends and I was probably more successful socially in high school than I've ever been since.

I only lived in Crookston fifteen years, then I went away to Carleton College and never really came back except to visit my family. My parents wanted me to go to a girls' school because of my age, but I balked at that and I finally got them to agree to Carleton, which at that time had very strict rules and strict discipline. I went through Carleton never thinking about medicine as a career. I majored in chemistry and math, but the only thing open to a woman then, particularly one who was only nineteen, was teaching. And I thought marriage was the end of everything. I wanted a career, so I took education too and got my license to teach. But that was the depths of the Depression and I just couldn't get a job. I went around the state interviewing for high-school jobs, and they'd take one look at me and I didn't look any older than the students.

Then I got a job in Chicago for $85 a month, working for the

Winthrop Chemical Company. This turned out to be a secretarial job, working for a doctor who was investigating drug complications. I was supervising the record-keeping for the detail men, who went out to sell the drugs to doctors and pharmacists. Winthrop was having a lot of unexplained deaths from one of their drugs. My boss would go out to investigate them. It was purely secretarial work, but it opened my eyes to the drug world. Living in Chicago was kind of a jolt for me, coming from a protected background. I wanted to be self-supporting, which I was. I didn't get any help at all from my father. To live on that salary and compete in the business world was not easy. That was just enough to make me realize that I wanted to go into medicine. So I wrote to my father and he said, OK, I'll see you through. So he put me through school.

Because I was living in Chicago, I applied at Northwestern and I got turned down on the basis of a quota system. They wrote me a nice letter that they had already filled their quotas of four women, four Jews, and four blacks. They actually *said* that! The interesting thing is that at the time it didn't even occur to me that it was strange. But I did get into the University of Minnesota at the last minute. Medical school was fun. You think you have some troubles, but you don't really.

There were only eight women in a class that started out at two hundred. There was a high mortality rate; they really weeded us out in the first year. We ended up with a class of about 150, but all the women hung in there and we were some of the best students. We were very much a group. We didn't really feel discriminated against at the time. When I look back on it now, I realize there was a lot more discrimination than I was aware of. Some of the teachers were rough on women—one never gave a woman higher than a C in physiology. And there were the usual jokes at the expense of the women. Now the female medical students walk out of class when there's stories they object to. We had to meekly take it. I guess I assumed that this is the way of the world and I've got to put up with this. It's this or nothing else, and I'm lucky to be here. I always assumed a woman would have to do a little bit better, work a little harder and get better grades to get an internship. It was *very* competitive to get good internships and residencies. Boy, you really had to work harder than the men did.

I started off in medical school thinking that I'd go into general practice like my father did. But this was the age of specialization, and I realized that you had to specialize if you wanted to get anywhere. In my senior year I went down to the Mayo Clinic and applied in person for a fellowship before I went east to intern. I got one in internal medicine that would start two years after graduation. Four of us in my class got internships in New Jersey, at the Jersey City Medical Center. I wanted to get out of Minnesota. I thought the further away I can get, the better, just to see what the rest of the world was like. I wanted a big hospital, a city hospital, because you get to do more.

I enjoyed my internship, but it was grueling work. I get mad now when I think of how we were exploited. All we got was room and board and our uniforms; we didn't get a nickel. Financially, it was hard. I could have asked my father for money, but I was proud, and I thought, I'm on my own now and I'm going to make do. But it was a good education. You learn a lot in emergency rooms, and riding ambulances you see *everything!* Jersey City is kind of the dregs of the earth down on the wharfs, and always we had a policeman at our side. I remember I had to ride on both Christmas Eve and New Year's Eve, and those were the two busiest nights of the year. The suicides were awful—you'd walk into an apartment and somebody would be hanging there. Just *unbelievable!* That was still the Depression.

I married Frank Quattlebaum while I was an intern. He didn't have any money either; his father had been dead many years and he went through medical school on borrowed money. We didn't want to borrow any more, so essentially we lived on nothing for two years. After our internships, Frank got a residency in surgery at the University of Minnesota and I was in Rochester at the Mayo Clinic, which was ninety miles away, so we'd get to see each other maybe twice a month. After about a year at Mayo, they asked me to change to obstetrics and gynecology. They wanted women in the field and I'd been doing gynecology and liked it very much. I became aware of the problem of unwanted pregnancies right from the beginning of my internship in Jersey City.

After I left the Mayo Clinic I did general practice for a year and a half in Florida. This was during the war, and Frank was assigned by the Army to a huge orthopedic hospital for convalescents in Daytona Beach. He spent the rest of the war there. I looked for something to do and found an eighty-two-year-old doctor in New Smyrna Beach, about twenty miles away. This was a small town, about half black, and they were *desperate* for doctors. Dr. Henry was being worked to death and was looking for help. I went down and interviewed and told him my training was in "Ob–Gyn" but I'd gladly do anything. He said, Fine, wonderful. And he died that night. I came over the next morning to work, and here his poor widow was crying.

Dr. Henry had this big house, and Frank and I moved in upstairs. Frank commuted to Daytona Beach; he'd come home at night and I'd put him to work. I walked into this absolutely unprepared, and I was just deluged. The phones were ringing, the doorbell was ringing all day and night, and I never worked harder in my life. The office was set up with a black waiting room in the back and the white waiting room in the front, and we would go back and forth. I think it would have been hard to change things, in that town, at that time. People couldn't believe that I would go out in the black neighborhood and make house calls. If I wanted to hospitalize a black patient, I had to send him a hundred miles to St. Augustine: The city hospital in Daytona Beach would not admit blacks. It's hard to realize now that segregation existed back then, but it was terrible. We would have stayed in New Smyrna Beach after the war ended, but the city council voted for golf links rather than a hospital, so we said, Let's get out of here!

We decided to go back to Minnesota, but everybody was coming back from service and there was a surplus of doctors. So we decided that we'd just open up for ourselves. We couldn't get into the Medical Arts building in Minneapolis, so we came over to St. Paul, where we could get space. We just opened up and hoped that somebody would find us. For a woman it was easy, because women were just beginning to realize that they'd like a woman doctor, particularly in my field. They just preferred women. So I had no problem, I had patients very soon. It was harder for Frank in surgery, because it's referred so much, and it took him longer to build up. We worked very hard, and I was gynecologist for the health service at the University of Minnesota. We started in 1947 and I had my private practice right up until 1972.

I got involved in abortion issues in the 1960s. I realize now that it had been bothering me in the back of my mind, and I was doing my best to help with the problem. My decision to challenge the abortion law was very gradual, it was an evolution in my mind. I didn't have any dying desire to overthrow the abortion law. But it gradually dawned on me that this was lousy medicine we were all practicing, and something ought to be done about it. But I never thought I'd see it in my day. I thought it would take forever. I knew it was bad medicine; I wasn't giving my patients good medical care. I just became more and more aware of it.

Then I was asked in 1968 to serve on a committee of the state medical society to study the Minnesota law, which was one of the worst in the country, to suggest modifications to the legislature. The committee had nineteen members, and nobody could agree on anything. We met over a period of several years and we got nowhere, really. It was just a continual argument over who's going to judge, who's going to make the decision. The idea of everybody having the right to an abortion didn't occur to me at first. I thought, It has to be qualified; we have to control it somewhat. I was as bad as the rest of them, really. We finally came up with the conclusion that abortion would be legal if it was approved by a five-man committee of doctors. That was the best we could do. It never even got to the legislature, because the heads of the medical society were so opposed to it and abortion was a political hot potato in Minnesota.

But that opened my eyes to the problem, because I studied about England, which passed their Family Planning Act in 1967. I studied the British system in detail and saw the difficult time they were having with their committee system. That didn't seem the answer. There seemed to be no solution—nobody wanted to grant the right to decide to anyone other than doctors themselves. It was just an impasse. I remember a good friend of mine on the committee, an older man; he and I finally agreed the only solution was total legality, with no restrictions whatever. But he said to me, Jane, you and I will never live to see this. It'll probably take a hundred years, but eventually the law will change. I agreed with him, and felt that at least we could try to help improve the law.

Then I became aware of the Clergy Counseling Service, which was so tremendous. They were very active in this area. I was so happy to have a place to refer patients. They would work out the details of referring them to Mexico City or Canada or California, and New York in 1970 made it easy when they made abortion legal on demand. I was using the Clergy Counseling Service almost entirely, because I was very, very busy. I couldn't personally arrange for each of these women. Prior to that, there had been *nothing* we could do for women who wanted abortions. I got more than my share of them, because I was a woman. Patients came to me because I never would turn anybody away for lack of the fee or anything. I was just deluged, really, with young women from all walks of life with problem pregnancies.

It was so hard for me to see these young women, many of them college girls, sacrificing their whole future. I long ago learned that marriage was not the solution; in fact, we tried to discourage them from that. It was just a daily problem. I would warn them, I know you can get an abortion done, but you're going to end up with trouble, and I'd explain what it would be. And sure enough, they would be back in my office, bleeding, and I knew they had gotten a criminal abortion. Some of them were so terribly sick, and we saw them die. Our city hospital would always have a few real bad ones on the wards.

So it was very frustrating. I was testifying, and speaking before medical groups about the problems, particularly in regard to teenage pregnancy and the problems of poor women. I saw case after case of the hardships involved. We made studies of the number of women leaving the state of Minnesota; between 100 and 150 a week were leaving and being referred out. Having to get medical care outside the state entailed much greater risks for these women. I think what spurred me on was New York's passage of their law and how well it was working. It passed in March 1970, just about the time I was thinking about challenging our law.

That was why I was looking for the ideal case and thinking, What should she be? She should be married and preferably have other children and be a model mother, because that wouldn't have bothered so many Minnesota citizens. And the legislature could swallow it a little better. And it just happened that Nancy Widmyer walked into my office, early in April of 1970. She came in requesting an abortion because she had been exposed to rubella early in her pregnancy. All three of her children had gotten rubella and she had the rash and all the clinical symptoms. We related well and she seemed to understand. I explained the whole thing to her and let her think about it. She promptly decided, yes, she had to do it. She had already made up her mind that she wanted an abortion. I could have sent her to Canada or somewhere else, like I ordinarily had been doing if a woman could afford it. If she couldn't afford it, she'd probably go to some local abortionist.

A lot of people asked me why I didn't just take Nancy to my hospital, like I had done with a few others. And the point is that I was sick and tired of the hypocrisy of it. The doctors' wives and doctors' daughters often took that route, usually through psychiatric indications. It was the inequity of it and the double standard that got to me. I was continually called by doctors: So-and-so is a very important person and is pregnant; can't you do this for her? I was just fed up with our way of handling it.

Things moved very quickly then. I notified the Clergy Counseling Service that I had found a test case, and they said they would provide a lawyer who had agreed to take it on at no expense. So we moved right ahead and filed a suit in federal court asking for a declaratory judgment that the law was unconstitutional, and also granting me the right to go ahead and do the abortion. I pointed out that time was of the essence because Nancy was then almost twelve weeks pregnant and the risks would increase so much after that. This was early in April and I wanted permission to do it before the first of May.

The federal court declined to do anything about it, on the basis that I was in no jeopardy and the law had never been enforced as far as doctors were concerned. In other words, everybody was looking the other way. The judge was a well-known Catholic here in the community and I wasn't at all surprised. So there was nothing to do but go ahead with the abortion, which I did. I had ample consultation—I think five physicians, three from the Mayo Clinic. Fortunately, everything went well and Nancy went home without any trouble.

It didn't take any doing to get arrested and indicted. Everybody had their eye on what I was doing; there had been so much publicity when I first sought permission in federal court. I was indicted at the end of April in 1970 for performing an illegal abortion. The police came into my office and took me to the police station and I had to go through the usual booking, being treated like an ordinary criminal—fingerprinting and everything else. So I went back to the federal court a second time, asking them to intervene on my behalf, now that I *was* in jeopardy. At that point they said, Sorry, lady, it's too late! You're in state court now and we don't have jurisdiction. So they got off the hook very easily. It was then that we appealed to the United States Supreme Court, which required sending a formal legal brief, asking them to hear the case and postpone the state court trial until they decided if the Minnesota abortion law was constitutional. I was really disappointed that Justice Douglas was the only one that voted to hear my case.

My trial on the abortion charge took place in October 1970. The American College of Obstetrics and Gynecology was meeting in Minneapolis at that same time, and I was very disappointed that the national president refused to testify for me. I was so let down. Here I had an impeccable record, my credentials were beyond question, I was a board-certified specialist, I wasn't a quack, and I had expert witnesses that were all qualified. Yet he would not even testify in the slightest degree on my behalf. There was a lot of division in the College at that time; there was a very strong anti-abortion faction. The College has gradually changed its attitude, but doctors really have to be led kicking and screaming to make any social progress. They like the status quo; there aren't many who are willing to take a second look at what they were taught in medical school.

Judge Plunkett, who presided over my trial, was a Catholic with eight children. But he was fair, and I appreciated very much his allowing us to put on all our witnesses. I realized enough about law to know that he could have refused all the witnesses we called, all the writings we introduced, and our films of children that had been affected by rubella and were born with horrible defects. On the other hand, some pro-lifers from Chicago, some terrorists who go around the country showing these horrible films of fetuses, wanted to appear and show their slides. My lawyers objected, and Judge Plunkett went along and wouldn't let them show their pictures. These people had never done any abortions, so it was a fair ruling. He let the show go on about as long as we wanted. It was a very scientific presentation.

We didn't choose a jury in this case. I was doing it on an intellectual basis and I thought it was far better to trust the judgment of a judge than an emotional jury; it would be easier to educate the judge. I really *wanted* to come to court—I thought that was the only way to educate the legislature. I expected the legislature would promptly pass a new law! But it didn't work out that way.

Judge Plunkett found me guilty and sentenced me to thirty days in jail and probation for a year, although he stayed the jail term pending appeal. Everybody in the community was terribly interested in my case; it was in the headlines for days as the trial proceeded. I got lots of phone calls, and there were some patients I never heard from again. I had a lot of Catholic patients. The threatening calls didn't bother me much, because I realized they were usually from ignorant people. The thing that's so amusing is that once they get into a similar situation, they're often the first to come around asking for an abortion! I've seen that turnabout so often, with doctors and active anti-abortionists.

I *was* concerned about losing my license after my conviction. I was on probation and I had to be darned careful what I did. I could still refer patients out, and I did continue to refer them to New York and California. But I didn't *dare* perform an abortion, even on patients who were obviously spontaneously aborting. Practicing good gynecology in a strong Catholic community is not easy, and I'd run into problems early in my practice. I had used St. Joseph's Hospital for quite a while. I remember taking care of a woman who was a good Catholic. She'd already had twelve spontaneous abortions; she wanted a pregnancy desperately and I wanted to help her. This woman was in her thirteenth pregnancy. We thought we had it made—she was over four months. She came into my office with no symptoms of labor and I examined her and realized that the fetus was hanging by the cord in her vagina and that she could expel the whole sac at any time and hemorrhage.

So I got her in my car and took her to St. Joseph's and scheduled her for surgery to remove the placenta and terminate her pregnancy. We were waiting for the operating room to be ready, and the priest came up to her bedside and they told me, He canceled your surgery. They thought I was deliberately aborting her. I was *so* incensed at the idea that he could go in and cancel my orders. I put her in my car and took her to a Protestant hospital. I later got that priest by the nape of the neck, I had him up against a wall, and I said, If you *ever* interfere in my practice again, I'll have you sued for practicing medicine without a license. I was so *angry* with him; and he got transferred shortly after that and he was out of my hair. After a while you get to the point of frustration and you can't even be reasonable in your dislike of people like that. This male-dominated hierarchy and what it has inflicted on the women of their church! They don't realize what agony they put women through. I had so many Catholic patients and dried their tears and tried to teach them to use rhythm. When I think of the basal temperature charts I've gone over with women and tried to figure out when and if they got pregnant, or how they could avoid pregnancy!

The Minnesota Supreme Court heard my appeal in the fall of '71 and I knew I'd have to wait for a decision. In fact, they waited until the U.S. Supreme Court decided *Roe* v. *Wade* in January 1973, and then my conviction was reversed. I went to Washington, D.C., in the spring of '72 to become the medical director of the Preterm Clinic, which had only been in operation about nine months. It was quite a challenge and a great experience for me. I went there not knowing *anything* about outpatient abortion services and I learned a lot. Our patients were a cross section of the whole country, from all over the United States. At that point, only New York and California were available for legal abortions. Women would walk in off the street and have their abortion and go to the airport, back to Arizona or someplace.

It was a totally different concept of medical care at Preterm. I was trained, and all doctors were at that time, that you *never* invaded the uterine cavity without the utmost sterile precautions, capping, gowning, gloves, in a sterile operating room, patients scrubbed and prepped, the skin shaved and painted. It took a little courage to change after you'd been trained over the years. But this outpatient procedure and suction equipment had demonstrated in other countries, Eastern Europe and England, that a lot of this was unnecessary and only increased the cost. We had a lot of foreign visitors, a lot of them referred from the White House, from Africa and England. I spent two days with Margaret Mead, who watched me abort patients. We kept very close records on more than twenty thousand patients and not one of them died, and there were very few complications. We did about a thousand a month. I felt that documenting the safety was the first way of dispelling the arguments of the 'antis.' Even some of the proponents of legal abortions were stumbling blocks: They wanted the procedure done in hospitals. But we proved the free-standing clinic was just as safe, and we published several papers based on our studies.

I got involved in the *Roe* v. *Wade* case through Sarah Weddington, the young lawyer who brought the case in Texas. She invited me to come down to Austin and talk to the student body at the university. While I was in Washington at Preterm, I went to hear Sarah argue the *Roe* case before the Supreme Court, and I celebrated with her afterwards. She did a very good job. She was only twenty-five years old at the time, quite pretty, with her long blonde hair down her back.

I thought *Roe* v. *Wade* was a *marvelous* decision! It was unbelievable, beyond my wildest dreams! I couldn't get over Justice Blackmun's perception of the whole thing. His opinion was so sound, medically, that we couldn't have asked for anything better. I was so impressed with it that I went to see him in his chambers. We had a mutual friend who arranged the visit. He talked with me for an hour and a half, and he couldn't have been nicer. I just felt I wanted to thank him; it's just one of those things you just *have* to do. He told me how hard it had been, ever since. He pointed to his wastebasket and said, Every day, the hate mail I get would fill that basket. And he told me how he couldn't help but have qualms sometimes about whether he had made the right decision. I hastened to reassure him that I felt that he *had,* and that was one reason I wanted to talk with him. I have no qualms anymore, ever! But I used to think, Maybe they *are* right, maybe this *is* wrong! Maybe I'm a cold, unfeeling person. Maybe I *am* a murderer! And then I'd see a patient, and that's all I had to do, and I'd say, There's no question about it, it *is* right! But Justice Blackmun didn't have the benefit of seeing those patients, and I thought because he is so isolated from the real world that he ought to know.

After I had spent two years at the Preterm Clinic in Washington, I wanted to come home. I had two teen-age daughters who hadn't seen much of me. There was plenty to be done, and I came back to St. Paul–Ramsey Hospital and I went full-time teaching and on the staff there, and started the fertility control clinic. I developed a clinic where we did a lot of the late-term abortions, because I figured the hospital was the one place where those could be done. I helped to develop techniques for second trimester abortions. Ever since then, my big object has been training the younger doctors, and I've trained a lot of very good people that are now outstanding in the field.

I got involved in the *McRae* case, which challenged the Hyde

Amendment ban on federal funding of abortions, while I was at St. Paul–Ramsey, where I was constantly seeing late abortions that were medically necessary, in the low-income group. We did not have the funds to do them and the hospital had no provisions for them, because we had a law in Minnesota that forbid spending any public money for abortions. You have no idea of the injustice of it. It would be heartbreaking sometimes. I helped to raise money, and we had a private fund that we used to help some of these women, and we did everything to help cut down on the cost in the hospital. But I was continually in conflict with the hospital heads over the charges they made. I'd be sailing into their offices every day with a conflict about the bills. It's a wonder they tolerated me, because I was always clashing with the administration over money.

I had testified as an expert witness in a number of abortion cases and I've done at least a dozen depositions. A witness gets to be known after a while, and the ACLU asked me if I would testify in the Hyde Amendment case. And I just jumped on it. I had testified before our state legislature umpteen times—to no avail, of course. Minnesota had passed a law prohibiting any state funding to women for abortions, and we had successfully challenged this law up to the federal court of appeals. It was pending there when I testified in the *McRae* case in New York.

My testimony was about the medical necessity for abortion. The government lawyers kept trying to pin me down as to medical indications, what would be justified, and I said there were none. They just spent *hours* on that. They really were shocked when I said that any woman's wanting to have an abortion was all that was necessary. That was the indication for abortion, that the woman *wanted* it! They didn't much like that. The government lawyers were an obnoxious crew. They always are! Unfortunately, the Supreme Court decision in the *McRae* case reversed our victory in Minnesota by declaring that the Hyde Amendment was constitutional.

Minnesota passed its parental notification law in 1981, and I became the lead plaintiff in the suit against it. I was then the medical director of three different clinics: Midwest Health Center for Women in Minneapolis, Planned Parenthood here in St. Paul, and we had just set up a clinic in Duluth. We had a lot of minors as patients, and their cases were particularly urgent. With our severe winters, you couldn't believe the problems they had, particularly the rural kids—having to hitchhike in the wintertime, or sleep in a car; not having any money; having to make two or three trips to go through a court hearing. We heard stories of sexual abuse, child abuse, beatings, all kinds of things. I remember this black girl who was deaf and her mother kept her chained to the bed; she wanted to get the abortion and her mother didn't want her to. It was horrible!

We had real problems at the clinics with parents who were off their rockers, who were fanatics. I've been threatened a few times. I remember one fellow who walked into the clinic and threatened to kill me if I aborted his girlfriend. I called the police and they arrested him for trespass. I went to court and spent an entire day, and the judge was another strong Catholic who listened to the whole thing and finally said, He had just as much right in a public building as the doctors did. So I got absolutely nowhere with that!

It looks now that our Minnesota case on parental notification might get to the Supreme Court, because the justices were split evenly when they decided a similar case from Illinois in December 1987. Justice Kennedy hadn't been confirmed then, so the Illinois case didn't set any precedent. We won the Minnesota case in the federal district court and court of appeals, and got excellent opinions from the judges. The state has stated they will appeal, so it's likely that our case will decide the issue. We'll just have to wait and see, particularly at how Justice Kennedy will vote on abortion issues.

Looking ahead to the future, I'm optimistic. Abortion is a personal issue: Only the individual can decide, and that's what people have to face up to. Now, with surrogate motherhood and frozen embryos, all of these things are new issues, and abortion has become commonplace. People talk about it openly. I remember when you didn't even *use* the word in polite society. I used to steel myself every time I'd go back to Washington and the cabbie would always say, What do you do? I'd say I was in family planning or something. Finally, I decided that was hypocritical and I'd say, I'm an abortionist! At first, it was hard. At that time, nobody was an abortionist who wasn't a criminal. Now, people don't even flicker an eyelash when you say you head up abortion clinics.

I know there are a lot of fanatics out there, but the old ones will die off, and some will get off on other subjects. There were fanatics as far as anesthesia and immunizations and things we take for granted nowadays. It may take a long time, and there will be setbacks, I suppose. When I first got involved in this issue, I really didn't foresee all the complications. I was naive. But I haven't any regrets. I wouldn't do it any differently. I realize how slowly things change, and maybe it's just as well they do.

I've become more a feminist, by far, as time goes on, because I really see that abortion is a women's issue. Women have been the ones who have suffered so much from unwanted pregnancies. I know how important this issue is to women's control of their lives, to economic equality and political equality, all along the line. If women can control their reproduction, equality can be achieved. But unless they do, they're a *long* way from getting equality.

12

Demetrio Rodriguez
v. San Antonio

Demetrio Rodriguez sued San Antonio, Texas, school officials in 1968 to challenge the property-tax finance system that kept poor children in poor schools. *Courtesy of* San Antonio Express-News, © *Express-News Corp.* *1988*

I.
"The Poor People
Have Lost Again"

The name of Demetrio Rodriguez appeared first among those on the complaint filed in the federal court of San Antonio, Texas, on July 10, 1968. Six other parents of children in the Edgewood Independent School District, located in the sprawling Hispanic barrio on the West Side of San Antonio, added their names to the suit against a long list of school and state officials. The suit charged that Edgewood children, and those of all other poor families in Texas, suffered from inferior education because of the inequitable property-tax basis of the state's school financing system. The Edgewood parents asked the federal court to find the system in violation of the U.S. Constitution and to order the state to equalize the funding of all 1,000 school districts in Texas.

Demetrio Rodriguez was the logical choice to head the list of plaintiffs in the complaint. The forty-two-year-old Navy and Air Force veteran had worked more than fifteen years at Kelly Air Force Base, just south of his Edgewood home. Demetrio and his family lived in a neat white house on Sylvia Avenue, a street with no sidewalks or storm sewers. Roosters crowed in his neighbors' yards. Three of his four sons attended Edgewood Elementary School, just a block away across a dusty playing field. The school building was crumbling, classrooms lacked basic supplies, and almost half the teachers were not certified and worked on emergency permits. Demetrio feared that Edgewood schools would not prepare his sons to compete for the good jobs that "Anglos" controlled in San Antonio. He became a grass-roots community activist and helped to organize the Edgewood District Concerned Parents Association.

The parents group met with frustration in asking Edgewood school officials to improve the district's twenty-five schools, which enrolled 22,000 students. Dr. Jose Cardenas, the district superintendent, explained sadly that he had no money to rebuild crumbling schools and hire more qualified teachers. Behind the gloomy financial figures lay ethnic statistics. More than 90 percent of Edgewood students were Hispanic, 6 percent were black, and fewer than one in twenty came from the Anglo community that dominated San Antonio's business and political leadership.

San Antonio was a booming Sun Belt city in 1968, brimming with confidence and eager to attract high-tech industries to balance the city's dependence on livestock production and military spending at its three air force bases. San Antonio won a national "Cleanest City" award in 1967, and bulldozers cleared a downtown slum area to make way for HemisFair '68, the exposition that city leaders hoped would bring millions of tourists and create thousands of jobs. Visitors would flock to see the historic Alamo, whose Anglo defenders fought and died in 1836 at the hands of Mexican troops; and the brand-new Tower of the Americas, soaring 750 feet above the city. The exposition did lure tourists to San Antonio, but few of them visited the Hispanic barrio that housed more than a third of the city's half-million residents. Four miles from the Alamo, Edgewood parents fought to protect their children from Anglo legislators in the state capitol of Austin who refused to correct the imbalance in school funding.

Just before HemisFair opened in 1968, Demetrio Rodriguez led a group of Edgewood parents to Arthur Gochman's law office in downtown San Antonio. Well-known for defending civil rights, Gochman was also well-connected in the city's business and political elite. Born in 1931, he graduated from Trinity University in San Antonio, and the University of Texas Law School. Gochman welcomed the Edgewood parents, who first raised charges of financial hanky-panky in the district's schools. After listening patiently to their complaints, Gochman explained that the real source of poor schools for poor families was unfair funding, not fiddling with the books. He had recently read a federal court decision which struck down funding disparities between schools in Washington, D.C. Although this decision was limited to schools within one district, Gochman felt that its holding could be expanded on a state-wide basis.

Gochman assured the Edgewood parents that he would help them challenge the state's property-tax system. Knowing that his new clients had little money, he hoped to enlist support for the suit from the Mexican American Legal Defense and Education Fund, which copied its name and purpose from the NAACP lawyers' group headed by Thurgood Marshall. Gochman sent MALDEF a legal memo on the Edgewood case, but internal political factors intervened and the group declined to participate. MALDEF was then a small organization and had decided to focus on individual cases of police brutality or job discrimination. Suits against the state of Texas, on behalf of millions of Mexican Americans, would have drained the group's limited resources. Gochman accepted the MALDEF decision and went ahead, funding the Rodriguez case from his own pocket.

Arthur Gochman prepared the complaint with great care. The case rested upon two major claims, neither of which had been accepted by any federal court. One was that the Fourteenth Amendment to the U.S. Constitution included education as a "fundamental right" which states must provide on an equal basis to all students. The other was that poor families constituted a "suspect class" which deserved special judicial protection against discrimination by state officials. Gochman added a third claim: Mexican Americans were a distinct racial and ethnic group and were included, like blacks, in the "suspect class" category. If the federal court accepted *any* of these claims, judicial precedent required that Texas officials present a "compelling" reason to justify the property-tax basis of school funding. Gochman knew that these claims rested on shaky legal foundations, but he supported each with a rock-solid factual argument.

Because the Rodriguez case challenged a state law on federal grounds, it came before a three-judge panel which would rule without a jury. There would be no courtroom dramatics in this case. Gochman knew that his strong suit would be statistical evidence, which by its nature was dry and dull, and he assembled a high-powered crew of six expert witnesses. Five came from San Antonio, including Dr. Cardenas, the Edgewood superintendent, and two Trinity University professors. The sixth was Dr. Joel Berke, director of the Education Finance and Governance Program at Syracuse University, perhaps the nation's leading expert on school financing.

The case began slowly and wound through the court like a dry creekbed. Lawyers for the state asked the judges to dismiss the complaint, arguing that there was no legal basis for relief to the Edgewood parents. More than a year passed before the judges denied the motion on October 15, 1969. The state then argued that the Texas legislature, which would not convene until January 1971, had authorized a committee study of school financing and should be allowed to act on the study. The state's lawyers predicted that legislative reform would equalize funding among districts and provide relief to the parents. Aware that the legislature that convened in January 1969 had adjourned in May without acting on similar reform proposals, the judges reluctantly granted the state's go-slow motion, directing the defendants to advise the court every 90 days of progress by the committee.

Despite these assurances, the Texas legislators came to Austin in 1971 and left without acting on school finance reform. Judge Adrian Spears of the federal panel lectured the state's lawyers at a hearing in December 1971: "I think it is a little disconcerting to a court, when it abstains and does it on specific grounds that it wishes for the legislature to do something about it, and with education as important as it is to the citizenry of our state and our nation, for the legislature to completely ignore it. It makes you feel that it just does no good for a court to do anything other than, if it feels these laws are suspect, declare them unconstitutional." Judge Spears, a Democrat placed on the federal bench by President John F. Kennedy, lived in Alamo Heights, an independent city inside San Antonio's borders. Spears knew very well the disparities between schools in Edgewood and Alamo Heights.

Preparing for the long-delayed trial with his expert witnesses, Arthur Gochman decided to dramatize the issues by contrasting Edgewood, the poorest of the county's seven systems, with Alamo Heights, its most wealthy district. The names alone illustrated the division—the Hispanic district at the city's edge, and the Anglo district on its heights. Wealth looks down on poverty in most cities and, despite its modest hills, San Antonio is no exception to this rule. Lawyers, doctors, and bankers lived in Alamo Heights; 54 percent of its male workers held executive or professional positions in 1970, against just 4 percent in Edgewood. Three of every four Alamo Heights residents had completed high school. The Edgewood figure was less than one in ten.

Gochman drove home the disparities with simple charts, extracted from more than 100,000 pages of documents. School funding began with local property values: The 1970 figure for Edgewood was only $5,429 per student, while the Alamo Heights figure was $45,095. Even though Edgewood parents taxed themselves at the highest rate in the city, property taxes provided only $26 for each pupil. State funding added $222 and federal programs contributed $108, for a total of $356 for each Edgewood student. Parents in Alamo Heights, eight times as wealthy in property, taxed themselves at the city's lowest rate and still raised $333 for each student. The state program added even more for Alamo Heights than for Edgewood, $225 per student; and federal funding of $26 gave a total of $594. With almost twice as much to spend on each student, Alamo Heights could afford better teachers; 40 percent had masters degrees, as opposed to just 15 percent in Edgewood. Each school counselor in Edgewood had six times as many students to help as those in Alamo Heights.

Gochman put his case into a nutshell with this figure: Edgewood parents would have to tax themselves at twenty times the rate of those in Alamo Heights to match their revenues from property taxes. This would require a tax of almost $13 for each $100 of property value. But the state imposed a property tax ceiling of $1.50. "The Texas system makes it impossible for poor districts to provide quality education," Gochman concluded.

Two days before Christmas in 1971, more than three years after the Edgewood parents filed their suit, the three-judge panel, like the Wise Men of old, brightened their holiday with a ruling that the Texas school-finance system violated the "equal protection" guarantee of the Fourteenth Amendment. The judges held that "wealth" discrimination was "suspect" under the Constitution and that education was a "fundamental" right, as Gochman had argued. The panel also ruled that not only had Texas been "unable to demonstrate compelling state interests" in basing school funding on property values, but it had failed "even to establish a reasonable basis" for the existing system. This latter holding meant that the state had flunked even the most simple test for judging laws. But the brightly-wrapped Christmas package was empty: The judges granted the state two more years to reform the unlawful system.

Texas had been given, between the suit's filing and the court's grace period, six years to put its schools in order. But the state had not expected the federal court ruling. "The initial reaction in Texas was one of surprise, bordering on shock," wrote Mark Yudof, a University of Texas law professor who had helped Arthur Gochman in the case. "The Attorney General's office had been spreading the word that the *Rodriguez* suit was frivolous and need not concern educators or politicians." With the state's pocketbook at risk, the Attorney General hired one of Yudof's colleagues to argue an appeal before the U.S. Supreme Court. Charles Alan Wright had become, at the age of forty-three, an acknowledged expert on federal litigation. He also had close ties with the Republican establishment, and belonged to exclusive social and country clubs in Austin and New York. Wright was an ideal choice to defend the state's enormous financial stake in the *status quo*.

Other states and their nervous bondholders had stakes in the case as well. The attorney generals of twenty-five states filed "friend of the court" briefs with the Supreme Court on the side of Texas; twenty-three high-powered (and high-paid) bond lawyers joined another brief. Minnesota broke ranks to support Demetrio Rodriguez and the Edgewood parents, along with the American Civil Liberties Union, the NAACP, the National Education Association, and California's state controller, a Democrat who lined up against the state's Republican attorney general. Most unusual and ironic was the brief submitted by the San Antonio Independent School District, urging the Supreme Court to uphold the lower-court ruling: The district was in fact the nominal defendant and was represented by Charles Alan Wright, whose argument the brief asked the justices to reject. Politics makes strange bedfellows; litigation sometimes kicks them out of bed.

Wright began his Supreme Court argument on the morning

of October 12, 1972. Only eight justices filed out through the red velvet curtain behind the bench; Justice Thurgood Marshall was ill that day. Wright began with a strategic concession that the Texas school-finance system was "imperfect" and produced substantial disparities between districts. But he then claimed that the lower-court ruling to eliminate these disparities "would impose a constitutional straight jacket on the public schools of fifty states." Wright urged that "the rational basis test is the appropriate test" of the Texas system, although the lower court had flunked the state on that easy test.

Wright also argued that "very little is to be left of local government if the decision below is affirmed," although the local government he supposedly represented now asked for affirmance. Wright faced a final question from Justice William O. Douglas, who noted that the case record "pretty clearly demonstrated" that Mexican Americans suffered from unequal school funding. "The racial issue is in this litigation," Wright admitted. Although the case was brought by "particular plaintiffs who are Mexican-American and who live in a district with low taxable resources," Wright argued that racial and ethnic factors were simply "a happenstance" in the case.

Arthur Gochman then replaced Wright at the podium and quickly pointed out that "the poorest people live in the poorest districts and the richest people live in the richest districts." The heart of the case, he argued, was that district wealth "perfectly correlates" with district school funding. Gochman was questioned about his claim, adopted by the lower court, that education was a "fundamental right" under the Constitution. What about police and fire protection, or health facilities, one justice asked. "Where would you grade them, with respect to public education? Higher? Lower?" Gochman responded that "education affects matters guaranteed by the Bill of Rights." Unlike protection against crime, fire, and disease, education "is related to every important right we have as citizens."

Gochman gave a heated rebuttal to Wright's cold statement that Texas was only required to give Edgewood students a "minimum" level of education. "What kind of morass is Mr. Wright asking you to get into? What is a minimum? Are we going to have two classes of citizens—minimum opportunity students, and first class citizens?" Gochman ended his argument by noting that

Wright's ostensible client, the San Antonio school district, "after seeing the decision of the trial court, and the equity involved, and the vast discrimination, filed a brief in support of the decision of the trial court."

Wright had reserved six minutes of the half–hour he was allowed for argument. He used the time for courtroom diplomacy. "I admire the devotion and the ability with which Mr. Gochman has persevered in this case," he said. Wright also lauded Demetrio Rodriguez and the other Edgewood parents. "These people have opened the eyes of the whole country to a very serious problem." Preaching the gospel of judicial restraint, Wright finally asked the justices to "look to legislatures to provide remedies" for the nation's poor children. Wright's argument included the unintended prophecy that he might make an entirely different claim about legislative powers "the next time I am up before you on a different case." His next client was President Richard Nixon, who tried without success to withhold the incriminating Watergate tapes from legislative committees. Wright certainly did not look to legislatures for remedies to Nixon's legal ills.

The legal and financial stakes in the *Rodriguez* case were reflected in the length of the Court's opinions, which covered 137 closely printed pages. Ruling by a one-vote margin, the Supreme Court reversed the lower court and upheld the property-tax basis of America's public schools. The ruling was issued on March 21, 1973, two months after Richard Nixon's second—and final—inauguration. Nixon had appointed four justices during his first term, and all four voted for Texas and its bondholders. The Warren Court had given way to the Burger Court, which almost invariably upheld the powers of state and local officials. Justice Potter Stewart, who joined the Nixon appointees in this case, was a fellow Republican and predictable supporter of fiscal stability.

Chief Justice Warren Burger asked Justice Lewis Powell to write the Court's majority opinion. Powell was a perfect choice for the task, a former corporate lawyer from Richmond, Virginia, whose firm represented many owners of school bonds. The only senator to vote against Powell's confirmation in 1971, Fred Harris of Oklahoma, was a prairie populist who feared that his patrician background would give Powell little sympathy for poor litigants before the Court. "In fact," wrote a later biographer of the wealthy justice, "it has been in the area of classifications based on wealth that Justice Powell has been the least receptive to Equal Protection arguments."

Powell's opinion dutifully and diligently canvassed the factual record of the *Rodriguez* case, finding "substantial disparities" in the funding of Texas school districts. Powell considered the proper judicial test more important than facts. "Texas virtually concedes," he wrote, that its school-finance system "could not withstand the strict judicial scrutiny" that the lower court employed. Powell's approach, however, found "neither the suspect-classification nor the fundamental-interest analysis persuasive."

Powell first addressed the issue of wealth as a suspect classification. The Court's previous opinions striking down laws which discriminated against poor persons, he noted, affected only individuals. The problem with poor people in Texas was that they belonged to "a large, diverse, and amorphous class, unified only by the common factor of residence in districts that happen to have less taxable wealth than other districts."

Powell continued with a denial that education constituted a "fundamental right" that was essential to effective citizenship. He noted that education "is not among the rights afforded explicit protection under our Federal Constitution." Two months earlier, Powell had joined an opinion holding that the Constitution protected a "fundamental right" to abortions, a term also not mentioned in the Constitution. Powell agreed that education was essential to citizenship, but the Constitution did not "guarantee to the citizenry the most *effective* speech or the most *informed* electoral choice."

Powell's opinion raised the ultimate question, the specter of socialism. Future cases, he wrote, might expand the claim of equal funding for education to claims for all of life's necessities. "How, for instance," Powell asked, "is education to be distinguished from the significant personal interests in the basics of decent food and shelter? Empirical examination might well buttress an assumption that the ill-fed, ill-clothed, and ill-housed are among the most ineffective participants in the political process," and deserve special protection by federal courts. Powell and the Court's majority shrank from such suggestions, made four decades earlier by President Franklin D. Roosevelt. Rejecting the New Deal promise, Powell sent the poor to forage for food, clothing, and housing on their own.

Justice Thurgood Marshall had been ill during arguments in the *Rodriguez* case, but the Court's opinion sickened his conscience. Marshall, who had argued the *Brown* case before the Supreme Court, denounced the Court's opinion in the *Rodriguez* case as "a retreat from our historic commitment to equality of educational opportunity" for poor children of any racial or ethnic minority. Marshall answered Powell with citations to more than fifty Supreme Court decisions upholding claims to "fundamental rights" that the Constitution did not spell out in explicit words. Marshall then quoted Chief Justice Warren's holding in *Brown* that education "is the very foundation of good citizenship." Demetrio Rodriguez did not ask, Marshall suggested, that the Edgewood schools should make his children the *best* citizens in San Antonio, only that they should become *good* citizens.

Justice Marshall ended his dissent with disparaging remarks about Justice Powell's faith in Texas legislators. He wrote with obvious sarcasm that Powell's remarks "will doubtless be of great comfort to the schoolchildren of Texas' disadvantaged districts, but considering the vested interests of the wealthy school districts in the preservation of the status quo, they are worth little more." Demetrio Rodriguez spoke for Edgewood parents in responding to the Court's decision: "The poor people have lost again."

Twelve years later, in 1985, Demetrio joined another suit—this one filed by the Mexican American Legal Defense and Education Fund—which challenged the school-finance system under the Texas state constitution. During those twelve years, the courts of six states had ruled that property-tax school funding violated state constitutions. Supreme Court Justice William J. Brennan, Jr., whose home state of New Jersey joined this parade, had urged lawyers for years to use state constitutions in seeking wider rights for their clients. Ruling on April 30, 1987, Judge Harley Clark of the Texas district court in Austin followed Brennan's lead: "If one district has more access to funds than another district," Clark wrote, "the wealthier one will have the best ability to fulfill the needs of its students."

Many things changed in San Antonio between 1968 and 1987. The city elected its first Hispanic mayor, Henry Cisneros, in 1981, and returned him to office in the next three biennial elections. The number of high-school graduates in Edgewood doubled within a decade, from 9 percent to 22 percent. But some things changed for the worse. The income gap for families with children in Edgewood and Alamo Heights widened from $4,000 in 1960 to $36,000 in 1980.

Demetrio Rodriguez has retired from his Air Force job, and his sons have graduated from Edgewood's schools. But his daughter Patty is still in school—and Demetrio is still in court, seeking an education for his daughter equal to that of the banker's daughter in Alamo Heights.

II.
"Education Is the
Best Thing"

I was born in 1925 in a small town in Texas that doesn't exist anymore. The name of it is Valley Wells. It was between Cotulla and Carrizo Springs, down near Laredo in Dimmit County, near the Rio Grande. It was a farming town; mostly winter vegetables. My folks lived in Valley Wells, and from there they went to Crystal City, then they moved to Hondo and Uvalde. Most of my brothers are in Uvalde now. My great-grandfather was a born Texan, my father was a born Texan, but my mother came from Mexico. She met my father in Eagle Pass, down on the border.

My father was a migrant worker—he worked in the fields. He would settle in a town until there was no more work, and he'd move to another town. In the early years, when he was young, he used to clear land. They would go around in buggies and wagons and sleep out in the fields. He used to tell me that they'd go into a town, and they'd tell him, Mexican, don't let that sun set on you here! They had guys riding on a horse with a gun. But he wasn't much of an activist; maybe he thought they had the right to do that. My dad never held a grudge against the Anglos or the gringos, which I sometimes call them. He had a lot of respect for the Anglo people, and he couldn't understand a lot of things the young people, Mexican Americans, were doing in the '50s and '60s—when they had movements here in Texas, like Cesar Chavez and the Farmworkers and La Raza Unida, all

294

those young people who were rebelling and trying to focus on the problems.

I came to San Antonio with my brother to go to school here in 1931, when I was about six years old. I had an uncle here, and he suggested to my father that maybe we could get a better education here in San Antonio, because where we were living then the school was segregated. They had one school and one teacher for the Mexican children. We had an Anglo teacher. She was a good teacher, trying to help us out, but it was hard for her, all by herself. I don't think she could speak Spanish.

When I came to San Antonio I spoke one time to my brother in Spanish and the teacher told me, No, don't speak like that! She told me, It's better that you speak English. But my teachers here in San Antonio were very understanding. The schools here were not segregated, but they had different groups in each grade, A and B. A was mostly Anglo kids and B was Mexican kids. At that time the blacks couldn't go to school with white people. Mostly all the Mexican kids were in the B class. When I passed to the second grade they put me with the advanced kids in the A class. I still remember this Anglo kid named Harold. He was the dumbest thing you could think of, but they put him in the A class even though he couldn't compete with us. That was the name of the game; we had to compete with the Anglo kids.

When I was a kid we used to come down to the Haymarket in San Antonio. They had little stands there, selling food and flowers. They had a lot of people singing, and people playing the guitar and accordian. The ladies selling food and flowers were nicknamed 'Chili Queens.' The Haymarket is now known as El Mercado, The Farmers' Market. It was part of our culture, growing up in San Antonio. That was fun for a kid. It's more sophisticated nowadays.

My brother and I would go back in the summer and work on the farms. We would bunch carrots, cut corn; we'd go to pick cotton in West Texas. We had to make a little money with my dad. I worked in the fields when I was ten, eleven, twelve. They used to put us like a bunch of cattle in a big truck and drive out those dusty roads. I still remember going out at the Christmas holidays one year, and they took us to the fields to bunch carrots. We'd wrap them up with string. It was muddy and really cold, and my hands would freeze and hurt. The old people would say, No pone las manas en la lumbre—Don't put your hands in the fire, they'll crack. Wash them in cold water and they'll get warm. And they did.

The farm kids would look at us. We came from San Antonio and we knew a lot of things that they didn't know. They used to ask us a lot of questions. They wanted to know, How are you making it there? Those people were very simple, but they were good people. They would do *anything* to help you. They didn't have too much, but they would share everything with you. We lived in a little house, two rooms. Sometimes we'd have to make our food outside in a fire, because we didn't have kerosene for the stove. There's a comedian from Mexico who jokes about that: When I was young, he says, we used to cook inside and go to the outhouse. Now they all want to cook outside and use the toilet inside!

I went to about the tenth grade—then I was drafted into the Navy in 1944, when I was eighteen. My brother and I were the only two kids from that little town in the service. The Anglo kids stayed there because their fathers were farm owners and got them exemptions. I served in the Pacific, in the Marshall and Gilbert islands, in a carrier aircraft-service unit, like a maintenance squadron. I learned sheet-metal work in the Navy. I didn't even know what a plane *looked* like before that. To me the Navy was a good experience. It helped me quite a bit, and I learned how to eat like a gringo—like shit on a shingle. You know, chipped beef on toast. I came back after the Navy and started working for a company that manufactured toilets and wash basins.

I got married in 1951, and my first wife died. We had a boy in 1953, David. Then I got married again and we got divorced. Then I married my third wife. We had a son, Alex; then Carlos; then James; and Patricia, she's the youngest, she was born in 1971. We have the same birthday, December 22. She's very quiet, not like me. When she goes to school, I ask her, Do the teachers know who you are, Patty? Do you tell them I'm your dad? No, she doesn't tell them. One time I went to pick up Alex at school and they said, Is Alex your son? He never told us anything. Well, he didn't want to. David and Alex are both married and they each have two kids.

I served in the Air Force in 1951. I was in the reserves and they called me to active duty during the Korean War. After I came back from the Air Force I made an application for federal civil service, and they called me and told me I had passed the exam. I was an aircraft sheet–metal worker at Kelly Air Force Base here in San Antonio. We would manufacture parts for aircraft, mostly old B-52s. They were real old aircraft and the aluminum corrodes on them. The parts that were needed were no longer being manufactured. That was our job, to manufacture exact duplicates. Later on I advanced to quality control, where I was an inspector for the last five years that I was there. It was hard work, and I put in thirty-nine years, with my service time. I don't get much of a pension, but I make a living. My house is paid up. Of course, it isn't a mansion, it's in a poor district. But I can live on what I'm getting.

It was kind of rough when I started working at Kelly. The ones in the top jobs were mostly Anglos. I saw a lot of abuses— not physically but verbally. Ever since I was a kid I noticed there was something wrong, but I couldn't pinpoint it. I'd say, How the heck can I do anything? Maybe I should take a gun and start *shooting* these people. Really! I'll tell you the truth, that's the way I felt about it. I knew there was something wrong but I didn't know how to do anything about it.

So when I came back from the service I joined some organizations, like LULAC, the League of United Latin American Citizens, and the American GI Forum. At that time we had people who were educated, they had degrees—like Albert Peña, who's now a municipal judge; and Richard Casillas, he's a regional director for Immigration and Naturalization Service. Those are some of the people who were in the American GI Forum, very active in trying to integrate the schools in small towns like Hondo, where they had the schools segregated in the '50s. When the *Brown* case came out of the Supreme Court, that's when they broke that up. They used to have one elementary school for the Mexican kids in the small towns. Very few Mexican kids went to high schools then. I learned a lot from those organizations in the '50s, although I was just a member.

I moved into Edgewood in about 1957. This is the southwest part of San Antonio, near the Air Force base where I worked. Edgewood used to be mostly a Belgian area; they were farmers with gardens. When Mexican people started coming they sold them lots, very small, about forty by a hundred and fifty feet.

They called it Las Colonias, The Colonies. That's funny. They didn't have any drainage, and the streets were dirt. We had a lot of problems in Edgewood; the schools were all shot. A lot of people realized their kids weren't getting a good education, like the kids on the north side of San Antonio were getting, where the Anglos lived. So they kind of rebelled against the schools. We blamed the problems on the superintendent. He was an Anglo who had been in Edgewood for many years.

The Edgewood elementary school was an old school, all beat up and falling down. It had a lot of bats, and they could only use the first floor. Sometimes bricks would fall down. We had a lot of problems in that school, teaching problems and disciplinary problems; they didn't care what the kids were doing. A lot of parents got together in 1968. We didn't know each other, but we got to know each other. We organized a group we named the Edgewood District Concerned Parents Association. The organizer was a very active lady named Mrs. Alberta Sneed; she was one of the plaintiffs in the case. From there we started having meetings and trying to organize the people to have some kind of dialogue with the school board, with the superintendent. They didn't want to listen to us, so we had a little demonstration, with people marching in front of the school. It got to where the media got caught up in it. I think the media has helped us a lot.

Willie Velazquez heard about it; he's director of Southwest Voter Registration. He got us together with a lawyer named Arthur Gochman. Arthur is a real down-to-earth man; he's got a lot of money but he doesn't show it. We started talking about why we had problems in Edgewood. Arthur told us, The problem's not your superintendent; your problem is the way the state finances your schools. It's a very complicated thing for a layman to understand. Even now there's a lot of things I don't understand. So I asked Arthur, What are we *doing* here? So he said, Well, I'm willing to file a suit against the state of Texas, but we need people, plaintiffs. All I need is for the people to support me, get me signatures from parents. And I said, If that's what you need, I'm willing to sign, to put my name there. What the heck, there's nothing they can do to *me!* So I was the first plaintiff to sign. I didn't know that I was going to be the lead-off plaintiff. I knew there was going to be a case filed: Arthur explained what a class-action suit was. He said, It's going to be all the citizens of Texas that are being discriminated against in school financing, not only the ones that sign; it's going to be everybody against the state of Texas. It was a good conversation. In my mind I thought, I ain't got nothing to lose; I think maybe we could do some good. I didn't envision that it was going to be something this big, that it would take *this* long!

Then I went around, trying to get more people. For a couple of weeks I walked the streets in Edgewood, trying to get people to sign. So we got about fifteen parents. Some of the people didn't want to sign. They said, We sign that thing and they'll just forget about it. I told them, Well, we can try—at least we're doing something. When it came out in the press, a lot of people found out at work that I filed a suit against the state of Texas and they said, You can't do that. You're a civil service employee; you're under the Hatch Act. I said, That's baloney. I can do anything as long as I take the route through the judicial system. A lot of the Anglo guys used to argue with me; they didn't like it. They thought I was a Communist. I told them, I'm no more Communist than you are. I'm using the judicial system and I don't care what you say. I told them, You know why I'm doing this? Because I've *been* the victim of discrimination.

I always thought about the discrimination that I've been through. When I was in the Navy I came back to visit my brother in Hondo. I was in my Navy uniform, very proud, with my Donald Duck cap. I went into a restaurant and they told me they couldn't serve me—I'd have to go back in the kitchen. I went to a theater in Hondo; they told me I couldn't sit there, I had to sit on the side for Mexicans or in the balcony with the blacks. When I was a boy, we went to pick cotton in West Texas and there was no restaurant you could go in. You could go order something at a little window in the back, but you couldn't eat in the restaurants. My boy says, Dad, I heard that story so many times and it's the same story you always tell. I said, It's the same story because I went *through* it, dammit! And I'll never forget it! I was a kid and I went through those things.

It never came to my mind that this case would go on for so long or go up to the Supreme Court. Arthur had a lot of lawyers to help him out. Warren Weir, Manuel Montez, Rose Spector, they did most of the work. Once in a while he'd call me to his office and kind of brief me on what was happening, what they were doing. We got together once in a while in Edgewood. After the case was in the courts from 1968 to 1972, I couldn't find a lot of the plaintiffs; I guess they forgot about it. After we filed the class-action suit, the three-judge panel ruled in favor of us. We felt optimistic after this, but Arthur told me, This is going to be appealed by the state, no doubt about it. It's going to take a long time, more paperwork, more briefs and all that. You're just going to have to hold on. And I said, As long as it takes, I'm here with you. If you need me for anything, just call me. I'll take off from work.

When the case came out of the Supreme Court and we lost, it surprised the hell out of me. I was sure the Supremes (my nickname for the Supreme Justices) were fair and would rule in favor of the case, because they could see there were discrepancies in the school financing in Texas, and the state had been trying to solve this problem for too many years. The state of Texas had the best constitutional lawyer in the Supreme Court; his name is Charles Alan Wright. They tell me he's a genius at constitutional law. After the Supreme Justices decided against us, we had a gathering at one of the schools to let the people know and explain it to them. It was sad. We even saw our lawyer, Arthur, cry about it. I guess it showed how much he cared. He told us that maybe, in ten years, the case would be reversed.

The schools in Edgewood didn't get any better after our case. They had to build a new elementary school because the old one was falling down. It's named the Oscar Perales school. He was a founder of LULAC, a very active person. It's sad to say this, but the Edgewood district is mostly used by teachers that need experience to find better jobs. Also, equally as sad is the claim by Pablo Escamilla, a former school board member here. He claims that ninety percent of the Edgewood teachers are from very little to extremely illiterate. The best teachers don't stay in the district. They change teachers one year to another, and the kids don't get settled. I guess it's natural for a person to try to make a better living in some other place. They want to go to northeast San Antonio or Alamo Heights. And they don't have the tools in the Edgewood schools, the equipment that other schools have, such as science equipment. They change principals at Kennedy High School about every year.

My daughter is an honor student at Kennedy. I hope she goes on to college. But they don't test those kids to know their ability;

they don't have any counseling. I was talking to one of the teachers last night at this meeting and I said, My daughter is a sophomore and they haven't even tested her to know what she's good for. They're not guiding her. That's one of the main problems we have in the Edgewood district. The counselors think that it's not necessary. They say they don't have the money for those tests. That lady last night opened my eyes: I'm going to approach the board and say, If I want my daughter to take that test, can I pay for it? Twenty dollars is *nothing* compared to what she's going to get out of it.

Edgewood hasn't changed too much since I moved here twenty years ago. We still don't have no sidewalks, no drainage. When the kids go to school they have to walk on the street and they get wet. Yesterday, when it was raining, the kids were coming out of the Kennedy High School and walking along McMullen, which has a lot of traffic coming in and out of Kelly. The streets are flooded and the cars come by and throw water on the kids. That kid ain't going to school, so then we don't get as much state aid, which is based on ADA, average daily attendance. But we developed a homeowners' association, and the last two years we started to work with the city councilman to bring us money for drainage. We got a bond passed; we're going to have $18.4 million for that area. We're going to get drainage, and sidewalks and streets resurfaced, over the next five years.

I'm working in the community now to get school-board members that know more about our problems. We're trying to get board members that went through the school system. Right now we have three members that went through the Edgewood system, so we have people that know more about the district and can help out. I was appointed to the board in 1969 for seven months. Then I ran and I lost by nineteen votes because the other guy had more money. I ran because most of the people on the board were the more entrenched, older people. Some young guys asked me to run on their ticket; they said I'd help them just by running with them. So we ran and one of them won, but I lost by nineteen votes. And we started an organization that's called CARE, Committee for Alternative and Relevant Education. After every election we start preparing for another one, so now we have a majority on the board that are trying to help the schools.

We want to get young people involved in politics, because that's going to bring the best of what we have. Young people get more educated, even Mexican American, they're more sophisticated. Of course, they're turning more to the right, they're getting very conservative. They haven't been victims of this discrimination, like we were. My boy James, he's a paralegal, and we argue about discrimination. He says, Dad, there's no such thing as that. Nowadays we don't have that. I tell him, Yes, you do. You haven't been out of San Antonio. Wait 'til you go out there and hustle; try to get a job and compete. He says, I don't think they should have affirmative action where they give the minorities jobs because they were minorities. I said, They *had* to do that, at that time. We didn't have the education; we had to fight for it and some of us didn't get it because there was obstacles thrown in front of us. Oh, we had big arguments about that. I hope we erase all these things, and the time comes where we can compete equally. Give me the chance, give me something to defend myself with. Education is the best thing you can have, and we have more kids that are getting educated.

But it's still not that good. We still have a lot of obstacles thrown in front of us. Not only the blacks and Mexican Americans, but a lot of poor people are being put on the back burner, where nobody wants to think about it or do something about it. Like in the Appalachian mountains. It's a shame that we have such a rich country, that we're not sharing with a lot of these people. It's bringing this country down. If you don't educate your citizens, something's going to happen and it's not going to help this country. We talk about the Communist takeover from South America—they're going to cross over the Rio Grande and all that baloney. We don't *have* to have the Communists come over here! We are doing the harm to this country by not having equal education. That's the only thing you can give a poor people. Give them an education and they'll be better citizens; they will help this country more. The more education that you have, the better it's going to be for your country. We need intelligent people to work, especially now that you have computers.

Some people are complacent—not that they want to be—because their educational background doesn't help them to understand these things. There's a lot of things I don't know about the school system, being that I don't have a high-school education. And some people don't want to get involved in legal matters, something that's going to go to court. Some of these people are afraid. They don't understand that this is a free country and you can file a suit. As long as you use the judicial system, it's there for you, to protect you. I don't say it helps us *all* the time. It hasn't helped us much in Edgewood, but it helped a little in our problems.

One thing we did about four years ago was file another suit against the state of Texas, this time in the state court. We had all the governors make committees to study the problems of school financing and promote some reforms. Connally and Shivers and Briscoe, they all made these committees. When Briscoe was governor we made a march in Austin and he promised us that he was going to do something about financing the schools; he'd go to the legislators and present a good package to bring about reforms. It never *has* happened! I don't think it's going to happen until the courts rule on the state level, like Judge Clark did in our case. I think it's a good thing what he said. That case was started in the Edgewood district and I'm one of the plaintiffs. We won that case and it's being appealed by the state of Texas. The organization that is handling the case is the Mexican American Legal Defense and Education Fund.

This country has been growing, and we have a lot of problems. I think they can be solved, but it will take years to do it. I guess I'm going to die and not get to see this thing resolved, these problems that we have. The Establishment doesn't want to make any waves for the people that got the money, the districts with money. But one of these days we're going to solve it; maybe it will be another fifty years. I hope with all the actions we're taking in the courts, to bring up the schools and the college system, all these things will bring changes. And the outlook of the Mexican American people here is positive. I'm better off than my parents were, my kids are going to be better off than I am. Of course, you have to hustle, you have to be aggressive. I tell my kids, You have to be aggressive like a gringo! He's aggressive! If he doesn't get in there, he'll push himself in.

But things are getting better in this country for everybody. And I *like* San Antonio! This is my home town. This is where I made my living, where my sons and daughter were born. This city has been growing. We're going to get drainage in our area in five years; it's going to be better. I think we'll have better schools. I *know* it's going to be better.

13

Jo Carol LaFleur
v. Cleveland Board of
Education

Jo Carol LaFleur was a junior-high teacher in Cleveland, Ohio, who challenged in 1970 a maternity-leave rule that forced pregnant teachers out of their classrooms. *Courtesy of* Cleveland Plain Dealer, © *1988*

I.
"There Is No Harm in Climbing Stairs"

Jo Carol LaFleur, a teacher at Patrick Henry Junior High School in Cleveland, Ohio, went to see her principal, Henry E. Wilkins, on the morning of December 17, 1970. Both principal and teacher were new to their jobs; Wilkins had just taken over at the inner-city school that did not have a single white student. Jo Carol was in her first full year of teaching, assigned first to English classes and then to a "transition" class of troubled girls with emotional and educational problems. Jo Carol informed Wilkins that she was pregnant and was expecting a child the next year in July.

The principal was dismayed by news that most people would consider an occasion for congratulations. Under school-district rules, he informed Jo Carol, she could not teach after her fourth month of pregnancy, in March 1971. She would then have to go on unpaid maternity leave and could not return to her job until the semester after her child was three months old. This would keep her from teaching until January 1972. Even then, she could be assigned to any school in the city, which included some twenty junior highs. Jo Carol expressed her objections to this policy, but she returned to her classroom and nothing more happened until March 12, 1971. Wilkins then looked at his calendar and called Jo Carol to his office for another chat.

Tempers flared at the second meeting of principal and teacher.

Wilkins insisted that Jo Carol sign the leave forms he thrust at her. She refused, explaining that her pregnancy did not interfere with teaching and that she wanted to complete the school year. Wilkins finally completed the form without her signature and informed Jo Carol that she was suspended from teaching. She stormed out of the office, returned to her classroom, and told her students that she would not willingly leave them.

Just five weeks after her suspension, Jo Carol faced the Cleveland school board in the federal courtroom of Judge James C. Connell. Two young lawyers, Carol Agin and Lewis Katz, had filed a complaint asking Judge Connell to hold the mandatory leave policy unlawful and to order that Jo Carol be returned to her classroom. The complaint alleged that the board's policy discriminated against women teachers and violated their "privileges and immunities" under the Fourteenth Amendment. Another pregnant Cleveland teacher, Ann Elizabeth Nelson, who taught French at Central Junior High, joined the suit with Jo Carol LaFleur. Behind the case was the Women's Equity Action League, a feminist group founded in 1968 to sponsor litigation and lobbying aimed at employment and education discrimination. Jane M. Picker, a Yale Law School graduate and professor at Cleveland–Marshall Law School, worked with WEAL and recruited Agin and Katz to try the case.

The trial before Judge Connell began on April 19, 1971, and took just two days. Crusty and conservative, Connell did not conceal his disdain for the feminist challenge to the school board's paternalism. Connell was seventy-three years old, a former county prosecutor and municipal judge appointed to the federal bench in 1954 by a fellow Republican, President Dwight Eisenhower. The school board's lawyer, Charles F. Clarke, shared Connell's party affiliation but differed in demeanor. Courtly and courteous, Clarke was a partner in Cleveland's largest corporate firm and devoted much time to community health and welfare groups; he served on the boards of the Free Medical Clinic and the Cleveland Welfare Federation. But Clarke, who also headed the national association of railroad trial lawyers, conceded nothing to his courtroom opponents and salted the trial record with objections to testimony which might damage his case.

Carol Agin and Lewis Katz challenged the mandatory leave policy as unduly rigid. An inflexible rule which banned teachers with normal pregnancies from the classroom made no sense, they argued to Judge Connell, who heard the case without a jury. Dr. Sarah Marcus presented their primary medical case against the rule. Chief of obstetrics at Women's Hospital in Cleveland since 1958, Dr. Marcus began her practice in 1923 and had treated thousands of pregnant women. She peppered her testimony with wry humor. Carol Agin first asked whether women should work during pregnancy. Women with normal pregnancies could work "up until just before they are ready to go into the hospital for delivery," Dr. Marcus answered. "I did," she added. What about physical activities like climbing stairs in schools? "I tell them to be careful and not run up the stairs all at one time, but there is no harm in climbing stairs. It is good activity."

Charles Clarke pricked himself on the doctor's sharp tongue. Unable to budge her from allowing pregnant women to continue teaching, he moved to farm work, which Dr. Marcus also approved. Clarke went on. "What about the mortality of the mothers when the babies were dropped in the field?" She obviously considered that an irrelevant question and answered curtly. Clarke took another plunge. "What about working as a steel worker," he asked, "climbing up on beams for a new steel building?" Dr. Marcus conceded that high-steel work "is hazardous, even for men." Clarke asked why she thought so. Dr. Marcus did not hide her incredulity at his question. "I watched them through the window falling off the Terminal Tower one time," she explained, "and when they got to the bottom, they weren't alive." She ended this exchange on a testy tone: "I wouldn't expect my pregnant mother to be a construction worker."

Clarke defended the board's mandatory leave policy with testimony by Mark Schinnerer, who wrote the regulation in 1952 as Cleveland's school superintendent and was now retired at the age of seventy-two. "We had some very embarrassing situations where women who were pregnant would stay too long in the classroom," he explained. Pregnant teachers "were subjected to humiliations" by students "who giggled about it." Clarke prompted Schinnerer to recall one example of student hilarity at the sight of teacher pregnancy. "It was reported that the children in the classroom in the junior high school were taking bets on whether the baby would be born in the classroom or in the hall." Schinnerer also explained why he wanted women teachers to stay at home for at least six months after childbirth. "I am a strong believer that young children ought to have the mother there" to take "tender care of the babies." Many of America's problems, he suggested, stemmed from working mothers who neglected their infants.

In the 1955 film "Blackboard Jungle," Sidney Poitier played an inner-city teacher who feared his students: "My pupils are the kind you don't turn your back on, even in class." Clarke intimated that pregnant teachers in Cleveland schools were also the likely prey of predatory students. He asked high-school superintendent Julius Tanczos how many students had assaulted teachers in the past year. Judge Connell overruled an objection to this question. School records showed a total of 256 student assaults on teachers, Tanczos stated. Clarke then asked how many guns and knives had been confiscated from students. Connell overruled another objection, and Tanczos said that forty-six guns and eighteen knives had been confiscated that year.

Clarke countered Dr. Marcus with another obstetrician, Dr. William C. Weir, whose practice spanned thirty-five years. The board's lawyer tried to turn the classroom into an emergency ward, leading the doctor through the possible complications of all nine months of pregnancy. Women in the first three months faced "spontaneous abortion, nausea and vomiting, and headaches," Dr. Weir stated. Complications in the next trimester included toxemia, which might cause convulsions, and placenta previa, resulting in serious hemorrhaging. The major complication of the third trimester, Dr. Weir said, would be spontaneous premature delivery.

Dr. Marcus had portrayed pregnant women as capable of most kinds of exertion and exercise. Dr. Weir portrayed the pregnant woman as a virtual cripple. "Her whole center of gravity changes," he stated; "her shoulders are further back, she is subject to more backaches, and due to the weight increase she is much more awkward and can't move around as quickly as she could before." Clarke then asked about the fears of pregnant women. Dr. Weir cited worries about miscarriage, labor difficulties, and abnormalities in their children. "What about an environment," Clarke continued, "in which the pregnant lady might be in fear of a physical assault?" Such fear could induce premature labor, Dr. Weir answered. Informing his witness that 256 Cleveland teachers had been assaulted by students the prior year, Clarke asked his opinion on "the wisdom and reasonableness" of the board's mandatory leave policy. "I think it is a very reasonable rule," Dr. Weir concluded.

Judge Connell agreed with Dr. Weir. His written opinion, issued on May 12, 1971, restated the testimony of Clarke's witnesses and made no mention of witnesses called by Agin and Katz. Before adoption of the board's rule in 1952, Connell wrote, pregnant teachers "suffered many indignities" which included "children pointing, giggling, laughing and making snide remarks" about their condition. Connell cited the testimony of Julius Tanczos about assaults on teachers and confiscation of guns and knives. He then painted a grim and gruesome picture of toxemia, placenta previa, and other complications of pregnancy which could lead to hospitalization or even death. "In an environment where the possibility of violence and accident exists," Connell wrote, "pregnancy greatly magnifies the probability of serious injury."

Judge Connell brushed aside the argument that imposing a mandatory leave policy only on women violated the "equal protection" clause of the Fourteenth Amendment. Far from harming the pregnant teachers, he ruled, the board's rule was designed to protect them. Connell went back to 1908 for Supreme Court precedent, quoting at length from an opinion reflecting the paternalism of that era: "The two sexes differ in structure of body," the Court had written, "in the functions to be performed by each, in the amount of physical strength, in the capacity for long continued labor, particularly when done standing, the influence of vigorous health upon the future well-being of the race, the self-reliance which enables one to assert full rights, and in the capacity to maintain the struggle for subsistence." Six decades later, this brand of Social Darwinism still appealed to Judge Connell. He concluded that the mandatory leave policy was "entirely reasonable" and did not discriminate against pregnant teachers.

Judge Connell's old-fashioned opinion did not surprise the teachers' lawyers, who asked the federal appeals court in Cincinnati to reverse the decision. In addition to WEAL and other feminist groups, other organizations considered pregnancy leave an important issue. The American Civil Liberties Union, United Auto Workers, National Educational Association, and a federal agency, the Equal Employment Opportunity Commission, joined as "friends of the court" to support the Cleveland teachers. The three-judge panel that heard and decided the appeal included a retired Supreme Court justice, Tom Clark, who remained on the bench and still heard an occasional case.

Judge George Edwards, a former auto worker and union lawyer who was placed on the court by President John F. Kennedy, wrote the panel's opinion in July 1972. Edwards read the trial testimony very differently than Judge Connell. He quoted Dr. Weir as admitting that many of his patients had worked past the fourth month of pregnancy without any problems. Dr. Weir's agreement that "each pregnancy is an individual matter" undermined the board's inflexible policy, Edwards noted. He did not share Connell's horror at "giggling" students: "Basic rights such as those involved in the employment relationship," Edwards wrote, "cannot be made to yield to embarrassment."

Judge Connell had dismissed as having "no weight" the argument that the board's policy discriminated against women. Judge Edwards disagreed, finding it "a rule which is inherently based upon a classification by sex." Although male teachers could not become pregnant, "they are subject to many types of illnesses and disabilities" but not to mandatory leave rules. Finding the rule "arbitrary and unreasonable," the appellate court reversed Judge Connell.

Losers in the second judicial round, the Cleveland school board asked the Supreme Court to review the case. Jo Carol LaFleur and Ann Nelson were joined by Susan Cohen, a Virginia teacher who had lost a similar case. Partly to resolve the difference between the lower federal courts, the justices voted to review both decisions and set the cases for argument on October 15, 1973. The issue of mandatory pregnancy leave reached the Supreme Court at the crest of the feminist wave. Pressure by women's groups had secured passage of "protective" laws during the Progressive era. But these laws, mostly upheld by the Supreme Court, did not give women equality with men; they reflected views of women as the "weaker" sex.

Spurred by the victories of black Americans in the 1950s, the feminist movement grew in the 1960s and gained its own victories in the early 1970s. Congress adopted the Equal Rights Amendment in 1972; more than half the state legislatures ratified the measure in the next few months. Congress approved the Equal Pay Act in 1973. The Supreme Court granted feminists their fondest wish in 1973 by upholding a right to abortion. Later that year, the Court came close to ruling that women belonged to a "suspect class" like blacks. Although the majority shied away from that holding, four justices declared their support for this position. The Burger Court, hostile to criminal defendants and the poor, seemed even more friendly to women than the Warren Court had been. Women's groups which had launched attacks on all forms of legal discrimination had every reason to feel optimistic in 1973.

The pregnancy-leave cases picked up new friends on both sides as they approached the Supreme Court. Delta Air Lines, which at that time fired pregnant stewardesses, joined the Virginia schools that had fired Susan Cohen. The Nixon administration, represented by Solicitor General Robert Bork, sided with the teachers against the school boards. Ironically, in the same month the cases were argued, Bork was badly burned in the Watergate "firestorm," when he obeyed Nixon's order to fire special prosecutor Archibald Cox.

Charles Clarke defended the Cleveland school board in the Supreme Court. Justice Blackmun, who authored the *Roe* v. *Wade* opinion, was "a little curious" as to why the board picked four months from conception as the time for leaving the classroom. Former superintendent Schinnerer considered that to be the time "it became apparent that the teacher was pregnant," Clarke replied. "I suspect that just as you pointed out in the *Roe* case," he told Blackmun, "medieval theology" had chosen four months as the time of "quickening" of the fetus. Schinnerer certainly reflected medieval thought about women.

Blackmun returned the argument to modern times and asked why teachers could not choose to teach until one month before giving birth. Clarke pointed to medical testimony about the "complications, disorders, and discomforts of pregnancy." Blackmun interrupted this litany of ills: Was that testimony before the Cleveland board in 1952 when it "made up this rule"? Clarke admitted it was not. The board picked the date "out of the clear blue," Blackmun suggested. Clarke could only suggest that pregnant teachers "began to swell" in the fourth month and that students might giggle at this sight.

Justice Potter Stewart wondered why the board needed a mandatory rule. Clarke replied that pregnant teachers had refused to go on unpaid leave before the rule was adopted. Teachers asked to leave after seven or eight months of pregnancy, he said, "just would not do it." Justice Blackmun followed up with a question about Jo Carol LaFleur: "Mr. Clarke, is it accurate to say that without the rule she might have finished the term without any difficulty?" Clarke conceded the point, but returned to his medical ace. "The evidence is undisputed on Dr. Weir's testimony that a schoolteacher, four months pregnant, is not an able-bodied person." Clarke did not mention Dr. Marcus, who had disputed this testimony with fifty years of experience.

With his medical testimony under question, Clarke abruptly changed his argument. "The rule was not enacted for the welfare of the teachers," he now claimed. "The rule is for the administrative convenience of the school," which could more easily replace pregnant teachers with substitutes. Despite his new legal tack, Clarke could not resist a recital of his medical horror stories. The pregnant teacher "urinates more frequently because of the pressure of the fetus on her bladder. She is more susceptible to headaches. She has the three classic fears of pregnancy, of a miscarriage, of her own death, of a deformed child."

Jane Picker, a specialist in constitutional law, took over for the teachers in the Supreme Court. She first aimed her argument at stereotypes about women. Her target was the 1908 decision that Judge Connell had cited as a "protective" measure. "Woman's frail nature historically has been an excuse for protecting her in ways which have affected her adversely," she stated. "In fact, if pregnancy is a valid reason for discriminating, we can discriminate in such a manner as to protect all women out of jobs." Picker then attacked Clarke's claim that the board's rule ensured continuity in the classroom, noting that Jo Carol LaFleur was assigned to her "transition" class to replace another pregnant teacher. "It requires the fingers of only one hand," Picker said, to count the three teachers the students met that year because of the board's policy on pregnancy. She reminded the justices that they had rejected "administrative convenience" claims in recent decisions involving women, and argued that no teacher's "employment rights should be taken away from them in order to shield children from the facts of life."

The last questions from the bench opened a new legal door. Jane Picker was first asked if this was a case "exclusively involving the Equal Protection Clause." She agreed it was. The next question was a chivalrous gesture: "You do not view it as involving the Due Process Clause at all?" The question was not academic, because recent Supreme Court opinions—including the *Roe* case—held that women had the "liberty" to make decisions about bearing and raising children under the Due Process Clause. "Your Honor," Jane Picker candidly admitted, "we did not think to plead that originally." Then she rushed through the open door and made the Due Process claim.

The Court's opinion, written by Justice Potter Stewart and handed down on January 21, 1974, ushered the teachers through the door the justices had held open for them. "This Court has long recognized," Stewart wrote, "that freedom of personal choice in matters of marriage and family life is one of the liberties protected by the Due Process Clause of the Fourteenth Amendment." Policies that acted to "penalize the pregnant teacher for deciding to bear a child" placed a "heavy burden" on constitutional rights. Stewart made a further point about the rigidity of the leave policy: "The rules contain an irrebuttable presumption of physical incompetency" of pregnant teachers. Branding such presumptions as "disfavored" by the Court, Stewart noted that the Cleveland board's medical witness, Dr. Weir, agreed "that each pregnancy was an individual matter."

Stewart's use of the "liberty" interest of the Due Process Clause, which neatly avoided questions of gender discrimination, troubled Justice Lewis Powell. Although he concurred in the result, Powell feared that broader "liberty" claims might push through the Court's open door. "As a matter of logic," he wrote, "it is difficult to see the terminus of the road upon which the Court has embarked under the banner of 'irrebuttable presumptions.'" Powell did not identify any groups which might wave this new banner, but gay and lesbian activists were among those who read the Court's opinion with interest and began to shape new legal challenges to "presumptions" that their sexual preferences were symptoms of moral or physical disease. The challenge did not reach the Court for another decade, but Powell was determined to block the road.

The Court's decision troubled two justices even more than Powell. Justice William Rehnquist wrote for himself and Chief Justice Warren Burger in dissenting. "All legislation involves the drawing of lines," Rehnquist wrote, and some people who are otherwise able to perform a function will be disadvantaged by lines that fence them out. Forcing administrators to make an "individualized determination" in each case would lead to chaos. The dissenters imagined "a twenty-year-old who insists that he is just as able to carry his liquor as a twenty-one-year-old" coming to court and waving Stewart's opinion. What really upset the dissenters, though, was the prospect of challenges to mandatory retirement laws for public employees. Rehnquist and Burger shrank at the imagined sight of older workers waving Stewart's opinion and demanding "individual determinations of physical impairment and senility."

In a sense, the *LeFleur* decision represented the high-water mark of the feminist movement in the Supreme Court. Following the decision, state laws and federal agencies barred private employers from withholding leave and disability benefits from pregnant workers. But as the feminist wave began to recede, and the Equal Rights Amendment became stalled in state legislatures, the Court stepped back from *LaFleur* and struck down such laws and regulations. Congress reacted by passing the Pregnancy Discrimination Act in 1978, which overrode the Court's restrictive rulings. Employers challenged the law and asked the Court to bail them out. But Congress had spoken loudly on the issue, and the Court decided in 1987 that a California bank must return Lillian Garland, who sued the bank, to the job she held before going on pregnancy leave. Judges and lawmakers no longer giggled at pregnant women after Jo Carol LaFleur took Cleveland to court.

II.
"Go Home and Have Your Baby"

I was born in Richmond, Virginia in 1947, and I grew up in a working-class family. My father worked for Western Union as a supervisor of equipment for thirty-five years and retired. My mother stayed at home most of the time to raise the three daughters. When I was a junior in high school, she went to work as a secretary at a college in Richmond, where she still is. I was the middle daughter, and I was always quite the adventurous, independent little cuss in the family.

Neither of my parents had gone beyond high school, but all three of the daughters have college degrees. My parents didn't really push me to go to college, but most of the folks I went to school with talked about going to college, and I just assumed that I would go. I did well in school, although I didn't particularly like to study. The College of William and Mary was a nice place to go, fifty miles from home, so I could live in a dormitory and be on my own. I really enjoyed that.

I had my first taste of social activism during college, which I entered in the fall of 1964. So I'm very much a product of the JFK era, and what I'd like to think was a more altruistic period in this country. During the summers while I was in college, I lifeguarded back in Richmond at all-black public pools. Even though public, they were in black residential areas. That experience of spending an entire summer as one of only two white staff members in a black-run public pool, making friends among black community residents that ordinarily you were not exposed to in segregated Richmond, made quite an impact on me.

I was raised as a Southern Baptist in an all-white Baptist church, in a community that was now becoming integrated, as our schools had become integrated. The first summer I was a lifeguard, my church refused to allow black children to come to the vacation Bible school. They had invited me to be a guest lecturer in the adult education class, and I did a whole talk about how disgusting and un-Christian that was. I related this to the special place that children had in the Bible, in the New Testament in particular. I remember concluding, You are keeping children out of this Bible school because of the color of their skin and this just *sickens* me. And I started to cry. I finished with a prayer and I left. Afterwards a number of people told me that I was right; that they deserved to hear that. But of course they didn't mean it enough to change the vote. That was one of my first public statements about matters that had become important to me.

So when I left William and Mary with a degree in sociology I figured I would save the world by becoming a social worker, sort of one person at a time. I married a man who was from Cleveland. He got a job teaching at a Jesuit high school there, so we moved to Cleveland the summer after I graduated from college. I wanted to get a masters degree in social work, and the Cuyahoga County welfare department had a program where if you worked for a year they would send you to Case Western Reserve School of Social Work.

I didn't even last the year. It was such bureaucracy. I hated doing clerical work, and that's about all you did—change food-stamp allotments, change addresses. I got very discouraged, so I decided maybe I should teach. I called every private and Catholic school I could think of, because I wasn't certified, to see if I could start teaching. I was hired at St. Ignatius Elementary School in December to complete a school year because a teacher was getting married. So I started teaching right away, a class of thirty-eight first-graders. I walked in, I'd never taught in my life, and I *loved* it.

But I really thought I'd like to teach high-school English, and I got accepted in the John Carroll University Master of Arts in Teaching program. In the six months I spent in the welfare department, I got to visit homes and the public housing projects, primarily in the black ghetto in Cleveland, and I really enjoyed that experience. I liked working with these folks, and I thought that that was where I could do the most good teaching. John Carroll had a very specialized little program, geared only to inner-city teaching. Because I was not an English major in college, I had to take a semester of supplemental work in English. I graduated in 1970 with a masters degree in teaching English to ghetto children.

It worked out beautifully. In January of '70 I did an internship semester at Patrick Henry Junior High in Cleveland. I walked in the first day of the spring semester to five English classes and a study hall, with no teacher there but me, and I said, I'm Mrs. LaFleur, I'm the new teacher, hello! And it was just go from there. Patrick Henry had 2,200 black students in a school made to house about 1,500, with one Chinese girl, Judy Yee. Very, very poor students, mostly from single-parent families. I had a delightful time teaching there.

Patrick Henry was a school where you were expected to use paddles and beat the children. The first day I was there I had at least three young men come up and ask if they could make my paddle in wood shop, and I said, *What!* And one of them showed me a model of a *huge* paddle, like an inch thick. I said, What do you want me to do with this? And he said, You got to beat us to make us mind. I said, If I have to beat you I don't think it's worth teaching you. And he said, But what'll you do to us if we don't mind? I said, I'll talk to your parents, we'll have detention after school, we'll talk about things. And he said, Can't you just hit us? I said, No, I'm not going to hit you!

When I came back in the fall, I started teaching English classes again. But just after Christmas I was asked to teach what was called a transition class, a class of seventh-grade girls who were having problems with adjustment, behavior, motivation—a difficult class. They had just had a teacher leave through pregnancy, creating the opening for me. They were low achievers who had already lost one teacher, and the thing they needed most was stability. I taught them the core curriculum, English and social studies and related subjects, and I was with them from morning until after lunchtime. And they were wonderful, so I figured that I'll teach this class the rest of the year.

I learned around January of 1971 that I was pregnant, with a child due to be born around the end of July. Teaching out the school year made perfect sense to me, so I told people all about it. It was delightful for my class. They were primarily children born out of wedlock. I remember one particular girl had just turned twelve and was pregnant. I had a ninth-grader in my study hall who had two children. I thought I was actually contributing, partly by being a good role model. I thought, This is pretty good—I'm a married woman, having a baby, going to a doctor, getting good care; I can do some good. We would sit around talking about prenatal care, and they were planning a shower for me and they had clothes they wanted to loan me. It was really a delightful experience.

Little did I know that you could not teach in the Cleveland schools past the fourth month of pregnancy. It had not even occurred to me. Finally the principal, Mr. Wilkins, called me into the office about the first of March. Mr. Wilkins was a very inadequate human being. Everytime he would go outside in a snowstorm the children would all pelt him with snowballs. He was pathetic. He had no control. He was terrible, terrible.

When I went to his office, Mr. Wilkins said, I understand you're having a baby in August. I said, Yes, I'm having a baby. And he said, You've got to go on maternity leave; you've got to fill out your papers. I said, I don't have to do that, because I'm not leaving. I'm just going to teach until the end of the year. He said, You can't do that; we have rules. I said, My baby isn't scheduled to be born until the summer. I just want to teach school. This class that you just put me in has already lost one teacher. And I teach students who are pregnant. He just said, Too bad, you have to go. He wouldn't fire me. He said, You're a good teacher. I'm not going to fire you, but you've got to take this leave. Mr. Wilkins filled out the maternity leave papers for me, because I wouldn't fill them out. He filled in the due date, which was a month off, so I actually taught through my fifth month. And then they stopped paying me.

I was very defiant after this happened, because I couldn't believe that anybody would yank from an inner-city school a person who was specially trained to teach there and who *wanted* to teach. Many of the white teachers in the inner-city schools taught there for the first couple of years until they could get seniority and transfer out to middle-class, white schools. But many of the new teachers got assigned there, and it was a place you escaped *from!* And I wanted to stay there. I couldn't believe this.

I really thought initially that I could talk Mr. Wilkins out of it, but he would not be moved. I was a member of the teachers' union, so I went to the union building leader, and said, I've got to have help here. These people are trying to kick me out. It's ridiculous, I'm perfectly fine. The union leader, who was a man, said, Oh, Mrs. LaFleur, just go home and have your baby. I said, No! I want to have my baby, but I don't knit, I don't crochet, I don't want to sit home, I just want to teach. It was clear the union had no interest or sympathy whatever, which made me angry. It was very discouraging that your union would not support you.

My fellow teachers were split. On the whole, they were not real supportive. Many of the younger women supported me, but the men and the older women really didn't. We had a woman in the building who had taught there a number of years, probably in her fifties, who was still raising the issue at faculty meetings that women ought to be required to wear girdles. When I began teaching there women were not allowed to wear pants to teach. Miniskirts, yes, so you could be practically disrobed in the class, but you couldn't wear pants. I finally was part of a group that got together and said, This is ridiculous. It is wintertime, it is cold, we're all going to wear pants tomorrow—they'll either have to send us all home or change the rule. And a number of us came in pants and they didn't send us home; they let us stay and they changed the rule.

I found myself getting sort of radicalized by this process. I was just this nice little teacher, I thought. I finally got desperate and called the local chapter of the American Civil Liberties Union. I had heard of the ACLU, in Nazi-related matters, and issues related to schools—like black armbands for students. They will help me, I thought, because they take on causes. But they wouldn't take my case. They said, We have too many other cases going that are winners. If you were a student, we'd help you, but— sorry. I talked to the local director at least two, maybe three times, and I wrote a letter or two, and I was getting stonewalled. I was not going to get anywhere there.

Finally, in an act of sheer desperation, I called *The Cleveland*

Plain Dealer and asked for the library. The woman who answered said, This is the library; what can I do for you? I need the name of a women's lib group, I said. And she asked, Who do you have in mind? *I don't know!* I was not a member of any women's-rights groups. I thought that individual rights were provided by the Constitution and that civilized people allowed people to work. I'd never had been in that radicalized situation. I said, Just *any* names, I figured you would know some. And she gave me the names of two or three groups.

One of the groups I called was the Women's Equity Action League, WEAL, and they referred me to a couple of lawyers, and I ended up with Jane Picker, who was teaching constitutional law at Cleveland State University Law School. The first time we ever met, Jane said, This child will probably be old enough to read the decision before we ever get a final verdict in this case. No matter the outcome, it's going to end up at the U.S. Supreme Court. And she said, There will never be any cost to you, any attorneys' fees, if you're willing to just stick it out with us.

Mr. Wilkins had given me a deadline to leave—near the end of March—so I was trying to scramble to get some kind of help that could prevent them from acting at the deadline. I had a feeling that once they kicked you out, it's a lot harder to get back in. I told the children, They're trying to make me leave because I'm having this baby. The children could not understand it; they thought it was ridiculous. Here *they're* pregnant, their classmates are pregnant. They were so good to me, and I said, I am refusing to give in. There may come a day when I am not here. If so, it's because they have barred me from the class. I will *not* tell you goodbye. I will continue to come and teach because I am *not* going to show that kind of weakness.

Jane tried to get an injunction in the federal court against the schools, to prevent them from barring me from my class. The district court judge, whose name was Connell—elderly, in his seventies—said at the injunction hearing, Mrs. LaFleur will get exactly what she deserves, and she doesn't deserve an injunction. Since we knew he was the trial judge, Jane said, This doesn't bode well. Jane pondered whether she should file an affidavit of bias against Judge Connell, but she decided not to.

So there was no way to defeat them at the time. I did show up at the school, on Jane's advice, for about two weeks after they kept me out, ready to teach. I reported to the principal's office and said, I'm ready to go down to my class. Any problem? Can I go down to my class and teach? After about two weeks we stopped those efforts. There was no point in doing this every day. It was clear the principal was not going to let me teach.

The whole thing just made me so sad. I was perfectly healthy. I never had any morning sickness; I had a perfectly normal pregnancy. I enjoyed teaching so much that after they wouldn't let me come back to the Cleveland schools I applied in Lakewood, Ohio, where we were living. This is an old suburb just west of Cleveland, a middle-income town. They had no requirement that you leave and they were wonderful people. They said, You love to teach, we need substitutes, come on. I taught regularly on a substitute basis in the junior and senior high. That's where I ended up teaching for three years.

The district court trial in my case was very interesting. I had just turned twenty-four, but I was like a babe in the woods. I'd never been in a courtroom for any reason. I found it quite intriguing, just being there, sitting at counsel table, being called to the witness stand. It was quite an experience.

The school board put on a doctor, a male obstetrician, whose testimony I found really annoying. He was talking about all of the horrible complications that were possible with pregnancy, like placenta previa. There was absolutely *no* data that showed that the act of teaching made it more likely that you would have one of these conditions. In fact, if I was not teaching, I would be home by myself. And if I had placenta previa and my placenta tore loose, I would much rather be in a school with people who can help me than be in my own home and all of a sudden start hemorrhaging and maybe pass out before I got to a telephone. So if they're worried about your health, putting you in a place of isolation—I remember thinking that their logic didn't make a lot of sense.

It was almost hilarious, in a very pathetic sense, listening to testimony about all of the possible complications of pregnancy. It's a wonder women *ever* have babies, if all of these horrible things happen. Talking about not being able to complete a class because you have to go to the bathroom all the time (which was not true for me), the inability to pick up books, and your center of gravity shifting so you couldn't walk. I had never encountered any of these problems. The week before my son was born I played nine holes of golf and I played a set of tennis. The only thing I didn't do was jump the net.

There were also some statements, from the time when the maternity leave rule was adopted in the early 1950s, that children would giggle and point at pregnant teachers, that they would be embarrassed to see them in the classroom. Judge Connell bought that. That was the part that seemed so ludicrous, because that did simply not occur. The judge was of an age where that might once have been true. But in 1970, that was not happening. Pregnancy was very open. The children and I talked about it. I was just beginning to look pregnant, and it would have been nice to have had that total experience with them, especially in some prenatal concerns, because I taught so many pregnant and unwed mothers. But nobody laughed. It's almost hard to think that this only happened fifteen years ago.

As a little aside—I was invited back to the Patrick Henry summer faculty picnic at the end of June, just before my son was born, the 22d of July. I arrived, and they had a volleyball net and I was over there playing volleyball. I'm jumping up and down, and who walks up but the principal, Mr. Wilkins! He could not *believe* this! And I thought, Just look at me. I'm doing just fine. You're not even out here playing volleyball.

After Judge Connell ruled against me, we filed an appeal with the Sixth Circuit Court of Appeals. I went to the hearing in Cincinnati, which was very interesting. Jane had asked me to bring my son, Michael, down to the argument. She said, It can't hurt, if people see that this child is healthy and looks loved. When we got to the courthouse, Michael and I and my husband rode up in the elevator with this older gentleman. He was saying, He's a cute little guy, and I said, He's a sweetheart. When the court comes in, it was Justice Tom Clark of the Supreme Court! I'm going, Oh, my gosh. It's a good thing I wasn't yelling at Michael or he wasn't having a tantrum. I thought, Anybody who's the father of Ramsey Clark and who raised Ramsey would have to be with us. So I thought we'd only need one more. And my lawyers had good feelings about Judge George Edwards—they thought his track record indicated that he would go with us. It was exciting to sit there and listen to them argue, though I don't remember the substance of that argument. I was so much overwhelmed by the event and the experience. My lawyers were right—We won in the court of appeals, and both Tom Clark and Judge Edwards voted for me.

The Supreme Court was much iffier. We weren't at all sure we would win, since the Court had become much more conservative than in the Earl Warren years. But it was really very exciting to be there. I'd never been inside the Supreme Court. My mother and sister came up for the argument. It was a packed courtroom, with tourists lined up to come in, and I looked around and I thought, Gee, this is *my* case. I can't believe this is *my* case!

In fact, when my case was argued, it was delightful. I remember Justice Blackmun asking the question of Jane Picker, whether she really saw any difference between a man losing his job because he refuses to shave a beard, and a woman losing her job because she's pregnant. And she stood up there, and she put her hands on both hips and she said, Your Honor, that analogy is ludicrous. Simply *ludicrous!* What's the remedy for a man? You shave! For a woman it's abortion, to get rid of the problem. It's a little different, Your Honor. And I could see her husband at counsel table, with his head in his hands—Jane, you shouldn't *say* such things! But Blackmun voted for us.

While we were waiting for the decision, there were external things happening that were saying this is a big case that will be important for women. My case was funded by the Ford Foundation to start the Womens Law Fund, and other lawyers were calling Jane Picker for her research and her briefs. Certainly by the time it was at the Supreme Court, I realized that I'm either going to assist in making an important statement on behalf of women or I'm assisting in a giant step backward.

The decision itself was 7–2, and I was surprised the margin was that wide. Not surprisingly, Rehnquist and Burger dissented, and I remember Rehnquist was distressed that we would have to treat teachers as individuals. He said, If we have to treat teachers as individuals, we're going to have to treat other groups as individuals, like retired people. What is this going to do to mandatory retirement? I was thinking, You're right, we *should* treat people as individuals!

I remember the day the decision came down. I was teaching a social-studies class in Lakewood, and we were discussing death and dying. I had a guest speaker from the Cleveland Memorial

Society, talking about preplanned funerals, when I got called out of the class for a telephone call from a radio station that wanted my opinion on the decision. I didn't want to call the radio station back, so I called Jane's office. They said, The only thing we know is that you won. We don't know what it says, we don't know the vote, but at least we know that you have won.

I went running back to my class, doing these *jetes*, these giant leaps down the hall. I went into my class and I calmed down, and I said, Mr. Smith, could I have just one moment? I need to tell the class something. They knew I had been waiting every day. *We won!* Thank you, please resume. He doesn't know what's going on. The kids are screaming, *All right!* It was a pretty exciting day.

After I won my case, the Cleveland school board had to offer me another position, and I knew if they offered me my old job back at Patrick Henry, I had to take it. I did not want to take it; I really preferred substitute teaching when my son was so little, a couple of days a week, and that's what I did in Lakewood. But I would have gone back as a matter of principle, because I'd been saying, It's wrong to do this, not to let teachers go back. As it turns out, the job they offered me was in one of only two Cleveland junior highs in which I would not teach, because there was no control—an incredible pattern of violence against teachers and against students. It was hard to believe that with as large a faculty as Patrick Henry had, there would not have been an English opening. So I turned them down. I was very angry at that system.

I taught at Lakewood until 1975, when I came out here to Salt Lake City. I had thought a little bit about going to law school when I was teaching, and one day getting to be a juvenile-court judge. A lot of the children I worked with had some problems and appeared in juvenile court, and others were there because of neglect, not of fault. I really enjoyed the one-on-one contact with troubled children, both at Patrick Henry and at Lakewood. I must have at some point said something about that to Jane, and she was very encouraging. She said, You really seem to have a sense of what these pleadings are about, understanding what the issues are. Frequently you have to lead plaintiffs by the hand, and they don't understand what is going on.

Jane was very encouraging, and I got accepted at Cleveland State in their evening program. I wasn't ready to make a full commitment yet—I wasn't sure about all of this—but I was able to teach school during the day at Lakewood and go to law school three nights a week, which I did for one year. But it nearly killed me. The last week of school, I was taking exams in contracts and torts, giving exams and grading papers for my juniors and seniors, and Michael came down with chicken pox and just wanted Mommy to hold him. I said, This is more than I can do.

My husband was thinking of getting a masters degree in public administration. So we sold the house and I transferred to the University of Utah. I had never been here, but I wanted the mountains and he picked Salt Lake City. It was not quite what I expected, but it's been very pleasant. We were divorced after we moved here, and I have remarried and my last name is now Nesset-Sale.

I took constitutional law at the University of Utah. Professor Ed Fermage taught the con-law class, and he called me into his office a couple days before we got to my case. It had been quite a thrill when I bought my con-law textbook and there's Cleveland Board of Ed versus LaFleur. He said, Jo Carol, I don't want to embarrass you, but it sure would be a treat if, instead of just having the next student assigned to do a case, you would just talk a little bit about the personal side of LaFleur and how you felt about it. So I did that, and as an old teacher and old ham, I felt just at home talking to them. And the students came down afterwards with their pens and asked me to autograph their case-books.

I practiced in the public defender's office for eight-and-a-half years after I finished law school. There were only two attorneys that ever stayed longer than I stayed in the defender's office here. I was doing felony trials in the capital homicide division. About three years ago I defended a man who was a serial killer of children, who kidnapped and killed five little boys over a four-year period, who eventually confessed to all of them. He solved every missing-child case in Salt Lake. He was executed in June of 1988. That was hard. I became quite hated for that around the state.

What I liked most about legal defense work was never the research and writing, it was the oral advocacy and the negotiation with the prosecutors and the interaction with clients, having them come to trust me and be glad that I represented them, so that every time they got in trouble, they'd say, I want Jo Carol.

Now I'm the bar counsel for the state bar association, counseling and prosecuting lawyers. I think attorney discipline is the most important work that a bar association can do. I have a real commitment to attorney ethics and to prosecuting those who are not upholding high standards. At the same time, it does involve some counseling and trying to make people winners. I seem to have good human skills.

I wanted to be a judge—still do—but it's clear that the governor and the judicial nominating committees do not pick from old defense lawyers to be judges at any level. We are thought to be anarchists, anti-law and order, pro-crime, which is very unfortunate. It's just a shame. I have, I think, an insider's view of crime and criminals that would be very helpful in making fair and tough decisions. I think it's harder to be conned by people in sentencing phases. But when I made some discreet inquiries, some folks on the judicial nominating committee told friends of mine that the community was not ready for a child-killer's attorney to be appointed a judge; that I was too notorious for representing people who had done very bad things. But that was my job.

Looking back, I'm not quite sure why I started my case. I keep thinking, There must have been a lot of other women who were affected by this rule. Why hadn't somebody before me said, This is wrong! I don't know why. When I got pregnant, I knew I wasn't sick. I knew I wasn't ill. How could a male-dominated school system say to me, Even though you're not ill, and pregnancy is a perfectly normal condition, you are unfit to teach. The fundamental unfairness of it seemed morally wrong, not just stupid but wrong; and that men were making the decisions didn't help, because they didn't know what it was to be pregnant. It wasn't fair, and it made me angry.

For somebody who's come from such a normal, little conservative Southern background, I seem to always be out there on the fringe. I lifeguard at pools where they wouldn't expect to find a little white girl; I teach in inner-city schools; I represent persons who have done heinous things. When I was in college, I wanted to join the Peace Corps, although I couldn't convince my fiancé at the time that we should just get married and join the Peace Corps. But that phrase about, Ask not what your country can do for you—for those of us between certain ages it really made some difference, as well as the assassinations of Martin Luther King and Bobby Kennedy, and the riots in Hough and Watts and the ghettos. I had grown up in a segregated society, and these social ills just seemed wrong and un-Christian. Maybe that's why I started my case, even though it wasn't the most important case the Supreme Court ever decided. When I went to law school, LaFleur was a leading case in the con-law text, and now it's just a footnote. Fame is so fleeting!

But I'm glad I did the case. The only thing that was sad during the whole time of the case was contact with folks who thought it was wrong to be pregnant and want to stay in a classroom. I got a few letters and phonecalls from folks who said, How *dare* you go in front of a class with a big belly? People like you should be shut up in some room!

But I got postcards from people all around the country that made up for that. A woman sent me a little medallion—there's a patron saint of pregnant women whose name I don't remember, not being Catholic, but it meant a lot. And I took an exercise class here in Salt Lake with a woman who said she was pregnant and a teacher. She said, I remember when they used to make people get out, but somebody fought that and thank goodness, I can keep my job. I didn't tell her *I* was the plaintiff who did that, it wasn't appropriate. But on the inside I was bubbling and saying, How neat! It's been sort of exciting.

14

Elmer Gertz
v. Robert Welch, Inc.

Elmer Gertz is a Chicago lawyer who bested the John Birch Society in a lengthy battle over false charges in 1969 that he headed a "Red" crusade against the police. *Photo by Gene Lovitz, courtesy of Elmer Gertz*

I.
"A Good Reputation as a Lawyer"

On March 22, 1969, someone thrust a pamphlet into the hands of Mary Giampietro while she strolled through a shopping mall in Chicago, Illinois. Only after she returned home did she browse idly through the unsolicited literature. The pamphlet bore the title, "Frame-Up, Richard Nuccio and the War on Police." Mary learned from small print that the pamphlet was a reprinted article from a magazine known as *American Opinion*. The article's author, Alan Stang, was identified as "a former business editor for Prentice–Hall" who had "just returned from an investigative trip to Chicago, where he conducted extensive research into the Richard Nuccio Case." Flipping through the pamphlet, Mary was shocked to find a picture of her husband Wayne's employer, Elmer Gertz. The caption under the picture read, "Elmer Gertz of Red Guild harasses Nuccio."

Within hours of Mary's shopping trip, Elmer read the pamphlet she brought him. What prompted Stang's article, Elmer discovered, was the murder conviction in August 1968 of a Chicago policeman, Richard Nuccio, for the shooting death of a young man named Ronald Nelson. What prompted Stang's charge against Elmer Gertz was the Chicago lawyer's role in representing Nelson's family in a civil damage suit against Nuccio. Stang drew a conspiratorial connection between the two separate cases. His article accused Elmer of active participation in "the Communist

War on Police," a national conspiracy aimed at destroying local police "so that Communists can impose their totalitarian dictatorship." Portraying Elmer as the mastermind of the "carefully orchestrated" campaign to frame Officer Nuccio for Nelson's murder, Stang labeled the Chicago lawyer as a "Leninist" and "Communistfronter." Stang's evidence for these charges, and "the only thing Chicagoans need to know about Gertz," was Elmer's association— no dates were listed—with "the Communist National Lawyers Guild."

The pamphlet did not identify the organization that published *American Opinion* and that paid Alan Stang for his article. Elmer Gertz quickly discovered that Stang's journalistic assault had been sponsored by the John Birch Society. During the 1960s, the Birch Society was the largest and most active of the Radical Right groups that were spawned by McCarthyism and fed on Cold War paranoia. Notorious for their "Impeach Earl Warren" campaign and their crusade against American membership in the United Nations, Birchers consciously adopted the tactics of their enemies and set up "fronts" which promoted their goals under cover of innocuous titles. Birch fronts often promoted fringe causes, like the "Committee to Warn of the Arrival of Communist Merchandise on the Local Business Scene," which opposed Polish hams and Czech glassware. Others tried to exploit more popular causes. The "Support Your Local Police" campaign, which peddled bumper stickers and 86,000 copies of Stang's article on the Nuccio case, allied the Birchers with an issue of widespread public concern.

Among the Radical Right groups, Birchers specialized in tossing around "treason" charges. Robert Welch, who had worked for a family confectionary business in Boston, abandoned candy to attack Communists in 1958, when he founded the Birch Society. Welch had no partisan bias in labeling American leaders as traitors. In the two-day speech that he delivered at the founding Birch meeting, and repeated every two weeks to Birch recruits, Welch accused President Franklin Roosevelt of "pure unadulterated treason" for his wartime agreements with the Soviets. Welch later branded President Dwight Eisenhower a "conscious agent of the Communist conspiracy." Although Welch soon disavowed this charge, it sent shivers through conservatives like Barry Goldwater, who slithered away from Welch's endorsement of his 1964 presidential effort. With friends like Welch, conservatives did not need enemies.

Although the Birch Society kept its membership figures under wraps, observers estimated that some 50,000 Americans became Birchers in the early 1960s. Three California congressmen admitted Birch affiliation, although each fell victim to the voters after his membership became an election issue. Birchers had an insatiable appetite for exposures of "treason" in high places. *American Opinion,* a glossy monthly, fed this appetite with articles by a stable of free-lance authors. Alan Stang, who wrote more than a hundred pieces for the Birch journal between 1963 and its demise in 1985, excelled at the kind of cut-and-paste, hit-and-run journalism that drew on newspaper snippets, quotations from Communists, and the indexes of congressional Red-hunting panels. Stang had no time for subtlety or nuance in his Radical Right writings. He favored three-word sentences and "treason" charges. Stang could not resist linking Elmer Gertz with the "traitors" who marched in Chicago against the Vietnam War.

The Birchers had not anticipated libel suits from their victims. Supreme Court precedent made it difficult for well-known figures to recover damages in defamation suits. But the Birchers had also not anticipated Elmer Gertz's reaction to Alan Stang's charge that he was a "Leninist" and "Communist-fronter." Only a few weeks after Mary Giampietro brought him the Birch pamphlet, Elmer sued the Birch Society's corporate body, Robert Welch, Inc. Wayne Giampietro, a young lawyer who had recently joined Elmer in law practice, filed the suit in Chicago's federal court. Elmer's complaint stated that he had practiced law in Chicago since 1930, that he belonged to many "professional, literary, historical, religious, educational, philanthropic and civic" organizations and had "received awards and citations for public services from several groups." The complaint added, without undue modesty, that Elmer "has deservedly enjoyed a good reputation as a lawyer and citizen" and that he "has always been a loyal and respected citizen of the United States."

The editorial tag-line to Stang's article claimed he had conducted "extensive research" into the Nuccio case. Stang's research, however, stopped short of talking with Elmer Gertz about his involvement in the case, or his background. This proved to be a fatal mistake for the Birch Society. The most cursory research would have disclosed that Elmer had never been a Communist, had never supported the Communists, and had in fact actively opposed the Communists on many issues. Stang had picked the wrong

person to libel. Elmer *had* once belonged to the National Lawyers
Guild, but he left the liberal group more than fifteen years before
Stang's article appeared. Three members of the U.S. Supreme
Court had also been Guild members, along with many lawyers—
some of them Communists—who rejected the conservative positions of the American Bar Association. Elmer had certainly never
been a "Leninist" of any sort, and Stang's "guilt by association"
tactics had no factual basis.

Because the Birch Society was based in Massachusetts, Elmer
was entitled to file his libel suit in federal court under the "diversity"
rule that governs disputes between citizens of different states.
But these diversity cases are decided on the basis of state law,
and Illinois judges had given Elmer an advantage—which he and
Wayne Giampietro well knew. Prior decisions by Illinois courts
made clear that falsely accusing someone of "Communist" membership or sympathy was libelous, regardless of motive or mistake.
The reason for what judges called the *per se* rule of libel was
that Communist activity was criminal in Illinois, and false accusa-
tions of criminal behavior would certainly damage a person's reputation.

Elmer's suit against the Birch Society faced one major obstacle:
the U.S. Supreme Court. As far back as 1925, the Court had
ruled that the First Amendment cast its protective shield over
journalists of both the Left and Right, and that press restraints
were suspect. More recently, in *New York Times* v. *Sullivan,* the
Court ruled in 1964 that the First Amendment protected even
false statements about public officials from libel suits. Only those
untruths that were made with "malicious" intent or with "reckless
disregard" for the truth could be punished. Supporters of Martin
Luther King had placed a full-page ad in the *Times* which included
false statements (the errors were minor) about the treatment of
civil-rights demonstrators by city officials in Montgomery, Alabama. The city's police commissioner, L.B. Sullivan, sued the paper
and won a huge libel judgment from an all-white Alabama jury.
Writing for the Supreme Court, Justice William J. Brennan reversed the ruling against the *Times* and proclaimed the nation's
commitment to "uninhibited, robust, and wide-open" debate on
public issues. Brennan's opinion held that some "erroneous statement is inevitable in free debate" and "must be protected" against
libel suits, at least those brought by public officials against their
critics. Subsequent decisions extended this protection to "public

figures" who did not hold office but whose activities exposed them to the media's spotlight, and to issues of "public interest" that involve private citizens.

Elmer's suit against the Birch Society put two rights into conflict. On the one hand, the law gave citizens legal protection against false statements which might damage their reputations and professions. Calling a respected lawyer a "Communist" might well scare away present or potential clients. On the other hand, threatening the press with huge damage claims for errors made in the heat of polemical battle might lead to editorial timidity and journalistic tiptoeing around issues. The judge who first handled Elmer's case faced an unenviable task in balancing these contending rights.

Elmer's suit came before District Judge Bernard M. Decker. The quirks of Chicago politics led a Democratic president, John F. Kennedy, to appoint Decker, a Republican, to the federal bench. But in Chicago, politics has many quirks, and lawyers considered Judge Decker competent and fair. Decker first ruled in Elmer's favor, denying the Birch Society's motion to dismiss the case. James A. Boyle, a respected Chicago lawyer with no Birch ties, argued without success that calling someone a Communist, even falsely, could not damage them enough to bring a case under federal jurisdiction. Judge Decker cited Illinois cases which upheld claims based on damage to professional reputation. "An allegation of Communist affiliations," Decker held, "must necessarily cast grave doubts" on a lawyer's adherence to American law, and fitness to practice. He set the case for trial before a jury and put the Birch Society in the dock.

Alan Stang, who stuck the "Leninist" label on Elmer Gertz, did not appear at the trial. The Birchers rested their defense on Scott Stanley, managing editor of *American Opinion*. Stanley had asked Stang, he told the jurors, to visit Chicago and determine whether "the Nuccio murder trial and the publicity around it were part of a continuing Communist effort to blacken the reputation of America's police officers." Not surprisingly, Stang reached the conclusion that Stanley had suggested. The article's purpose, Stanley testified, was to support the Birch Society's "national Support Your Local Police campaign."

Wayne Giampietro, who represented Elmer at the trial, hammered at Stanley's quick-and-dirty editorial work. Under Illinois law, editorial negligence would suffice for libel damages. Stanley admitted that because of deadline pressures he sent Stang's article to the printer "within twenty-four hours" of its submission. Wayne asked if Stanley had any personal knowledge of the facts in the article. "No first-hand knowledge," the editor confessed. "I relied upon Mr. Stang." Had Stanley ever heard of Elmer Gertz before he read Stang's article? The answer was no. Did he personally check any of the charges about Elmer before the article went to press? Again, the answer was no.

Wayne pressed Stanley on whether Elmer's former membership in the National Lawyers Guild justified calling him a "Communist-fronter." Stanley tried to distance himself from the term. He preferred to call the Guild "a Red organization." Weren't the terms synonymous, Wayne asked. Red was known "as early as the French Revolution as the color of International Socialism," Stanley explained. Calling someone a French Revolutionist would not be libelous. But any claim that Elmer had Communist sympathies, Stanley knew, exposed the Birch Society to libel damages. Stang's article, of course, made just that claim.

The next witness caught Boyle and Stanley by surprise. Michael Kachigian identified himself as a Chicago lawyer who knew Elmer Gertz personally. Wayne asked if he knew Elmer's reputation among other lawyers for honesty and integrity. "Very good," Kachigian answered. What about Elmer's reputation as a loyal American? "Excellent." Kachigian had never heard Elmer espouse any Communist ideas. Wayne then asked the witness if he knew Officer Nuccio. "Yes, I do, as his attorney." Wayne then asked if Elmer had been "involved in any way in any prosecution or harassment of Mr. Nuccio." Kachigian had no knowledge of any involvement. Wayne then asked, "Did you ever hear of a man named Alan Stang?" Kachigian's answer struck Boyle and Stanley like a brick. "I don't believe so." Wayne pressed on. "Did Mr. Stang ever contact you about the Nuccio case?" "No." Boyle was so shaken by this testimony that he only asked Kachigian one question: "I'm sorry, I didn't hear your name?"

The trial testimony left Boyle without much defense on the facts. His closing argument reflected this reality. "I think you are entitled," Boyle told the jurors, to presume "that Stang wasn't right in all respects in this case. I don't think there are any two ways about it. As I stand here today, I can speak on behalf of my client and say that we don't think that Elmer Gertz is a Communist." With that concession, and Stang's article on the record, Judge Decker instructed the jurors that Elmer had been libeled and directed them to assess damages. The jury returned quickly with an award of $50,000 against the Birch Society.

Judge Decker promptly took the check out of Elmer's hands. Ruling before the trial that Elmer was not a "public figure" under Supreme Court standards, Decker did not require him to prove "malice" on Stanley's part. After the trial, Decker changed his mind. The murder prosecution of Officer Nuccio, Decker wrote, "commanded wide public attention and interest." Stang's article reflected that interest. "By representing the victim's family in litigation brought against the policeman, Gertz thrust himself into the vortex of this important public controversy." Although Stanley's failure to check the accuracy of Stang's article was negligent, Decker held that "Stanley clearly did not act with actual malice or with reckless disregard for the truth."

Elmer asked the federal appellate court in Chicago to return his award. The judges sat on his appeal for eighteen months and then ruled against him in August 1972. Judge John Paul Stevens, later appointed by President Gerald Ford to the Supreme Court, agreed with Judge Decker that a false statement on a matter of public interest "is protected unless made with knowledge of its falsity or with reckless disregard of its truth or falsity." Stevens noted Stanley's "failure to verify Stang's facts" and his "apparent disposition" to believe that any lawyer who filed suit against a policeman might be a "Communist-fronter." But the trial record showed "no evidence that Stanley actually knew that Stang's article was false," Stevens wrote. Without proof of malice, Elmer could not recover damages for the admitted libel. "We cannot," Stevens concluded, "apply a fundamental protection in one fashion to the New York Times and Time Magazine and in another way to the John Birch Society." Judge Roger Kiley concurred in the decision "with considerable reluctance" because he felt that Stevens had "pushed through" the "outer limits of the First Amendment" and had stripped ordinary citizens of "their personal privacy."

Having won the trial but lost the verdict in both lower courts, Elmer asked the Supreme Court to reverse those decisions and reinstate his award. His appeal came before the justices on November 14, 1973. Wayne Giampietro, making his first Supreme Court argument, stressed his claim that Elmer had been neither a "public official" nor a "public figure" during the prosecution of Officer Nuccio. Elmer had done "absolutely nothing" in connection with the state's murder case. The basic issue for private citizens, Wayne argued, was "the right to be let alone, the right to privacy." Protection from libel was just as important as protection from unlawful search and seizure.

Wayne professed to have no quarrel with the right of the press to report on controversial issues. But there "must be some check upon that right" in order to protect citizens against falsehoods which damage their reputations. "I think in some areas the press ought to have to stop and consider what they are about to do to an individual," Wayne added. Addressing the possible risk of press timidity, he suggested that "such self-censorship is not entirely a bad thing" if it deterred the publication of falsehoods.

The Birch Society had retained a new lawyer to make the Supreme Court argument. Clyde J. Watts, a sixty-five-year-old former Army general from Oklahoma City, did not hide his Radical Right sympathies. Watts had earlier argued and lost a libel case before the Court, representing former General Edwin A. Walker, who sued the Associated Press in 1962 for reporting his role in the rioting at the University of Mississippi. Walker, who commanded the Army troops that enforced the 1957 integration of Central High in Little Rock, had noisily opposed the integration of Ole Miss by James Meredith. Watts chose to defend the Birch Society by pushing the conspiracy theory of Alan Stang's article. The article "documented and established," Watts claimed, "a strategy by the Communist enemy to downgrade the police by false charges of police brutality." His continued references to "the persecution of Officer Nuccio" prompted a skeptical inquiry: "Is this the same police officer that was found guilty?" Watts agreed, but charged ahead with his "persecution" claims.

Watts displayed an almost invincible ignorance of the trial record. Asked if James Boyle had conceded that Stang's article had libeled Elmer Gertz, Watts replied that "I was not at the trial" but professed to find "an inference that the article was not libelous" despite its falsehoods. The Birch Society lawyer would not concede what the record showed and the lower courts had held. "I suggest again that there is nothing in that article that says that Mr. Gertz was a Communist," Watts stated. Taking issue with the record was hardly the best response to questions about issues of press freedom. Asked to suggest the limits of the Court's holding in the *Times* case, the former general complained that "I am being ordered" to do something "which I just, frankly, feel incompetent to do."

The Supreme Court found it difficult to strike the precise balance on the constitutional scale of the conflicting rights of press and privacy. Seven months elapsed from oral argument until the nine justices issued six separate opinions on June 24, 1974. Justice Lewis Powell, who often spoke for the Court in close cases, admitted that the Court "has struggled for nearly a decade to define the proper accommodation" between libel law and the First Amendment. After a lengthy canvass of cases which protected the press, Powell held that private citizens deserved protection from libel. Public officials and figures usually have access to the media to rebut falsehoods about them. "Private individuals," Powell wrote, are "more vulnerable to injury, and the state interest in protecting them is correspondingly greater."

Justice Powell took issue with Judge Stevens over the issue of Elmer Gertz's involvement in the Nuccio case. "He took no part in the criminal prosecution of Officer Nuccio," Powell wrote. "He plainly did not thrust himself into the vortex of this public issue, nor did he engage the public's attention in an attempt to influence its outcome." Because the trial judge had not required Elmer to prove fault and the damages he suffered, Powell sent the case back to Chicago for a new trial. Chief Justice Warren Burger and Justice Byron White, who wrote dissenting opinions, actually sided with Elmer and voted to reinstate the jury award without a new trial. The Court's two most consistent supporters of press freedom, Justices William O. Douglas and William J. Brennan, dissented on grounds that writers should not risk punishment by jurors who consider their views offensive, regardless of the truth or falsity of their facts.

The Court's muddled opinions put Elmer back where he began in 1969, facing a new judge and new jurors. Another seven years passed, marked by Birch Society foot-dragging, before District Judge Joel M. Flaum convened the second trial in April 1981. A former state and federal prosecutor whom President Gerald Ford placed on the bench, Flaum turned the Supreme Court decision upside down before the trial began. The Court had held that Elmer only needed to prove negligence to recover damages, but Flaum ruled that Elmer must prove malice toward him by the Birch Society. Flaum based his ruling on claims by Alan Stang and Scott Stanley that the "Communist-fronter" charges against Elmer came from government publications and were therefore immune from libel claims. Wayne Giampietro argued against this decision but went ahead to prove that Stang and Stanley showed a "reckless disregard" for the truth or falsity of their charges against Elmer. Elmer won a second verdict, this time from jurors who proved more generous: The Birch Society was ordered to pay him $400,000 in damages.

Two more legal hurdles remained, and two more years passed, before Elmer received his check from the John Birch Society. The Birchers first asked the federal appellate court to reverse the judgment, arguing that the record lacked sufficient proof of malice. Ruling that Judge Flaum had incorrectly applied the malice standard, the appellate judges held that Elmer had met that standard anyway. The judges found the "slipshod and sketchy" research that went into Stang's article to be "evidence of actual malice." The Birchers lost the last round on February 22, 1983, when the Supreme Court issued a two-word order: "Certiorari denied."

Two years later Robert Welch died. Within months of its founder's death, *American Opinion* folded. The Birch Society limps on, no longer feared by the targets of its conspiracy charges. Elmer Gertz savored his victory, and continues to practice law in Chicago.

II.
"I'm a Legal Landmark"

I was born September 14, 1906 in Chicago, and I've lived in Chicago most of my life. I was born on Blue Island Avenue, on the East Side of Chicago, an area where many immigrant Jews lived in those days. My father, Morris, was a presser with Hart, Schaffner & Marx, and later he opened his own clothing shop. I was the fourth child of six, the third son in a close-knit family. We later moved to the 'Back of the Yards' area of the stockyards and slaughterhouses that Upton Sinclair wrote about in *The Jungle*.

My mother died when I was ten, and my younger brother Bob and I were sent for a while to the Jewish Orphans Asylum in Cleveland. Although I later found it difficult to tell people I had lived in an orphanage, it had an excellent school, where I developed my lifelong love of books, and we went to see Tris Speaker and Babe Ruth play baseball at the Indians' park.

Like every good little Jewish boy, I was interested in law. Two experiences in particular helped to push me in that direction. At the time I was about to graduate from high school, I got a bond as a gift. Somewhere in the chain of title, the bond had been stolen. Of course, I knew nothing about it and the person who gave it to me didn't know it. One day in 1924 while I was taking care of my father's clothing store, two plainclothes men who looked like they were going to hold me up came in and arrested me. 'Come with us, kid!' was all they said. They took me to another part of the city—didn't permit me to call my father and tell him that I had to leave the store. They must have violated about every right of mine. This was at the time that Loeb and Leopold had been picked up for the kidnapping and murder of Bobby Franks. The captain in the police station noticed I was about the same age as Loeb and Leopold and began talking to me about the case, and was apparently interested in what I had to say. After midnight, he permitted me to call my father. The next day the theft charge against me was thrown out. That had a great effect on me.

A little later, the Sacco–Vanzetti case had a profound impact on me. I was deeply moved by the case of the two immigrant anarchists charged with murder, and I studied all the literature on the case. I felt then and I feel now that they were innocent, and when they were finally killed in 1927, I was terribly shaken. Those two things did more than anything else to steer me to law. At the same time, all my life I had been writing, since I was a little kid. I was also interested, strangely enough, in architecture. So I didn't know whether I was going to be a lawyer, a writer, or an architect. Somehow, circumstances led to me going to law school. But I have never been *only* a lawyer. I've always been a writer, and I was always involved in housing. I was president of almost every housing group; I fought for veterans' housing, housing for the poor. The Post Office used to send me mail that was addressed just to 'Mr. Housing, Chicago.' And I'm still interested in architecture, everywhere I go.

Law wasn't in the background of my family. In my family, practically nobody had even gone to college. My oldest brother had gone to college briefly, studying mechanical engineering, but nobody in my family had gone through college. I was virtually the first one to go. I went to the University of Chicago. At that time, in 1924, if you were going to college in Chicago and were Jewish, you thought of going to the University of Chicago as a matter of course. There was no problem getting in. All you had to do was enroll and be able to pay tuition. The only exam they gave was in English composition, but no IQ test or any of the tests they give now. But as soon as I got in, even though the tuition was very low, I had very real problems paying tuition. At one time somebody suggested to me that I sell my Galsworthy letters—I had corresponded with John Galsworthy, the English writer—to get tuition; and I did. They paid for a year's tuition. And my last year I wouldn't have had money if I hadn't gotten a scholarship. So it was a real problem.

I graduated from law school just a few months after the stock-market crash of 1929, and it took me four months to get located in a law firm. I got all of fifteen bucks a week as a lawyer, but it was a politically well-connected firm, the Epstein and Arvey firm. I handled *every* kind of case. They paid me in compliments rather than money! They used to say that I could handle anything in the field of law. I used to get down there at seven in the morning and they'd scold me: 'Who expects you to *work* so hard?' I was working to become a lawyer. I handled everything under the sun, and had some very interesting experiences. We had a very big estate that was highly contested, and one day we went to court when the case was being tried. I was carrying the briefcase of the senior partner, McInerney, and when the case was called, McInerney answered, Ready!—and then to my shock he turned to me and said, It's *your* case, Elmer. I was fortunate enough to win the case.

I did estate work, and I was the assistant to two masters in chancery. I also got involved in other things. I did what was once a famous pamphlet of mine, 'The People Versus the Chicago *Tribune.*' But it wasn't really until I left the firm after fourteen years that I got into the cases of mine that aroused great interest—the Leopold case and Jack Ruby's case and many others. I got involved in the Leopold case through the Civil War. People think I'm pulling their leg, but it's true! I was one of the founders of the Civil War Roundtable. For a pacifist, I was much interested in the Civil War. One of the members turned out to be the oldest brother of Leopold, who used a different name, of course. He often told me of the family tragedy. In the first effort to get Leopold out of prison, I was sort of an advisor to the brother, rather than lawyer. After his brother died, Leopold wrote me and asked me to visit him. That was when he had written his book, *Life Plus Ninety-nine Years.* I became the attorney in connection with that book, and Leopold said he would like me to represent him in his efforts to get out of prison. I said, I'm not a criminal lawyer, even though I had many criminal cases. That's why I want you to be my lawyer, he said—because you're *not* a criminal lawyer.

Even before I went to college, I knew Clarence Darrow. I attended lectures of his and corresponded with him. I saw him on behalf of Frank Harris, who asked me to arrange for him to be defended by Darrow if he came to this country and were arrested

because of *My Life and Loves*. Darrow agreed to do so. I took
very seriously what Darrow had said many times, that you had
to be not only a lawyer for your clients, but a friend. And I
became that. Some of my dearest friends were clients. I always
was very careful in preparation. In the *Tropic of Cancer* case, the
head of Grove Press, Barney Rossett, said the extent of my preparation was almost terrifying. In every case, I would never think in
terms of what I could afford. I have always worked very hard.
Throughout my entire practice, I was always embarrassed by having to charge fees. I never knew what to charge. I was always
glad when there was a conventional fee, an hourly fee, or a percentage. My son, who's a very good lawyer in a different field, makes
several times more than I ever made in my practice.

I have never been a dogmatic Jew. I've been emotionally Jewish
but without any belief in any of the dogmas, or God, or immortality.
But I have felt intensely Jewish and have been much influenced
by the Old Testament prophets, by the Psalms of David. And
my father, though almost completely uneducated except for He-
brew school as a young man, was probably a socialist in his viewpoint. And I always had freedom from prejudice. In college I
formed the first interracial, interethnic art and literary group.
We couldn't meet in white homes or white restaurants. So always,
without thinking of it, I was against prejudice. The absence of
prejudice has always been very advantageous for me.

I have always been opposed to capital punishment. Part of this
came from my Old Testament readings. Even under the Sanhe-
drins, nobody could be sentenced to death just on circumstantial
evidence. That kind of teaching had a very great effect on me.
And I also knew from my experience in Chicago that race was a
major factor in who was sentenced to death. There was hardly a
day for fifteen years when I didn't try to persuade someone that
chance, or the wrong color of skin, were more likely to decide
who lived and who was executed. For many years Willard Lassers,
who is now a judge, and I monitored every death-penalty case
in Illinois. We made certain that everyone under sentence of death
was properly represented on appeal, even if we had to handle it
ourselves. In that period of years, nobody was executed in Illinois.

My best-known death-penalty case was the Witherspoon case,
which went to the Supreme Court. His original lawyer asked me
if I would handle the effort to get executive clemency for Bill

Witherspoon, who had killed a police officer in tragic circumstances. I filed a very strong clemency petition with the governor and had lined up impressive witnesses. And then Witherspoon did exactly what I told him not to, he filed a habeas corpus petition in the federal court on his own behalf, without consulting me. This petition finally led to the Witherspoon ruling by the Supreme Court, that prohibited prosecutors from automatically barring jurors who had conscientious scruples against capital punishment, to produce what Justice Stewart called 'hanging juries' in death cases. Bill Witherspoon was finally paroled, very successfully, with my assistance. He now lives in Michigan and works to help those in difficulty, and he's very happily married. We're still close, and I hear from him now and then.

My libel case started this way, in 1969. I knew a young woman, Ralla Klepak, who was a lawyer with a criminal practice and who was interested in literature and the theater. She was retained by the family of Ronald Nelson, who was killed by a police officer, Richard Nuccio. She had represented Ronald when he was being persecuted by the police when he was still alive. She asked if I would associate myself with her in the case. I knew nothing about the circumstances of the case, but when she told me what it was all about, I readily agreed, and then I took the lead in the case.

The circumstances of the case were simply outrageous! Ronald Nelson, who was a white kid, may not have been a nice kid in some respects. He and a group of friends that you might call young hoodlums used to frequent this hot-dog place across from the Cubs' park, Wrigley Field, and the owner called in the police. A judge in the juvenile court ordered Nelson and his friends not to go there for six months, and he violated the order, which the judge had no right to enter. When they appeared again, the owner called the police and this Nuccio, who had harassed young Nelson on other occasions, responded. Nelson took off down the alley, and he was ninety feet away when Nuccio shot him in the back and killed him. There was no reason for this cop to think his life was in danger. And the cops planted a knife nearby to cover up the murder!

Shortly after I became attorney with Ralla Klepak the wife of my associate, Mary Giampietro, called me up, all excited. She had been shopping and a pamphlet, a reprint of an article from *American Opinion*, the Birch Society magazine, was thrust upon her. She looked at it and there was a picture of me, and an article dealing with me. So I asked her to come down, and I was very much upset and angered and shocked by this thing. The article accused me of being part of a Communist conspiracy to undermine respect for the police across the country, and being part of a conspiracy to frame Officer Nuccio for Ronald Nelson's murder. The article based these totally false charges on my former membership in the National Lawyers Guild, and referred to me as a 'Leninist.' A large part of my practice was not civil rights—they were property cases, estates, business matters. I thought that many of my clients could have been prejudiced by these claims about me, so I decided to sue the Birch Society.

My only role in the case was to help Nelson's family get a civil judgment against Officer Nuccio, which we did, but they never recovered because Nuccio had nothing. It was an *absurdity* for the Birch Society to say that I had anything to do with Officer Nuccio's criminal indictment or prosecution or conviction. I didn't have the *slightest* thing to do with it! One of the paradoxical things was that I had been the director of public relations for the Illinois Police Association. I had represented the police on many occasions, including some McCarthyite police, because I thought their civil rights were violated. So it was an absurdity for anyone to say that I was the architect of a communist conspiracy to frame a police officer for murder.

I had no advance knowledge of this article. I was never interviewed, and nobody connected with me had been interviewed. It was just a complete shock. If they had done the slightest research, looked at *Who's Who in America,* looked at any of my books, they would have known that, while I had a liberal orientation, basically I was opposed to collectivism. I believed in the largest measure of individual freedom, and I still do. I was sympathetic to the New Deal and other efforts in behalf of the ordinary man, but I don't have romantic illusions about collectivism. My reason tells me that the surest way *not* to help the ordinary man is through collectivist efforts. You have inefficiency, tyranny, corruption.

I was never connected with any socialist group, even though I was a staunch New Dealer. Like many liberals, I was very sympathetic to the Russian Revolution until the purges in the 1930s. Now, with the persecution of the refusniks and Jews in general, I could very easily be a Red-baiter. The only thing that keeps me from being violently anti-Soviet is the necessity to preserve world peace. I think nothing's more important than that. I've been to the Soviet Union three times. Once, the National Conference for Soviet Jewry sent me. The first time we went there, in 1966, we visited my wife Mamie's aunt and cousin in Kiev, and it was a wonderful visit. We took Mamie's old aunt to lunch in our hotel, and we bought a bottle of wine, and I remember her toast: For the brotherhood of all men, and peace everywhere! And it was genuinely meant. There were revealing signs of friendship with the American people everywhere.

My role in the National Lawyers Guild had a direct effect on my libel case, because the Birch Society article claimed that I actively supported the Communist cause as a Guild officer. I was outraged because they didn't have sense enough to check. Actually, I had not been a Guild member for fifteen years, although I had once been president of the Guild in Chicago, and national vice-president. I became involved almost at the beginning of the Guild in the late 1930s, when Arthur Goldberg was president of the Chicago chapter and the Guild was a very respectable organization. We had presidents of the United States and senators and justices of the Supreme Court speaking at our meetings. I was consulted as the Guild president by the Navy and the State Department about applicants for jobs.

I left the Guild later. When it was attacked by the Un-American Activities Committee, I felt I ought to remain in there. When the Lawyers Guild was admitting blacks and was concerned with New Deal legislation, it was a very useful organization. The American Bar Association and other lawyers' groups wouldn't admit blacks. But when foreign affairs became the Guild's preoccupation, I felt it was losing its effectiveness and I became increasingly impatient. Now, if I had remained a member, I would understand its concern with Vietnam, Central America, and other things, where I feel those foreign-affairs issues are really domestic issues as well.

What concerned me about the Communists in the Guild was their deceit, rather than anything else. One of those in the Guild whom I used to admire greatly was Lee Pressman. Whenever we'd have meetings, Lee would call a group of us together and discuss economic affairs and public affairs with us, almost like a pundit. Never once did he even hint that he was a Communist.

When he finally admitted to his membership, I was outraged that he could have deceived people like myself who were friends. There were others who wouldn't deceive, like John Abt. He was a classmate of Leopold, and when I was trying to get Leopold out of prison I wrote to all his classmates to join in a petition. Abt wrote back, You'd better not ask me because my Communist affiliations would hurt rather than help. Many of the Guild members, like Thurgood Marshall and Charles Houston, I admired greatly. The Lawyers Guild did all kinds of useful things. But I felt I could accomplish much more through the American Jewish Congress, the Decalogue Society of Lawyers, the housing organizations that I headed.

After I learned of the Birch Society article, my associate, Wayne Giampietro, and I did some research and concluded that we would have a good cause of action for libel. We weren't thinking of the fourteen-and-a-half-year history that would follow. Wayne was a brilliant young attorney whom I had hired originally in connection with the appeal of Jack Ruby from his death sentence for the murder of Lee Harvey Oswald. Wayne was a law student then, and I was so impressed by him that I asked him to join me when he finished law school. This suit illustrated for me what time and place mean. First of all, if they had defamed me at the time of the Leopold case, which was before the Supreme Court decision in New York *Times* versus Sullivan, I was clearly a public figure. I couldn't go anywhere in Chicago without being instantly recognized. People would stop me on the streets and say, How's your client getting along? And then I receded into being an ordinary lawyer. I was well-known in my profession, but nobody on the jury panel had ever heard of me. And if the article had appeared a few weeks later, I would have been a public official, because I was elected as a delegate to the Illinois Constitutional Convention. I learned later that nobody expected me to win, but I did!

One interesting thing about the case is that actually my earnings did not decrease. They went up! And I was elected to public office. But nonetheless, by the Supreme Court test of humiliation, embarrassment, injury to reputation, I did suffer greatly. Nobody knows how many clients I may have lost because of this article. I learned later that some of the board members of the Chicago Bar Association said maybe I was a Communist. Undoubtedly, it had an adverse effect in many quarters.

I've often analyzed, Why did I file this suit? It was a very complicated process. I knew the John Birch Society had called General Marshall and Eisenhower, and others I respected, Communists or Communist influenced. And I felt that *somebody* ought to call a halt to that kind of thing. In a sense, I nominated myself to do the job. If I had been defamed by some obscure group, I might not have done it. But it was the John Birch Society. I knew the effect of Red-baiting and McCarthyism. I never had the feeling that I was a brave character, going forth to fight the John Birch Society. Never in my life did I have a martyr complex. But once I got involved in the case, I was determined to carry it through.

When my case was first tried, I felt pretty confident the jury would rule in my favor. Wayne Giampietro tried the case, and we didn't have any trouble showing that the Birch Society statements about me were false. The judge, Bernard Decker, instructed the jury that I was not a public figure and that if they concluded the statements were false, they should decide on the amount of damages. The jury very quickly returned with a verdict for me of $50,000. Then Judge Decker, after the trial, changed his mind and set aside the verdict and the award, ruling that while I was not a public figure, I was involved in matters of public interest and therefore would have to prove malice on the part of the Birch Society.

I was outraged that once I had gotten a verdict against the Birch Society, a judge who was my friend set aside the verdict. He decided that the Supreme Court was heading in the direction of deciding that any case involving public issues be subject to the New York *Times* rule. John Paul Stevens, who is now on the Supreme Court, wrote the first opinion for the court of appeals that upheld the dismissal of my suit. Then President Ford named him to the Supreme Court, and the governor of Illinois had a dinner in his honor and invited my wife and me to the dinner. I'm not a table hopper, but I figured I ought to go to the table where Stevens was sitting. When he saw me coming, he had a big grin on his face. He said, Elmer, we decided the case the way we did because that was the direction we thought the Supreme Court was going. Then he said a very interesting thing. He said, You're the only lawyer who ever overruled me in the United States Supreme Court.

I didn't attend the Supreme Court argument in my case, because

I didn't want to make Wayne nervous or embarrassed. But I did get a tape recording of the argument. Interestingly, Chief Justice Burger stressed one thing during his questioning from the bench that we should have stressed, but didn't. This was the matter of Birch Society accusing me, in effect, of criminal activity. A conspiracy to convict someone was a criminal offense. Burger was very much impressed by the file the police department was supposed to have on me. And Wayne instantly took up on that. I don't have a great admiration for Burger, but he said in his opinion that I was in effect a role model for lawyers and an advocate in the highest tradition of the law. My colleagues here say I'm the only lawyer in Illinois who has been certified by the Supreme Court for good reputation.

The Supreme Court ruled for me in 1974, and my reaction to winning the case was one of intense joy. For one thing, I was going to realize my lifelong ambition to go around the world. Strangely enough, even the media, who were opposed to libel actions, in some instances had editorials commending the result. The Chicago *Sun-Times* said, We cheer the result. I think this was partly because of my long involvement in civil rights and freedom of expression, and partly because I had been defamed by the Birch Society.

But my case wasn't over when the Supreme Court ruled that I had been defamed by the Birch Society. The case was remanded for a retrial under the new standard the court had established for persons who were not public figures. This time, ironically, the trial judge ruled that I had to prove malice on the part of the Birch Society. This was a higher standard than the judge applied in the first trial.

The second trial didn't take place until 1981, partly because the defendants dragged the proceedings out as long as possible. I can't help thinking that they hoped my demise might end the case—after all, I wasn't a young man, and libel actions don't survive the plaintiff. I worked out one strategy for Wayne at the trial. The Birch Society had said in its article that there was so big a file on me in the Chicago police department that it took a big Irish cop to lift it, which was an absurdity. The file was just a couple of sheets, which told such terrible things like I had presided at a dinner to honor Albert Einstein, and that I was a pallbearer at Jack Ruby's funeral. I said to Wayne, Here's what you do in your closing argument. Have a couple of sheets of paper and say to the jury, 'I'm not Irish, I'm Italian, and I can very easily lift these two sheets of paper.' I thought the jury would conclude that if the Birch Society could lie in that extravagant fashion, they'd lie about everything else.

Wayne's little demonstration must have worked. When the jurors began their deliberations, I went with Wayne to his office, and we got a call from the judge in about an hour that the jury had brought in a verdict. So Wayne and I walked to the courthouse, and when we reached the entrance, I turned to him and said, The jury is bringing in a verdict in my favor. They're going to allow me a hundred thousand dollars compensatory damages and a half million dollars in punitive damages. Wayne looked at me as if I were nuts! And they came in with a hundred thousand compensatory, three hundred thousand punitive! I learned later that some of the jury had been holding out for five hundred thousand. I also learned that the jury had concluded within minutes that the John Birch Society had deliberately, knowingly defamed me.

The Birch Society appealed the case, which dragged on until 1983, when the Supreme Court upheld the award. To pay the award, which had increased with interest to almost a half million dollars, the Birch Society had to sell their headquarters building. My wife, Mamie, and I took a long, around-the-world cruise after we received the award payment, and we used to make a toast at every port we stopped in, to the John Birch Society for giving us the means to see the world.

There have been over two hundred law-review articles that deal with my case, and chapters in books and treatises. My case is cited in almost every libel decision. I'm cited more now than New York *Times* against Sullivan, largely because one of the dicta in my case about opinion not being actionable. That's cited as much as the main holding about the distinction between public and private figures. I tell my students at John Marshall Law School that I'm no longer a person, I'm a legal landmark. You do have a feeling of intense pride and satisfaction that you've helped in the development of the law. Strange as it may seem, I'm a humble person, even though there's another part of my brain that says, I deserve the nice things people say about me.

I'm not a First Amendment absolutist. I lecture each semester to journalism students at the Medill School at Northwestern, and I make the point that the press ought to be held to a *higher* rather than lesser standard in libel cases, because they're capable of doing greater mischief. I think reputation is as important as injury to your limbs. People ask me why I'm opposed to obscenity prosecutions but favor libel cases. I think they're clearly differentiated. There's no demonstrated proof that obscenity has an adverse effect. In fact, during the *Tropic of Cancer* case, one of the Kinsey Institute researchers told me that their studies indicated that it may even have a therapeutic effect.

I'm still very active. I teach as an adjunct professor at John Marshall Law School, and I still handle a number of cases, such as my effort to get Paul Crump paroled from prison. And I have a church–state case against the Illinois House of Representatives, which passed a resolution to create a prayer room in the state capitol. I filed a proceeding for a client, attacking this, and I won in the federal district court. The state has appealed it, and I'm working on the appeal in that case. Whenever I get a complicated case, my wife raises hell! I make innumerable speeches and I write books and articles; Mamie and I travel around the world; and I do a lot of grandfathering. So I'm very, very busy—and I enjoy it all!

15

Ishmael Jaffree
v. George Wallace

Ishmael Jaffree of Mobile, Alabama, took school officials to court in 1982 over the classroom prayers that his children's teachers recited over his protests. *Atlanta J. Leviton/People Weekly © 1985 Time Inc. All rights reserved*

I.
"My God, What's Wrong with That Man?"

Five-year-old Chioke Jaffree was confused and upset when he came home from his kindergarten class at the Dickson School in Mobile, Alabama, on September 16, 1981. Chioke told his father, Ishmael Jaffree, that his teacher led the class in a musical grace before lunch every day. Charlene Boyd, a young black woman in her second year of teaching, had the children sing, "God is great, God is good, Let us thank Him for our food; Bow our heads we all are fed, Give us Lord our daily bread. Amen!" The children sang this grace before they marched from the classroom to the cafeteria. The first day of school that fall, Chioke told Ms. Boyd that he objected to singing the prayer. She told him he did not have to sing with the other children, but the musical prayer continued every day.

Ishmael Jaffree worked as a lawyer with the Legal Services Corporation of Alabama, a federally funded agency which helped poor people in civil matters such as housing and employment. He and his wife, Mozelle, had three young children in Mobile public schools, and four-year-old twins in a private preschool program. The Jaffree family was divided on religious issues. Ishmael's Baptist mother raised him as a child preacher, but he became an agnostic in college. Mozelle belonged to the Bahai faith, a sect with Middle Eastern roots which preached religious and racial tolerance and had endured both Christian and Moslem persecution. Both Ishmael and Mozelle agreed that their children should be raised to choose their own religious faith—or to choose none. The Jaffrees differed on the question of God's existence, but they agreed that the Mobile schools should not engage in religious indoctrination.

Ishmael listened to Chioke's complaint and told him to inform Ms. Boyd that school prayer had been declared unlawful by the U.S. Supreme Court. Chioke delivered the message, but his teacher ignored him and continued to lead her class in prayer. Eight-year-old Makeba reported that her teacher, Pixie Alexander, led the class in the Lord's Prayer. Julia Green, nine-year-old Aakki's teacher, also led her students in prayer. Because Chioke, an outspoken little boy, had provoked some tension with his teacher over prayers, Jaffree decided to raise the issue first with Charlene Boyd, and he visited her classroom in early December. Ms. Boyd was less concerned about prayer than with Chioke's sabotage of Santa Claus. Her students were about to have a Christmas program, she told Jaffree, and she didn't want the other children to learn that Santa was a fantasy, as Chioke was telling them.

Chioke's father and his teacher later differed in court over whether they had even spoken in December 1981. Ms. Boyd did not recall any discussion with Jaffree until the following March. Any argument over Santa Claus, Jaffree claimed, would logically have come before Christmas. But they both agreed that Chioke delivered a hand-written letter from his father to Ms. Boyd on March 10, 1982. This letter stated that Jaffree had learned from Chioke that the lunch-time prayers had continued, denounced them as unlawful, and asked for a conference to discuss the matter. Charlene Boyd promptly took the letter to her principal, Betty Lee, who told the troubled young teacher that she would consult with school officials. In the meantime, the principal said, Ms. Boyd could continue with the prayer.

Jaffree sent another letter that same day to Abe Lincoln Hammons, the Mobile school superintendent. This letter stated that the teachers of all three of Jaffree's children led classroom prayers on a daily basis. Jaffree noted that participation in the prayers was voluntary; he added that this did not save any religious exercise from its basic constitutional defect. Hammons first ignored the letter. Jaffree then began to besiege the principals and Hammons with telephone calls, asking for a ruling on his demand that prayers be halted. Hammons refused to return Jaffree's calls. Two weeks later, the superintendent's secretary told Jaffree that a response had been drafted and that he could pick it up at the office.

Jaffree had expected the superintendent's letter. The school board's legal counsel, Hammons wrote, had carefully examined the prayer issue and had determined that voluntary prayer did not violate any Supreme Court rulings. Teachers in the Mobile schools had not been directed to lead students in prayer, and no students were forced to join the prayers. Jaffree could request that his children be excused from the prayer exercises, but the teachers would continue to ask God's blessings on their students.

Jaffree and the Mobile schools had reached an impasse. On May 28, 1981, Jaffree filed suit in Mobile's federal court against his children's teachers and principals, superintendent Hammons, and Mobile school-board members. His complaint alleged that the prayer exercises constituted an "establishment of religion" and violated the First and Fourteenth amendments to the U.S. Constitution. Ronnie Williams, a former Legal Services lawyer who was now in private practice in Mobile, filed Jaffree's complaint and represented him in court.

When he moved from Ohio to Alabama in the 1970s, Ishmael Jaffree had little idea that Mobile was such a religious city. Established by French traders in 1702, the Gulf Coast port had grown by 1980 to a thriving city of 200,000, whose residents endured the pungent odors of paper manufacturing, the city's primary industry. Mobile also manufactured religion. Some fifty-six denominations, from mainstream groups like Episcopalians to Pentecostals on the fringe, had churches in Mobile in 1980. Baptists were by far the largest religious group, with 192 churches in the Mobile area, ranging from tiny Primitive Baptist churches with only a dozen members to the gigantic Cottage Hill Baptist Church, whose 8,500 members sang to sound facilities that rivaled those of the Radio City Music Hall in New York.

Jaffree's lawsuit provoked both politicians and preachers. Alabama Governor Forrest "Fob" James denounced Jaffree in a televised address and urged a more-than-willing state legislature to put prayer in the schools by official act. The governor's son, "Fob"

James III, a young Mobile lawyer, drafted the prayer that the legislature adopted: "Almighty God, You alone are our God. We acknowledge You as the Creator and Supreme Judge of the world. May Your justice, Your truth, and Your peace abound this day in the hearts of our countrymen, in the counsels of our government, in the sanctity of our homes, and in the classrooms of our schools. In the name of our Lord. Amen." Teachers were permitted to lead "willing students" in this prayer; the law made no provision for excusing those who objected. Once the legislature acted, Jaffree amended his suit to include the governor as defendant.

The legal prospects of the defendants looked grim. The U.S. Supreme Court had ruled twenty years earlier, in an opinion written by a native Alabaman, Justice Hugo Black, that a state-composed prayer "breaches the constitutional wall of separation between Church and State." Later decisions barred recitation of the Lord's Prayer and Bible verses in schools. Justice Tom Clark spoke for the court in writing that "in the relationship between man and religion, the state is firmly committed to a position of neutrality." Perhaps no other Supreme Court decisions have been so widely excoriated and evaded. "Eighty percent of the American people want Bible readings and prayer in the schools," said evangelist Billy Graham in 1963. "Why should the majority be so severely penalized by the protests of a handful?" Graham was correct in his figures: Surveys have consistently shown overwhelming public support for school prayer.

But the Supreme Court decisions remained the law, and were binding precedent on lower courts. It would take a courageous, or foolhardy, federal judge to rule against Ishmael Jaffree. But Mobile had such a judge. Born and raised in Mobile, W. Brevard Hand practiced law and Republican politics in his home town from 1949 to 1971, when President Richard Nixon placed him on the district court. Described by one observer as "the last surviving Confederate," Judge Hand believed so firmly in states-rights doctrine that he was willing to lead a one-man charge against the Supreme Court.

Robert Campbell III, the school board's lawyer, lacked the zeal of a true believer in defending school prayer. But the Religious Right, encouraged by Judge Hand's well-known position, saw the case as a vehicle for broader purposes—not only to promote school prayer but also to attack "secular humanism," which fundamentalist Christians considered the Devil's doctrine. Religious Right activists crusaded to purge schools of books which promoted evolution in biology, "logical positivism" in math, and "values clarification" in social studies—all part of "secular humanism" and subversive of traditional morality.

Pastor Fred Wolfe of Mobile's Cottage Hill Baptist Church led the Mobile crusade: He signed up 624 churchgoers and asked Judge Hand to make them "intervenors" in the case. Ronnie Williams and Robert Campbell opposed the motion, but Hand allowed Wolfe and his followers to join the case and call witnesses. Thomas Kotouc and Barber Sherling, Alabama lawyers with ties to the Religious Right, represented the intervenors. Much of the money for their efforts came from the National Legal Foundation, set up by television evangelist Pat Robertson, himself a Yale Law School graduate, and later a Republican presidential candidate.

Judge Hand called his courtroom to order on November 15, 1982, for the trial—without a jury—of Ishmael Jaffree's suit. Two very different trials, with different witnesses and issues, took place at the same time. The Mobile schools were attacked from both sides, by Jaffree for promoting religion in class and by Pastor Wolfe and his flock for excluding religion from school texts. The board's lawyer, Robert Campbell, often looked bemused as testimony by Wolfe's witnesses became esoteric. Betty Jane Mahoney, the court reporter, struggled with the names of philosophers, spelling two of them "Frederick Nichy" and "George Hagel."

Ronnie Williams called all three teachers of the Jaffree children. Charlene Boyd explained why she taught Chioke's class her musical grace: "It was one I had learned when I was in school." Why did children need to thank God for their food? "That's who I thank." Ms. Boyd recalled that Chioke Jaffree "objected the first time we did it. He told me he could not say it." Chioke, she said, "is a very outspoken child, and whatever is on his mind, he lets you know." Ms. Boyd then recalled her meeting with an outspoken Ishmael Jaffree: "He said he hated to discuss this with me because I was black, but I was doing something that was against the law. He said I could go to jail for what I was doing." According to Ms. Boyd, Mozelle Jaffree, who taught at the same school, later called her aside and said "that I probably misunderstood her husband; that sometimes he has a hard time explaining himself."

Pixie Alexander, Makeba's second-grade teacher, admitted leading her students in the Lord's Prayer. "Did you ever explain to your class," Williams asked, "that if anyone did not want to participate they did not have to?" The answer was no. What values did she want the children to gain from the prayer? "Respect for authority and recognition of their place in life." How did Makeba respond? "Makeba was very respectful, would put her hands together and bow her head with no direction." Williams asked the teacher why her students needed to pray aloud. "The power of life and death is in the tongue," she answered. Julia Green, Aakki's teacher, explained that Jaffree's letter of complaint upset her so much that she stayed home for two days. She also stopped leading her class in prayer. "I had several parents ask me why the children didn't do it anymore," she added. "I explained to them what happened and they say, 'My God, what's wrong with that man?'"

Williams then called Ishmael Jaffree to the stand. "Mr. Jaffree, we will get right to the point. Why did you file this lawsuit?" This was not a simple question, and Jaffree's answer covered more than thirty pages of the trial transcript, punctuated with objections from the board's lawyers. Judge Hand let Jaffree outline his views on religion and his efforts to persuade school officials to end the classroom prayers. Jaffree related how Chioke came home from school and told him that Ms. Boyd continued with prayers over Chioke's objection. "Chioke was perplexed. And he was upset over this. I was extremely upset that this was happening. I tried to resolve this matter informally and that reached a stalemate. No one cared. I was at my wit's end. I didn't want to bring this lawsuit. I realize this is a very conservative area and people have grown up with the Bible from Day One."

Jaffree explained that he had nothing against children praying. "I think children on their own should be free to pray before meals, at any time they want to." He simply wanted to free his children from the influence of teachers who preach. Children "accept what they hear" from teachers, Jaffree said. "They would accept a belief in the tooth fairy, just because it is told to them by adults." But the purpose of prayer, he added, was to proselytize. "What they are being exposed to," Jaffree said, "is basically a fundamentalist, Christian philosophy." What he wanted for his children was not indoctrination but inquisitiveness. "I want my children not to accept everything that is told to them and be free to examine, to explore, to ponder, to think about, to be exposed to different philosophies."

Before he left the stand, Ishmael Jaffree described the price of his stand. "My children have experienced all types of abuse from neighbors. Some of the children in our neighborhood, which is mostly white, have stopped playing with my children, and other children laugh at them. I have learned from others who have filed similar lawsuits," he continued, "that the children suffer immensely after the lawsuit is over. If it is ultimately successful, then my children will be forever stamped as the children of the father who tried to take religion out of the public classrooms. How are my children going to handle this? I don't know. I have suffered emotionally myself and it has drained me. My future here in Mobile is going to be drastically altered because of this lawsuit. I'm perceived as an outsider that is disrupting Mobile's quiet tranquility."

The witnesses called by the intervenors hardly mentioned school prayer. Their sights were on bigger game, "secular humanism" and the Supreme Court. Barber Sherling asked two "born again" Presbyterian ministers what bothered them most about textbooks used in Mobile schools. One objected to "logical positivistic views," which he defined as the claim that "all truth must be verified" by scientific methods. His second target was evolution. "This is very, very important because without evolution humanism cannot stand. In fact, the major philosophical viewpoint in the West today is humanism, and the major one in the East is Communism. They both stand on the single pillar of evolution which is necessary for both." The other minister argued that Christian parents needed Christian prayers for their children. "Non-Christian prayer would be offensive to the Christian," he said. Ishmael Jaffree's effort to remove prayer from schools "ought to make everybody stand up in horror."

The intervenors asked Rousas John Rushdoony to make the major attack on "secular humanism." Little known in Mobile, Rushdoony is a central figure in the so-called Reconstructionist movement, centered in the Chalcedon Foundation that he heads in California. This movement aims at "reconstructing" America from a secular to a theocratic state whose laws would be based on biblical commands. The intervenors' lawyers shied away from asking Rushdoony to discuss his views, which include advocacy of the death penalty for adultery, perjury, and juvenile disobedience of parents. Rushdoony's task in Mobile was to convince Judge Hand "that Humanism is a religion," as he stated. John Dewey and Horace Mann bore the blame, Rushdoony said, for infusing schools with "the religion of Humanism."

The major hurdle for the intervenors was Supreme Court precedent in prayer cases. Their legal challenge rested with James McClellan, a former University of Alabama political science professor. More important, McClellan had served as legislative assistant to Senator Jesse Helms, who led the political fight against the Supreme Court's prayer rulings. One month before the Mobile trial, the Senate had rejected Helms' bill to bar all federal courts from hearing cases concerning "voluntary" school prayer. McClellan came to Mobile to enlist Judge Hand in the battle against the Supreme Court. His weapon was history. With copious reference to letters and speeches of the Founding Fathers, McClellan argued that their intent in adopting the First Amendment "was to prevent the national government from usurping the powers of the states" in religious matters. McClellan also claimed that the Fourteenth Amendment, which barred states from abridging the "liberty" of citizens, had not included First Amendment liberties. States were free, McClellan assured Judge Hand, to permit school prayer or even to establish a state religion.

Judge Hand did not disappoint the Religious Right. His written opinion, more than 20,000 words long, credited McClellan for demonstrating "that the First Amendment was never intended to be incorporated through the Fourteenth Amendment to apply against the states." Alabama was thus free to promote school prayer. Hand accused the Supreme Court, and his fellow Alabaman, Justice Hugo Black, of historical error and judicial tyranny. But Hand knew that his opinion would most likely be reversed by appellate judges—so he concluded with a warning: "If the appellate courts disagree with this court in its examination of history," Hand promised to "hunker down" and "purge from the classroom" those books that denied the "Christian ethic" and promoted "the secular humanistic ethic."

Judge Hand led a gallant charge against the Supreme Court,

but he suffered the same fate as his Confederate ancestors. Judge Joseph W. Hatchett, a black Democrat from Florida whom President Jimmy Carter had placed on the appellate bench in 1979, chided Hand for his judicial defiance. Federal judges "are bound to adhere to the controlling decisions of the Supreme Court." The Supreme Court had repeatedly struck down school prayer laws, and Judge Hand must follow those rulings. Judge Hatchett, a judicial liberal, quoted Supreme Court Justice William Rehnquist, a judicial conservative: "Unless we wish anarchy to prevail within the federal judicial system, a precedent of this Court must be followed by the lower federal courts no matter how misguided the judges of those courts may think it to be."

By the time the Mobile case reached the Supreme Court for argument on December 4, 1984, new names appeared on court papers. George Wallace had replaced "Fob" James as Alabama's governor and also as the principal defendant. John Baker, a Louisiana lawyer, had replaced all the defendants' lawyers. Paul Bator, a Harvard Law School professor on leave, represented the Reagan administration in supporting the defendants. Only Ronnie Williams, appearing for Ishmael Jaffree, remained from Judge Hand's courtroom.

The legal issues in the case had narrowed since the case left Mobile. Baker knew that defending the Lord's Prayer in schools was a lost cause, so he retreated to a less exposed position, defending the Alabama law that allowed silent prayer in classrooms. No student would be forced to do anything, Baker claimed, but stand silently for one minute. "During that minute he is in no way embarrassed, he is in no way coerced to do anything." Baker's argument was hardly the states-rights charge that Judge Hand had launched at the Supreme Court. Sensing defeat, Baker sat down well before his time expired. Paul Bator, appearing as "friend of the court" for the pro-prayer Reagan administration, admitted his ignorance of the trial record and stumbled around the issues. Pressed by Justice Thurgood Marshall as to why students needed a law to let them pray silently, Bator admitted that "long before this statute, after this statute, children have a right in the Alabama schools to pray silently." Ronnie Williams, sensing victory, took just enough time to acquaint the justices with the Jaffree family. "The children were being taught one thing at home and something else in the public schoolroom," he said, "and it is just not the business of the state" to pit teachers against parents in matters of religious belief.

Six members of the Supreme Court voted in June 1985 to demand Judge Hand's surrender. Writing for the Court, Justice John Paul Stevens noted Hand's "remarkable conclusion that the Federal Constitution imposes no obstacle to Alabama's establishment of a state religion." Without mentioning James McClellan, Stevens rebuked his reading of constitutional history and stated that "the individual freedom of conscience protected by the First Amendment embraces the right to select any religious faith or none at all." The Court's three dissenters—Chief Justice Warren Burger and Justices Byron White and William Rehnquist—wrote separate opinions, but agreed that Alabama schools could allow voluntary prayer. Justice Rehnquist, whose lengthy opinion recited much of McClellan's historical data, argued that the First Amendment was designed solely "to prohibit the designation of any church as a 'national' one." Nothing in the First Amendment "requires government to be strictly neutral between religion and irreligion," Rehnquist concluded.

Unlike his Confederate hero, General Robert E. Lee, Judge Hand refused to hand over his judicial sword to the Supreme Court. His first move was to convert Pastor Wolfe's parishioners from intervenors to plaintiffs in a new suit against the Mobile schools. Hand had promised to "hunker down" over Mobile's textbooks, and in March 1987 he ruled that forty-four books promoted "the religion of secular humanism" and must be removed from the city's schools. Television reporters filmed Mobile students turning in banned textbooks to their teachers. Three days later, federal appellate judges in Atlanta suspended Hand's order; five months later, they dissolved his ruling.

Reactions to Judge Hand's second defeat reflected predictable positions. Arthur Kropp, speaking for People for the American Way, which joined the American Civil Liberties Union in opposing Judge Hand's ruling, called the appellate decision "just plain good sense." The Religious Right denounced the decision as a "tragedy" for Alabama's children. Robert Skolrood, who directed Pat Robertson's troop of fundamentalist lawyers, denounced the decision: "It is clear Christians no longer have equal standing before the court," he declaimed.

Like no other legal issue, the prayer issue simply will not surrender to judicial edict. More than two decades after the Supreme Court banned school prayer, teachers lead their students in prayer in more than half of America's ten thousand school districts. Senator Jesse Helms has not abandoned his effort to cripple the federal courts in this area. At its heart, the prayer issue tests America's tolerance for difference and diversity. Five years after Ishmael Jaffree brought his suit, a Mobile hotel clerk glared at him and hissed: "That's the man who caused all the trouble in our schools." She did not mention the trouble the Mobile schools caused Ishmael Jaffree and his family.

II.
"Tell Them About My Children"

I was born on March 28, 1944, in a home for unwed mothers in Cleveland, Ohio, the first and only child of my mother. By reference to where I was born, she clearly was unwed at the time of my birth and she remained unwed. The name my mother gave me was Frederick Hobbs. I never did know my father. She told me that my father had died before I was born. It wasn't until I was grown that I found out that wasn't the truth. My mother was poor; she did domestic work for white people and she only made about $30 a week. In the early years of my life, I never had anything new. My clothes were purchased from Goodwill, and we ate mostly pork and beans and wieners. Unlike many only children, I didn't have everything that I wanted. I had very little of what I wanted because my mother couldn't afford it.

I started very early being different from other children—sort of a nonconformist in certain areas. This started even before I went to school. Somehow, I developed at a very early age an independent pattern of behavior. I didn't even conform to the behavior patterns of my mother. However, my mother did early-on influence me with respect to religious matters. She was a Baptist, but she was somewhat hypocritical in her religious precepts. Her being religious did not stop her from socializing with married men. Her being religious did not stop her from going into a restaurant and stealing the silverware. She claimed that she had paid for it in the cost of the meal and that justified her taking it. I observed this hypocrisy in my mother and vowed that I would never be a religious hypocrite.

Despite my mother's hypocrisy, she wanted me to be a minister. She promoted the idea that I was gifted or a God-chosen person. There used to be an old wives' tale that any child that is in the mother's womb and the father dies before the child is born, that child is touched and special and one of God's chosen. Early on, I believed there may have been something to that, and so I thought that eventually I'll do something very positive in the religious area, that I would become either a minister or some influential religious person, and my mother sort of fostered that idea. In my early years I was very much a student of the Bible and I used to read it a lot. Very early in my childhood I used to go on the street corners and minister to the people and preach. I would take my Bible and tell people to repent and come right with God, that you are all sinners.

Even before my teenage years I sort of strayed from the straight and narrow. I became a petty thief and was stealing things from department stores. When I was only ten I was sent to a juvenile detention home for taking a machete from a truck. Later on I was judged to be a juvenile delinquent, and I served an eight-month term in a juvenile institution. When I was in the eleventh grade I was thrown out of high school. I had my hair processed, and they had a dress code that prohibited black males from processing their hair. I didn't think the school should tell me how to wear my hair, so I wore my hair processed anyway, something that is repugnant to me now but that I was into at the time. I wanted to appear to be older because I dated females who were older than me. I used to go to clubs a lot and dance, although I never drank. I've never had alcohol in my life, which surprises me at forty-three. I've never smoked pot or taken drugs; I've never gotten high that way. The way I get high is listening to music and dancing and talking to people. I like to talk.

But I continued to articulate strong religious views even after I enrolled in junior college. One incident that influenced my religious views occurred in a sociology class. The teacher was discussing how values are formed, how groups influence individuals. As part of that discussion she took a survey and asked all those who believed in God to raise their hand. Practically everyone did and I thought everyone had. Then she asked all those who don't believe in God, who are atheists, to raise their hand, and one female white student raised her hand. That was the first I came into face-to-face contact with someone who professed to be an atheist. And I remember that I instantly *hated* this woman and I couldn't understand her. I wondered how could she possibly raise her hand to deny the existence of a God that was responsible for her being here, responsible for her breathing. How could she turn her back on God and admit publicly that she did not believe? I felt she did not even have a right to live.

Some time later I started questioning why I was so angry just because this lady thought differently than I did. Later on I started taking courses in comparative religions, and all of a sudden my views started to change. As my views progressed, I adopted what we referred to as a black religion, a black theology. My concept of Jesus Christ became a black person, justified by passages in the Bible that suggested that Christ's hair was like wool. And from the country that he came from, he must have been black. I no longer believed that Jesus Christ had blue eyes and white skin. So I was part of a movement at this time, in the mid-sixties, that pushed the theory that Jesus Christ was black and therefore, of course, God was black. I wanted to encourage black people to accept that concept.

When I got into regular college in 1968, at Cleveland State University, I started to waver in that theology. I started thinking that maybe God is just an image, an energy force perhaps, and doesn't have to look like any particular person or be any particular color. And then I started questioning whether God exists at all, and started thinking about how I formed my ideas and how religious ideas got formulated in the first place. How an early Cro-Magnon person was afraid of fire because he couldn't understand it and ascribed supernatural qualities to it. I started thinking about how, through an evolutionary process, we got to where we are. Once I did that I became an agnostic, and I began to question everything.

I didn't come to that position because I was influenced by people or by writers. It was a gradual process, and it seemed like a common-sense approach. I realized that the mere fact somebody taught me something doesn't mean it's true. The fact that a large number of people believe something doesn't mean it's true.

At the same time I was going through an evolution with respect to my religious beliefs, I was going through an evolution with respect to my racial attitudes. I went from having a complex about being black to being proud that I was black. As a result of the sixties and seventies, I also went through a political metamorphosis in the sense that I went from being supportive of the military complex system to being opposed to the military and the war in Vietnam.

I never formally joined any groups. I had this aversion to joining groups. I didn't want to sacrifice my own individuality. Most groups had leaders and the rest of the people were followers. If I couldn't be in charge of the group, I wouldn't simply be a member of it. Even though I sympathized with the Black Panthers, I never joined the group because they had their members march around and wear certain clothes and just be little functionaries. I never wanted to do that. I also became very familiar with the Black Muslim movement and I had some friends in it, but I never joined for the same reason. I don't want to be simply part of a movement and have somebody tell me what I should do, what I should believe, how I should think. I didn't want to follow the dictates of some charismatic figure who suggested that this is the way we should go, this is what's best for us.

The way I became a lawyer goes back to when I was put out of high school. I worked after that for several years, at all kinds of jobs: I worked at restaurants as a busboy, and in an auto plant. Then I went back to an alternative-education school. What caused me to go back was that I used to watch Perry Mason on TV and became fascinated with him. And I thought, Gee, I'd like to be a lawyer, but in order to do that at least I have to finish high school. So I completed that and went on to junior college.

And about that time I got interested in politics, and I learned that a lot of politicians were attorneys, so that was further motivation to go to law school. I got involved in the campaign of Carl Stokes, a black man who ran for mayor of Cleveland. After he won, the second time he ran, I thought, Gee, I'd like to run for political office, and law would be a good steppingstone. Also at that time, in 1972, I changed my name from Frederick Hobbs to Ishmael Jaffree. Most black people's names came from former slave owners, and I rejected the slave-master path. I chose Ishmael because it means 'outcast,' and Jaffree came from a Cleveland State professor that I admired.

While I was at Cleveland State University, I became active in trying to encourage law schools in Ohio to recruit blacks. And after I finished college, I applied to several and got turned down because my law-board score was so low. I applied to NYU, Cornell, Ohio State, Case Western Reserve. I finally got accepted at Cleveland–Marshall College of Law, principally because they had balked at admitting black students. I was a hell-raiser in college, and I was protesting, and I threatened to go to the media. I met with the dean, who fancied himself as a civil libertarian. So they started a special program at Cleveland–Marshall for disadvantaged youths, and I was in the first group they admitted.

Law school was easy for me. When I was in law school, I was working full time at the Federal Trade Commission, and I'd go dancing in clubs at night. I never really studied very hard. I had this technique: The teacher may assign fifty pages and ten cases that we had to read and be prepared to brief the next day. I would read the first and second case and then raise my hand to be called on first. Or if somebody else was called on, I'd ask all kinds of questions about the case. Before exams, I would cram and read the stuff. I had a knack for law, and I took all the harder courses, like tax law. I never had a Black's law dictionary and I never used canned briefs in class. I didn't have difficulty passing the Ohio bar exam. When I came to Alabama, I didn't even study for the bar; I just took it based on the Ohio bar.

What I wanted to do after I finished law school was constitutional law. That was what I enjoyed the most in law school. What I *didn't* want to do was criminal law, which I thought was too easy. And I also didn't look forward to working in a system where people committed crimes and got off. I also had some biases. I couldn't represent somebody who had raped a woman, because that was repugnant to me. I couldn't even represent somebody that was selling drugs to the community, because my philosophy wouldn't tolerate that, even though I felt that these people needed representation. But I had values that wouldn't allow me to represent them, because my heart wouldn't be in it, and if I *knew* they were guilty I simply couldn't assist.

I had made a promise to myself in law school, to never charge anybody any money for any legal service that I provide. There were only two ways I knew that I could do that. I could work for some federal agency such as the Federal Trade Commission, but that was too limited. Or I could work for legal services, which

I had an interest in even before law school. So I knew that I would eventually wind up in a legal-services office, because I didn't want to charge any money and I wanted to ensure that low-income people had access to quality, competent, free legal services.

When I was in law school I heard about a program called the Reggie fellowships, the Reginald Heber Smith fellowships to support law-school graduates in legal-services work for one year. I applied, and at the time I had recently been married and my wife had gone to school in Huntsville, Alabama. I was tired of Cleveland, and I thought the civil-rights movement was moving to the South, and that's where all the action was going to be. So I moved to Huntsville, which is an attractive city; but there weren't many black people there or much social or political activity going on. After a year in Huntsville I moved to the legal-services office in Mobile in 1977. I heard that they had a voting-rights case that was very active, and that they had a few black attorneys here.

The reason I brought the school prayer case is that I wanted my children to be free from programmed thinking, conditioned thinking. I wanted them to be free to explore a wide variety of ideas and not have to go through the long and painful metamorphosis that I went through. The case started in 1981 when my son Chioke, who was five and had just started kindergarten, came home from school one day and I asked him what's going on in school. He told me his teacher, Mrs. Boyd, was having the class line up before lunch and bow their heads and sing this grace.

Chioke was going to the same school where my wife, Mozelle, was teaching. My daughter Makeba was then seven, and she was in the second grade; and my son Aaki was eight, and he was in a special program because he had academic and emotional problems. They were all going to different schools in Mobile. When Chioke told me his teacher was leading the class in grace before meals, I remember telling him, Your teacher is doing something that's not legal. I want you to tell her that what she's doing is not legal. And he said, Okay.

I didn't think anything about it at the time. And about two weeks later, he said, Remember I told you my teacher was leading the class in prayer? She's still doing it. I said, Did you tell her what I said? He said, Yeah, but she's still doing it; she didn't care. So I wrote a letter for him to give his teacher, saying that my son has advised me that you are leading your class in a prayer before meals. You should know that this is unlawful; that the Supreme Court ruled some time ago that this is unconstitutional.

I gave Chioke the letter to his teacher, and I asked him when he got back from school did he give it to her, and he said, Yeah. Did she read it? Yeah. Did she stop? No. I then went down to the school and talked to Mrs. Boyd, who was a black teacher. I said, Chioke brought you a letter, and he said you're still leading the class in prayer. I don't really want to make a big issue out of this, but you really ought not to do that. I told her that I had reached an agreement with Mozelle that we are not trying to promote religion in our household. Mozelle is a Bahai and she's very religious, and I don't subscribe to any religion, but I don't influence the children to my way of thinking. Here you are undermining that neutrality in our household by promoting your brand of religion, and it's really unlawful. I'm not making any children say anything, she said. Her attitude was one of shock that I would even complain about it.

Then I talked with the principal, and she said that she would talk with the superintendent of schools and get back to me. By this time, my other two children told me that their classes were doing it, too. And I talked with *their* principals, and they said they would have to check with the superintendent as well. When I called them back, they said they were told the teachers could lead the children in prayer as long as they didn't make them take part. So I wrote a very long letter to the superintendent, whose name was Abe Hammons, complaining about the principals and telling him about the separation of church and state and how this is unlawful.

Superintendent Hammons told me he would check with his attorney and get back to me. But all the teachers kept doing it. I realized that it was getting close to the end of the school year. I was getting angry, so I decided to file a lawsuit. I contacted the ACLU and they said they didn't have the money to hire an attorney. Then I got a bright idea and contacted Ron Williams here in Mobile, and I told him that I didn't want to lose my job at Legal Services but that I would do all the work in the background. He used to work for Legal Services as well, and had recently gone into private practice. So we quickly dictated a complaint and filed it in federal court.

I was naive at the time and thought that once it reached the federal attorney, he'd say, Let's settle this case and stop this practice. I thought it wouldn't last more than two weeks. But the school-board president, Dan Alexander, had political ambitions. They had a meeting and he told them, Either we are going to have to say that what the teachers are doing is wrong and they will stop it, or we'll have to fight this all the way. The board voted to fight it.

The governor at the time, Fob James, heard about my lawsuit, and he called a special session of the Alabama state legislature. He called the media in advance and told them he was having a special news conference. So he went on statewide TV and criticized me by name and said I had sued these three brave teachers who were doing nothing more than teaching the children of our state to pray. The governor submitted legislation to permit teachers to lead willing students in prayer, and it was passed within a week. The legislation included a prayer that was written by the governor's son. They are both religious fanatics. So I quickly filed an amended complaint to challenge this new law as well, and I added the governor as a party.

That's when the publicity really started. The school-board president thought he could make political points and he started attacking me, and the local media just had a field day. I got a lot of hostile reaction. The black community was up in arms that some black person had done this. I got portrayed as a person who was trying to take God out of the public schools. The talk shows in Mobile were filled with people who said, Why doesn't he go back to Africa where he came from. I got all kinds of nasty letters, and I got nasty phone calls at all times of night. I used to talk with people and try to let them understand why I did this—that it was a matter of principle and the schools shouldn't be promoting anybody's religion. People in the neighborhood stopped their children from associating with my children. My children got jumped on, laughed at, talked about in school. My children started turning against me; they said it was a stupid lawsuit. They especially turned against me when Judge Hand ruled against me. They told me the judge had said what I was doing was stupid.

This case was originally assigned to Judge Cox, who was a new federal judge in Mobile. Cases were assigned on an even-number, odd-number basis. Judge Cox would get all the even-numbered cases and Judge Hand would get the odd-numbered cases. This was an even-numbered case. Judge Hand learned about the case and he wanted it, so he just took it from Judge Cox and put it on his own docket. At first, I was glad Judge Hand took the case, because he had had his hand slapped by the court of appeals in a similar case in Alabama, where they had Bible reading over the school intercom and a course that promoted religion. Judge Hand dismissed the case, and the court of appeals ordered him to issue an injunction and a declaratory judgment against the school board. I knew about that case, and I thought Judge Hand knows the law now and so he's going to quickly rule in my favor.

All of a sudden, these people from the biggest Baptist church in Mobile, Cottage Hill Baptist Church, moved to intervene in my case. They wanted to be defendants and said they wanted prayer in the schools. They claimed it would be a denial of their rights of free exercise of religion to take prayer out of public schools. We objected to their presence, but Judge Hand said, I'll just let them stay in temporarily and hear what they have to say. We had a preliminary hearing and I subpoenaed Senator Holmes, who sponsored the law, and we got him to admit that he wanted to get prayer back into the schools.

Then the intervenors said, We have some people we want to testify—and they brought in this Baptist minister from Florida who said that our religion requires prayer to be said everywhere, including the schools. Then he mentioned secular humanism, which he had been talking about every Sunday on his television show. We objected, but Judge Hand said that it's about time the courts started looking at what he called the religion of secular humanism. So the other side got their clue, and they started making secular-humanism noises. And they said that if Jaffree is successful in getting an injunction against the Christian religion, we want an injunction against secular humanism as well.

Then they started having mass rallies at the Cottage Hill Baptist Church. They passed out circulars throughout the city and took out newspaper advertisements for mass rallies to keep God in school. At these rallies, they asked people to look in their children's school textbooks for anything they didn't like, and to bring that to the court. Judge Hand decided that he would first have a trial on my complaint, on whether the teachers were promoting prayer. But he let the intervenors put on all these witnesses who talked about all the books they didn't like, and they had a tableful of books. The state put on one so-called expert witness who said the Supreme Court had misinterpreted the Constitution and that states were free to establish a religion. We didn't think anybody would be foolish enough to buy that!

Judge Hand heard all of this testimony over our objections. Then he came out with this opinion saying that the teachers were promoting prayer but it didn't matter, because the states are free to establish a religion if they want to and the Supreme Court had erred; that he had studied some fresh historical analysis on this. And he put in this footnote that said if the Supreme Court overruled him, he had heard testimony that secular humanism was a religion and was being advanced in the schools. I'm going to hunker down, he said, and go through these books page by page, and you'll get censorship like you've never seen. I was really shocked! I had *no* idea he would come out from that angle.

As soon as Judge Hand ruled, *everybody* started having prayer sessions in school. The school-board president even called in the media and led children in prayer at lunch. This was all focused on my children. One of them used to bury his head when the media came around. We got more threats on my life. Some of the black people would see me at the mall and criticize me. I was considered a misfit. It wasn't until the court of appeals ruled in my favor that the attitude among blacks started to change slightly.

I didn't argue my case before the Supreme Court, but I knew the law so well that I programmed the attorney who did the argument. We had a session where I pretended that I was each of the members of the Supreme Court, and I put hypothetical questions to them. I studied opinions that all the justices had written, and when I wrote the brief I incorporated stuff they had said, to sort of lock them into positions on these issues. I tried to anticipate what they would say in light of what they had written before, and what kinds of questions they might possibly ask.

I had never been in the Supreme Court before, and I was aware of a sense of awe, the sense of serenity of the place, the power that these justices have. Everything was so solemn and quiet. It was like a church.

While I was there at the argument, sitting at the counsel table,

I really wanted to answer some of the questions. They asked whether the 'moment of silence' statute had ever been implemented, and whether the Jaffree children had suffered any injuries, and whether there was a case or controversy. I knew the answers to all of those questions, and it was frustrating that I couldn't answer them. I wanted to say something so they could see I was a real human being with flesh and blood, I wanted to tell them about my children. I'd kind of like to be there someday as a Supreme Court justice, but my life style would never permit that!

I thought I was going to lose. I had studied the Supreme Court enough that I didn't think it would say that schools could not even set aside a moment and tell students they could pray or meditate in that moment. Teachers leading students in vocal prayer—of course not. But telling students that they could meditate or pray silently, which they could do anyway, I didn't think the Supreme Court would find that constitutionally infirm.

By the time the Supreme Court ruled for me, the mood of the community had tempered somewhat. When Judge Hand's ruling had sunk in, some people had been embarrassed, because he had gone too far. I mean, he had reversed the Supreme Court, which he had no power to do, and said that the Bill of Rights didn't apply to the states. And nobody in Mobile was really excited about the meditation issue. What they really wanted was vocal prayer! So that didn't create the hostile reaction that the case earlier had.

The Supreme Court decision created a great deal of joy in my children. They suddenly realized that I had won, and that the whole case was over. That was it! The teachers in my children's schools stopped saying the prayers, although I found out they were still praying in other schools. But they are very careful not to pray in *my* children's schools, because they know that I, more than any other person in Mobile, would raise the issue all over again.

16

Michael Hardwick
v. Michael Bowers

Michael Hardwick challenged the Georgia law
against sodomy after his 1982 arrest in Atlanta for
having sex with a consenting male friend in his
own bedroom. *Photo by Bill Coore, Associated Press
for the* Washington Post, © *1986*

I.
"I Saw a Bedroom Door
Partially Open"

Early in the morning of August 3, 1982, Officer K.R. Torick entered Michael Hardwick's house in the Virginia Highland neighborhood of Atlanta, Georgia. Torick carried a warrant for Hardwick's arrest on a charge of failing to appear in court for drinking in public. Several weeks earlier, Torick had ticketed Michael outside the bar where he worked, for carrying an open beer bottle. Torick later claimed in his official report that when he arrived to serve the arrest warrant, one of Michael's housemates answered the door and admitted the officer. "The roommate told me he didn't know if Hardwick was home but said I could come in to look for him. While walking down the hallway inside the house, I saw a bedroom door partially open." Torick entered the bedroom and promptly arrested Michael and his male companion for violating the Georgia sodomy statute.

While Michael and his friend were dressing, Officer Torick searched the room and discovered a small amount of marijuana, which he confiscated. Handcuffing his prisoners, Torick drove them to the central police station, where they were booked, photographed, and fingerprinted. Officers then tossed Michael and his friend into the holding tank, informing both guards and prisoners in graphic terms of the charges against the two gay men. They spent most of the day behind bars before friends were permitted to post bail for their release. Torick never served the arrest warrant:

Three weeks earlier, Michael had appeared in court and paid a $50 fine for the public-drinking ticket, which wiped out the warrant.

Shortly after his sodomy arrest, Michael accepted an offer by the Georgia affiliate of the American Civil Liberties Union to begin a test-case challenge of the law. Michael understood the risks in this effort. Conviction for sodomy carried a maximum prison term of twenty years. Too, a college-educated gay artist like Michael would be torn apart by the human pit bulls in Georgia's prisons. Michael also risked the unwelcome glare of publicity—his lawyers could not guarantee they could keep his face off television screens and his name out of newspapers. After his first encounter with Officer Torick, Michael was attacked and badly beaten by assailants who knew his name. Wider publicity might expose him—and other Atlanta gays—to vigilante violence. Michael's greatest risk was legal defeat; his most formidable opponent was the U.S. Supreme Court. Despite the Court's approval of "privacy" rights for married couples, unmarried heterosexuals, and pregnant women, the justices adamantly refused to hear appeals by homosexuals for similar protection against state prosecution for their intimate activities.

Michael listened as his volunteer ACLU lawyers, John Sweet and Louis Levenson, described these risks and stressed that the case might take years to reach final decision. Although he had not been a gay activist, Michael worked in gay bars and knew the constant fear of harassment, arrest, and prison that pervaded Atlanta's gay community. After a few days of solitary reflection, Michael decided to go ahead. The ACLU lawyers first disposed of the marijuana charge with a misdemeanor guilty plea in Atlanta Municipal Court. As a felony charge, the sodomy case went before the Fulton County Superior Court after an initial municipal court hearing.

Sweet and Levenson actually hoped for a guilty finding against Michael. Without an adverse judgment, they could not begin the appellate route that led through state courts to the U.S. Supreme Court. Before the case reached trial, Fulton County District Attorney Lewis Slaton pulled the case from the court's docket by refusing to present the charges to a grand jury for indictment. Slaton, a sixty-year-old, no-nonsense prosecutor, declined to discuss his reasons for keeping the case out of court. Most likely, he did not want to arouse the Atlanta gay community and its enemies, who obeyed an uneasy truce in the Virginia Highland area and in Piedmont Park, where gays congregated and competed in softball leagues, complete with uniforms, raunchy team names, and cheerleaders. Slaton undoubtedly knew that Officer Torick's expired warrant, his earlier arrest of Michael, and disputes over how he gained entrance to Michael's house might embarrass the police and prosecutors.

Unlike many prosecutors who defended entrapment tactics and police sweeps of parks and gay bars, Slaton kept a relatively tight rein on his troops. Most of the gays arrested in public places like Piedmont Park, even if the police witnessed acts of sodomy, were simply charged with the misdemeanor offense of "public indecency." Slaton later explained his views to an Atlanta reporter: "Consensual sodomy should be a misdemeanor, not a felony," he said, "but nobody has the courage to push it that way." But the law remained on the books as a felony, and Michael Hardwick had been arrested for sodomy. Slaton's refusal to prosecute did not protect Michael from indictment at some time before the four-year statute of limitations expired.

Frustrated at the state level, ACLU lawyers shifted their attack to the federal courts. Kathleen Wilde, a twenty-eight-year-old graduate of Yale Law School, volunteered to take the case before District Judge Robert H. Hall. She decided to broaden the attack on the sodomy law, which subjected heterosexuals as well as homosexuals to prosecution and prison. Wilde recruited a married couple as additional plaintiffs and drafted a complaint which claimed that the law deprived Michael Hardwick and "John and Mary Doe" of their constitutional rights of "privacy, due process, and freedom of expression and association." She filed the complaint with Judge Hall under a statute which allowed federal judges to declare that state laws violated the U.S. Constitution and could not be enforced.

The Georgia law that Kathleen Wilde asked Judge Hall to strike down had been enacted in 1816. It provided that "a person commits the offense of sodomy when he performs or submits to any sexual act involving the sex organs of one person and the mouth or anus of another." Unlike the abortion laws the Supreme Court struck down in 1973, sodomy laws had deep roots in social bedrock. Abortion had not been a "common law" crime in England, and most American states did not outlaw abortion until late in the nineteenth century. But "the detestable and abominable crime against nature," as common-law judges described oral and anal sex, had been proscribed and punished for centuries. Hostility toward homosexuals had not, however, been universal or eternal. Many cultures tolerated or even encouraged homosexual behavior, and ancient Greeks gave their name to acts of sodomy. Until the thirteenth century, the Catholic church had no official policy of persecution; St. Thomas Aquinas first castigated homosexual conduct as "unnatural" and cast those who practiced sodomy into hell's fiery furnace. Criminal law followed church law, and the sin of sodomy became a crime.

All the original thirteen states had made sodomy a criminal offense when the Bill of Rights became part of the Constitution in 1791. As late as 1961, all fifty states had outlawed sodomy. Pressure to liberalize these laws first came from medical, social-welfare, and legal groups. The American Law Institute, an impeccably conservative group of establishment lawyers, urged state legislatures in the late 1950s to enact a Model Penal Code which decriminalized adult, consensual, private sexual conduct. Illinois became the first state, in 1961, to adopt the ALI code.

Homosexual organizations played a quiet role in the initial lobbying to repeal sodomy laws. Founded in 1951, the Mattachine Society represented gays for more than a decade. Its leaders first adopted a low profile, fearful of public hostility, but the black civil-rights movement of the 1960s stirred gays toward militance and activism. Franklin Kameny, a Mattachine maverick, argued in 1964 that gays should examine "the case of the Negro," whose gains in the ninety years after Emancipation "were nothing compared to those of the past ten years, when he tried a vigorous civil-liberties, social-action approach" to legal oppression.

Kameny's rhetorical spark did not ignite the gay movement until the hot summer night of June 27, 1969, when New York poilce raided the Stonewall Inn on Christopher Street in Greenwich Village. Beaten and abused, gays fought back in bloody battles which lasted for three nights. Out of the "Stonewall riots" came the Gay Liberation Movement, which soon moved its agitation from the streets to council chambers and courtrooms. Lobbying and litigation paid off: By 1975, more than half the states had repealed or invalidated their sodomy laws. But none of those states was below the Mason–Dixon line, where hostility toward gays fed on the "good ol' boy" Southern syndrome of exaggerated masculinity.

Kathleen Wilde filed her complaint against three Georgia officials: Attorney General Michael Bowers, a forty-two-year-old West Point graduate; Lewis Slaton, the Fulton County district attorney who refused to prosecute Michael Hardwick; and George Napier, Atlanta's police commissioner. Judge Robert Hall, who first ruled on the complaint, had been a Georgia official for many years. The sixty-two-year-old judge served in the state attorney general's office and on Georgia courts before President Jimmy Carter, a long-time friend, placed Hall on the federal bench in 1979.

Judge Hall had no desire to rule on the Georgia sodomy law. He looked for an easy out, and found one in the 1975 decision of a federal judicial panel which upheld Virginia's almost identical sodomy law. In a case called *Doe* v. *Commonwealth's Attorney*, the panel's majority denied that homosexuals shared the "privacy" rights of their straight neighbors. Supreme Court precedent, the majority held, provided these rights only to marital or familial relationships which states had legally approved. Because homosexual conduct "is obviously no portion of marriage, home or family life," Virginia could punish sodomy "in the promotion of morality and decency," the panel ruled. The two-judge majority added that "the longevity of the Virginia statute does testify to the State's interest and its legitimacy." Punishment of sodomy "is not an upstart notion; it has ancestry going back to Judaic and Christian law."

District Judge Robert Merhige dissented from the *Doe* ruling. He viewed the Supreme Court cases cited by his colleagues "as standing for the principle that every individual has a right to be free from unwarranted governmental intrusion into one's decisions on private matters of intimate concern." Judge Merhige would extend privacy rights to all consenting adults, regardless of gender: "A mature individual's choice of an adult sexual partner," he wrote, "would appear to me to be a decision of the utmost private and intimate concern." Merhige suggested that the sodomy issue "centers not around morality or decency, but the constitutional right of privacy."

Judge Merhige had pinpointed the conflict over sodomy laws,

with claims of "morality and decency" posed against the "right of privacy." The Supreme Court had refused to hear an appeal from the *Doe* ruling, and Judge Hall looked no farther for guidance. "The Virginia statute challenged in that case is quite similar to the Georgia legislation in question," he ruled on April 18, 1983, "and all the constitutional arguments made by Hardwick here were rejected in *Doe*." Dismissing Hardwick's complaint, Judge Hall also denied the challenge of "John and Mary Doe" to the sodomy law. Because District Attorney Slaton had not threatened them with prosecution, the Does faced no "immediate danger of sustaining some direct injury as a result of the statute's enforcement."

Kathleen Wilde took Michael's challenge to the federal appellate court in Atlanta, and they waited more than two years for the next decision. The result was worth the long wait. Writing for a two-judge majority, Judge Frank M. Johnson rejected the *Doe* case and declared that Michael had a privacy right that began in his bedroom. Appointed to the federal bench by President Dwight Eisenhower, Johnson had endured the hostility of fellow Alabamans for ruling that black children had the right to attend public schools with white children. Placed on the appellate bench by President Jimmy Carter in 1979, Johnson continued on his liberal course. He wrote for the panel that subsequent Supreme Court decisions had left the *Doe* ruling "an open question." Citing a 1977 Supreme Court opinion which struck down state restrictions on contraceptive sales, Johnson held that "private consensual sexual behavior among adults" was protected from punishment. Covered by the "privacy" blanket, Johnson wrote, were all kinds of "intimate associations" based on consent and caring. "For some," he added, "the sexual activity in question here serves the same purpose as the intimacy of marriage."

Georgia officials recoiled from Johnson's decision and asked the Supreme Court to reverse his ruling. Confronted with a rejection of its *Doe* ruling, the Court agreed to hear the state's appeal. Georgia's brief answered Michael Hardwick with two millennia of Christian morality. Attorney General Bowers distinguished between straight and gay relationships, arguing that "marriage is the bedrock of society, the essential and elementary unit upon which even government depends." Bowers reminded the justices that they had "many times held that morality and decency constitute legitimate and compelling state interests" which justified restrictive state laws. For more than 150 years, he argued, Georgia's legislators had agreed that "it is the very act of homosexual sodomy that epitomizes moral delinquency."

Bowers was not the first prosecutor to present a "parade of horribles" to the Supreme Court. His brief claimed that "homosexual sodomy leads to other deviate practices such as sadomasochism, group orgies, or transvestism, to name only a few." Bowers made no effort to link Michael Hardwick to any of these activities. Waving newspaper headlines before the justices, Bowers adopted scare tactics in his brief. Claiming that homosexual sodomy was often practiced in "gay baths" and "gay bars," he concluded that Georgia lawmakers "should be permitted to draw conclusions concerning the relationship of homosexual sodomy in the transmission of Acquired Immune Deficiency Syndrome." Suggesting a link between AIDS and Georgia's sodomy law, Bowers neglected to note that the law was enacted more than 150 years before the AIDS virus was discovered; the fear of AIDS could hardly have prompted the law. Prosecutors often ignore such uncomfortable facts.

Among the numerous groups that filed *amicus* briefs with the Supreme Court, most impressive was the joint brief of the American Psychological Association and the American Public Health Association. Much like the original "Brandeis brief" on which it was modeled, this document included ninety-one citations to medical and social-science literature. The brief first noted that oral and anal sex, outlawed by Georgia, was practiced by at least 80 percent of all married couples. As early as 1948, the Kinsey Report estimated that 95 percent of American males had engaged in oral sex and violated sodomy laws. Gays were no more likely to violate sodomy laws than their straight neighbors, nor did gays suffer any more than straights from emotional illness. In fact, the brief claimed, "there are great similarities among homosexual and heterosexual couples—in emotional makeup, significance of the relationship to the individual, and in the role sexuality plays in the relationship."

The brief of the health groups tackled the AIDS issue head-on. Sodomy laws added nothing to campaigns against AIDS, they claimed. "The threat of prosecution actually *harms* the public health effort by driving the disease underground where it is more difficult to study and by impeding the flow of information about prevention from public health experts to the population at risk." Fear of prosecution for sodomy contributed toward "internalized homophobia," the brief argued—self-hatred on the part of gays which might lead to rejection of "safe sex" efforts to curb AIDS.

The state's appeal came before the Supreme Court on March 31, 1986. Michael E. Hobbs, a thirty-five-year-old deputy to Attorney General Bowers, defended the Georgia officials. Hobbs spoke first and framed the issue as "whether or not there is a fundamental right under the Constitution of the United States to engage in consensual private homosexual sodomy." Less than a minute later, Hobbs faced a barrage of questions. Why had the Atlanta district attorney not sought to indict Michael Hardwick? "I do not know what was in the mind of the District Attorney when he decided not to prosecute this case," Hobbs confessed. Had any married couple ever been prosecuted for sodomy in Georgia? "Not to my knowledge," Hobbs replied. Would such a prosecution be lawful? "I believe that it would be unconstitutional," Hobbs responded.

Once the state's lawyer had fielded all the questions, he urged the justices to avoid creating a "constitutional right which is little more than one of self-gratification and indulgence." Hobbs warned that striking down the sodomy law would open a "Pandora's box" and lead eventually to attacks on laws "which prohibit polygamy; homosexual, same-sex marriage; consensual incest; prostitution; fornication; adultery; and possibly even personal possession in private of illegal drugs." Against the "crack-in-the-door" challenge of Michael Hardwick, Georgia stood firmly for "a decent and moral society." In opening Michael's bedroom door, "Georgia is not acting as a big brother," Hobbs concluded, but "is adhering to centuries-old tradition and the conventional morality of its people."

Laurence H. Tribe took the podium for Michael Hardwick. Professor of constitutional law at Harvard and author of the most influential treatise in the field, Tribe had appeared before the justices in more than a dozen important cases, with an impressive victory record. Often listed as a likely Supreme Court nominee by a future Democratic president, the forty-five-year-old Tribe began by reshaping the issue Hobbs had framed: "This case is about the limits of governmental power." Michael's case had nothing to do with polygamy, bigamy, or incest, but with Georgia's power to dictate "how every adult, married or unmarried, in every bedroom in Georgia will behave in the closest and most intimate personal association with another adult."

Justice Lewis Powell moved the discussion from bedrooms to "a motel room or the back of an automobile or toilet or wherever." Could Tribe define the "limiting principles" of his claim that consensual sodomy was beyond the bounds of state proscription? Tribe reminded Powell that bedrooms in homes had special constitutional protection from police invasion, far more than public places. The colloquy between Tribe and the justices resembled a law-school seminar, as the professor discussed jurisprudential concepts of "minimum rationality" and "heightened scrutiny" in reviewing claims of rights against state regulation. Justice Powell interrupted to chide Tribe for evading his "public toilet" question. Tribe conceded that states had some rights to regulate behavior in public places. Urging that "there is something special about a home," he added that "Robert Frost once said that home is the place where, when you go there, they have to take you in." Poetry had no force as precedent, but Tribe hoped his evocation of home and hearth would turn the Court's mind away from public toilets and AIDS.

Three months after the argument, on June 30, 1986, a sharply divided Court announced that Georgia could punish its citizens, straight or gay, who engaged in sodomy. Justice Byron White, a former All-American football star and a stern judicial moralist, wrote for the majority. White framed the question in the same words Michael Hobbs had used: "The issue presented is whether the Federal Constitution confers a fundamental right upon homosexuals to engage in sodomy," he wrote. Not surprisingly, White and Hobbs agreed on the answer. Cases which granted privacy rights to relations of "family, marriage, or procreation" did not extend those same rights to gays. White based his opinion not on precedent or the present status of gays in American society, but on the "ancient roots" of criminal penalties for sodomy. He answered Tribe's argument that bedrooms were "special places" by listing the horrors inside Hobbs' "Pandora's box" of perversions.

Granting gays the right to practice sodomy in their homes might hinder prosecution of "adultery, incest, and other sexual crimes" which are committed in homes. "We are unwilling to start down that road," White stated.

Two weeks before the Court's decision, Chief Justice Warren Burger announced his retirement in July, after sixteen years at the Court's helm. Michael Hardwick's case gave Burger his last chance to speak from the bench on issues of personal rights, and he added to White's opinion a short sermon which reflected the unbending morality of his Lutheran forebears. Adopting the ancient definition of sodomy as "the infamous crime against nature," Burger found its condemnation "firmly rooted in Judeo–Christian moral and ethical standards." A judicial holding that sodomy "is somehow protected as a fundamental right would be to cast aside millennia of moral teaching," the Chief Justice concluded. In an even shorter concurrence, Justice Lewis Powell agreed that "there is no fundamental right" to practice sodomy—but he was troubled that Georgia provided a twenty-year maximum prison term for conviction. Powell hinted that if Georgia had prosecuted and sentenced Michael Hardwick, he might have voted to reverse the conviction and the law.

Writing for the four dissenters, Justice Harry Blackmun virtually accused the majority of judicial homophobia. "Only the most willful blindness," he wrote, "could obscure the fact that sexual intimacy" is central to healthy personal relationships of all kinds. The Court's majority refused to recognize that "a necessary corollary of giving individuals freedom to choose how to conduct their lives is acceptance of the fact that different individuals will make different choices." Blackmun also reminded the Chief Justice, his boyhood friend, that Biblical precepts had been used to justify not only sodomy laws but Southern racism.

The final paragraph of Blackmun's outraged dissent looked to history for an ominous parallel and possible redemption: "It took but three years for the Court to see the error" of its 1940 decision which upheld the expulsion of Lillian and William Gobitis from school for refusing to salute the flag, Blackmun wrote. The Court's opinion had unleashed a wave of violence against Jehovah's Witnesses and forced the reversal of the *Gobitis* decision in 1943. "I can only hope that here, too, the Court soon will reconsider" its approval of sodomy laws, Blackmun urged, "and conclude that depriving individuals of the right to choose for themselves how to conduct their intimate relationships poses a far greater threat to the values most deeply rooted in our Nation's history than tolerance of nonconformity could ever do. Because I think the Court today betrays those values, I dissent."

The source of Blackmun's feeling of betrayal surfaced two weeks after the Court's decision. "Powell Changed Vote in Sodomy Case," revealed *The Washington Post* in a front-page headline. Quoting "informed sources" who were not identified, the *Post* claimed that Powell had voted at the Court's conference to strike down the Georgia law. Before the decision was announced, Powell had changed his mind and his vote, a right which justices enjoy but rarely exercise. Such voting switches are never announced; reporters had never before "opened the door" of the Court's conference room.

Blackmun's hope for the Court's redemption and reversal of the *Hardwick* decision remains alive. Justice Powell retired in 1977, and Justice Anthony Kennedy took his seat in February 1988. That same month, a federal appellate panel in San Francisco struck down the Army's ban on gay soldiers. The Army had discharged Sgt. Perry Watkins after sixteen years of service, although Watkins had admitted his sexual orientation at the time he enlisted in 1967. Writing for the panel's majority, Judge William A. Norris looked to Blackmun's dissent for guidance in his opinion. Even the dissenting judge, Stephen Reinhardt, expressed his hope that the *Hardwick* case, which he felt bound to follow, "will be overruled by a wiser and more enlightened Court." Government lawyers prevailed in June 1988 in asking for a rehearing of this decision by a larger appellate panel. Whatever the outcome of this review, the Watkins case will almost certainly reach the Supreme Court for final decision. Michael Hardwick might yet win his right to keep his bedroom door closed to the police and prosecutors.

II.
"What Are You Doing in My Bedroom?"

I was born in Miami in 1954 and raised in Miami. My mother is a very wonderful and intelligent and sensitive woman. My father was a very intelligent and crafty-type man. He was a fireman and worked during the Cuban missile crisis with fallout shelters and radiation. My parents divorced when I was twelve years old and I lived with my mom until I was seventeen. I went to high school here and it was pretty normal, just like high school anywhere.

I have two sisters and a brother that are all older than me. My older sister is forty and she is a lesbian. She has a daughter who is sixteen and she's been a strong influence on me all my life. I have an older brother who is straight and married and has children.

I wanted to be a landscape architect, and I went to school in botany and horticulture at Florida State University in Gainesville. I spent three years up there, pretty much as a spiritual recluse. I was seriously considering becoming a Buddhist monk, and I was into a very spiritual frame, as far as Karma and all of that. My family was all Catholic, so they were rather disturbed about this. They were actually relieved when I told them I was coming out instead. Their attitude was, Thank God!

From Gainesville I went up to Atlanta and met this man that I fell in love with. When I met this guy it seemed like a perfectly normal thing and that was that. Things didn't work out between me and this man in Atlanta. He had a lover, which I didn't know, so I left and went to Knoxville, Tennessee. I went there because I had a girlfriend I had originally gone up to see in Atlanta, who was also gay, and she and her girlfriend were moving to Knoxville. They were telling me, You've got to do something; you're a mess. So they brought me up there and nursed me back to mental health. I was totally devastated for about six months. All I did was listen to Billy Holliday and have The Blues. When I got my balance I went to Gatlinburg, up in the Smoky Mountains, and I really loved it there. It was good for me inside, soul-searching and putting things back into perspective. I really liked the place.

Then I left and went back down to Miami and told my mother and my sister I was gay, and they were very supportive. I was twenty-one years old at the time. And I've been out since then. My mother was very accepting. She has become very independent for the first time in her life. She's now living all by herself on fourteen acres of land up in Gainesville, and she's loving it. She's been great all along.

I started working in Miami, and I opened a business called Growth Concept Environmental Design. Because I had bar-tended in a private gay restaurant, very elite, I knew all these top designers. So when I opened my business I immediately had an excellent clientele. I worked for about a year and a half and I finally decided I needed more time by myself. I had questions that I really hadn't worked out. So I sold my business to my junior partner and I moved back to Gatlinburg because I was so taken with the Smoky Mountains. I opened a health-food store and I hiked about forty miles a week. I was there for two years and I lost my ass in the health-food store, but at the same time I gained a lot of knowledge of myself and became a friend to myself, which is what I was really seeking to do.

This girlfriend that had pulled me out four years earlier was living in Atlanta, so I went down there to visit her, which is how this whole case started. I had been working for about a year, in a gay bar that was getting ready to open up a discothèque. I was there one night until seven o'clock in the morning, helping them put in insulation. When I left, I went up to the bar and they gave me a beer. I was kind of debating whether I wanted to leave, because I was pretty exhausted, or stay and finish the beer. I decided to leave, and I opened the door and threw the beer bottle into this trash can by the front door of the bar. I wasn't really in the mood for the beer.

Just as I did that I saw a cop drive by. I walked about a block, and he turned around and came back and asked me where the beer was. I told him I had thrown it in the trash can in front of the bar. He insisted I had thrown the beer bottle right as he pulled up. He made me get in the car and asked me what I was doing. I told him that I worked there, which immediately identified me as a homosexual, because he knew it was a homosexual bar. He was enjoying *his* position as opposed to *my* position.

After about twenty minutes of bickering he drove me back so I could show him where the beer bottle was. There was no way of getting out of the back of a cop car. I told him it was in the trash can and he said he couldn't see it from the car. I said fine, just give me a ticket for drinking in public. He was just busting my chops because he knew I was gay.

Anyway, the ticket had a court date on the top and a date in the center and they didn't coincide; they were one day apart. Tuesday was the court date, and the officer had written Wednesday on top of the ticket. So Tuesday, two hours after my court date, he was at my house with a warrant for my arrest. This was Officer Torick. This was unheard of, because it takes forty-eight hours to process a warrant. What I didn't realize, and didn't find out until later, was that he had personally processed a warrant for the first time in ten years. So I think there is reason to believe that he had it out for me.

I wasn't there when he came with the warrant. I got home that afternoon and my roommate said there was a cop here with a warrant. I said, That's impossible; my court date isn't until tomorrow. I went and got my ticket and realized the court date was Tuesday, not Wednesday. I asked my roommate if he'd seen the warrant and he said he hadn't. So I went down to the county clerk and showed him the discrepancy on the ticket. He brought it before the judge, and he fined me $50. I told the county clerk the cop had already been at my house with a warrant and he said that was impossible. He said it takes forty-eight hours to process a warrant. He wrote me a receipt just in case I had any problems with it further down the road. That was that, and I thought I had taken care of it and everything was finished, and I didn't give it much thought.

Three weeks went by, and my mom had come up to visit me. I came home one morning after work at 6:30 and there were three guys standing in front of my house. I cannot say for *sure* that they had anything to do with this, but they were very straight, middle thirties, civilian clothes. I got out of the car, turned around, and they said 'Michael' and I said yes, and they proceeded to beat the hell out of me. Tore all the cartilage out of my nose, kicked me in the face, cracked about six of my ribs. I passed out. I don't know how long I was unconscious. When I came to, all I could think of was, God, I don't want my *mom* to see me like this!

I managed to crawl up the stairs into the house, into the back bedroom. What I didn't realize was that I'd left a trail of blood all the way back. My mom woke up, found this trail of blood, found me passed out, and just freaked out. I assured her that everything was okay, that it was like a fluke accident, these guys were drunk or whatever. They weren't drunk, they weren't ruffians, and they knew who I was. I convinced her everything was okay and she left to go visit a friend in Pennsylvania.

I had a friend come in a few days later who was from out of town, in Atlanta to apply for a government job. He waited for me to get off work, we went home, and then my roommate left for work. That night at work, another friend of mine had gotten really drunk, and I took his car keys, put him in a cab, and sent him to my house, so he was passed out on the couch in the living room. He did not hear me and my friend come in. I retired with my friend. He had left the front door open, and Officer Torick came into my house about 8:30 in the morning. He had a warrant that had not been valid for three weeks and that he didn't bother to call in and check on. Officer Torick came in and woke up the guy who was passed out on my couch, who didn't know I was there and had a friend with me.

Officer Torick then came to my bedroom. The door was cracked, and the door opened up and I looked up and there was nobody there. I just blew it off as the wind and went back to what I was involved in, which was mutual oral sex. About thirty-five seconds went by and I heard another noise and I looked up, and this officer is standing in my bedroom. He identified himself when he realized I had seen him. He said, My name is Officer Torick. Michael Hardwick, you are under arrest. I said, For what? What are you doing in my bedroom? He said, I have a warrant for your arrest. I told him the warrant isn't any good. He said, It doesn't matter, because I was acting under good faith.

I asked Torick if he would leave the room so we could get dressed and he said, There's no reason for that, because I have already seen you in your most intimate aspect. He stood there and watched us get dressed, and then he brought us over to a substation. We waited in the car for about twenty-five minutes, handcuffed to the back floor. Then he brought us downtown; brought us in and made sure everyone in the holding cells and guards and people who were processing us knew I was in there for 'cocksucking' and that I should be able to get what I was looking for. The guards were having a *real* good time with that.

There was somebody there to get me out of jail within an hour, but it took them twelve hours to get me out. In the meantime, after they processed me and kept me in a holding cell for about four hours, they brought me up to the third floor, where there was convicted criminals. I had no business being up there. They again told all the people in the cells what I was in there for. It was not a pleasant experience. My friend was freaking out, and when I got out of jail I came back within an hour and got him out. He decided because of his government position he could not go on with the case.

I was contacted about three days later by a man named Clint Sumrall who was working in and out of the ACLU. For the last five years, he would go to the courts every day and find sodomy cases and try to get a test case. By this time, my mom had come back into town and found out what had happened. We had a typical mother conversation—she was saying, I *knew* I shouldn't have left! So she went with me to meet with Sumrall and this team of ten lawyers. I asked them what was the worst that could happen, what was the best that could happen? They explained to me that the judge could make an example out of me and give me twenty years in jail. My mom was saying, Do you realize I'll be *dead* before I see you again? So they said, Just think about it for two or three days.

I realized that if there was anything I could do, even if it was just laying the foundation to change this horrendous law, that I would feel pretty bad about myself if I just walked away from it. One thing that influenced me was that they'd been trying for five years to get a perfect case. Most of the arrests that are made for sodomy in Atlanta are of people who are having sex outside in public; or an adult and a minor; or two consenting adults, but their families don't know they are gay; or they went through seven years of college to teach and they'd be jeopardizing their teaching position. There's a lot of different reasons why people would not want to go on with it. I was fortunate enough to have a supportive family who knew I was gay. I'm a bartender, so I can always work in a gay bar. And I was arrested in my own house. So I was a perfect test case.

I immediately met with these ten lawyers and decided on two of them to represent me. I chose John Sweet and Louis Levenson. They told me I had to get prosecuted and have a conviction from the superior court in order to get into the federal courts and be a test case. There was also a small amount of marijuana in my room, so there was a misdemeanor charge and a felony. So I had to go into the municipal courts before the superior court.

So here I go, marching into municipal court with two of the best hot-shot lawyers in Georgia on a possession-of-marijuana misdemeanor. Officer Torick got up there and said he had been let into my house; he didn't realize it had been twenty-one days since the warrant, and he was acting under good faith. The only question my lawyers asked him was why he stood there for thirty-five seconds before he identified himself. He answered that the lights were low in the room and he wasn't sure what was going on. The judge kind of chuckled and asked my attorneys how I pled, and they said 'Guilty' with no argument. We didn't want them to get suspicious as to what we were up to.

The transcripts went up to the superior court level, and when the prosecutors saw who was representing me, and saw that I pled guilty on the marijuana charge, they got suspicious. They sensed that something was coming and they didn't want to get involved in it. So they refused to set a court date for me, which would have meant that I would have four years of the case pending. Once the time had run out, I would not be able to start a federal suit. At that point it was very touchy. I'd been meeting with my lawyers about once a week for two or three hours while they were preparing me for testimony. So we met, and they said, You can let things ride, but what we really need to do—and we're taking a *very* large chance—is to push it. So I agreed to do that, and we insisted that the district attorney prosecute me, because I did not want this pending over me. They wrote back a letter saying they had no intentions of further prosecution, which was in itself a judgment from the superior court.

At that point, Kathy Wilde came into the case as my lawyer, working with the ACLU, and I ended up getting very, very close to her. She was the perfect lawyer to work with me and we saw eye-to-eye on everything. We started at the federal level, and we filed a complaint that I was suing the police commissioner of Atlanta and the state attorney, Michael Bowers. There was also a John and Mary Doe who joined my case. They came in through Kathy as co-plaintiffs, stating that the reason they were pursuing this was because the officer coming into my house had had a chilling effect on their own personal relationship. They did not want to be identified. So we went to the federal court, and Judge Hall saw that this was going to be a major thing. So he immediately dismissed the case and said that I did not have a case. My lawyers had assured me that was okay. Then we went to the court of appeals. They decided two-to-one in my favor.

I didn't realize when I went into all of this that I was going to be suing the police commissioner, nor did I realize that while in the federal courts I had to continue to live in a city where the KKK was rather strong. The case lasted about five years, and in that time I moved and got an apartment in someone else's name—my phone bills, electric bills, everything was in someone else's name. I was still working as a bartender, plus I had opened up a floral shop with a friend of mine, but all in his name again, because I didn't want them to have any way of tracing me, especially after the beating. I lived very incognito for the rest of the five years.

After the appeals court decided in my favor, the state brought it into the Supreme Court. At that time I wanted to get out of the city. I'd been living there in fear for three years and I just wanted to leave the city, but my lawyers said it might hurt the case in the Supreme Court, and there was only six months to go. I stuck it out for about five more months and moved down to Miami about a month before the case was argued before the Supreme Court.

Then I went to the Supreme Court and was there for the hearing. No one knew who I was. At that point, I had not done any interviews or speaking in public. The issue was privacy, and I wanted to keep it a private issue. My lawyers had informed me from the very beginning that it would be better to keep a low profile because we did not want the personal aspects of the case to come into it, which I agreed with. They thought that if there was a lot of personal publicity it would affect the decision of the Supreme Court.

It was an education to be there. I had forty-two lawyers working on my case, plus Laurence Tribe of Harvard Law School arguing the case for me. I had met with all of them early that morning for breakfast, and we were kind of psyching each other up. I was going to be sitting with one of the people who wrote the *amicus* brief for Lamda, which does gay legal defense in New York, and they once again assured me that no one knew who I was. So I sat in the Supreme Court as a completely anonymous person. The whole omnipresence of the room, the procedure of the judges coming in, is sort of overpowering. I expected the room to be huge, but it wasn't; it was a very small room. You could see the judges' faces and their expressions no matter where you sat.

The guy from the state came up first and argued for about five minutes and he was an idiot. He kept going on about how the state *did* have a justified government interest in continuing to enforce the law because it prevented adultery and retarded children and bestiality, and that if they changed the law all of those things would be legal. He made absolutely no sense. I think it was Justice Burger who asked why, if they had my head on a silver platter, if they had such a justified government interest in enforcing this law, did they refuse to prosecute me. At which point, his answer was that he wasn't at liberty to discuss that. The nine justices and the whole place cracked up and he pretty much ended his argument.

Then Laurence Tribe got up and articulately argued for about forty-five minutes. He was incredible. I've never seen any person more in control of his senses than he was. When he got done, everyone was very much pre-victory. They were *sure* I would win. About forty of us went to lunch around the corner, and everything seemed very positive and optimistic, and I flew back to Miami to work. Then came the waiting period. That was the worst phase for me, because we never knew when the decision was coming.

I would be on pins and needles, and every time the phone rang I'd be jumping. They made it the last decision of the year, of course. They waited until just after all of the Gay Pride parades around the country.

I was at work when I heard about the decision. I cater a complimentary buffet for about a hundred people a day, so I go into work about four or five hours before anyone else gets there to do all my prep work. On this particular morning I could not sleep, and I got to work about nine o'clock. A friend of mine had been watching cable news and had seen it and knew where to find me and came over. When I opened the door he was crying and saying that he was sorry, and I didn't know what the hell he was talking about. Finally I calmed him down and he told me what had happened: that I had lost by a five-to-four vote.

I was totally stunned. My friend took off and I was there for about four hours by myself and that's when it really sunk in. I just cried—not so much because I had failed but because to me it was frightening to think that in the year of 1986 our Supreme Court, next to God, could make a decision that was more suitable to the mentality of the Spanish Inquisition. It was frightening and it stunned me. I was scared. I had been fighting this case for five years and everyone had seemed so confident that I was really *not* expecting this decision the way that they handed it down.

So I called Kathy Wilde and I called Laurence Tribe. I think he was more devastated than I was. Nobody expected it. I was calling for some kind of reaffirming that everything was going to be okay and that something could be done. But they said, That's it! There's nothing we can do. I learned later that I originally *had* five votes in my favor on the Supreme Court. Justice Powell came out a week later and said to the press that he had originally decided in my favor. I *still* don't understand why Powell changed his mind in my case. What a half-assed decision!

At that time, everyone thought I was still in Atlanta. And I thought this was okay, I'll just get through this personally. People who knew what I was doing kept coming into the bar and saying, I'm sorry. And I'd say that I'd rather not talk about it. I figured the best place for me would be behind the bar, because it would make me pull myself out of it.

About eight o'clock that night, in comes this woman from Channel 11 news, with a man behind her with a camera on his shoulder.

This is in a gay club. I was stunned. All of a sudden it sunk in that they could find me. I asked her how she knew where I was, and she said she was very resourceful. She wanted to do an interview, and I immediately left the bar and went upstairs. I was shaking. She got pissed off because she couldn't do an interview with me, and on the eleven o'clock news she's talking about Michael Hardwick, and the whole time she has the camera focused on the bar I worked at.

About two days went by where I was just kind of stunned. There wasn't anything I could do to change the way I feel, and I'm normally a very positive person. It wasn't that I was negative, I was just nonresponsive to anything. Then all of a sudden I started getting pissed off, angry. Kathy called me two days later and she said that *Newsweek* magazine just came out with a national poll that said 57 percent of the people were opposed to the decision. And she said, By the way, Phil Donahue called and wants to know if you'll do his show. She was very clever, letting me know the nation was behind me, and then hitting me with the Donahue show. Up until then, they had all advised me to keep it private. But she said, This is one approach you can take: You can come out and let people know this was not a homosexual decision, as they tried to put it out, but that it affects everyone as individuals, as consenting adults. And the only way you're going to get that across to them is to use this opportunity.

That was the first time I'd ever spoken publicly. Donahue called and said he was putting me on with Jerry Falwell, and I said I wouldn't do the show—it wasn't a religious issue. So he called back and said, We got rid of Falwell, but you'll have to do the whole show by yourself. Okay. So I flew up there and did that, and that was probably the hardest thing I've ever done in my life. But it went very well, and everyone who saw the program said I was a good spokesman. That started something I had never anticipated. I did a lot of talk shows after that, a lot of newspaper interviews.

They told me after Donahue that in a month I'd be old news, but this has been the most hectic year of my life. Just about the time the whole thing died out, we started on the two hundredth birthday of the Constitution. I did a special with Bill Moyers on PBS, and one with Peter Jennings. And I've been speaking at a lot of rallies.

In the last three months I've done about twenty-four round

trips to various areas, usually in one day. It's very draining, because I work two full-time jobs. I bartend full time to support myself, and I also have my work as a sculptor. I just started about a year ago, but I'm doing very well with my art, getting a lot of exposure. So that right there is about seventy hours a week. And usually on the weekends I'm going to New York or Washington or Columbus, Ohio. I consider this an obligation on my part. It's something I started, and I had no idea it would go to the Supreme Court.

When I started this, I didn't even know there *was* a sodomy law! My lawyers basically laid it out to me, and I met with them about once a week for the first six months. In that process I was educated about procedures and court levels, so that I would be articulate when it came to testifying—which never really happened. Once I started studying the system and realized I was getting actively involved in the system, it kind of sparked an interest, and I did a lot of independent reading on the legal system and past cases. My lawyers were always reeling off these cases, and then I would go and research it and read. In fact, I recently got an honorary degree, with robes and everything, from the City University of New York Law School. They were all kidding me, like 'Are you ready to take the bar exam?'

I actually *have* considered going to law school. Once you get involved in the legal system, you realize the implications. People have no idea about these nine justices who sit up here and make decisions that affect their daily life in millions of ways. Once you start to study that and you realize how important it is, you can't help but develop an interest and get into it. Reagan is stacking the courts like nobody's business. He wants to make sure that he'll prevail for the next twenty years.

When I started this case, people had never heard of AIDS, and that all developed as my case developed. And all the negative impressions that society and the media have been producing for the last three years had just about reached a high point when the decision came down and they asked me to come out nationally. That affected me a lot. When I first started speaking I thought that some crazy fundamentalist was going to blow my head off. Once I overcame that fear and a month or two went by, people would stop me and say, I'm not a homosexual but I definitely agree with what you're doing. This is America and we have the right to privacy, and the Constitution should protect us. They were supportive once they understood the issue and how it affected them.

The more I got this support the more I realized the importance of the position I had been placed in as a spokesman. This is something I started and something I have to follow through. It would be easy to say that I've done my bit and now I'm going on with my personal life. But as long as there is a need for me to speak, as long as I can help work toward changing the negative impression the society has right now about gays, I'll continue to work in that direction.

Gays are just a step up from drug addicts in the way society treats us. We're second-class citizens. I would fight to my dying day to defend my rights as a homosexual. I am a perfectly well-adjusted person. I am very productive, I am very talented. I refuse to be suppressed, I refuse to be treated as a second-class citizen. There's no *way* the Supreme Court can say that I can't have sex with a consenting adult in the privacy of my own bedroom.

Because of my personal perspective in life, I have a tendency to dwell on the positive instead of the negative. I feel very fortunate I was given the opportunity to do it. Speaking and coming out nationally was a very healthy experience for me, because it made me develop a confidence I never would have had if I had gone along with my individual life. It also gave me a sense of importance, because right now there is a very strong need for the gay community to pull together, and also for the heterosexual community to pull together, against something that's affecting both of us. I feel that no matter what happens, I gave it my best shot. I will continue to give it my best shot.

Epilogue

"Doesn't Anybody Remember the Spanish Inquisition?"

Sixteen cases, sixteen stories, sixteen voices. Each has told us about a struggle to turn a piece of paper, our Constitution, into a living document which will grow as America grows—in population, in diversity, in complexity. And, hopefully, as we grow in tolerance of each other's difference. If there is one common thread to these stories, it is that each case began with an act of intolerance. Lillian Gobitis professed a different religion than most of the residents of Minersville, and their intolerance prompted her expulsion from school. Michael Hardwick practiced a different form of sexual intimacy than most people in Atlanta, and their intolerance is written into Georgia's sodomy law. The stories in between those of Lillian and Michael—who are themselves very different in belief and behavior—all express the heavy cost we pay for intolerance.

Studies of tolerance among Americans offer some hope for the future. The earliest surveys, conducted by Samuel Stouffer during the Cold War years of the 1950s, painted a chilling picture of widespread public hostility toward political dissenters. While the public voiced agreement with the abstract norms of tolerance, large majorities would deny Communists, atheists, and other non-conformists the right to speak, teach, or hold public office. Two decades later, having lived through the turmoil of the civil-rights era and the Vietnam War, Americans expressed more willingness to tolerate dissenters. A repetition of Stouffer's study reported an increase of the "tolerant" public from 31 percent in 1954 to 55 percent in 1973. The authors were pleased that "citizens who are most supportive of civil liberties have emerged as the majority in our society—and they are not a 'silent majority.'"

Before we congratulate ourselves on this progress, let us keep in mind that the glass is almost half empty. Close to a majority of the public remains intolerant. And agreement with the words of the Bill of Rights does not mean the same as acceptance of those who differ in religion, race, ethnicity, politics, or life style. A more recent study of the 1980s revealed that political tolerance does not extend to social tolerance; those who "subscribe to the general norms of civil liberties and tolerance" indicate a desire to maintain their "social distance" from those whose views they dislike.

We have considerable evidence that generalized tolerance—what people tell pollsters—is spread like a thin veneer over our fears and prejudices, and that attitudes can shift as rapidly as news headlines. Opinion about gays illustrates both the shallowness and volatility of tolerance. The Gallup Poll's first sounding of opinion in 1977 showed that the public was evenly split over legalization of homosexual relations between consenting adults. Five years later, in 1982, those who opposed legalization dropped to 39 percent. But the AIDS epidemic and the fear it spread among the public turned these figures around in 1986: Only 33 percent favored legalization, and more than half now opposed it.

Declines in levels of tolerance often produce increases in overt acts of intolerance and violence against those who are perceived as threats to health, jobs, property values, and national security. Hard figures are hard to find, but the gay community has reported an increase in assaults on gays, harassment on the streets, and other forms of intolerance since the AIDS epidemic became a source of public hysteria. Even on college campuses, gays and lesbians have complained about an epidemic of verbal and physical assault. The men's room in the Rutgers University history department was defaced with this graffiti: "Faggots and commies burn in hell!" This linking of macho and Cold War hostilities with violent religiosity tells us much about the sources and persistence of bigotry.

Intolerance can lead to such extremes of violence as murder, bombings, and arson. History courses at all school levels largely ignore America's violent past: The forced removal of Native Americans along the "Trail of Tears," during which thousands died in the 1830s; the lynching deaths of 2,000 blacks between 1882 and 1903, and hundreds more in later decades; dozens of deaths—thirteen women and children burned alive in the Ludlow Massacre of 1914, and ten strikers shot in the back in the Republic Steel massacre of 1937—in workers' struggles to organize unions. Even in the past decade, intolerance has spawned violence: Ku Klux Klan terrorists in Mobile, Alabama, murdered a young black man, Michael Donald, in 1981; two jobless Detroit auto workers mistakenly thought Vincent Chin was Japanese, and beat him to death with a baseball bat in 1982; Dennis Malvasi received a seven-year prison term in New York City in 1987 for bombing abortion clinics. The Supreme Court can proclaim rights, but it cannot act as policeman or peacemaker.

Intolerance can also produce intimidation. In January 1988 the Yonkers, New York, city council held an open meeting to discuss a court-ordered plan to construct low-income housing which would add blacks to the largely white city. The only Yonkers resident to defend the plan was Laurie Recht, a thirty-four-year-old legal secretary, who was verbally abused at the meeting and later was deluged with death threats. The next month, hoodlums spray-painted a swastika on her apartment wall. "It's a cowardly act by insecure people who don't have the guts to discuss the issue or face me," Ms. Recht told a reporter. "I really feel sorry for them."

Valerie White, a young lawyer in Hyde Park, Vermont, filed a suit in 1987 to remove a cross from the local courthouse lawn. The tradition of Yankee tolerance has eroded among her neighbors. "In a small, close-knit town like this," one hostile person said, "I don't see how she will survive six months." Ms. White is angry at those who harass her: "Doesn't anybody remember the Spanish Inquisition, the Holocaust, even the Irish troubles now? Most people just don't think about those things." Another Vermonter, Beth Phillips, was run out of town by intolerance. As the high-school librarian in Vergennes, she balked in 1977 at removing controversial books from the shelves, and joined an ACLU lawsuit. Ministers denounced her in sermons and circulated petitions demanding that she be fired. Ms. Phillips lost the suit, and moved away to escape further harassment. "It took me several years to heal," she later said. "Parts of me have never healed. I have anger inside me I have never let go. I just hope I never have to face something like this again."

Half of the people in this book endured actual or threatened violence because of their constitutional stands. Lillian Gobitis had rocks and fists thrown at her; J.D. Shelley's daughter was pushed around; Daisy Bates was the target of dynamite bombs; people spit on Robert Mack Bell; Mary Tinker, Dr. Jane Hodgson, and Ishmael Jaffree all received death threats; and Michael Hardwick was badly beaten.

What kind of people have the fortitude to face this kind of abuse, and to endure the years of waiting and the uncertainty of a Supreme Court case? Each person in this book lost his or her case at one or more judicial level; eleven lost in the trial court; and six lost in the Supreme Court. They all faced discouragement, delay, and potential defeat.

In my opinion, four common factors unite this very disparate group. First, almost all come from working-class families. Their fathers include farmers, garment workers, loggers, firemen, printers. Even the three "professionals" among the fathers—a small-college professor, a deposed minister, and a small-town doctor— were hardly affluent. Second, they all developed a strong set of ethical values. Some drew these values from religious training, others from their own life experiences. Third, they all learned to become assertive, to be outspoken, to question authority. Finally, and perhaps most important, every one of them was raised to consider racial discrimination both wrong and sinful. They were all raised to be tolerant. It is hard to exaggerate the significance of this last factor; even those who grew up in the white South knew that racism was wrong.

Can we paint a collective portrait from these common traits? I hesitate to draw generalizations from such a small group. But in talking with these sixteen remarkable people I learned two things: first, that they are all "ordinary" Americans; second, that they have extraordinary strength of conviction and character. Dr. Willard Gaylin, a psychoanalyst who interviewed imprisoned draft resisters in the Vietnam era, concluded that they shared two characteristics: "a high degree of ego strength" which produced a strong sense of self; and an equally strong "super ego" which placed conscience above conformity. What Dr. Gaylin wrote about the war objectors who chose prison (I was one of his subjects) also fits those who began these constitutional cases: "In sociological terms they were service-oriented individuals who believed that a man must be judged by his actions, not his statements, and that ideals and behavior were not separable phenomena." Broadening this insight to include women, its aptness to the people in this book is striking. They all had inner strength and outward concerns.

What of the future? With tolerance of diversity subject to political crusades and the public's fears, can we rely on courts to protect the Bill of Rights from the Religious Right, from racial bigots, from a revival of McCarthyism? Predicting the future is always difficult, but the prognosis for a "living Constitution" is especially hard to provide. All judges swear to uphold the Constitution, and federal judges are protected by lifetime tenure from the political pressures that twist the arms of many state judges. Attachment to precedent, the principle of judicial restraint, and the general conservatism of judges all combine to suggest that the Warren Court's expansive rulings will survive the Rehnquist Court's chipping and trimming.

But we cannot rely on judges alone to defend the Constitution against its enemies. Looking to the future, we must recall the recent past. During his first six years in the White House, President Ronald Reagan placed 290 judges on the federal bench, almost 40 percent of all sitting judges. "By the end of his second term President Reagan should pass the 50 percent mark," writes Sheldon Goldman, our leading judicial analyst. Goldman's figures show that more than 90 percent of these judges are white, wealthy, male, and Republican. A Columbia Law School study in 1986 of Reagan's appointments to the federal appellate bench reveals their right-wing leanings. Ruling on discrimination claims, the Reagan judges voted for plaintiffs only 24 percent of the time, contrasted with 69 percent for judges appointed by Democratic presidents. In cases which raised issues of constitutional rights, the Reagan judges agreed in only 38 percent, while the Democratic judges upheld the claim in 66 percent. Most of the Reagan judges were under fifty years old when they donned their robes, and will most likely serve into the next century.

What kinds of issues will face judges as we approach the next century? Issues of religion and race, protest and privacy, will not vanish from judicial dockets. Most Americans now accept—often grudgingly—the rights of Jehovah's Witnesses to knock on doors, blacks to attend public schools, Communists to appear on ballots, and married couples to use condoms. Beyond these established rights, however, tolerance has limits. The constitutional issues of the future are likely to include the limits of AIDS testing, surrogate parenthood, the rights of aliens, privacy in the workplace, and the boundaries of the public forum. How state and federal judges, and the Supreme Court, will rule on such issues is impossible to predict. All we can hope is that Americans like the people in this book, people with both courage and conviction, will continue to bring these issues to the courts, and that judges will look behind the "masks of the law" to see the many faces of America.

Let us listen finally to Perry J. Watkins, whose case might reach the Supreme Court before this book is printed. He joined the Army in 1968 and rose through the ranks to staff sergeant, receiving annual commendations. The Army discharged him in 1984 for being gay, although Watkins from the start told his superiors of his homosexual orientation. Ruling in February 1988, the U.S. Court of Appeals in San Francisco reversed the Army's action. His discharge cost Perry Watkins more than his job. Unable to find work in Tacoma, Washington, he was reduced to "shivering in his rented house, which was unheated because he was unable to pay his utility bills." The appellate judges who decided his case all voiced the hope that the Supreme Court would reverse its *Hardwick* decision of 1986 and uphold the rights of homosexuals.

Perry Watkins is less optimistic. "I don't hold out any great hopes for winning with the Supreme Court," he confessed. But he remains determined to pursue his case to the end. Who will win this battle between the state and the individual, between conformity and conscience? We must wait and see. In the meantime, and in years to come, the vitality of the "living Constitution"—the heart and soul of our nation—will depend on Americans with the courage of their convictions.

Sources and Further Readings

The sources for the essays in this book are many and varied. Much material comes from newspapers, magazines, journals, biographical directories of judges and lawyers, and other sources available in good libraries. Quotations from judicial opinions are mostly from official reporters (collections of published opinions) which many college libraries and all law-school libraries have. Some material is from unpublished or hard-to-find sources, such as transcripts of some Supreme Court arguments, available only in the U.S. Supreme Court Library in Washington, D.C. To help readers who want to delve more deeply into these cases, I list below for each the citations to judicial opinions and published accounts of the cases and the issues they involve.

First, a note about judicial citations: Supreme Court opinions are officially published in *United States Reports,* cited by volume and page number. For example, the opinions in *Minersville v. Gobitis* are found at 310 U.S. 586—which is to say volume 310 of *United States Reports,* at page 586. Opinions of the federal courts of appeals are in *Federal Reporter, 2d Series,* also cited by volume and page number. The appellate decision in *Gobitis* is at 108 F.2d 683. Federal district court opinions are in *Federal Supplement;* the *Gobitis* opinion is at 21 F.Supp. 581. Opinions of state supreme courts are found in regional reporters. All cases in this book with state court opinions are in one of four reporters: *Southwestern Reporter, Second Series; Northwestern Reporter, Second Series; Pacific Reporter, Second Series;* and *Atlantic Reporter, Second Series.* These are also cited by volume and page number. For example, the Missouri Supreme Court opinion in *Shelley* v. *Kraemer* is at 198

S.W.2d 679. It looks forbidding, but it's really a simple citation system.

Let me also list several books which provided material for more than one case, and several that are good background reading in American law. The most important source is Bernard Schwartz, *Super Chief: Earl Warren and His Supreme Court—A Judicial Biography.* This massive work includes accounts of every important case decided by the Warren Court, from 1954 to 1969; especially helpful are accounts of discussions at the Court's secret conferences, reconstructed from the notes of several justices. Another essential source is the series edited by Philip B. Kurland and Gerhard Casper of the University of Chicago Law School, *Landmark Briefs and Arguments of the Supreme Court of the United States: Constitutional Law.* These volumes include all the briefs and many transcripts of oral arguments in important cases. All the cases in this book are included in this series except for the *Bates, Epperson, Tinker, Hodgson, LaFleur,* and *Gertz* cases. Most law libraries have on microfiche the official records and briefs of these cases, although they do not include transcripts of oral arguments.

This book does not pretend to be a treatise on American constitutional law. For that I commend to readers the book of that name (now available in a second edition) by Prof. Laurence H. Tribe of Harvard Law School. Nor is this book a constitutional history. For that I recommend Melvin I. Urofsky, *A March of Liberty: A Constitutional History of the United States, Vol. II: Since 1865.* This is an admirably well-written book. Chapters 31 to 40 cover the time period treated in *The Courage of Their Convictions.*

Listed below are judicial citations and suggested readings for the cases in this book.

1. *Gobitis* v. *Minersville*

The Supreme Court opinion is at 310 U.S. 586; the court of appeals opinion is at 108 F.2d 683; the district court opinion is at 21 F.Supp. 581.

Two books recount the *Gobitis* case and also deal with the *Barnette* case that overruled it in 1943: David R. Manwaring, *Render Unto Caesar;* and Leonard A. Stevens, *Salute! The Case of the Bible vs. the Flag.* Manwaring's book is more detailed and scholarly (it is a revised dissertation), and Stevens has written a journalistic account which is more readable. The Justice Department officials who investigated violence against Jehovah's Witnesses after the Supreme Court ruling in the *Gobitis* case put their report into print in Victor W. Rotnem and F.G. Folsom, Jr., "Recent Restrictions Upon Religious Liberty," *American Political Science Review*, 1942, p. 1053. The Supreme Court's opinion in the *Barnette* case is at 319 U.S. 624.

2. *Hirabayashi* v. *United States*

The Supreme Court opinion is at 320 U.S. 81; the federal district court opinion is at 46 F.Supp. 657.

The primary work about *Hirabayashi* and the other wartime internment cases is my own book, Peter Irons, *Justice at War*. I have also edited a book of documents about the reopening of these cases in the 1980s, Peter Irons, *Justice Delayed*, which includes a lengthy essay about the *coram nobis* effort, the petition submitted to the district courts, and the judicial opinions in the *Korematsu* and *Hirabayashi* cases. A good account of the internment is in the 1982 report of the Commission on Wartime Relocation and Internment of Civilians, *Personal Justice Denied*.

3. *Shelley* v. *Kraemer*

The Supreme Court opinion is at 334 U.S. 1; the Missouri Supreme Court opinion is at 198 S.W.2d 679.

The only substantial work about the racial-covenant cases is Clement Vose, *Caucasians Only: The Supreme Court, the NAACP, and the Restrictive Covenant Cases*.

4. *Barenblatt* v. *United States*

The Supreme Court opinion is at 360 U.S. 109; the federal court of appeals opinions (there were two) are at 240 F.2d 875, and 252 F.2d 129.

There is no account of the *Barenblatt* case, but several books deal with the McCarthy period and congressional investigations of Communist activities. Victor Navasky, *Naming Names*, focuses largely on Hollywood but is a chilling analysis of the informer mentality. Ellen Schrecker, *No Ivory Tower: McCarthyism and the Universities,* provides a good account of this aspect of McCarthyism, but has little about legal challenges. Walter Goodman, *The Committee*, is a good journalistic report on the House Un-American Activities Committee. Carl Beck, *Contempt of Congress*, deals with the *Barenblatt* case and other contempt cases of the 1940s and 1950s.

5. *Bates* v. *Little Rock*

The Supreme Court opinion is at 361 U.S. 516; the Arkansas Supreme Court opinion is at 319 S.W.2d 37.

Daisy Bates has written her own story of the Little Rock school crisis in *The Long Shadow of Little Rock: A Memoir*. Her book is exciting and inspiring, but it deals only briefly with her Supreme Court case. A University of Arkansas law professor, Tony A. Fryer, discusses the legal aspects of the Central High integration case in *The Little Rock Crisis: A Constitutional Interpretation*. However, his brief account of the Bates case includes numerous errors. A useful article about Daisy Bates' husband, L.C. Bates, is C. Calvin Smith, "From 'Separate But Equal' to Desegregation: The Changing Philosophy of L.C. Bates," *Arkansas Historical Quarterly*, August 1983, p. 254.

6. *Bell* v. *Maryland*

The Supreme Court opinion is at 378 U.S. 226; the Maryland Supreme Court opinion is at 176 A.2d 771.

Surprisingly, there is no full-length study of the sit-in movement, and no account of the sit-in cases. The best works to consult on the Student Nonviolent Coordinating Committee (which came out of the sit-in movements but was not involved in the *Bell* case) are Howard Zinn, *SNCC: The New Abolitionists;* and Clayborne Carson, *In Struggle: SNCC and the Black Awakening of the 1960s*. The sit-in movement actually began in the 1940s with the Congress of Racial Equality; see August Meier and Elliott Rudwick, *CORE: A Study in the Civil Rights Movement, 1942–1968*.

7. *Seeger* v. *United States*

The Supreme Court opinion is at 380 U.S. 163; the federal court of appeals decision is at 326 F.2d 846.

For a contemporary account of the anti-draft movement (which does not mention the *Seeger* case), see Michael Ferber and Staughton Lynd, *The Resistance*. The treatment of conscientious objectors during World War II (with brief discussion of World War I) is recounted in Mulford Q. Sibley and Philip E. Jacob, *Conscription of Conscience: The American State and the Conscientious Objector, 1940–1947*. Daniel Seeger has outlined his own views and philosophy on war and peace in *The Seed and the Tree: A Reflection on Nonviolence*, Pendle Hill Pamphlet 269, available from Pendle Hill Publications, Wallingford, PA 19086.

8. *Elfbrandt* v. *Russell*

The Supreme Court opinion is at 384 U.S. 11; there are two decisions of the Arizona Supreme Court, at 381 P.2d 554, and 397 P.2d 944.

There is no good account of the loyalty-oath controversy from a national perspective. The best book on one state's experience is David P. Gardner, *The California Oath Controversy*. Ellen Schrecker's book, *No Ivory Tower*, listed above under the *Barenblatt* case, deals in part with loyalty oaths for college teachers, although not for high-school teachers.

9. *Epperson* v. *Arkansas*

The Supreme Court opinion is at 393 U.S. 97; the Arkansas Supreme Court opinion is at 416 S.W.2d 322.

The *Epperson* case is discussed in a general history of the legal battles over evolution, Edward J. Larson, *Trial and Error: The American Controversy Over Creation and Evolution*. Another book to consult is Marcel C. LaFollette, ed., *Creationism, Science and the Law: The Arkansas Case*, which deals with the 1981 challenge to the Arkansas "equal-time" law. An article which recounts the origins of the Arkansas antievolution law is Cal Ledbetter, Jr., "The Antievolution Law: Church and State in Arkansas," *Arkansas Historical Quarterly*, Winter 1979, p. 299.

10. *Tinker* v. *Des Moines*

The Supreme Court opinion is at 393 U.S. 503; the federal court of appeals opinion is at 383 F.2d 988; the federal district court opinion is at 258 F.Supp. 971.

Surprisingly, there is no good history of the Vietnam antiwar movement, particularly of its grass-roots tactics and strategies. The best account of opposition to the war, largely at the national level, is Thomas Powers, *The War at Home: Vietnam and the American People, 1964–1968*. There is nothing substantial in print about the last seven years of the antiwar movement.

11. *Hodgson* v. *Minnesota*

There was no Supreme Court opinion on the case Dr. Jane Hodgson brought to challenge the Minnesota antiabortion law. The federal district court opinion that dismissed her case is in *Doe* v. *Randall*, at 314 F.Supp. 32. The Minnesota Supreme Court opinion that reversed her criminal conviction (after the U.S. Supreme Court decision in *Roe* v. *Wade*) is at 204 N.W.2d 199. The U.S. Supreme Court opinion in *Harris* v. *McRae*, the challenge to the Hyde Amendment that Dr. Hodgson joined as a plaintiff, is at 448 U.S. 297. The federal district court opinion in the McRae case is at 491 F.Supp. 630.

The only full-length account of the legal struggles over abortion is Eva R. Rubin, *Abortion, Politics, and the Courts: Roe v. Wade and Its Aftermath.* This book is not well organized and does not discuss Dr. Hodgson's criminal case or deal adequately with the legal and political strategies of the movement to legalize abortion. Other books worth consulting, although they skimp on legal issues, are Frederick S. Jaffee, Barbara L. Lindheim, and Philip R. Lee, *Abortion Politics: Private Morality and Public Policy;* and Rosalind P. Petchesky, *Abortion and Woman's Choice: The State, Sexuality, and Reproductive Freedom.*

12. *Rodriguez* v. *San Antonio*

The Supreme Court opinion is at 411 U.S. 1; the federal district court opinion is at 337 F.Supp. 280. (There was no appellate court decision.)

Sad to say, very little has been written about the significant issue of public-school financing and legal challenges to the property tax system. The best available source is Betsy Levin, ed., *Future Directions for School Finance Reform.* This book includes a good essay on the Rodriquez case by Mark G. Yudof and Daniel C. Morgan, "*Rodriguez v. San Antonio Independent School District:* Gathering the Ayes of Texas—The Politics of School Finance Reform."

13. *LaFleur* v. *Cleveland*

The Supreme Court opinion is at 414 U.S. 632; the federal court of appeals opinion is at 465 F.2d 1184; the federal district court opinion is at 326 F.Supp. 1208.

There has been virtually nothing published on the problems of pregnant schoolteachers (or of pregnant women in general, for that matter). One good law review article is "Love's Labors Lost: New Conceptions of Maternity Leaves," *Harvard Civil Rights–Civil Liberties Law Review*, Vol. 7, p. 260.

14. *Gertz* v. *Robert Welch, Inc.*

The Supreme Court opinion is at 418 U.S. 323; the federal court of appeals decision in the first round of the Gertz case is at 471